THE MAKING OF

Black Detroit
in the Age of
Henry Ford

THE MAKING OF

Black Detroit in the Age of Henry Ford

BETH TOMPKINS BATES

The University of North Carolina Press
CHAPEL HILL

Designed and set in Calluna types by Rebecca Evans
Manufactured in the United States of America

The paper in this book meets the guidelines for permanence and durability of
the Committee on Production Guidelines for Book Longevity of the Council on
Library Resources. The University of North Carolina Press has been a member
of the Green Press Initiative since 2003.

Bates, Beth Tompkins.
The making of Black Detroit in the age of Henry Ford / Beth Tompkins Bates.
p. cm.
Includes bibliographical references and index.
ISBN 978-0-8078-3564-7 (cloth : alk. paper)
1. African Americans—Michigan—Detroit—History—20th century. 2. African
Americans—Michigan—Detroit—Social conditions—20th century. 3. Migration,
Internal—United States—History—20th century. 4. Detroit (Mich.)—Social
conditions. 5. Detroit (Mich.)—Race relations. I. Title.
F574.D49N428 2012   305.896′077434—dc23   2012007161

16 15 14 13 12   5 4 3 2 1

FOR TIM

CONTENTS

ILLUSTRATIONS

ACKNOWLEDGMENTS

The Making of Black Detroit in the Age of Henry Ford, a history of a community in formation, could not have been written without the generous contributions of a community of scholars, activists, scholar-activists, archivists, autoworkers, colleagues, family, and friends. While I cannot possibly recognize all who helped make this effort possible, I want to name a few who helped me along the way.

I am indebted to all the scholars who have studied the history of African Americans in Detroit as well as Henry Ford's influence on the city. Many of the published and unpublished works on these two subjects are cited in my bibliography. One group bears special mention for rescuing me when I hit a wall trying to grasp Henry Ford's racial policies. The pioneering research of economic historians Christopher Foote, Thomas Maloney, Warren Whatley, and Gavin Wright, working with data from the Ford Motor Company, clarifies the true nature of Ford's compensation policies for black workers. This book has greatly benefited from their research efforts.

My interest in this topic grew out of the experience of living and working in Detroit, especially teaching African American history in the Department of Africana Studies at Wayne State University. Seeds for the project were planted in my history classes as I grappled with what had been going on in early twentieth-century black Detroit and tried to reconcile the written record with what I was learning from interviews with veterans of Detroit's labor struggles, including General Baker, Grace Lee Boggs, Mike Hamlin, David Moore, and Quill Pettway. Seminars sponsored by Walter Edwards, director of the Humanities Center at Wayne State University, allowed the seeds to germinate and led to a "Working Groups" grant, making it possible for Professors L. Todd Duncan, Kathryne V. Lindberg, and me to interview race and labor activists for our project, "Detroit Voices."

Once my questions were formulated and my research was under way, many archivists helped with materials. In Detroit, the staff of the Archives for Labor and Urban Affairs at the Walter P. Reuther Library never failed to amaze me with their dedication and efficiency, locating not only what I requested, but other materials related to my topic as well. In this regard, thanks go especially to Tom Featherstone, Louis Jones, William Lefevre, and Mary Wallace. Mark Bowen successfully conducted numerous, invaluable searches in the basement of the Burton Historical Collection, often for mere shards of evidence without which it would have been impossible to document the formation of the black community during the 1920s. Karen L. Jania and Malgosia Myc were extremely helpful with my searches at the Bentley Historical Library. Thanks also go to Peter Kalinski at the Benson Ford Research Center and the librarians and archivists at the Labadie Archives and the reference desk of Harlan Hatcher Graduate Library of the University of Michigan. Among the efficient staff of the Purdy/Kresge Library of Wayne State University, Markeesha Barnett and Regan Rodriguez deserve special recognition for helping me locate materials.

In addition to those mentioned above, a community in the larger Detroit area dedicated to preserving its history provided connections and suggestions that have proved invaluable. Special appreciation goes out to Marti Alston, David Arsen, Steve Babson, Melba Boyd, Ron Brown, John Bukowczyk, Angela Dillard, Todd Duncan, Elizabeth Faue, Carol Forsythe, David Goldberg, Robert Hensleigh, Larry John, Tom Klug, Marian Kramer, Scott Kurasige, Lilian Lai, Maggie Levenstein, Beth and Bruce Morrow, Rudy Nelson, Charles Simmons, and Stephen Ward. I also want to acknowledge the recent loss of three intrepid souls who dedicated their lives to preserving Detroit's past. The work and collegiality of Tom Featherstone, Kathryne Lindberg, and David Moore enriched this book and my life in countless ways.

As the project was taking shape, I was fortunate to have had questions, suggestions, and reactions from colleagues who commented on drafts, conference papers, and other fragments that later became part of the whole. To Martha Biondi, Grace Lee Boggs, Melba Boyd, Alan Brinkley, Matthew Countryman, Angela Dillard, Todd Duncan, Tami Friedman, Maggie Levenstein, David Levering Lewis, Robert Self, Fran Shor, Robyn Spencer, Thomas Sugrue, Pat Sullivan, Cynthia Taylor, Jeanne Theoharis, Stephen Ward, Calvin White, Victoria Wolcott, and Komozie Woodard I extend special thanks. I am especially grateful to Timothy Bates, Eric Foner, David Goldberg, and Quill Pettway, who took valuable time away from their busy schedules to read the complete manuscript. Their suggestions were indispensable and helped me bring the parts and the whole into better alignment as I entered the final phase.

I am very glad this manuscript caught the eye of Chuck Grench, who launched the project at the University of North Carolina Press, and has guided it through its various mutations, providing necessary encouragement and patience at every turn. Katy O'Brien helped me at an early stage, and Sara Cohen has carried the project forward, answering questions both technical and literary on a moment's notice. My thanks go to Dino Battista, Jennifer Hergenroeder, Beth Lassiter, and Ron Maner for their assistance. The final product has benefited enormously from the wisdom and advice of Paul Betz, who shepherded the manuscript through its final stage. Eric Arnesen and Steven Reich, readers for the Press, reviewed the manuscript with great care, offering extremely constructive suggestions for revisions. The book is much better thanks to their collective scholarly critiques.

My greatest debt is to Timothy Bates, who believed in the project from its inception, cheered me on during protracted periods of research and writing, critiqued several drafts, and kept me focused and fit to the finish. This book is dedicated to Tim for devoting his professional career to research that has led to the removal of some of the barriers to equal economic opportunity. The fact that his expertise is in such demand today is a reminder to us all that the struggle for racial and economic justice, documented in this book, is far from finished nearly a century later.

Asheville, N.C.
October 2011

ABBREVIATIONS USED IN THE TEXT

For abbreviations used in the notes, see page 257.

ACD	Americanization Committee of Detroit
AC	Associated Charities
AFL	American Federation of Labor
AWU	Auto Workers Union
BSCP	Brotherhood of Sleeping Car Porters
BTWTA	Booker T. Washington Trade Association
CIO	Congress of Industrial Organization
CRC	Civic Rights Committee [Detroit]
DCL	Detroit Citizens League
DPW	Department of Public Welfare [Detroit]
DUL	Detroit Urban League
FMC	Ford Motor Company
ILD	International Labor Defense
IWW	International Workers of the World
KKK	Ku Klux Klan
MUC	Mayor's Unemployment Committee
NAACP	National Association for the Advancement of Colored People
NAPFE	National Alliance of Postal and Federal Employees
NIRA	National Industrial Recovery Act
NLRB	National Labor Relations Board
NNC	National Negro Congress
NRA	National Recovery Administration
NUL	National Urban League
SWOC	Steel Workers Organizing Committee
UAW	United Auto Workers
UAW-CIO	United Auto Workers–Congress of Industrial Organizations
UNIA	Universal Negro Improvement Association
WPA	Works Progress Administration

INTRODUCTION

THIS IS A STORY ABOUT DETROIT, a city whose name evoked the promise of America as the land of opportunity in the early years of the twentieth century. Henry Ford promoted that image with the progressive industrial policies and maverick business practices he put into place at the Ford Motor Company (FMC). The unfolding narrative is anchored to Henry Ford and his desire to revolutionize the world through the production and sales of his Model T, affectionately known as the Tin Lizzie. Ford succeeded—perhaps beyond even his expectations—in transforming how Americans in the twentieth century worked and played. From the agrarian rhythms characterizing the world of work in the nineteenth century, Ford retooled industry, reconstructing how the production process would be orchestrated—even as he strove to expand and enrich the world workers inhabited during their leisure time. His innovative strategies for having workers manufacture cars from interchangeable parts along a moving assembly line produced automobiles more efficiently, uniformly, and faster than the world had ever imagined.

Ford's mass-production strategies and industrial policies spawned a revolutionary business model, redefining the road to success under industrial capitalism. By linking prosperous workers to productive markets, Ford's formula helped shape a consumer-based economy. The more cars Ford produced and sold, the lower the cost of producing each car, making the car affordable to the workers who produced them, leading to more sales and increasing demand, which in turn lowered production costs further. When Americans purchased a Ford, they drove into a "new era."[1] Ford's Model T, created for the "great multitude," shaped modern America by expanding the nation's cultural horizons, changing social behavior, and altering expectations about what was possible.[2] By the early twenties the Ford name was synonymous with the word "car," and his renown, resulting from his mass-production techniques and the cars rolling off his assembly line, was international in scope.[3]

Despite Ford's identity as an international icon for shaping the auto industry, surprisingly little notice has been paid to another revolutionary practice he initiated. After World War I, Ford hired thousands of African American men to work for the FMC, a policy decision that launched black workers on the road to modernity so they, too, could take part in Ford's "new world." The narrative that follows aims to capture how African Americans in Detroit used the foundation provided by jobs at the FMC to build their lives anew.

Entry into the new-age automotive industry represented a quantum leap forward for black workers, who were routinely excluded from high-wage positions, considered to be "white" men's jobs. In the early part of the twentieth century, many of the "best" jobs for African Americans were in the service industry, illustrated by the fact that highly educated black men often had few opportunities in the broader economy apart from work as porters, catering to the needs of white travelers on sleeping-car trains for the Pullman Company. In 1920, the Pullman Company was the single largest private employer of African American men in the nation. White men were hired as conductors; black men as Pullman porters. Black men would shine shoes, turn down beds on the sleeping cars at night, change sheets and remake beds in the morning, iron clothing, and attend to any other needs of the traveling public on the Pullman Sleeping Cars, but they never exchanged money or issued tickets, jobs reserved for conductors, all of whom were white. The position of Pullman porter was little more than that of a servant working for tips. Nonetheless, highly educated black men—engineers, ministers, and lawyers—worked for the Pullman Company because more often than not that was the best they could do in the segregated economy.

Ford challenged the stereotype of the black man as servant when he put out the welcome mat for African Americans two decades before General Motors and Chrysler hired blacks for any but foundry or janitorial jobs. By opening the door to economic opportunity for black Americans on a wider, more inclusive scale than any employer had before, Henry Ford turned into a mythic figure of immense proportions in black America. The jobs he offered were not "black" jobs, but the same jobs open to both black and white workers. During the twenties, Ford not only hired large numbers of African Americans; he also placed many in skilled positions, such as crane operator, mechanic, electrician, bricklayer, and tool-and-die maker. The possibility of gaining access to jobs across the occupational spectrum at Ford, on the heels of migrating North in search of greater opportunity, marked more than entrance into the industrial mainstream of the economy. By rejecting the notion that better jobs were for white men only, Ford raised expectations and hope about what was possible, suggesting a corner had been turned in the ongoing black struggle for inclusion as full-blooded Americans. In this regard, Ford's policies sparked a transformation in the lives of black workers and their families, helping lay a foundation for a labor-oriented civil rights agenda, and, ultimately, providing a base for the formation of the urban black middle class.

This book traces relations between Henry Ford, the FMC, black workers, and Detroit's black community as they were formed and transformed during the years between World Wars I and II.[4] The objective is to follow relationships that grew out of the interests of black Detroiters and those of Ford in order to discern how African Americans made a living and a life for themselves as pioneers navigating their way across the new economic frontier. I argue that the power of raised expectations played a significant role in turning the wheels of history between the wars in Detroit. Henry Ford was a major catalyst for raising those expectations, and his policies provide a means for examining how black migrants used this experience to improve their lives.

When Henry Ford began hiring African Americans during World War I, he was bringing into his factories men who were new to the industry and new to the North. While many migrants had a taste of urban living, Detroit was generally their first sustained experience with northern urban life. Black transplants did not view Detroit as yet another way station; they hoped to put down roots in the bustling, burgeoning metropolis that the city had become by the late teens. The opportunities Henry Ford extended to black workers raised the bar for what was possible for African Americans in the United States. The black Americans journeying North during World War I and after carried with them vivid memories of restrictions excluding them from participation as equals in American life. That exclusion shaped both their motivations for leaving the South and their expectations for what they might accomplish in the North. African Americans in the postbellum South may have slid a step back for every step forward, but the quest for full inclusion in the American polity never faded.[5] Promises raised in 1863 by Lincoln's Emancipation Proclamation and inscribed into law with the Thirteenth, Fourteenth, and Fifteenth Amendments were the stars that guided the descendants of slaves who trekked North during the Great Migration.

Ford, too, was shaped by an antislavery ideology. Born on 30 July 1863 in Greenfield Township, near Dearborn, Michigan, Ford grew up in an agricultural region exemplifying the rock-ribbed Republican Party values expressed by "free soil, free labor, free men." He interpreted his high-wage jobs as a way to offer greater independence and freedom to workingmen, a principle that had rarely been extended to black Americans.[6] The relationships between Henry Ford and African Americans took shape as the nation struggled with labor radicalism, civil repression, and the triumph of a racist definition of Americanism in the aftermath of World War I.[7] The narrowly circumscribed context, which excluded blacks from much of the nation's industrial and civic life, drew Ford and black Detroiters into a bond of interdependency, shaped as much by the political state of the nation as the respective hopes and visions of the two parties.

Henry Ford had a vision for where and how the black community and black workers would fit into his work process; the black community had clear expectations of their own regarding their place in Detroit. While displaying ambivalence in his personal racial beliefs, Ford claimed he hired black men, in part, because he thought it was the responsibility of the "superior" race to open up jobs to African Americans.[8] But Ford's interest in African Americans also overlapped with his hope that blacks might turn out to be ideal workers for his open-shop movement, his "American Plan." The black community took Ford's American Plan very seriously, for they, too, had a plan, one that led to inclusion in the American Dream. Cementing the bond was the question of allegiance, an issue dear to both. Ford stood at a crossroads when he arrived at his decision to hire large numbers of recently migrated black workers to help run operations at his newly constructed River Rouge plant. Several issues challenged his enterprise during the spring of 1919—labor racialism, strikes against his suppliers, and more than $50,000,000 owed in dividends and interest to his stockholders—pushing him to seek even greater control over his company.[9] In return for opening up jobs to African Americans, Ford expected loyalty and allegiance from black workers and their families to bolster his defense against the threat of unionism.

The question of allegiance was very much on the minds of African Americans who journeyed to Detroit during World War I. They came for jobs at the FMC hoping to fit into the expanding high-wage industrial economy. Black workers seized the chance to work at Ford Motor because at the time it represented a giant step toward greater economic opportunity.[10] World War I—the war to make the world safe for democracy—intensified the longing to escape the tyranny of the southern caste system and be included in the promise of America. Despite considerable dissent, most black Americans viewed the war as an opportunity to demonstrate allegiance to American democracy. Thus did the desire to participate in American democracy fuel the migration process, connecting it to the larger, ongoing black freedom struggle and the quest to move beyond the shadows of second-class status.[11]

PROBING THE QUESTION of allegiance necessarily challenges conventional views that assume rather than explore black allegiance to Ford. The portrayal of black Detroiters between the wars has been largely one of a community lacking independent political expression. This portrayal is put forth by scholars interested in understanding how the United Auto Workers (UAW), one of the new unions affiliated with the Congress of Industrial Organizations (CIO), was able to unionize the FMC, given the fierce loyalty of black workers and the black community to Henry Ford. While the question has puzzled historians for years, one thing is clear: between the wars, sentiment in black Detroit changed from pro-industrial to pro-union. The question is why. In one pioneering exploration put forth in August Meier and Elliott Rudwick's *Black Detroit and the Rise of the UAW*, we are told that the FMC "enjoyed the virtually unanimous admiration of the city's black community."[12] Yet the body of evidence supporting this claim consists of a cursory glance at the twenties and early thirties, accepting at face value the alleged loyalty of leading ministers, such as the Reverend Robert Bradby, whose Second Baptist Church was known as Ford's church within black Detroit. Closer investigation of Rev. Bradby reveals a conflicted character, fraught with ambivalence toward the FMC.

The traditional examination of the shift from an anti-union stand within black Detroit to a pro-union position argues that loyalty to Ford precluded a pro-union position among black Ford workers. Much like looking at only one side of the moon, this dichotomy is filled with assumptions about the issue of allegiance. Viewing the question of allegiance only through the lens of the labor organizing drives of the mid- to late 1930s suggests, on the one hand, that because black Ford workers appeared to be loyal to Henry Ford, they were opposed to unions, positing the issue in either-or terms. At one level, this seems reasonable. Given the lack of opportunity for black men elsewhere in Detroit, why wouldn't black Ford workers be loyal? Besides, Ford demanded loyalty. The price for high wages and access to jobs included surveillance of one's personal habits and beliefs and manipulation of black institutions, all part of Ford's overbearing paternalism. To bring the activities of black Detroiters out of the realm of conjecture, we need to extend the range of our chronology and look at the formation of black Detroit from the perspective of those who built it during the twenties and thirties.

Upon closer inspection, when the question of loyalty is placed within the political and social context of black life in Detroit between the wars, the issue of allegiance becomes more complex. The assumption underlying this question—that Henry Ford's control, concealed in his gloved fist, kept black Detroiters in line—does not hold up, especially when we examine black support for Frank Murphy, a prominent political leader and a staunch opponent of Henry Ford's agenda. Leaving the larger history of community formation in the shadows obscures complicated and conflicted evolving relationships between Henry Ford and black Detroit. Conflicts rooted in the great migration and urban settlement process deeply influenced the perspective and agenda of African Americans, which, in turn, transformed the metropolis that became their new home. Exploring how African Americans adjusted to life in Detroit during the 1920s and 1930s gives us a clearer picture of subsequent shifts as they occurred in their relations with Henry Ford and the FMC.

THE STRUGGLE FOR HOUSING was front and center. It did not take long for African Americans to realize that inclusion in the American economic dream was not going to extend to housing within the city of Detroit. When black migrants got off the train at Detroit's Central Station, they were steered toward overcrowded, segregated neighborhoods in Black Bottom. The city's black population, which increased over 600 percent between 1910 and 1920, was squeezed into limited, decaying housing stock as the walls of the emerging ghetto rose. Detroit's Real Estate Board forbade sales to blacks in white neighborhoods, and racial covenants severely restricted areas where blacks might develop their own communities. Another way blacks were kept in their "place" was through the brutality of Detroit's largely native-born, white police force.

Despite these setbacks, expectations raised by Ford gained traction when African Americans took part in Frank Murphy's campaign for judge in 1923, an election that pitted the traditional, Protestant industrial elite—Ford interests—against the larger population of Catholic immigrants and blacks. Murphy, a lawyer and activist in the Democratic Party, had big ambitions, especially for an Irish Catholic politician in a city controlled by Anglo-Saxons. The business elite had traditionally used Detroit's judicial system to, in effect, criminalize poverty. Murphy launched his political career by appealing to those who had been brutalized, excluded, and pushed aside. About more than reforming the court system, Murphy's campaign used the legal system as a means to free the city from what he called the "tyranny" and "autocracy" fostered by the "upper crust." Appealing to African Americans and white ethnics, the coalition of voters that would help put Franklin D. Roosevelt in the White House a decade later, Murphy called for a new day in Detroit politics, one that would overturn the control of the industrial elite and counter the weight of the Ku Klux Klan, which also held sway over Detroit's politics. The votes of black Detroiters helped elect Frank Murphy to the judiciary, thus launching his stellar political career—mayor of Detroit, governor of Michigan, U.S. attorney general, and U.S. Supreme Court justice. Murphy never forgot the support he got from black voters in 1923; black Detroiters' participation in Frank Murphy's "new deal" coalition over the next decade shaped and expanded their expectations for equal treatment.

The question of allegiance sheds light on how African Americans understood their relationships with Henry Ford and evaluated their options as they adapted to Ford's labor policies while simultaneously challenging the racial status quo politically. Mutually beneficial relationships between black Detroit and Frank Murphy in the twenties led to a self-conscious use of the black vote to influence public policy. As black Detroiters forged close relationships with Murphy, they gained access to levers of power and created networks within the community that became launching pads for the rise of protest politics in the thirties.

When Frank Murphy first ran for mayor in 1930, black political networks were up and running on a moment's notice to campaign for him. We see in these networks a self-reliant community of activists charting their own course. Before the appearance of Roosevelt's New Deal, black Detroiters, in an alliance with Mayor Murphy, helped shape a new political era in the city. The Reverend Robert L. Bradby, most often remembered as minister of the largest of the so-called Ford churches in black Detroit, actually helped weaken the bonds between Ford and black Detroiters. While Bradby used his church effectively as a hiring hall for jobs at the FMC, his close affiliation and support for Frank Murphy's reform agenda revealed that Bradby's expectations for black Detroiters included much more than inclusion in the mainstream industrial job market. Indeed, Rev. Bradby's close working relationships with both Henry Ford and Frank Murphy exposed his deep ambivalence toward Ford.

Henry Ford wanted allegiance and control over his African American workers not only at the auto plants but within the community as well. When Frank Murphy ran for reelection for mayor in 1931 against Henry Ford's candidate, Rev. Bradby took a decisive stand supporting Murphy in defiance of Ford's interests. Bradby believed that when Henry Ford dictated whom the black community should vote for, he stepped over a sacred line. In this case, allegiance to Frank Murphy and what he stood for trumped Bradby's loyalty to Henry Ford. Although he was reprimanded by a top Ford official, Bradby defended his right to support and vote for the candidate of his choice.

Even in the case of a person as invested in sustaining close connections with the FMC as Rev. Bradby was, the question of loyalty to Henry Ford has to be viewed from within the context of black Detroit. On one level, allegiance to Ford and his labor policies was merely a matter of economics, comparing opportunities gained by working for the FMC with the exclusionist hiring policies at other firms. Nevertheless, the black community exhibited tremendous loyalty to Frank Murphy at the start of his political career, a loyalty that only grew over time. By the early years of the depression, the politics of these two figures—Henry Ford and Frank Murphy—provided bookends to the range of approaches considered for improving economic, political, and social life in Detroit.

When we attempt to discern causes of the final dissolution of the ties binding black Detroiters to the FMC, actions of the Communist Party complicate the picture. Many leaders of black Detroit were characterized as "conservative." Yet these alleged conservatives sometimes supported activities sponsored by the communists. The question of the influence of the Communist Party in the UAW labor organizing campaigns of the mid- to late thirties drives some narratives, putting the political strategies and activities within the black community on the back burner.[13] To argue, as one scholar has, that the most important factor in the shift to a pro-union stand by black Ford employees was the work performed by the Communist Party is to dismiss the activism of black Detroiters between the two world wars.[14] Such a narrative reduces African Americans to the role of following the lead of the communists. Too often, black leaders, activists, and networks have been captured for the historical record at one point in time, as though history can be reduced to a still life. The perspective of black community activists is assumed, rather than interrogated. Without investigating the political and economic agenda embraced by black Detroiters, we cannot know what weight to assign to communist influence in rejecting the paternalism of Henry Ford toward his employees and the larger black community.

None of the above suggests that the communists did not play important roles in the political transformation of black Detroit. Close relationships with communists did influence the transformations in the thirties, yet this observation only marks the starting point for an investigation of the impacts of communist activism. The question is why were black Detroiters so willing to accept radicals into their networks if they, indeed, were merely loyal subjects of King Henry? How do we bridge the gap from blacks regarding loyalty to Ford as a vehicle for realizing the American Dream of upward mobility to blacks welcoming radicals who aspired to undermine American capitalism? So-called conservative, traditional black leaders repeatedly demonstrated little discomfort working with professed radicals—such as those with the International Labor Defense (ILD)—on campaigns to raise money to protest injustices of the southern legal system. How should we explain Rev. Bradby's endorsement of Maurice Sugar, a union activist, very public "fellow-traveler" of the communists, and candidate for judge in Detroit's courts in the mid-thirties? What drew such unlikely bedfellows together?

THE QUESTION OF ALLEGIANCE runs like a river through this portrayal of black Detroit's political and economic evolution. This question is the entry point for exploring how Ford's industrial policies shaped the black migrant community and raised their expectations of what kind of life was possible in urban industrial America. Insight into how African Americans adapted to life in Detroit gives us a clearer understanding of the shifts that occurred in the relationships between black Detroit, Henry Ford, and the FMC, and how the black community moved from a pro-Ford to a pro-union position. The question of allegiance also serves as a heuristic device to link relationships between Henry Ford and black Detroiters to their larger "civil rights" agenda. The vectors carrying the narrative forward—one economic and one political—ground the story of black Detroit in the soil of the larger black freedom struggle. Inclusion at Ford raised expectations about broader economic rights; participation in Frank Murphy's emerging political coalition expanded expectations for equal treatment. In this latter sense, the question of allegiance is a tool for locating the coordinates that shaped the racial geography of Detroit, those boundary lines that help us understand how so many allegedly "docile" black workers at Ford's massive River Rouge plant had by the early forties become the mighty UAW Local 600, the power of which sent shock waves through the national leadership ranks of the union. Wondering what lay behind this dramatic change in community identity drew me to this project.

Although I was never satisfied with traditional explanations about steadfast allegiance to Henry Ford, I carried with me several stereotypes about the roles played by various black leaders into the archives and was taken by surprise at what I learned. Because so much had been written about Henry Ford's paternalism, I imagined a black community virtually choking under its influence. I certainly did not anticipate the degree to which political activism flourished in the Black Bottom and Paradise Valley neighborhoods in the twenties and the thirties.

Kevin Boyle's exemplary history of the Ossian Sweet case, *Arc of Justice*, has helped paved the way for bringing the political activism of black Detroiters out of the shadows. He is joined by several other scholars who excavated parts of the settlement process that created black Detroit.[15] Despite such efforts by the pioneers who pulled back the curtain and opened a window on the myriad ways black Detroiters were pursuing their own interests during the interwar period, the enduring popular image of black Detroiters' relationship with Henry Ford is one largely of dependency. As a result, few would regard black Detroit as a leader during this period for its role in putting the black freedom struggle on more solid footing. Yet, I argue, what emerged after black Detroiters wrestled for two decades with the demons they faced on their new political and economic frontiers was such a model. The road taken in Detroit helped point the way toward utilizing a labor-oriented civil rights agenda to challenge racism within the union movement as well as in the larger community.[16]

In their pathbreaking "Opportunities Found and Lost," Robert Korstad and Nelson Lichtenstein boldly suggested the value of stepping back in time in order to better understand the power of unionization as a pro-cess. When coupled with the "evolution of late New Deal labor legisla-tion," union organizing gave working-class blacks "an economic and po-litical standard" for legitimating their demands and laid the foundation for the civil rights unionism that emerged in the late thirties.[17] This book builds on their analysis, but pushes the clock back to World War I and the early years of the 1920s, hoping to isolate seeds of change present within a northern black community before the arrival of the UAW or the New Deal. This exploration of the evolution of relationships between Henry Ford, black Ford workers, and the black community—as sentiment shifted from pro-Ford to pro-union—is intended to contribute to the conversation on the long civil rights movement and civil rights unionism.[18] The narrative addresses the settlement process of southern blacks in a northern urban area during the first wave of the Great Migration. The "expansion of urban, black communities," Steven A. Reich observes, "made possible black po-litical mobilization and realignment" and fostered a "new mentality and outlook among African Americans that ultimately proved instrumental in the grassroots assault on Jim Crow later in the twentieth century." The vast relocation of people, as Jacquelyn Dowd Hall notes, transformed the "racial geography of the country" and gave rise to the "long civil rights movement."[19]

Extending the time line to the 1920s, I explore black urbanization as a social, economic, and political process as it unfolded in Detroit in order to isolate the "long arm" of the civil rights movement. The settlement process shaped black Americans as they endeavored to realize new op-portunities and challenge restrictions in urban areas. For at least a decade before Roosevelt's New Deal, black Detroiters cultivated their version of an American plan, an experience serving as a tutorial for utilizing the tools of democracy to challenge exclusion from its promise. Collectively devel-oping their agenda was a big step forward for black Detroiters. While dis-cussions will continue about whether the glass was half full or half empty for African Americans in terms of what was done *for* black America during Franklin Roosevelt's New Deal, this study argues that what black progres-sives did for themselves within Detroit was a model for enhancing the power of African Americans to demand inclusion.

Finally, the Detroit story reveals that the path forward was far from smooth, challenging accounts of civil rights history that view actors through a traditional political lens as radical, conservative, or moderate.

The quest for economic justice drew black Americans to Detroit and was a critical part of all phases of the local civil rights movement between World War I and II. But the efforts of many were required to carry the movement forward, and Detroit's black community was not a monolithic bloc. Alliances formed across political boundaries that may not have been possible in another historical context. In order to put our finger on the pulse of the movement, we must trace its aims, agenda, and aspirations over time and from diverse perspectives. As a result, this study also contributes to the history of the Great Migration, black religion, and New Deal politics at the local level; all played essential parts in shaping this history.[20] That said, the primary focus is relationships between Henry Ford, black Ford workers, and the black community. Ford's influence permeated life in black Detroit to such a degree that the Reverend Charles Hill, a voice for change in black Detroit, viewed the FMC as the "battleground for the civil rights movement whether you worked for it or not."[21]

Traditional explanations of anti-union, black Ford loyalists joining the mighty UAW in 1941 ignore the great distance they had traveled in the previous two decades. During the period between the wars, black Ford workers and the community experimented with political and economic strategies that they hoped would lead to a better way of life. While taking part in Ford's select family of workers raised the black community's expectations about what was possible, involvement in Frank Murphy's progressive political coalition laid the foundation for accepting industrial unionism in 1941. Ultimately, the struggle for inclusion in the march toward the promise of America forged the labor-oriented civil rights agenda embraced by black Detroiters on the eve of World War II.

CHAPTERS 1 AND 2 provide context for the social and economic world that greeted African Americans arriving in Detroit during World War I and its aftermath. Henry Ford and other industrials had constructed a new social order on the eve of the Great Migration with an eye to transforming foreign-born workers into a united work force and good American citizens. Henry Ford's idea of including African American workers in his American Plan for the 1920s was not just unique for its time, but also differed in some important aspects from the industrial policies that Ford launched in 1914 for his immigrant workers.

Chapters 3 and 4 trace the settlement process in the 1920s as black Detroiters came of age politically with their support for Frank Murphy, participation in campaigns against the KKK, and challenges to the restrictive racial housing market. Chapters 5 and 6 examine Henry Ford's and Frank Murphy's different responses to the national economic crisis, the Great Depression, and the shifting of loyalties within black Detroit. Chapter 7 examines the rise of self-reliance within black Detroit, focusing on efforts to carry the battle for inclusion forward as new approaches to old concerns, such as jobs and unions, were shaped between 1933 and 1935.

Chapters 8 and 9 carry the narrative from 1935 to 1941, as black Detroiters and black Ford workers laid the foundation for their version of civil rights unionism; the principles guiding the black community's shift culminated in support for the UAW-CIO in the spring of 1941.

CHAPTER ONE

With the Wind at Their Backs

MIGRATION TO DETROIT

With ever watchful eyes and bearing scars, visible and invisible, I headed North, full of a hazy notion that life could be lived with dignity.

—RICHARD WRIGHT, *Black Boy*

EARLY IN THE TWENTIETH CENTURY, the social, economic, and political landscape of Detroit was dramatically transformed as the automotive industry turned this medium-sized city, known for its peace and beauty, into a whirlwind of activity. The siren of new Detroit was "motion . . . the motion of . . . life and energy and unceasing prosperity." People were drawn to the city, it was said, because it was known as "a land flowing with milk and honey and opportunity."[1] What had been a moderately diversified manufacturing center in 1900 was, by 1920, the urban area most committed to manufacturing in the nation, driven increasingly by one industry. By 1919, the automobile industry employed 45.4 percent of the manufacturing workforce, a pattern that continued for decades, making Detroit more specialized in motor vehicle manufacturing by 1940 than Pittsburgh was in iron and steel or Washington, D.C., was in government. Detroit placed fourth in the nation in terms of dollar value of manufactured goods in 1916, moving to third, after New York and Chicago, in the early 1920s.[2] The hub of this wheel of fortune was the Ford Motor Company (FMC). In 1915 the company marketed four times as many cars as its closest competitor, Willys-Overland.[3]

The new automotive industry required enormous numbers of workers, boosting Detroit's population ranking from thirteenth in the nation in 1900 to fourth in 1920, with 1,165,153 people in the metropolitan area. Growth was the result of both internal and foreign migration. Newcomers came from American farms, mines, lumber camps, the rural South, and an increasing number of different countries. Although the percentage of foreign-born Detroiters had been decreasing since the 1900s, the diversity of countries represented in the migration flow increased between 1900 and 1920. Poland was the birthplace of the single largest group of foreign-born Detroiters in 1920 (19.6 percent); Canadians were second (19.1 percent). Germans, Russians, Britons, Austrians, Italians, and Hungarians contributed smaller but significant proportions. When World War 1 cut off nearly all foreign-born immigration, the demographics shifted as the migration of southerners, especially blacks, increased several fold beginning in 1916.[4]

Detroit's black population increased 611.3 percent—from 5,741 in 1910 to 40,838 in 1920—the most rapid growth for any large city and three times faster than the average for other metropolitan areas. The greatest swell in black migration occurred between 1916 and 1920, as industrialists sought a new group of workers to fill positions previously held by immigrants.[5] Forrester B. Washington, the first administrator of the Detroit Urban League (DUL), recorded "1,000 Negroes a month . . . arriving in the city" during May, June, and July of 1917. He estimated that by 1920 the figure was over 1,000 a week. The postwar economic downturn did little to stem the flow, and the black population doubled again between 1920 and 1925 to 81,000, with an estimated 15,000 new residents arriving in 1923 alone. By 1930, the 120,000 black Detroiters accounted for nearly 8 percent of the city's population, up from 1 percent in 1910, or a 2,000 percent increase in African Americans since 1910.[6]

Coleman A. Young, Detroit's first black mayor (elected in 1974), and his family were among the 15,000 African Americans arriving in 1923. The Young family, like many others who moved to Detroit, came from Alabama, traveling, most likely, on a one-way ticket. The northern destination was determined by the placement of the rail lines as well as job possibilities. For that reason, the majority of black Detroiters traveled from rural areas and towns in Alabama, Mississippi, Tennessee, Georgia, South Carolina, and Florida.[7] The decision to migrate was usually made after years of frustration with the South's racial restrictions.[8] Young described the Great Migration as not so much an orchestrated, collective movement as a "cataclysm of personal watersheds."[9] The migration process represented, he recalled, "the accumulation of generations of social degradation and economic despair, of lynchings and whippings and fires and rages, of second-class citizenship and third-world living conditions . . . of ruthless planters cheating their sharecroppers at the autumn settlement . . . of mud floors, of trampled spirits."[10]

Nationally, the pool of migrants came largely from the first generation of black southerners to grow up free from the shackles of slavery. Yearning for the chance to realize the promise of Emancipation, they were most impatient with the restoration of the old order of white supremacy in the post-Reconstruction South.[11] Asa Philip Randolph, who at the age of twenty-two migrated to Harlem on the eve of World War I, believed that actual emancipation could no longer be denied, that it was time to complete "the unfinished task of emancipation."[12] Despite the nation's retreat from the hopes raised by Emancipation and Reconstruction, a political culture, grounded in self-determination and independence from white control, took hold in the latter part of the nineteenth century beyond the surveillance of whites within black communities across the South.[13] By 1916, as James R. Grossman observes, the new generation turned to "industry, to the city, and to the North for access to the perquisites of American citizenship."[14]

Coleman Young's recollections corroborated data collected for a 1920 survey by Forrester Washington, director of the Detroit Urban League, who looked explicitly at why African Americans decided to migrate to Detroit. Using only black investigators, Washington limited his study to heads of black families who had recently migrated and were living in Detroit. When families were asked why they left home, the overwhelming majority cited social factors. Within the category of "social factors," 73 percent noted "unbearable conditions," and another 17 percent cited "oppression." Of the 190 heads of families surveyed, 148 stated that social reasons caused them to leave.[15] Nevertheless, more is needed to understand the Great Migration; inhumane treatment was not new.

Unprecedented opportunity for industrial employment, which opened up with World War I, was new. As the United States closed the door to European immigration, industries geared up to supply the war effort, creating a critical shortage of workers in the North. The labor crisis, in turn, opened the door to economic opportunities for African Americans in meatpacking plants, steel mills, and the foundries of the automotive industry, all areas where industrialists had traditionally employed European immigrants. From an all-time high of 1,218,480 in 1914, total immigration fell to 110,618 in 1918, more than a 90 percent drop.[16] Northern industrialists took a sudden interest in African Americans, sending labor agents to entice black workers to leave the South. Some 400,000 blacks left the South between 1910 and 1920, followed by close to a million more in the twenties, almost all of them heading for the large cities and industrial centers of the Northeast and Midwest, areas rich with economic opportunity.[17]

Both "push" and "pull" factors galvanized the refugees fleeing southern oppression, seeking increased wages, better educational opportunities, voting rights, escape from violence, and a chance to participate as equals in society.[18] Writing in the *Negro Year Book* (1918–19), sociologist Monroe N. Work noted that no event since "Emancipation" had "so profoundly influenced the economic and social life of the Negro." If the "Thirteenth Amendment granted physical emancipation, the conditions brought about by World War I made for the economic emancipation of the Negro," because the war had made it possible for the first time to find "employment along a great many lines, many of which had hitherto [been] closed entirely to him." Many referred to their escape from the South in terms of the "Second Emancipation."[19] The impulse connecting the Great Migration to Emancipation was reinforced as the nation mobilized for World War I under the rubric of making the world safe for democracy. African Americans amended the patriotic call, emphasizing the need to "fight for citizenship at home" as well as across the sea.[20] The ethos unleashed by the war lived on in the hearts and minds of African Americans and fueled the hope that World War I would mark a significant turning point in the black freedom struggle. However southern blacks may have expressed their reasons for migrating, their aim was to secure independence from the oppressive social relations that structured life in the Jim Crow South and to pursue the chance to begin life anew in the North.[21]

Coleman Young's family had to leave Alabama because his father had "used up his southern options," a reference to his "bad" attitude, demonstrated by selling and circulating prominent black newspapers—the *Pittsburgh Courier* and the *Chicago Defender*. When Young's father was advised by a white friend to leave, the family wasted little time packing their bags for Detroit.[22] Social reasons also drove the family of David William Lamar Moore—a future leader in the labor movement in Detroit—from their home in Beech Island, South Carolina, in 1923. Though his father was a locomotive fireman, a position coveted by black men, Moore's family left abruptly to escape Jim Crow sanctions after Moore befriended a young white girl from an elite family in the neighboring town of Aiken, a clear breach of socially acceptable behavior. Moore, who was eleven at the time, remembered fleeing during the dark of night to catch a train in Atlanta that took his family to Columbus, Ohio, where they had relatives. After a few years in Ohio, the family moved to Detroit in 1927, drawn by the hope of working at the FMC.[23]

C. J. Young (no relation to Coleman Young), from Port Arthur, Texas, told the Detroit League on Urban Conditions Among Negroes in 1917 that he had wanted to go North in order to "make a 'man' of himself." An Alabama resident connected the terror of a recent local lynching with his desire to leave. Another Alabamian attributed his desire to migrate to the fact that he was "counted no more thin a dog" where he lived. A Georgian, in his forties, said he was trying "to make an honest living and all of it seems to be a failure." He heard that better treatment and higher wages could be found up North. A resident of Sanford, Florida, wanted to go to another part of the country where he could "better my condishion" while "beaing asshured some protection as a good citizen under the Stars and Stripes."[24]

Skilled and educated along with uneducated agricultural and manual laborers were subject to a southern racial code designed to diminish the humanity and independence of blacks. The successful were debased and humiliated by a system that locked them into a dangerous paradox: the more African Americans succeeded in pulling themselves up by their bootstraps, the greater the chance white supremacists would attack them for being uppity. Ida B. Wells-Barnett identified the conundrum when she exposed the lynching of three successful black businessmen in Memphis, Tennessee, in 1892. They were, as Wells-Barnett argued, lynched for the crime of stepping out of place, "getting too independent." The Memphis incident opened her eyes to what lynching was all about: "An excuse to get rid of Negroes who were acquiring wealth and property and thus keep the race terrorized and 'keep the nigger down.'"[25]

The racial code sought to reign in uppity blacks, to define in hundreds of ways on a daily basis the inferiority of African Americans and the limited spaces where blacks could live their lives. By the end of the nineteenth century, as the number of lynchings of blacks increased dramatically, white supremacists operated outside of the law with an abandon expressed by Ben Tillman, governor of South Carolina in the 1890s and later a senator. The *Congressional Record* recorded Tillman saying that he was proud South Carolina had disfranchised so many African Americans. "We have done our level best," he declared. "We have scratched our heads to find out how we could eliminate the last one of them. We stuffed ballot boxes. We shot them [blacks]. We are not ashamed of it."[26]

More than hunger for increased wages mobilized black migrants. Five decades after President Lincoln signed the Emancipation Proclamation, as Isabel Wilkerson reminds us, "they still had to step off the sidewalk when a white person approached, were banished to jobs nobody else wanted no matter their skill or ambition, couldn't vote, but could be hanged on suspicion of the pettiest infraction."[27] They migrated to put distance between themselves and the racial code of the Jim Crow South; they sought self-determination and inclusion in the American social compact, regardless of the challenges the North might present. A migrant from Mobile, Alabama, spoke for most when he said he was "anxious to leave this part of the country and be where a Negro man can appreshate beaing a man at the present time."[28]

ARRIVAL IN DETROIT

Detroit had been on the short list of desired destinations for black southerners since long before the Civil War. The city's proximity to Canada made it an attractive place for slaves escaping from bondage in the American South. African Americans in antebellum Detroit and the sizable black communities that developed across the river in Windsor and Chatham, Canada, often collaborated in the antislavery crusade. When Frances E. W. Harper, a poet and novelist, stopped off in Detroit in 1858 as part of her lecture tour for the abolitionist cause, she was hailed as the "greatest female speaker ever" on both sides of the border. John Brown met with his co-conspirators in Detroit and Chatham to plot the final stages of the armed insurrection he carried out in October 1859 against the United States Arsenal at Harpers Ferry.[29] Detroit remained on the short list in 1916 as the forces unleashed by World War I, the Great Migration, and industrialization converged with the city's need for hundreds of thousands of new workers. Black southerners were ready to pack their bags, letting the winds generated by war fill their sails and carry them North to industrial jobs and a chance to realize the dream of equal opportunity.

Upon arriving in Chicago, Richard Wright recalled seeing "black faces trying vainly to cope with a civilization that they did not understand." He "knew that this machine-city was governed by strange laws" and wondered if he "would ever learn them."[30] Arrival in Detroit was no less disorienting, and a similar insecurity gripped black newcomers attempting to negotiate the new terrain without a map. In addition to experiences black Detroiters shared with new arrivals in other northern, industrial destinations, they encountered one feature that distinguished the city from other municipalities.

During the 1910s, Detroit's industrial magnates became, Olivier Zunz argues, "active social leaders," as they attempted to construct a "new social order based on a unified work force." The aim was to bring order and efficiency out of the phenomenal growth and diversity in population that had fueled the explosive industrial production since the turn of the century. By the time black newcomers arrived in large numbers, industrialists had spent several years grappling with how best to manage a diverse, largely foreign-born workforce. Adopting the image of a melting pot, industry leaders envisioned a society united by the new American identity that would replace ethnic affiliation.[31] Henry Ford led this endeavor with his Americanization campaign to organize and control his overwhelmingly immigrant work force. He developed labor policies and devoted considerable resources to his effort to assimilate foreign-born laborers in the years leading up to WWI. Although the Americanization campaign preceded Ford's hiring of African Americans in large numbers, it provides a context for understanding the setting at the FMC once black workers were a critical part of Ford's operations.

The social activism of Detroit industrialists extended to the public sector as well. In the late teens, they reformed the city charter with considerable support and money from the FMC. The new city charter was designed to organize the municipality, unifying and harmonizing the body politic in the new social order, by removing inefficiencies inherent in the democratic process. Reform measures in city hall drew from the Progressive impulse to run government with business-like efficiency—popular policies throughout the nation during this era. Detroit's approach was distinctive for its high degree of coordination between reform in the private and public sectors and the unity of managers committed to running "the city as a corporation."[32] While the inspiration for the new social order in 1912–13 was the multiethnic workforce, by the end of the war the presence of large numbers of black workers and residents challenged the intentions of businessmen. Was their aim to assimilate all diverse groups, or was there a separate plan for African Americans? The question—where and how were blacks to fit into the new order in Detroit—probably ranked high among first impressions held by black newcomers seeking to understand the political landscape of their newly adopted city.

HENRY FORD'S AMERICANIZATION CAMPAIGN

Between 1910 and 1913, the FMC dazzled the world with its innovative mass production system based on the idea of an assembly line designed so that work would move while workers stood still. It was hailed as a revolutionary approach for drastically increasing the volume of auto production, which it did, but not to the satisfaction of Ford executives.[33] Soon after the assembly-line production system was launched, management noted a major flaw in the process. Simply put, Ford's workers were not content to stay in place, "doing one job over and over again, and always in the same way," as Henry Ford described the workers' tasks. Ford confessed that the thought of working that way was nothing short of a "terrifying prospect." "I could not possibly do the same thing day in and day out, but to other minds, perhaps I might say to the majority of minds, repetitive operations hold no terrors." The worker Ford hoped to attract "wants a job in which he does not have to think."[34]

By 1913 the quit-rate and absenteeism among assembly-line workers reached crisis proportions, prompting Ford and his executives to reconsider the value of labor in the manufacturing process. Production worker requirements that year were about 13,600, yet the company needed to hire over 53,000 workers to replace what amounted to a labor turnover rate of 370 percent. On any given day, the average absentee rate was 10 percent of the entire workforce.[35]

Management declared that the very diversity of Ford's workforce undermined the efficient operation of the mass production line, contributing to lagging productivity. By 1914, almost three-quarters of the 14,000 workers at Ford's main plant, Highland Park factory, were foreign-born. One source identified over fifty nationalities. Simple miscommunication between non-English-speaking workers and English-speaking foremen could disrupt the continuous flow of moving parts through the factory. According to Ford executives, a new degree of cultural conformity was needed to facilitate the uninterrupted flow of materials. Ford officials also flagged the work habits of foreign-born workers for dragging down productivity and diluting the "American Standard of Living," both at work and at home.[36]

In order to manage the human element of production more effectively, Ford introduced the second phase of his industrial revolution, aimed at Americanizing his largely foreign workforce, by prescribing a standardized way for his workers to live and work by.[37] Ford called it the Five Dollar Day, Ford Profit-Sharing Plan. When it was unveiled in January 1914, the world was stunned. Ford workers would receive a five-dollar-a-day wage, more than double the average wage in the auto industry at that time. When compared to lower prevailing wages in other industries such as steel, meatpacking, or coal mining, the Ford proposal was even more astounding. Simultaneously, the FMC reduced the workday from nine hours to eight hours.[38]

The idea that the basic rate for a nine-hour shift, which had been $2.34 a day, was raised to $5 per day for an eight-hour shift seemed too good to be true. Had the general public and journalists paid closer attention to the devil in the details, they would have realized that Ford's plan was much more complicated than it first appeared. The eight-hour-day policy was straightforward. Less clear was what the FMC meant when officials reminded workers that to receive the Five Dollar Day they were required to take part in a plan the company called "profit-sharing," which was not to be confused with a wage increase. The basic pay for an eight-hour shift was $2.34, just what it had been for a nine-hour shift (which, of course, did amount to an increase in wages). However, in order to "earn" the remaining $2.66 per day—and take home $5 per day—workers had to agree to transform themselves into worthy profit sharers. Investigators from the Sociological Department, created to implement Ford's Americanization program for workers, determined whether individual workers were worthy, a process that often took months.[39]

To clarify the plan and explain what many people had missed, the company issued a pamphlet, "Helpful Hints and Advice to Employes [sic] to Help Them Grasp the Opportunities which Are Presented to Them by the Ford Profit-Sharing Plan." Wages were defined as that "which the Company will pay . . . for his services and labor." Share of profits "meant that sum which is put into the pay envelopes each pay day over and above the sum earned and paid as wages." To underscore the distinction, workers' pay envelopes had the amount of wages and the amount of "profit" recorded separately. A Ford employee could count on the basic wage for services and labor rendered to the company. What a worker could not count on was his share of the "profits." To receive his share of the profits ($2.66 per day), a worker had to demonstrate that his lifestyle would be "of permanent benefit" to himself, his family, and the FMC. In other words, the worker was rewarded with a share of the profits if he proved to be a reasonable investment for the future of the company. Thus the profit-sharing plan, embedded within the Five Dollar Day, used the lure of profit sharing to alter the behavior and control the lives of Ford workers in ways determined by and considered appropriate by Henry Ford.[40]

The Five Dollar Day, Profit-Sharing Plan sought to increase worker productivity and reduce turnover and absenteeism by offering a larger paycheck at the end of the day, but only if the worker was able to conform to a narrowly defined work culture. The Sociological Department was organized to carry out extensive investigations of Ford workers and their families, friends, and neighbors. Laborers were evaluated in terms of personal cleanliness, sanitation, "thrift, honesty, sobriety, better housing, and better living generally." Investigators looked through family Bibles, passports, and other government documents; they questioned ministers, priests, and members of fraternal organizations. If the worker "passed" inspection, he received the Five Dollar Day. If not, the company held back the profits for six months, the time allowed for the employee to raise himself up to Ford's standards with the aid of "free" counseling from a sociology adviser. If the employee still did not measure up, the company let him go.[41]

Investigators had lots of advice and very little tolerance for what it called "bad homes" located in "bad neighborhoods." In case there was any doubt, the company literature declared it was "by no means the intention of the company to dictate the neighborhood in which the employe [sic] shall live," yet, in the same breath, added "it does insist that the neighborhood be decent and the home wholesome, clean and sanitary."[42] The company justified its intrusive labor policy by explaining that it did not feel it ought to underwrite the business of saloons and brothels with its profits. By paying out profits to its workers it had a right to demand a fit, sober labor force.[43] "Helpful Hints" further explained that its requirements were made for the good of "each employe," that he might "make the most of his or her life."[44]

The requirements also helped realize Henry Ford's larger vision, "to make men in this factory as well as automobiles," as he put it in 1913 to the Reverend Samuel S. Marquis, the minister of St. Paul's Episcopal Cathedral in Detroit, the church Ford attended.[45] Making men as well as automobiles captures, in short form, the spirit that gave birth to Fordism as the economic system based on mass production and mass consumption. Allen Nevins and Frank Ernest Hill call mass production the "womb in which modern industry was to be reshaped."[46] If they are correct, then the Five Dollar Day, Profit-Sharing Plan spawned the mass consumption without which Fordism would have died. At one level, Ford wanted to make consumers out of the men who made his cars. The idea that high wages would lead to high sales volume, once workers could afford to buy what they produced, revolutionized the philosophy of business by demonstrating, twenty years before John Maynard Keynes articulated the idea, the importance of rising consumption in fueling economic growth.[47]

At another level, Fordism was about making a new breed of workers: men, for the most part, who lived according to Ford's ideal of an "American Standard of Living," the guide for his profit-sharing plan. That plan not only sealed the pact between employees and the FMC, but also gave birth to Ford's vision for a new era. He hoped to make a new American worker through the "regenerating power of work . . . [that] is given a just return. . . . the kind [of contractual situation] that helps a man to help himself."[48] That was one way Ford promoted his own agenda by appealing to the self-interest of workers, especially those who wanted to be included as highly paid workers in Ford's "new era." The profit-sharing covenant also stifled union activity, as the intrusion of investigators from the Sociological Department posed a serious challenge to any form of labor organizing.[49]

The total compensation package consisted of the basic wage, about half of the five dollar day, which paid for the way a worker made a living. Slightly more than half of the five dollars came from the profit-sharing part of the plan, which "paid," in essence, for the way a worker conducted his life.[50] Ford's new labor contract or covenant, designed to usher in his new era, was embedded in the profit-sharing part of the plan. It was the hook that drew workers into Ford's orbit, nurtured a new culture at work and social order at home and in the larger community. By virtue of taking part in the Ford profit-sharing plan, workers contracted to take responsibility for ensuring that their domestic, social, and civic lives measured up to standards set by Henry Ford. If they passed inspection, workers not only got the full five dollars a day, they became members of the Ford family of American workers.

Emphasis on cleanliness, housing stock, and personal habits was directly connected in Ford's mind to making Americans out of foreigners. As Henry Ford told the *New York Times*, "We will give every one time to correct his living conditions, but the tenement and the crowded rooming house must be eliminated." Ford employees who continued to live in squalid tenements would no longer be "Ford $5-a-day men." Ford explained, "They sell their labor to us and we give them a bonus." But the bonus is given for a reason. "These men of many nations must be taught American ways, the English language, the right way to live." Following Ford's plan was the path to becoming an American. Married men were warned not to sacrifice "family rights, pleasure, and comfort by filling their homes with roomers and boarders." Single men were expected to live under similar conditions. If they live "correctly," Ford reasoned, "we can make them good citizens."[51] Stephen Meyer calls the Five Dollar Day, Profit-Sharing Plan, Ford's attempt "to fit the immigrant worker into . . . [his] preconceived mold of the ideal American." A branch manager was told that Ford intended "to make better men and better American citizens and to bring about a larger degree of comforts, habits, and a higher plane of living among our employees."[52]

When Henry Ford appeared before the U.S. Senate's Commission on Industrial Relations in 1915, he explained his profit-sharing plan in terms of how it related to American citizenship and the advancement of the community. His sociological advisers, he told the commission, taught "American Ways and Customs, English Language, [and] duties of Citizenship. . . . The whole effort of this corps [the staff of the Sociological Department] is to point men to LIFE and make them discontent with a mere living."[53] The Five Dollar Day, Profit-Sharing Plan reduced turnover. In 1915 the FMC required only 2,000 replacements.[54]

A second institution, the Ford English School, taught English to foreigners, completing the Americanization process initiated through the social engineering carried out by the Sociological Department.[55] Samuel S. Marquis, director of the Sociological Department at the FMC in 1915, noted that the "first thing we teach them to say is 'I am a good American,' and then we try to get them to live up to that statement."[56] The lessons created for teaching the language were selected specifically around themes designed to inculcate the basics of American social and cultural norms as well as principles for learning how to be good citizens in an urban environment.[57]

The English School, established in 1914, was compulsory, meeting two times a week for an hour and a half. Lessons were given in personal hygiene and how to take care of the home. Great emphasis was also placed on teaching civics classes in city, state, and national government as well. Marquis maintained that the government recognized the value of the Ford curriculum by giving those who "hold a diploma from the Ford English School, their first papers without examination." Prior to 1952, naturalization required filing a Declaration of Intent, known as first papers, the first part of the two-step process for an immigrant to become a U.S. citizen. The preference was to teach classes that were mixed as to race and country, for "our great aim is to impress these men that they are or should be Americans and that former racial and national differences are to be forgotten."[58]

In order to celebrate the transformation of the foreign-born worker into an American, Ford's Americanization efforts included commencement exercises after a worker successfully completed his studies at the Ford English School. The following company report describes a typical graduation ceremony for some 500 employees. "Commencement exercises were held in the largest hall in the city. On the stage was represented an immigrant ship. In front of it was a huge melting pot. [The pot was 15 feet in diameter and 7½ feet high.] Down the gangplank came the members of the class dressed in their national garbs and carrying luggage such as they carried when they landed in their country. Down they poured into the Ford melting pot and disappeared. Then the teachers began to stir the contents of the pot with long ladles. Presently the pot began to boil over and out came the men dressed in their best American clothes and waving American flags."[59]

Ford's Americanization Plan became a model for other industrialists in Detroit and the nation. Although aspects of educating foreigners about the "spirit of true Americanism" can be found from the late 1890s onward, the issue of assimilating foreigners, shaping them to conform to the American way of life, did not begin to assume concrete shape until in 1912 the Progressive Party proposed federal action to promote the "assimilation, education and advancement" of the immigrant population.[60] Support came from business organizations, particularly when the United States economy heated up with orders from Allied forces after the start of World War I. As John Higham argues, "Many an employer saw in Americanization a means of increasing the efficiency, cooperation, and output of his present workers."[61]

Members of the Detroit Board of Commerce, an organization of in-

Henry Ford's "Melting Pot" ceremony in process, 4 July 1917. Note the newly matriculated "citizens" walking down the steps carrying the American flag in one hand and a diploma from Ford's English School in the other. From the Collections of The Henry Ford. ID#P.O.7227.

dustrialists, adopted Ford's approach to Americanization in 1915, setting up night schools throughout the city to teach English and forming the Americanization Committee of Detroit (ACD).[62] The ACD's purpose was "to promote and inculcate in both native and foreign born residents of the metropolitan district . . . the principles of American institutions and good citizenship" and to assist immigrants in learning English. John R. Lee, first director of the Ford Sociological Department, who was a director of the Board of Commerce and actively involved in forming and running the ACD, assured Henry Ford's imprint.[63]

With America's entry into World War I, Detroit's Board of Commerce led the way for the larger, national Americanization campaign that "blossomed into a great popular crusade."[64] As the obsession to be considered a 100 percent American heated up, freedom of speech was restricted, foreigners were regarded with suspicion, and patriotism meant undivided loyalty to country. Efforts by immigrants to retain elements of their culture, such as their native language, were considered "un-American."[65] The campaign raised questions about a citizen's origins and political allegiance across the country, challenging definitions of democracy in the process. While the anti-German campaign is well documented, the question of loyalty to America hung around every newcomer's neck. Black migrants in the North were no exception. They may have been citizens in name, but were they in deed?

African Americans understood that the desire to be accepted as part of the American family, and not as third cousins once removed, rested on a wing and a prayer. The issue had gained momentum and prominence in the pages of black newspapers, pulpits of ministers, and speeches of black leaders well before U.S. entry into the war.[66] W. E. B. Du Bois began educating *Crisis* readers about the significance of World War I for African Americans shortly after the outbreak of armed conflict in Europe. In a fall 1914 essay, he reviewed racial policies of the countries at war, concluding, "To-day civilized nations are fighting like mad dogs over the right to own and exploit . . . darker peoples." Although Du Bois did not consider any of the belligerents innocent, he suggested that the sympathies of black Americans should lie with the Allies—France and England.[67] The *Chicago Defender*, widely distributed in the South, also discussed questions of citizenship and war.[68]

By the time World War I was under way, concerns of Detroit industrialists and black southerners broadly converged over the question of what it meant to be an American. African Americans, determined to demonstrate their allegiance to American values, welcomed the opportunity to prove their loyalty to their native land. Black newcomers from the first generation of the Great Migration wanted, Richard Wright wrote, what others had, "the right to share in the upward march of American life." Migration North was, as Carole Marks noted, the first part of a larger plan "to become a part of the whole" of American life.[69]

That was, in many respects, just what Henry Ford wanted from his labor force. Black workers, driven by a desire for inclusion in modern industrial society, hoped to find a position in the new social order unfolding in Detroit by joining Ford's family of American workers. In turn, Henry Ford hoped the new social order would become a model for industrial society at work and within the larger community.[70] Allegiance to the American system and American values grounded the shape of the new order each group envisioned.

FITTING BLACK DETROITERS INTO
THE NEW SOCIAL ORDER

Ford's Americanization Plan, specifically constructed to fit foreign-born workers into his new order, assumed the "skin" of ethnic affiliation would be shed as foreign-born citizens united behind a new American identity.[71] But when immigration from Europe slowed to a trickle, the Detroit Board of Commerce beefed up its efforts to encourage the migration of southern blacks to take the place of foreign workers. Nevertheless, efforts to Americanize "hyphenated aliens" moved forward, with little thought given to fitting black Detroiters into the new social order. As a result, the racial status quo remained, and a color line was woven into the social fabric of metropolitan Detroit. We can trace the contours of that color line through the relationships that developed between black Detroiters, the Detroit Urban League (DUL), and the interests of industrialists on the board of Associated Charities (AC), a philanthropic organization.[72]

Well over 25,000 African Americans moved to the city in 1916 and 1917, but few institutions were prepared to serve the needs of this large group of newcomers. Eugene Kinckle Jones, aware of the problem as director of the National Urban League (NUL), went to Detroit in 1915 seeking help from the city's black community leaders in an effort to establish a branch of the NUL. When community leaders rejected him, Jones formed an alliance with the white elite through Henry Glover Stevens. From that alliance, the DUL was created.[73]

Stevens, a wealthy businessman who managed the Stevens Land Company, was vice president of AC, which was established in 1879 by Detroit's civic leaders to raise and disburse funds for the community's welfare. Stevens liked the idea of a partnership between industrialists and the local office of the NUL. The effort was a good way to promote civic harmony in a city whose only social welfare agency was for white migrants and whose industrial leaders were, according to Olivier Zunz, "clearly at a loss when faced with the continuous flow of southern Blacks into the city."[74] The alliance between Jones and Stevens was initially mutually beneficial. The DUL was formed as a "committee" of AC, its legal status from 1916 to 1924.[75] A DUL board, also a creation of AC, included representatives from Detroit's largest corporations, one of which was the FMC, and insisted on control over the DUL's policies in return for funding the organization.[76] Stevens, who served as president of the DUL, declared its aim was "trying to aid in the assimilation of these newcomers," noting in particular the need to "open to the Negro industrial and recreational opportunities."[77]

The DUL board hired an African American, Forrester B. Washington, as its executive director, or public face, in 1916. Washington's background at elite institutions, including Tufts, Harvard, and Columbia Universities, prepared him to carry out his job with skill and cultured grace as a liaison balancing the needs of industrialists with those of black Detroiters.[78] The agenda, driven by the interests of industrialists, was to acclimate the thousands of recent arrivals from the rural and small-town South, making them into efficient workers so they could fit into the new industrial culture.[79]

Washington ran day-to-day affairs at the DUL, under close supervision from Stevens and other directors, who could examine and question Washington's every office transaction, leaving him with little autonomy in terms of policy and practice. Washington focused his efforts on material surroundings, influences impacting migrants' "health, their morals, and their efficiency." A healthy, wholesome environment was necessary, for "you cannot grow lilies in ash-barrels." The first need, he said, is employment, in order to get the "Negro immigrant started off right." Besides, Washington added, "few land-lords will rent a house or rooms unless the prospective tenant has a job."[80]

Although the task was, in many respects, daunting, the program enacted by the DUL was hailed as a model for assimilating black migrants. The organization's activities were observed from as far away as New York City. An editorial in the *New York Evening Post* praised Washington for understanding that because "the human material coming from the South is plastic," with care migrants could be shaped into "industrious, law-respecting, and progressive" citizens. His time with recent arrivals was spent educating them in how to present a clean, sober appearance when interacting with white employers, save their money, and avoid the temptations of crime and vice.[81]

Washington and his successor, John Dancy, who took over as DUL executive director in 1918, were told to steer clear of any issues that would put in question the prevailing racial status quo.[82] Although Washington usually avoided public discussions of thorny issues such as housing, the ban did not stop him from producing a sound piece of research on the "Negro in Detroit," published in 1920. It was especially sobering for revealing difficulties black newcomers had as they searched for decent, affordable housing.[83] His task must have seemed Sisyphean. Washington put jobs and recreational opportunities, issues sanctioned by corporate leaders, high on his agenda.[84] Yet as he did so and as *The Negro in Detroit* documents, even approved topics exposed a disturbing level of tolerance for inequality by the industrialists dominant on the DUL board, which supported separate facilities both on the job and at recreational sites. Within the factory walls, discrimination against black workers was rampant. In the majority of industrial establishments, black workers were excluded from social activities such as participation with whites in bowling leagues, baseball teams, dances, and picnics. Washington also noted separate facilities for black and white employees in lunchrooms and bathrooms. In some factories, employers hung signs designating "white" and "colored" bathrooms. Washington came to the conclusion that "there are a few shops in the city in which the Negro is included in every recreational and welfare activity," which he referred to as "democracy" within the factory gates. But, in the majority of cases, Detroit's industrialists did not address social "democracy."[85]

HOUSING BLACK MIGRANTS

Although Henry Stevens declared that the aim of the DUL was to "aid in assimilation," his definition of the process never extended to housing, which Washington called "the most serious of the Negro's urban problems."[86] African Americans were immediately directed to the one part of town where most black Detroiters lived, the East Side, when they first arrived. Finding places for newcomers to call home assumed crisis proportions for blacks and whites alike during World War I, for decline in housing construction during the war added to the crowding produced by the continuous flow of newcomers. While new construction accounted for 16,489 additional buildings in 1916, it fell to just over 7,000 in 1918.[87] But if the housing situation for whites was dismal, that for African Americans was atrocious. What distinguished the settlement experience of black migrants from that of white ethnics was the immobility that ultimately fenced black Detroiters into a black metropolis housing African Americans from all social classes. Restrictive covenants, real estate codes, and racial prejudice were forces that prevented African Americans from exercising free choice when it came to housing.[88] During the first phase of the settlement process, the black ghetto was still in formation and not a fait accompli. But the barriers were rising, year by year, segregating African Americans into a separate city within the larger city.

Those barriers made a difference in how African Americans became urbanized. Lack of choice in where black Detroiters lived influenced how they were able to live—where they could and could not shop, what streets they could travel on in other parts of town, and what areas they could use for recreation. The black urbanization process shaped the racial geography of Detroit, the legacy of which is etched on the urban landscape of the twenty-first-century metropolis known as the Motor City. Although certain sections of neighborhoods housing white immigrants were slums, they never reached the level of overcrowding, unhealthy living conditions, and dilapidation blacks were forced to live in.[89]

Many reports—some filed by DUL executive director Washington, others by black sociologist George Haynes writing for a national audience—put Detroit on the map as a city in trouble well before the end of World War I. Haynes estimated that discrimination and lack of new housing stock were responsible for squeezing 12,000 to 15,000 black Detroiters into the East Side, an area that "formerly furnished housing accommodations for less than one-half that number." Some rooms were crowded to the point that the most efficient way "to dress was to stand in the middle of the bed." The official survey of black Detroit noted that the 1919 housing shortage was so acute that some paid for a chance to sleep in automobiles and on pool tables. The quality of the homes was "the least desirable in the city. Houses of 4 or 5 rooms crowded with people pay the highest possible rents." Many of the houses had no bath, and often no inside toilet.[90] Oliver Zunz points out that "all observers familiar with conditions in other cities reported intense crowding in Detroit."[91]

Although by 1920 about 70 percent of Detroit's blacks lived on the East Side in a neighborhood known as Black Bottom, only half lived in blocks dominated by African Americans. Most still shared city blocks with Jews, Italians, Czechs, and other East Europeans.[92] But they paid more for the same housing stock than other ethnic groups. Blacks living in the same duplex housing with other groups often paid as much as 50 percent more for the very same facilities. Generally, blacks did not protest rent gouging for fear the landlord might kick them out, leaving them with no other place to live.[93]

In 1918 the increasingly crowded black East Side neighborhoods caught the attention of members of the ACD, who asked John Dancy to take them on a tour of Black Bottom. The committee's report described blacks "living in shacks unfit for human habitation and paying for them excessive rents." Struck by their tour, the committee added a special section, "Negro Housing Problem," to its annual report and recommended that another committee "delve further" into the situation in order to "suggest a program of activity which at least in part would relieve this blot in the city's boundaries." Though shocked by the overcrowding, the lack of sanitation facilities, and the outrageous rents the area was able to command, the committee nonetheless ultimately declared that its organization was not concerned or responsible for the crisis in housing black Americans. The committee took no further action.[94]

For all the effort expended on ushering in a new social order, creating a unified society of American citizens out of the multiethnic population of workers, Detroit's industrialists did not intend to fit African Americans into the social matrix. The industrial elite concentrated their support on the DUL, the vehicle for assuaging the fears and trials of black migrants, cautioning Washington and Dancy to avoid at all costs efforts to assimilate blacks into Detroit's melting pot of diverse nationalities. The elite industrialists may have wanted to avoid residential integration of blacks in order to curb black political and social ambitions, or to placate the racism of the white working class. It is not clear what motivated the hands-off response to the housing crisis in Black Bottom. However, during this period, these same industrialists did not shy away from micromanaging reform of city government.

RESTRUCTURING DETROIT'S MUNICIPAL GOVERNMENT

In 1918 the Detroit Citizens League (DCL) reconstructed municipal government by rewriting the city's charter. Created by Henry Martyn Leland, founder and president of Cadillac Motor Car Company, the DCL led the effort to infuse city government with order, stability, efficiency, and morality. The major problem, according to Leland, was a council based on two representatives from each of the city's twenty-one wards. The forty-two councilmen were considered inefficient, and the process for selecting

them through partisan balloting, unacceptable. The result was a municipal system regarded by the professional and business elite as inept and
corrupt.[95]

In carrying out reform, Detroit industrialists waved the banner of efficiency that inspired the Americanization programs initiated for factory
workers. The corporate model was applied to City Hall with the aim of
redrawing the boundaries of the democratic process in a way that better
served the interests of industrialists and minimized the ward-based political strength of ethnic and lower-class citizens. Working in concert, the
Detroit Board of Commerce, the Employers Association of Detroit, and
representatives of Henry Ford produced a new charter that transformed
city government in 1918. The mayor and aldermen were voted in through
at-large, nonpartisan elections; the power of the mayor was strengthened;
and the new City Council consisted of only nine aldermen, restricting the
voice of the majority. The first mayor in the new order was James Couzens,
a former vice president of the FMC.[96]

The DCL reasoned that putting the reins of power in the hands of what
it considered the "better class" in Detroit was the means for leading voters to back policies to promote overall "civic progress." League leaders did
not hide their lack of faith in the majority. Pliny Marsh, secretary of the
DCL, said it was "very questionable" whether average people could create a
strong, efficient, well-run government. What such people needed was "the
leadership and financial support of men of broad judgment and ample
means."[97]

Henry Ford and his executives played a major role in publicizing the
plan for the new charter to his workers and other Detroit voters.[98] Like
those of most industrialists, Ford's interests were closely tied to the goal
of keeping Detroit an open-shop city by decreasing the possibility for political activism among workers. Ford's support of the charter was crucial
for capturing working-class votes for the new charter. Ten large meetings
were held at the FMC to pitch the virtues of the new charter over the old.
The company also included promotional literature about the charter in
employees' pay envelopes. Finally, Dr. Samuel S. Marquis of the FMC's Sociological Department and the DCL produced two cartoon films to highlight the benefits of a new smaller council.[99]

By the end of World War I, industrialists' discussions for a new order
began to include talk of physically expanding the city as a way to ad-

dress housing concerns. William P. Lovett, a leading member of the DCL, claimed a major aim of the new charter was to create an entity that would provide direction for the physical expansion of the city. Eliminating the ward system was a first step toward that expansion since it was regarded as a way to reduce intra-city factions, drawing "all classes, creeds, and kinds of people into one community relationship," one defined by the DCL.[100] Within a year of the new city charter, there were five real estate agents on the nine-man Common Council, and real estate interests continued to have a significant voice on Detroit's Common Council, later called the "City Council," between World War I and World War II.[101]

The new city charter, which increased the power of businessmen, may have assured the leaders that their multiyear project to shape a workforce imbued with decency and American values was on the right track. The DCL dared to imagine that it could lead "voters toward its version of the civic ideal."[102] It was not long, however, before their entire outlook was challenged as the city and the nation came to terms with problems washed ashore in the wake of World War I. The optimism of the industrial elite soon gave way to a fear of labor unrest and a Red Scare as many of the gains enjoyed during the robust years of the war became casualties of the postwar slump in the economy. The model for the good society was tested by unemployment, the rise of radicalism, and the inability to figure out how black workers would "fit" into the new order. The attempt to resolve that last concern would prove especially troubling in the years ahead.

BLACK DETROITERS MAP THEIR BOUNDARIES

During the first decades of the twentieth century, Detroit changed from a medium-sized manufacturing center into an industrial wonder of the modern world. Henry Ford's revolutionary approach to mass production, tethered to mass consumption, transformed the face of the city even as the technological success of Fordism swiftly turned Detroit into the automotive center of the universe. The highly productive system, fueled by incentives of the Five Dollar Day, Ford Profit-Sharing Plan, shaped a new industrial order and the workers to fit that order. The covenant that Ford offered to workers exhibiting traits of good American citizenship linked Fordism with his Americanization campaign. The campaign—coupled with his English School—became a model both for Detroit industrialists and for the country, as an obsession with one's claim to being an American grabbed the nation's attention during World War I. It did not take long for the country and the world to equate a newly coined term, to "Fordize," with "Americanize."[103]

As industrialists in Detroit moved forward with their efforts to harmonize the multiethnic makeup of its autoworkers, the demographic profile of the city was shifting. African Americans moved to the city in massive numbers during the first years of the Great Migration, seeking escape from Jim Crow and inclusion in the new social order that promised equal pay with little discrimination at the FMC. But the city was not prepared, nor was it preparing, to incorporate African Americans as equals in the new Detroit. Industrialists gave lip service to the idea of assimilating blacks, but their actions told another story. Whether by default or by design, a color line was etched into the city, shaping the boundary lines that restricted black citizens from all backgrounds to an increasingly congested part of the city. Thus, during the initial period of settlement, black Americans were consumed with housing issues. Racial prejudice decreased choice and mobility for African Americans and increased the price they paid for the same housing stock occupied by other ethnic groups.

As the walls of segregation in housing were raised, political expression was kept in check when the DCL successfully restructured city government. The new city charter, written to dilute the influence of the hyphenated majority, was supported by Henry Ford, who hoped it would douse the fire of political activism, spread during the Red Scare, and dampen the appeal of unionization efforts among his workers.

While African Americans had been drawn to Detroit by the magnetic pull of the North Star shining over the city's new-age automotive center, Henry Ford remained a figure of great promise and appeal to black workers. But it was not until 1919 that Ford began hiring African Americans in great numbers, carrying out the third phase of his revolutionary industrial design. When he did so, he demonstrated a way to "fit" African Americans into his new era.

Although African Americans were not allowed to put down roots in most neighborhoods when they arrived in Detroit, in the short run blacks focused on the huge gains they made in the industrial job market. Nowhere was the leap over past barriers in industry greater than at the FMC.

When Ford began hiring black workers in large numbers, he inaugurated a period not only of high wages for black workers but also high hopes that inclusion in Ford's family of American workers would bring other perks of citizenship. Ford provided the foundation for building a new life; for a while that was a sufficient reason to be loyal to Henry Ford and his company.

CHAPTER TWO

Henry Ford Ushers in a
New Era for Black Workers

I'm goin' to get a job,
Up there in Mr. Ford's place,
Stop these eatless days from starin'
Me in the face.

—BLIND ARTHUR BLAKE, "Detroit Bound Blues"

RUMOR HAD IT that "workin' in Mr. Ford's place" in Detroit was the route to inclusion for African Americans in the modern industrial American economy. Henry Ford's promise of a Five Dollar Day was not tainted with discrimination; blacks were paid a wage equal to that of whites. During the late teens, "the name *Ford* became synonymous with northern opportunity," recalled LeRoi Jones (Amiri Baraka), inspiring hundreds of black southerners to travel North with their sights set on a job at the Ford Motor Company (FMC).[1] During the first years of the Great Migration, few blacks landed jobs at the FMC, for the company was slow to hire large numbers of African Americans. By 1919, however, Ford took the lead, taking on 1,700 African Americans, compared to 926 at Packard, second in black employment in the auto industry. Ford kept its lead and held it, as Herbert Northrup noted, coming "closer to job equality" than any large corporation and remaining in the vanguard in terms of equal hiring policies within the automotive industry until World War II.[2]

Henry Ford embraced the idea of hiring large numbers of black workers as he came to terms with a host of problems threatening control over his automotive empire. By the end of World Word I in 1918, Ford's Five Dollar Day, Profit-Sharing Plan was on shaky ground as labor turnover, which had been curbed substantially between 1914 and 1916, increased and labor productivity decreased. Wartime inflation eroded the value of Ford's Five

Dollar plan and the incentives it had created to alter worker behavior through conformity to the Americanization campaign. By the war's end, a Ten Dollar Day would have had to be instituted to match the Five Dollar plan of 1914, but that was not forthcoming.[3]

In 1917 Vladimir Lenin's Russian Revolution shook the world and with it Ford's plan to create a new industrial worker to fit his new era. While Ford's revolutionary Five Dollar Day demonstrated one way to make workers and management partners in profit sharing or shareholders in capitalism, Lenin's plan did much the opposite. Not only did Lenin's Soviet plan make workers and bosses enemies, but, more importantly, it was thought, it put control over production in the hands of labor, an idea that caught the attention of workers at the FMC. Feeling the tremors from the social upheaval thousands of miles away in the Soviet Union, Ford looked in new directions for model workers.[4]

At the same time, the war expanded federal government power over labor relations. In order to boost productivity, the government trotted out its own incentives, often promising "industrial democracy" and reminding workers "the People ARE the Government."[5] Such patriotic slogans may explain the increasingly repressive labor policies Ford put into place on the shop floor and the company's surveillance of suspected dissident American and immigrant workers. While Ford's wartime policies silenced some and put fear into others, they also breathed new life into unions. Many reports filed by Ford informers noted the increase in radical ideas and alliances with labor unions. The Ford network of spies was both extensive and thorough. Having contributed their labor and wages to make the world "safe for democracy," some workers, Stephen Meyer writes, wanted to have a say in creating their vision of industrial democracy at the FMC.[6]

The optimistic spirit that drove the Five Dollar Day, Profit-Sharing Plan was gone by the end of the war, replaced with Ford's frustration over how to move forward. His zeal for social engineering had not, however, withered on the vine. He had lost faith not in the model for his new era, merely in the means for getting there. No longer interested in changing the attitudes and behavior of his foreign-born workers, whose allegiance he regarded as questionable, Ford turned his attention to hiring African Americans. Along with the labor unrest that erupted in 1919, an economic downturn raised issues of labor efficiency and control, and concerns over just how the war had undermined his Americanization campaign for foreign workers. Good American workers were never intended to be union members. Thus, World War 1 and the Russian Revolution shaped Ford's new American Plan, leading him to hire thousands of African Americans who would carry the torch for his new era in industrial relations into the future.

The war to make the world safe for democracy, which had spurred African Americans toward jobs and freedom in the urban North, ended with a renewed resolve, best stated by W. E. B. Du Bois, to "make way for democracy! We saved it in France, and by the Great Jehovah, we will save it in the United States of America, or know the reason why." More often than not, however, white resistance met black resolve. The increased incidence of lynchings, fewer jobs, race riots in twenty-five cities and towns, and the return of the Ku Klux Klan sent a definite message: the place for African Americans in the postwar world would continue to be subordinate to whites. The nationalization of the "maltreatment of Negroes," Carter Woodson had predicted, would be one of the consequences from the Great Migration as "poor whites of both sections . . . strike at this race long stigmatized by servitude but now demanding economic equality."[7] Thanks in part to Henry Ford, however, black Detroiters faired better than most African Americans in the immediate aftermath of the war.

FORD HIRED HIS first African American employee at the FMC, William Perry, on 9 February 1914. Ford had initially employed Perry in the 1880s to cut down trees on his property in Dearborn, and he sometimes shared the task with Perry when he took up the opposite end of a two-man cross-cut saw.[8] After the hiring of Perry, who stayed on the company's payroll until his death in 1940, Ford's policy for employing African Americans resembled that of other industrialists for several years. The 200 blacks working for Ford in 1917, for example, largely held janitorial or menial positions within the company.[9]

This changed in 1919 when Ford's hiring policies took a radical turn as he began employing larger and larger numbers of African Americans for positions throughout his Detroit-area factories. He soon became the largest single employer of blacks in the auto industry. He also initiated hiring black workers for jobs throughout his plant.[10] In August, Ford hired Eugene J. Collins to conduct tests on cast iron samples in the company's control analysis laboratory. As one of the first blacks with a white-collar job at Ford, Collins foreshadowed changes to come.[11] Within a short period

James C. Price, first black salaried employee at Ford Motor Company, was responsible for purchasing industrial diamonds for grinding machines. He is seen here inspecting emery wheels in the Rouge Motor Building (n.d.). From the Collections of The Henry Ford. #P.833.72372.

of time, black workers at the River Rouge, where the majority were employed, were present in all phases of the manufacturing operations; at no other plant in the auto industry was that the case.[12] In addition to being on the assembly line, black Ford workers had jobs in laboratories and drafting rooms; they worked as crane operators, mechanics, electricians, and tool-and-die makers. In 1924 Collins was put in charge of a unit working with die-casting machines in the electric furnace building, and James C. Price, hired in 1917, was given responsibility for purchasing abrasive and industrial diamonds and became the first black salaried employee at Ford in 1924. Collins supervised a mixed staff of over one hundred men; Price had an all-white crew working under him. One black foreman during the 1920s headed an all-Polish group of thirty-five men.[13]

Approximately 1,500 black workers were employed in 1920 by the FMC, a period when Ford's industrial labor force decreased to about the 1916 levels as the postwar recession set in. By 1922 the number of African Americans at the River Rouge plant was 5,354.[14] Such a sudden expansion suggests Ford's strong commitment to hiring black workers, for during this time of high unemployment, he had his pick of workers.

Automakers enjoyed brisk sales in 1919, but, by the end of 1920, they faced a weak economy and lack of customer purchasing power.[15] Inventories stacked up at auto plants and dealerships; the entire automotive industry slid into a sharp depression.[16] As the last of the automakers to accept the necessity of shutting down operations, the FMC carried out intensive cost-saving measures that included cutting the office workforce by more than half, merging some departments, eliminating others, and laying off thousands of factory workers. Finally, on 24 December 1920, Ford announced that the Highland Park plant was halting work but would reopen in early January. Of the approximately 176,000 workers employed in Detroit in September—most of whom were production workers—only 24,000 remained on the payroll at the end of December, a decrease of 86 percent in three months. About half the drop in employment occurred within the last week of December, when Ford closed its doors.[17] When Highland Park was reopened on 31 January 1921, and operations resumed at the River Rouge in February, production at the FMC was in the hands of a much larger percentage of black workers than ever before despite the abundance of white labor.[18] Why did Ford choose to hire and retain so many African Americans?

Among the many reasons, Henry Ford's obsession with keeping Detroit an open-shop, union-free city is a favorite. African Americans represented an insurance policy against labor unrest and unionism. We certainly know that during the union drives in the late 1930s and early forties, Henry Ford exploited racial antagonisms hoping to break the United Automobile Workers (UAW) union. David L. Lewis offers another explanation, pointing out that Ford's philosophy of an integrated workforce "was born at the end of a crosscut saw," referring to the times that Ford helped William Perry clear land on Ford's property in Dearborn. According to Lewis, when Ford expressed his progressive policies in 1919, he declared that his company had "learned to appreciate men as men, and to forget the discrimination of color, race . . ."[19]

Other theories focus on Ford's penchant for helping society's disadvantaged groups. African Americans were, according to August Meier and Elliott Rudwick, hired for the same reason that led Ford "to include in his labor force cripples, ex-convicts, and the blind." Blacks, like other disadvantaged groups, were stereotyped as "social outcasts" who needed Ford's help and would be grateful for the opportunities he provided for them.[20] When the five-dollar day went into operation, the company ordered the personnel department to consider all job applicants, even those who were physically impaired, unless they suffered from contagious diseases. In 1919, there were at least 9,000 handicapped and 600 ex-convicts working for Ford. Samuel S. Marquis, director of the Education Department (formerly called the Sociological Department), reported numerous cases reflecting Henry Ford's belief that "no problem was to be solved by the use of money when the solution could be reached through work." Ex-convicts and handicapped men, given a job in an employment climate in which most employers rejected them, showed "their appreciation by doing well the work given them." Ford took great pride in lifting "to the level of self-support hundreds of people who otherwise would have been living on the charity of others." Uplifting African Americans followed this pattern.[21]

All of these theories capture aspects of Ford's perspective toward African Americans, but none explains why the dramatic shift in hiring practices occurred when it did, right after World War I. Not surprisingly, no company documentation is known to exist spelling out the company's policy on recruiting black workers.[22] Ford made it a point to keep certain thoughts to himself. But as Hayward S. Ablewhite, a supervisor in the Sociological Department at the FMC, observed, Ford had a habit "of carrying a little pad in his vest pocket with a little, short, stubby pencil. Every once in a while he would take out this pad and pencil, and jot something down."[23] In one of those reflective moments, Ford wrote, "I'm going to see that no man comes to know me."[24] Although this was perhaps his intention, we can discern the nature of his new direction if we place his decision to hire African Americans in a larger context.

HENRY FORD AT A CROSSROADS: 1919–1921

Ford's sudden interest in employing black workers coincided with a period when the direction of his company was at a crossroads. From 1919 until 1921, Ford focused his attention on solving a series of crises that threatened to drive the company into the red, even as he relentlessly pursued his plans for an even bigger, brighter future for the FMC with the completion of his massive River Rouge factory complex. Much more than a mere postwar recession challenged Henry Ford in the months after the end of World War I. He faced strikes against his suppliers by workers in ports, railroad shops, steel mills, and coal mines; he owed more than $50,000,000 in dividends and interest to minority stockholders and taxes to the Internal Revenue Service; three of his ablest lieutenants resigned in the spring of 1919; and, lastly, construction on the River Rouge plant was delayed.[25]

Some aspects of the crisis were of Ford's own making; some were not. The millions the FMC owed were part of loans advanced to Ford when he bought out his stockholders. The complex transaction, including a $75,000,000 loan issued in 1919, made Henry Ford and his family sole owners of the FMC, with complete control over its organization.[26] Repayment of this huge loan was due in the spring of 1921. With only $20,000,000 in cash in the fall of 1920, Ford estimated that he needed an additional $55,000,000 to meet his obligations. These challenges tested the wit, tenacity, and steely resolve that had helped shape Henry Ford.[27]

When the FMC shut down operations in December 1920, rumors spread that the company was in desperate need of cash. A headline in the *New York Times* in January declared: "Ford Co. Said to Seek Loan of $50,000,000 or More." Reporters descended on Detroit speculating that several New York banks were trying to engineer a deal to bail out Henry Ford. This period of his business career—dubbed the "black winter"—was so critical that some thought he would have to borrow large sums of money from New York bankers, a horrifying thought to Ford.[28] He devoted an entire chapter in his autobiography to the topic of this crisis. He was careful to point out that he was not "against bankers as such. We stand very much in need of thoughtful men, skilled in finance. We have to have money. We have to have credit."[29] What he objected to was the way the plight of the FMC was sensationalized and broadcast to Wall Street as "evidence of impending failure," as reporters flocked to Detroit to magnify any signs of weakness found in the giant of the industry.[30]

During the shutdown, the idea circulated that if the FMC ever did open again, "they would be in new hands." Ford told one persistent New York banker he did not need to borrow any money. On the contrary, the banker replied, not only did Ford need a loan from his bank, but he also needed to transfer some control over the company's finances into the hands of the bank. For starters, the banker wanted to name "who the new Treasurer shall be." With that suggestion, Ford's showed the banker the door, telling him to "get out real quick!" Ford and his company survived the crisis—without borrowing from Wall Street—through a combination of creative accounting and coercion (his dealers were given a choice: either accept and pay for surplus new-car inventory—thus "advancing" a loan to the FMC with no interest—or else forfeit their franchises).[31]

Ford's distrust of bankers was about more than relinquishing financial control. During the First World War, Ford, a pacifist at the time, had come upon the idea that the "international Jewish banking power" (the Rothschilds and the Warburgs) had started the war. After the war, Ford broadcast his anti-Semitism in the pages of his newspaper, the *Dearborn Independent*. During 1919, its first year of publication, the newspaper focused on Ford's distrust of financiers, bankers, and the investment banking system, which concentrated too much power in too few hands.[32] Increasingly, diatribes against Jewish people took over the columns of the newspaper. By June 1920, as the sensational smearing of the entire Jewish population increased, Ford conflated Jewish people with bankers, equating "Wall Street finance capitalists" and "New York Jews." In July a series of articles introduced the "Jewish World Program"; a November essay was titled "The Struggle for Jewish Supremacy in the American Financial World."[33]

AFRICAN AMERICANS AND FORD'S AMERICAN PLAN

Ford's critical financial challenges between 1919 and 1921 and his intense, unrelenting ravings against Jews may offer a window on why Ford opened the doors at the FMC to African Americans at just this time. What connected these events were issues propelling Ford to reestablish his dominance in the auto industry after the postwar crisis. Ford reconsidered his Americanization Plan and his reliance on immigrant workers as he came to grips with the rise of radical labor domestically as well as internationally in the context of the Russian Revolution.[34] Even though the struggle against Germany and its allies led to victory, the battle against the Red Army and Soviet Communism was lost, thus shifting the tectonic plates previously defining the balance of power in the world. Industrialists and workers alike took note. On the one hand, the new fault lines made it harder for Ford to predict and plan for the future; on the other, many sympathetic American workers imagined the Soviet system as a model of economic democracy, one addressing the cry for industrial democracy that had gained momentum during the war.[35]

As Joseph A. McCartin argues, demands for industrial democracy were connected to larger expressions of American patriotism during World

War I. Answering the call to demonstrate their patriotism, workers often interpreted industrial democracy in terms of gaining more control over workplace decisions. By the end of the war, millions of American workers were rallying around the industrial democracy concept.[36] Government agencies reinforced workers' aspirations by calling for industrial democracy at home to match the nation's fight to "make the world safe for democracy" abroad, supplying the rationale to justify efforts to expand workers' rights. Rather than suppressing worker unrest as the government had intended it to, the phrase pumped life into aggressive labor organizing.[37] Union organizers emphasized "democracy in industry," portraying labor organizing as a patriotic act of good citizenship. By 1919, many workers assumed that the era for industrial democracy was at hand. Henry Ford, like other industrialists, was on a mission to appropriate the spirit of industrial democracy, repackaging it with his anti-union, open-shop movement, the American Plan.[38]

Ford and other industrialists in Detroit prided themselves on being ahead of the curve in terms of expanding the open shop. Before the war's end, the Employers' Association of Detroit had drawn up a contract called the "American Plan of Employment," whose declaration of principles included the right to work without interference, intimidation, or hindrance by those engaged in strikes.[39] Detroit industrialists may have been pioneers, but their agenda was similar to a wide range of experiments proposed by liberal-minded industrial engineers, politically active businessmen, and others during the postwar period. Their shared goal was to reconfigure the "architecture of power" at the work site through workers' councils, profit sharing, and relying on delegates from the shop floor to increase the sense that workers were participating at some level in the work process. The overarching concern was to rein in "costs of instability" generated, in part, by turmoil within the ranks of mass production workers not prepared to become "cogs" in automated production lines, like the ones at the FMC.[40]

The proximity of the United Automobile, Aircraft, and Vehicle Workers' Union (AWU), headquartered in Detroit at the end of the war, with its 40,000 members and commitment to industrial unionism, served as a reminder to Ford that he needed to be vigilant. Ford joined managers of Wadsworth Body Company in 1919 to break a strike called by the AWU. Industrialists hired spies to report on meetings of socialists, the Industrial Workers of the World (IWW), and the Detroit Labor Forum, a group established to hold public discussions of labor issues. The industrialists were aided by a special force of Detroit policemen who stood ready to resist any activities or functions that might promote the establishment of labor unions in Detroit. In addition, the FMC provided surveillance of suspected radical groups in order to screen the activities of workers and assess worker allegiance to company and country. A Ford spy reported that several Ford employees were among the approximate 1,000 attendees at a meeting of the AWU in October 1919.[41]

Radical labor activists on the national scene, including Emma Goldman, William D. Haywood, and A. Philip Randolph, made their way to speak at the Detroit Labor Forum during this time.[42] Shortly after the war, the *New Republic* addressed the "tests of unprecedented severity throughout the world" that faced democracy and concluded that democracy's future was dependent on "the capacity of employers and workers to harmonize democratic ideals of freedom with the voluntary self-discipline essential to efficient production."[43]

As Ford contemplated this new world order, he worried about the ramifications it posed in terms of labor relations. The inclusive Americanization of all workers that Ford had done so much to promote—with its uplifting, positive tone—turned into his increasingly negative view of the melting pot. The root of the problem lay with the "sweeping changes" immigration had undergone as a result of the war. The problem was not so much, as Ford's *Dearborn Independent* suggested, the concept of the melting pot as "with the base metal. Some metals cannot be assimilated, refuse to mix with the molten mass of the citizenship, but remain ugly, indissoluble lumps." Behind the unassimilated metal, Ford saw the red menace. Those indissoluble lumps represent "those aliens who have given us so much trouble," aliens like those "Bolsheviki messing up our industries and disturbing our civil life—these I.W.W."[44]

The newspaper called for "greater scrutiny of the immigration gateways in the interests of national welfare," pointing out that U.S. immigration policy had relied on the private sector to Americanize aliens before the war. Up to the present, "the greatest Americanization processes anywhere have been supplied by the big industrial establishments, where careful standards of work and living are enforced and where the development of personal self-respect and its attendant social and political consciousness, is warmly encouraged."[45] What was "immediately obvious" was the need to "watch the process of Americanization from first to last, just as any other process, in manufacture or elsewhere, must be watched."[46] The goal was to ensure the pot does not contain just "any and every sort of metal."[47]

Left unanswered was how to replace the great flood of cheap immigrant European labor, the kind that industrialists had relied on before the Great War, which would "automatically diminish" with the closing of immigration gateways. The "returned American soldier is not prepared, nor is he expected to take the place of immigrant labor." Who, then, will take the place of immigrants and be "willing to do the work immigrant labor was asked to do at the wages immigrant labor received for its work"?[48] The question occupied a prominent place in Henry Ford's mind as his prize project—the building of the River Rouge factory—neared completion.

Ford had been working on the River Rouge Plant, an "industrial colossus," since 1915.[49] By the time it was completed—blast furnaces were in full operation by 1923—it was the largest factory in the world.[50] But flow—not size—was its most distinguishing feature. One of Ford's goals when building the Rouge was to take the flow concept utilized in his moving assembly line to another level by addressing the need for continuous, reliable movement of materials to the point of production. As one trade magazine put it, Ford's model had shifted the focus of attention from the individual machine to the "process." The largest cost savings, therefore, were "likely to come from moving rather than making."[51] For Ford and his engineers, control over the supply of raw materials, especially iron and coal, the backbone of the automobile industry, argued for a plant with a harbor for large ocean-going vessels, railroads, and eventually a steel-making facility. Reduced to its basics, as Charles E. Sorensen, head of production for the River Rouge plant, noted, the process amounted to "raw materials" coming "in at one side, a complete motorcar" coming "out at the other."[52]

The operation required reliable, steady workers to guarantee uninterrupted flow of production, which partly explains why Ford expanded his employment of African American workers in the months after the war. As the Rouge production facility grew and the contours of the postwar industrial complex crystallized, Ford's labor needs shifted in both quantity and quality. He needed many more workers, but, just as important, he needed workers who would be wedded to his industrial plan, grateful for the opportunities opened up by a job at the FMC. Ford's genius was to realize that in many respects, African American workers were ideal for his new Rouge experiment. They hungered for inclusion in industry and carried

Overview of the River Rouge plant of the Ford Motor Company, Dearborn, Michigan, the largest integrated factory in the world by the mid-1920s. Within this single complex—which included its own steel mill—raw materials such as iron ore and copper were turned into cars. Image courtesy of the Walter P. Reuther Library, Wayne State University.

no idealized vision of industrial democracy in their heads as they flocked to Detroit. While a large presence from the black community of Detroit would not satisfy all his labor requirements, the inclusion of black workers offered the possibility of putting the FMC on the path to a new era in industrial relations, one that could make the difference between continuing success and mere mediocrity in coming years.

Ford's new policy toward African American workers represented his third revolutionary practice in the industry. Other automobile manufacturers viewed industrial relations through a rearview mirror, seeing a large black presence as potentially too volatile. Rather than confront white animosity toward blacks, other automotive industrialists let white racism drive their policies. Ford looked ahead, imagining that a policy of relatively superior occupational status, combined with large-scale employment of black workers, could anchor his new era in greater control over his workforce.[53]

Ford, like many other industrialists, had also redefined what it meant to be an American during this period: Americans were not pro-German, not socialists, not pro–Soviet Union, and certainly not in favor of the IWW. Divided loyalties toward the United States, rooted in the birthplace of many workers, emerged during the war: German and Austro-Hungarian workers sometimes expressed sympathies with their homelands; the Russian Revolution captured the imagination of others. The net effect was increasing discontent from immigrant workers, with a rise in labor turnover during the war, one of the factors leading to Ford's Five-Dollar-a-Day Americanization program in 1914. The labor turnover rate in 1918 was 51 percent in Ford's factories. While not nearly as high as in 1913, these turnover rates spurred Ford's desire to reduce his reliance on immigrant workers.[54] Rather than infusing American values in foreigners, why not start with English-speaking African Americans who yearned for the opportunity to participate as equals in Ford's workforce?

Ford's racial views included a belief in Anglo-Saxon-Celtic superiority and innate black-white differences that led him to support social and residential segregation. But he also believed, as he stated on "Ford's Page" in the *Dearborn Independent*, that the African American is "a human being," an American citizen, "and as a human being he is entitled to opportunities to develop . . . and enjoy his natural human rights." The races should be partners in work, with "the colored man at one end of the log and the white man at the other."[55] When African Americans were given a fair chance as workers, Ford wrote, they were a "community asset." When there are enough jobs to go around in this country, "when every man shall have opportunity to go forth in the morning to perform the work he is best fitted to do" and earn a wage that can provide "a secure family life, there will be no race question." On-the-job promotion, furthermore, should be decided by merit, not color. Black workers should be "given a chance, and should be regarded with full humanity and treated with entire justice." Ford regarded the "race question" as a question of employment opportunities. "The Negro needs a job, he needs a sense of industrially 'belonging,' and this it ought to be the desire of our industrial engineers to supply."[56] Indeed, Ford's journal editorialized, the "right to economically and culturally" better oneself demanded full and equal protection of the law. Nevertheless, "true friends of the Negro . . . must come to see," as the journal explained, that racial differences make "the assimilation involved in social 'equality' as impossible for the African as for the Asiatic elements of the population."[57] Ford's racial views were often as complex as they were convenient.

BLACK FORD WORKERS:
A BRIDGE BETWEEN TWO ERAS

Opening employment opportunities for black workers also helped Henry Ford lessen a conflict that lingered as he distanced himself from the benevolent characteristics embedded in his Five Dollar Day, Profit-Sharing Plan. Ford's American Plan unveiled in the aftermath of World War I, anchored by open-shop principles, emphasized loyalty to company over the welfare of employees.[58] To put his plan in place, Ford hired Harry Bennett in 1919 to direct the FMC Service Department, responsible for surveillance of workers, and placed operations at the River Rouge Plant under the command of Charles Sorensen, signaling the beginning of his new approach to industrial relations. Samuel S. Marquis, though an intimate friend of Henry and Clara Ford, quit as director of the Education Department of the FMC over the issue of launching this new era of labor relations. The company he had loved had sold its soul; Henry Ford had changed, and gone, he said, were "the old group of executives, who at times set justice and humanity above profits and production." The result was the end of "an era of cooperation and good-will in the company."[59] The humane employment policies were replaced by a ruthless accounting mentality by men like Sorensen, who rose to the top during the financial crisis of 1919–21. Sorensen represented what a later Ford executive called a new, "more hard-boiled" breed at Ford's that believed men are "more profitable to an industry when driven than led, that fear is a greater incentive to work than loyalty." Pay your workers well and "then see to it that you get your money's worth out of them" was the new policy.[60] Sorensen had little patience with projects designed to help humanity and focused his "demoniac energy" on keeping up with the furious growth of auto production forthcoming from the Rouge expansion, throwing his all into taming the monster, its machines, and its men.[61]

We know, however, from Marquis, that Henry Ford's desire to "serve the world" and, to some degree, "mold its thought" continued to capture his imagination.[62] Henry and Clara Ford were greatly disturbed after the publication in 1923 of Marquis's book, *Henry Ford: An Interpretation*, which did not present Ford in the most positive light. The Ford organization responded by trying to buy up all the copies, an indication of the value Ford placed on his legacy.[63] He once told Marquis that his wish in life was not for "things that can be bought with money." He wanted "to live so that the world will be better for my having lived in it." On another occasion, Ford said that his company will have "outlived its usefulness as a money-making concern, unless we can do some good with the money"[64]

When Ford turned his attention to black Americans and began hiring them in large numbers, more was at issue than his desire to help social outcasts, the impulse that guided his hiring of ex-convicts, cripples, and the blind.[65] Ford's embrace of black Americans served several needs simultaneously. African Americans had the potential to be model workers for Ford's postwar American Plan: they were eager, hard-working laborers, not inclined to support unions; they were American citizens who spoke English and demonstrated allegiance to the American Way. Allegiance to company and country, Ford may have reasoned, would keep black Americans from turning red or radical. It was no secret that white unions had rarely been friends of black labor.[66]

In addition, by the time Ford hired African Americans in large numbers, the stirrings of a struggle within Ford's mind between country and city, rural and urban life, had begun to take hold of the man who put the world on wheels, to borrow from Douglas Brinkley.[67] He romanticized who his African American workers were. As newcomers from the Old South, Ford seems to have reasoned African Americans surely must subscribe to certain values—such as a belief in hard, honest, productive work—principles he found sorely lacking in urbanites from fast-paced cities. Constructing an image of African Americans, shaped by simple agrarian values as the hewers of wood and haulers of water, the producers of the world, Ford likely pictured his black workforce in contradistinction to radicals, aliens, and especially the Jewish culture he held responsible for the erosion of the very virtues that "have made our civilization" in the United States solid and successful. While Ford was quick to point out that the Christian virtues he espoused did not condone prejudice or hatred, he believed the "genius of the United States of America" was "Christian" and the country's destiny was to remain "Christian." Ford's fantasy may have served his interests at the time, but it failed to account for the historical reality that had shaped black workers.[68]

Ford's streak of native populism, noted by several scholars, left him forever suspicious of paper money, middlemen, and the stock market.[69] He traced to "one racial source" the "marked deterioration in our literature, amusements, and social conduct . . . a general letting down of standards." A "nasty Orientalism [which may have been Ford's shorthand for unacceptable foreign influences] has insidiously affected every channel of expression—and to such an extent that it was time to challenge it."[70] Jazz was signaled out as an aberrant art form, inspired by Jewish culture, despite its origins within the African American community, revealing Ford's storied lack of concern with facts once his mind was made up.[71]

Initially, Ford appeared to be an ideal employer for newly arrived black Americans: he opened doors that, for the most part, had been shut; he treated black workers with more respect than any other large corporation at that time; and the FMC provided more than employment. A job at Ford was also an opportunity for black Americans to participate as both producers and consumers as they entered the middle ranks of the American working class. A job at Ford represented membership in the premier flagship driving the new-age economy, based on the mass-production assembly line, which, in turn, fueled mass consumption. When Henry Ford hired black workers, he expanded their purchasing power, increasing economic resources within the black community. For that reason alone, African Americans flocked to the FMC.[72] But black workers also seized the chance to labor at Ford because at the time it seemed to embody a democratic value—equal opportunity—they held most dear. In terms of economic rights of citizenship, Ford's plan for black workers pulled the curtain back, revealing possibilities for advancement in the Age of Henry Ford.

THE PULPIT AS HIRING HALL

Fortunately for Ford, his reputation as a benevolent employer among African Americans overshadowed reality. As a result, black recruits lined up and were hired in large numbers at the FMC, even as its industrial relations shifted decisively toward more adversarial relationships.[73] To fill the large number of positions opening up for blacks at the Rouge, new personnel procedures were initiated in 1919 for hiring African Americans. The company relied on recommendations from a select group of black ministers who screened black applicants for the FMC much like black clergy had done for management of the Pullman Company, of meatpackers in Chicago, and of steel mills in Pittsburgh.[74]

By cultivating close ties with the black clergy, Ford also gained control over racial problems in the workplace. As the number of black workers increased substantially in the early postwar era, fighting—often with knives—broke out on the shop floor between black and white employees.[75] Concerned that the company could not control the violent reactions of white employees frustrated with Ford's progressive hiring policy, Charles Sorensen invited the Reverend Robert L. Bradby, pastor of the Second Baptist Church, Detroit's largest and oldest black church, to lunch with Henry Ford and the FMC executives. The Ford officials sought Bradby's insight and suggestions for possible solutions to heightened racial tension within the plant.[76] In reaching out to Bradby, Ford officials no doubt knew of his remarkable accomplishments as a fund-raiser and a talented speaker. He began his career at Second Baptist in 1910 and within a few years had raised the spirits of his rapidly expanding congregation as well as paid for extensive renovations of the church. Church receipts, which were under $400 in 1910, were over $4,000 in 1915.[77] Over lunch in the fall of 1919, Sorensen showed Bradby a number of knives and other weapons found on black and white workers, and Henry Ford outlined the nature of what was referred to as "the Negro problem." Integration had disrupted the smooth flow of production, adding to costs of instability; Ford management needed Bradby's help to turn the situation around.[78]

Bradby assumed responsibility for settling black-white tensions on the factory floor and was given a pass to all of the firm's buildings so he could check up on conditions at his leisure. He also agreed to screen black applicants for the company, promising to recommend only "good Negro workers," "very high type fellows."[79] For more than two decades, Rev. Bradby was instrumental in brokering relations for black workers at the FMC, reporting to Charles Sorensen. By 1926, Bradby reported that things had "been moving . . . smoothly" and that there had been no fights or "any disturbance for over a year" at the Rouge.[80] It appeared that Ford's goal of instilling harmonious relations between black and white workers was successful.

Ford did not acknowledge the additional benefits his new hiring policy brought to the FMC. As part of his cost savings during the recession of 1920–21, Ford cut the staff of the Sociological Department as the company phased out the Five Dollar Day, Profit-Sharing Plan.[81] Ford's paternalism did not disappear so much as morph into a package of benefits and responsibilities better suited for the new era at the FMC.[82] As was noted above, the work culture shifted because the speedup on the assembly line and ruthless heavy-handed tactics became the tools of choice for enforcing labor discipline and increasing productivity. In addition, despite the largesse distributed to the black community over the years in the form of donations to black institutions like the NAACP branch in Detroit, Ford must have realized enormous cost savings by utilizing the established networks connected with the church to shape and sanction worker behavior.[83] Rather than pay the salaries of many investigators to keep records on the lifestyles and spending habits of each hourly worker, the company now dealt instead with a select group of black clergy.[84] During the initial phase of the arrangement, not many favors were required to keep the agreement running smoothly. Over time, as the black community put down roots, a more generous outpouring of Ford assistance was required to sustain the loyalty of black Detroit.

With the continued expansion of the FMC's African American work force, Sorensen thought the task of screening job candidates and monitoring black Ford employee behavior was more than one person could handle. In 1923 he enlisted the help of Father Everard W. Daniel, pastor of St. Matthew's Episcopal Church, who served the interests of Ford from within the black community until his death in 1939. The Reverend William Peck of Bethel A.M.E. Church, also tapped by Ford officials, participated to a lesser extent than Bradby and Daniel.[85] Alliances with black clergy put Henry Ford and the FMC in touch with several different interest groups within black Detroit. While Rev. Bradby's church was thought of as the "church for the laboring masses," Father Daniel's church, pastured by black Detroit's most educated minister, addressed a smaller congregation that was considered a "church for the classes." Rev. Peck's congregation was closer to Bradby's, including factory workers, carpenters, tailors, janitors, laundresses, and cooks.[86]

To further assist in the overall execution of Ford's revolutionary experiment in industrial integration, Harry Bennett, head of the FMC's Service Department, hired Donald J. Marshall, an African American ex-policeman in 1923. Because of his skills as a police officer, Marshall was picked to be a "service man" at the Rouge. Bennett was in the process of building up a cadre of agents who would for nearly two decades act as a force of spies and private police keeping watch over Ford workers both on the job as well as within their communities. Marshall served as Bennett's eyes and ears, spying on black workers and their families in order to keep a lid on union activities and enforce discipline.[87] A member of Father Daniel's church, Marshall also reported to Charles Sorensen.[88]

We have no record of Henry Ford's thoughts regarding fights between white and black workers, but we know he was sensitive to a potential "Negro" problem at the Rouge. Again, Ford's notepad offers a clue. In one undated entry, Ford posed the question, "what is the best way to handle the negro [sic]"? On the other side of that page, he jotted down, "colonelize [sic] the Negro." Both entries are clearly written by Henry Ford.[89] While it is impossible to assess accurately this provocative thought, it offers, none-theless, evidence that Ford was trying to work out how best to incorporate black workers into his new industrial order.

During the twenties, Henry Ford made substantial financial contri-butions to select black churches; ministers praised his largesse from the pulpit. In addition, Edsel and Eleanor Ford backed the NAACP with large financial gifts, and the Ford family, Sorensen, and Bennett cultivated rela-tionships with leaders in the black community. The networks established during this period nurtured the bonds initiated at the historic lunch meet-ing between Rev. Bradby, Henry Ford, and Sorensen. Those bonds were strengthened during the 1920s as the economic well-being of black Ford workers became the very cornerstone for the prosperity of the commu-nity's entrepreneurial and professional activities.[90]

African Americans who worked at the FMC wore their employee badges with pride, we are told, despite the new regime of speedups defining the pace of work.[91] Detroit's black population doubled between 1920 and 1925, growing in tandem with the appeal of Ford's promise of equal economic opportunity.[92] The company's public relations were validated by the fact that the Rouge plant truly did have black workers in practically every de-partment and occupational category. As black Ford worker David Moore explained it, "Ford . . . was more liberal toward the blacks. I shouldn't use the word 'liberal.' There was nothing liberal in the bastard. He had a strat-egy that was different than General Motors and Chrysler. . . . they didn't have blacks on any machine. The best you could do was work cleaning up the floors, mopping in the restrooms, and things like that. But Ford had a sprinkling of blacks here and there."[93]

By 1926, African Americans were among the students in the Henry Ford Trade School. Black men, locked out of training for the skilled trades by

Henry Ford, sitting in the front row next to his white straw hat, with students at the Henry Ford Trade School. Behind him are two African American students. 26 July 1936. From the Collections of The Henry Ford. ID#P.189.13360.

apprenticeship schools controlled by the American Federation of Labor, could hardly believe Ford actually let them in. According to Quill Pettway, among the first generation of black tool-and-die makers trained at the FMC, it was thought that securing a place in one of the Ford Trade Schools was to put oneself among the "very fortunate."[94] Even in the post–World War II era, white men could not just walk in and become a tool-and-die maker, a highly skilled occupation, without the recommendation of a union member. The Ford Trade School was yet another reason for African Americans to stick with Henry Ford's anti-union policies. Before the 1940s, a black man had little chance to get the required training to advance through the ranks from apprenticeship to journeyman unless he worked at Ford. Willis Ward, a full-time staff member of the Employment Department, went so far as to claim that he knew of "nowhere on this planet that a colored man could aspire to and become a tool-and-die maker excepting Ford Motor Company."[95] The Ford Trade School was exceedingly popular with black men in Detroit and received many more applications than places available. From its inception in 1916, Ford's school had a strong "uplift" character attached to it. Students spent one full week in the classroom followed by two weeks in the shop and, on the basis of need, received cash scholarships, which in 1928 ranged from a minimum of $450 to a maximum of $1,020 per year. Tuition was free. If a student wanted a high school diploma as well as a certificate from the trade school, he could attend night classes in the regular public school system. Approximately half chose to do so; how many of them were black Detroiters is not known. By the thirties, Ford had added two other schools: the Apprentice School and the Ford Training School, both of which admitted African Americans. Although there were disproportionately few black students in these schools, the FMC at least admitted black men to its prized training schools, giving those same students jobs in the company upon graduation.[96]

RACIAL BARRIERS AND THE FORD MOTOR COMPANY

Why did Ford break with custom by hiring black workers in large numbers and placing them in skilled as well as unskilled positions? In addition to the idealism and philanthropic concerns leading him to adopt his revolutionary experiment, Ford, always the astute businessman, was also driven by profit. The employment of blacks was profitable for Ford, which explains why, by 1922, 25.9 percent of the 20,665 Rouge workers were black, amounting to 5,354 employees, or approximately 27 percent of all black men with jobs living in Detroit.[97] By 1926, Ford had 10,000 black workers, representing 10 percent of his workforce. At the same time, Dodge's workforce was 3.5 percent African American, or 850 men; Cadillac's was 5 percent; Murray Body, 4 percent; Chevrolet, 3.5 percent; Timken, 2.5 percent, Chrysler, 1.5 percent, and Hudson, 1.2 percent. Fisher Body had only 40 black workers in its large Fisher Body plants in Detroit.[98] If employment of blacks was profitable for Ford, why didn't Cadillac, Dodge, Chevrolet, and Fisher Body break tradition and begin large-scale hiring of black workers?

The answer was related to the fact that many white workers, especially those from the South, did not want to work beside African Americans and regarded them as undeserving of the good jobs in the automotive industry. Why should they be employed at that time, in that place? The combination of a weak economy in the South and passage of the Immigration Acts of 1921 and 1924, which restricted the influx of foreign-born workers, brought larger numbers of white migrants from the American South.[99] By 1940, Detroit's more than 75,000 southern whites, mostly migrants from rural Kentucky, Tennessee, and West Virginia, amounted to 4.6 percent of the city's total population, more than double the percentage living in Chicago, Cleveland, Pittsburgh, New York, or Philadelphia. Because white southerners brought their Jim Crow culture to the North, managers were especially careful not to mix blacks with whites in the workplace.[100] To take on the task of integrating such diverse populations required a willingness and ability to swim in uncharted waters. How did Henry Ford navigate the riptides of race?

Ford's approach appeared to transcend racial animosity between black and white workers. Was he perhaps able to trump racial tensions by hiring whites at a higher rate of pay? Pioneering work by economic historians examining the employee records of the FMC for the period 1918–47 shows, however, that during this period wages for blacks and for whites were virtually identical. We get a glimpse of Ford's business acumen by looking not at wages, narrowly, but at working conditions, a non-wage feature of an employment contract. Christopher L. Foote, Warren C. Whatley, and Gavin Wright found black Ford workers disproportionately placed in "the most distasteful jobs, such as those in the metal foundry, where workers were paid the same as co-workers who worked in less onerous jobs." They conclude that Ford exploited the "negative wage differential" assigned to black labor by the outside market by "masking it with a positive differential for difficult work." As a result, Ford profited from discrimination elsewhere without creating any noticeable differences in the wages that his own black and white workers could observe.[101] Henry Ford's methods for dealing with race relations were subtle, creative, and multifaceted.[102]

He also exploited the racial barriers remaining at other automotive plants in Detroit by hiring the best black men for jobs most white workers would not tolerate. Economists Thomas Maloney and Warren Whatley show that Ford was able to attract a particular kind of black Detroiter—men who were disproportionately likely to be "educated, married, and willing to remain at Ford longer than Ford's white employees."[103] Even as the positions they occupied within the factory required intense effort, turning those workers into "Ford mules"—as they were called when they straggled "home from work all dirty and sweaty and beat"—they were not deterred from working at the River Rouge.[104] Benefiting from widespread discrimination in the Detroit labor market, the FMC was able to exploit a "large and stable work force of married black men who had no choice but to make the extra effort" that Ford demanded. He was less successful extracting the extra effort from married white men, who had other "employment opportunities where they could earn a family wage under more leisurely work conditions."[105]

Henry Ford benefited from the lack of alternatives open to black workers by being able to select young, married black men over older, single black men. We know that Ford gave high priority to married workers during his Five Dollar Day, Profit-Sharing phase, and we assume that he continued to have that preference because married men were more stable. Black married Ford workers in fact exhibited a higher degree of stability (lower labor turnover) than either white married men or single men. As a result, Maloney and Whatley explain, the determination of married black men to "support their families, coupled with the fact that Ford was virtually the only game in town, funneled to Ford a supply of black workers that was large enough to drown out the marital wage premium they should have earned."[106]

During the 1920s, even as Henry Ford remained a mythic figure for ushering in a new era for black workers, anecdotal evidence suggests the black community understood the high price extracted by working for Ford. One black worker later recalled that the Rouge was known as a "house of murder." As an example, he related how the men often had to be helped up the steps by their wives when they arrived home. On the streetcars, passengers might see twenty men asleep, and "everyone would say, 'Ford workers.'" Conductors routinely had to wake up men to tell them they were at their stop. "On Sunday Ford workers would sleep on the way to church."[107]

Walter M. Cuningham, who worked five years at the FMC in the 1920s, supplied another angle on this story. After the night shift, he woke up one morning on the streetcar one mile beyond his stop, with his head resting peacefully on a black woman's shoulder. "It's alright, white man," she said. She had seen his badge and knew he was a Ford man who just needed some rest. "My man he done work at Ford's, too, on de night shift, so ah knows how tired yo all is."[108] During an interview in the late thirties, Joe Louis, the world's heavyweight boxing champion and a native son of Detroit, referred to the awful job he had when he worked for the FMC.[109] Ford and hard work were synonymous. "If an employe [sic] is on the payroll at Fords, he works. The foreman, the strawboss and the machine see to that." While every muscle is aching, when nerves are breaking, and the brain is numb, the mantra, "Let's Go! Let's Go!" rings in workers' ears all day long. The noise, the piercing cry of the boss, and the coercion led to something called Forditis, or the "Ford stomach," which made it hard to eat properly.[110]

The FMC archives also contain documentation of the unrelenting pace that defined the "spirit" of the Rouge during the twenties, a spirit that was described as "repressive" by scholars Allan Nevins and Frank Ernest Hill. As the output of cars increased in the early part of the decade, a period of "hard driving" set in. Under the prodding of Charles Sorensen and William C. Klann, the foremen of each shift "tried lustily to outdo the production records of the shifts immediately preceding and following theirs." Charles Sorensen became known as a Simon Legree, after the slave driver in *Uncle Tom's Cabin*, the nineteenth-century novel that incited a clamor against slavery.[111] William C. Klann, in his reminiscences, called Ford "one the worst shops for driving the men," even though Klann was one of those drivers. Klann's remarks reveal a mean-spirited level of competition among the drivers.[112]

Ford could not but profit from the intense effort his foremen and managers demanded at the Rouge. The fact that African Americans were willing to make the effort to match the pace demanded helped Ford establish new benchmarks to gauge how far workers could be pushed. The same foremen who competed with each other when driving workers also employed competition between black and white workers to squeeze more out of both groups. Robert W. Dunn, writing in 1929, had a Ford foreman tell him that Ford liked to "work white men alongside the Negroes, for a certain competition would be set up inducing them both to make greater efforts and thus securing greater output from both."[113] Bill McKie, a Ford worker, recalled hearing a white foreman cry out to a white worker laboring beside a black worker: "Get a move on! Are you going to let this [Negro] get ahead of you?" And the black man understood that if he did not keep up with the white man, he would be shown the exit.[114]

The driving pace added to the already extreme discipline that characterized the entire Rouge factory. A hallmark of Henry Ford's style had always been to place a high premium on controlling his workers. Management's tight grip kept complaints from white employees about working with blacks at Ford to a minimum since they knew that the alterative might be not to work at all.[115] During the twenties, this aspect of Ford's discipline worked to the advantage of black workers, helping to integrate them into the larger production process.

WORK IN THE RIVER ROUGE FOUNDRY DURING THE 1920S

The foundry at the River Rouge has often been referred to as a "black department."[116] Although across the industry the majority of black automobile workers were assigned to the foundry, it is misleading to call the foundry at the Rouge in the 1920s a "black department." More black workers were assigned to the foundry at the Rouge than to any other department, but the number of employees required to operate the Rouge foundry far exceeded the 10 percent of total company employment represented by black workers in the 1920s. Between 1920 and 1932, black workers made up between 20 and 50 percent of Rouge foundry employment. Neither black nor white workers chose the foundry; they were assigned to it for lack of better employment.[117]

The dust generated in the process of performing all the various tasks of the foundry was responsible for the high rate of tuberculosis and other lung problems. The din and general noise level led to hearing loss. The grime that permeated each worker was so thick that it was often impossible to distinguish black from white workers. Pouring iron and tending the furnace required working in extreme heat; burn injuries were common; other operations required inhaling nauseous fumes. As scholar Lloyd H.

Bailer noted, foundry work had "a notoriously high death rate."[118] Though tuberculosis was considered the greatest hazard that foundry workers faced, pneumonia was their number one killer. A study by the Metropolitan Life Insurance Company noted that the high death rates from pneumonia led to the lower rates from tuberculosis. Tuberculosis may have resulted in a lower mortality rate simply because workers died of pneumonia before they could succumb to tuberculosis.[119]

Since the foundry was hot, dirty, and dangerous, white workers tried to avoid working there. To compensate for the hazards, the FMC paid a premium to all foundry workers through most of the twenties. The wage premium encouraged white workers to stay on the job even when they had alternatives. After controlling statistically for individual worker characteristics (age, tenure, and the like), Warren Whatley and Gavin Wright found the wage differential between white and black foundry workers in the 1920–27 period was less than 1 percent (0.7 percent). That changed during the 1928–32 period, when an 11.3 percent differential between white and black foundry wages emerged. According to Whatley and Wright, the shift toward a more segregated facility occurred during this period as "Ford learned . . . that blacks could be placed in the foundry without paying a foundry premium."[120]

The significant discrepancy between black and white foundry wages emerged in the aftermath of Ford's financial crisis in 1927, the year that marked the end of the Flivver—the popular name for the Model T. Even though Ford remained the leader in auto sales, Rouge officials had reason to worry as competition cast a shadow over the magic that once belonged solely to Ford. With the launching of the Model A, Ford rebounded, but not until late in 1928. Ford workers—black and white—tightened their belts as the company shut down the Rouge to retool for a new model. Thousands of unemployed Ford employees had to wonder whether Ford would be able to make a comeback. It was a preview of events to come after the Crash of 1929.[121]

HUSTLERS AND FORD MULES

By the mid-twenties, the FMC, though a "man-killing place," was not a place blacks could stay away from.[122] Black male workers withstood the hard driving pace, making that extra effort not just to earn a decent living, but also to pave the way, ultimately, toward a fuller life for their families, one they hoped would offer more choices in the future. Black workers at Ford represented economic hope for the future of black America. Before World War II, blacks could not be found on auto assembly lines—with perhaps a few scattered exceptions—except at the FMC.[123] Leaving Detroit was not an attractive option since other northern urban areas had many fewer opportunities for black workers. Philadelphia manufacturing firms, for example, rarely hired black workers until the late thirties.[124] In 1939 black autoworkers (including salaried employees) had average yearly earnings ($1,092) that surpassed the average for all workers in all manufacturing industries nationwide ($975), that were more than the average for all white manufacturing employees ($1,002), and that amounted to almost double the average for all black manufacturing workers.[125] By 1940, as Maloney and Whatley show, roughly half of all black men employed in the metropolitan area of Detroit worked at the FMC.[126]

The automotive industry was the main prop of the American economy by the mid-twenties, and wages from the FMC were the chief stimulant for the economic growth of black Detroit.[127] The paychecks of black workers at Ford provided the infusion of funds needed to buy goods and services, fueling the growth of black-owned businesses (professional services, personal services, retailing, publishing, banking, as well as the underground economy based on prostitution, Prohibition, and numbers), which, in turn, created more jobs within the black community. As Lloyd Bailer observed, "scarcely a Negro professional or business man is completely independent of income derived from Ford employees." In this way the "Ford entourage was able to exercise a dominating influence in the community" over black churches, fraternal bodies, and other organizations.[128]

The multiplier effect of Ford wages fortified and stabilized the aboveground economy even as it trickled down to the underground world of bootleg whiskey, gambling, and women of leisure. Coleman Young recalled that with Prohibition during the twenties, the black communities of Black Bottom and Paradise Valley were extremely prosperous. "The money was practically jumping from pocket to pocket in those days. If you weren't making any, you either weren't trying or were inhibited by an unusual code of lawfulness." As a young black man, Young had basically "two role models in those days—the hustlers, with their flashy clothes and money clips, and the Ford mules."[129] While Young's portrayal of prosperity presents a skewed picture, it does convey the interdependence of the two economies in sustaining life for African Americans and their families. As

Victoria Wolcott observed, "Ford mules," by spending their relatively high wages, "fostered a thriving informal economy during the height of Prohibition."[130] During that time, the second largest industry in Detroit after automotive production was the illegal sale of liquor.[131]

Henry Ford's new era for black workers extended only indirectly to African American women. As a Ford wife, a black woman benefited from the relatively steady and high wage for raising a family. But Ford's reputation for paying generous wages was exaggerated in the case of both black and white workers, especially after 1925. When distress or sickness fell upon a Ford family, a black woman had few options to supplement the household's earnings. She could take in boarders, which was fairly common, or she could work as a domestic servant, which was the major occupation of black female workers. Women also operated small businesses in the informal economy as beauticians, seamstresses, spiritualist mediums, or operators of restaurants or chocolate shops.[132]

Discerning the true nature of economic activity during a period when the formal and informal economies were joined at the hip is inherently difficult. The line dividing the formal from the informal economy was blurred, and as black urban identities were being formed and transformed, it was no less difficult to differentiate reputable from disreputable behavior. Coleman Young touched on the complexity when he recalled how a "local hat shop" served as a "front for the biggest numbers operation on the east side." Similarly, "Dave Winslow made whiskey in the rear of his sweet shop."[133] Black women who valued economic self-sufficiency more than loss of respectability in the eyes of the old guard pursued blues and cabaret singing, nightclub dancing, and numbers running.[134]

John C. Dancy, head of the Detroit Urban League, who assumed responsibility for reforming illicit commercial activities in the black community, may not have openly condoned many pursuits that fell under the "informal economy." But he rationalized the draw such economic activities presented. With "so many fields of endeavor closed to them," it was "not surprising that some Negroes of exceptional ability turned to gambling as a career." Often, Dancy continued, those who made a career of the numbers racket, "led exemplary personal lives, put their children through college, and acquired a nest egg that enabled them to switch to legitimate business fields." On the other hand, for those who were impoverished, and "could see no legitimate way out," the "investment of a few cents in a numbers ticket could bring at least a few hours of hope." [135]

Making an investment in hope was not restricted to the numbers racket. It was an impulse that galvanized the black community during the twenties, jump-started many small businesses, and built the social and economic infrastructure that defined black Detroit. Loyalty to Henry Ford's new era of economic opportunity was heavily infused with hope as well. In other words, during the interwar period in Detroit, more was at issue than making a living wage. For African Americans, working in the Rouge foundry was to labor on the front lines of a larger struggle, connecting their toil to the hope that advancement within the auto industry would be a means for attaining broader social citizenship. Work was hot, dirty, and dangerous, but if the cost to labor was high, so were the potential rewards. For this reason, until the Great Depression, black workers responded by making the effort required to fit into Ford's American Plan. Unparalleled success at the Rouge was the base that provided a foundation for black Detroiters as they shifted their attention to the political arena.

CHAPTER THREE

The Politics of Inclusion and the Construction of a New Detroit

The old Detroit . . . is disappearing and a new Detroit is
arising. What it will be, nobody knows.

—WILLIAM P. LOVETT of the Detroit Citizens League, 1923

ONCE THEY WERE EMPLOYED, African Americans put down roots in Black
Bottom, the highly congested neighborhood that increasingly became one
of the few areas where blacks were allowed to live. Segregated living may
have narrowed the range of possibilities but not the determination to
explore other ways to expand opportunities. Loyalty to Henry Ford remained high, and the black community, buoyed by the expectations Ford
had raised, found ways to make its voice heard politically. Ford workers
proudly displayed their employee badges, symbolizing the distance they
had traveled since leaving the South, even as some expressed their politics by joining Marcus Garvey's Universal Negro Improvement Association (UNIA). Other political statements were made through challenges to
institutional arrangements and through the ballot box. By the early 1920s,
activism by black Detroiters on several fronts revealed a community-wide
commitment to push back restrictions on their participation in shaping
the emerging new Detroit. During this period, black Detroiters laid the
foundation for the infrastructures of religious, civil, and political organizations and began building a political coalition whose agenda veered
from Henry Ford's vision for his black workers, their families, and their
community.

During the winter of 1917, leaders of the Good Citizenship League, a
small group of well-educated black Detroiters, set out to serve as an alternative to the Detroit Urban League (DUL), which its members called
the "White League on Urban Conditions." Jasper Henry Porter, head of

the Good Citizenship League, stressed its independence from mainstream white organizations as it went about criticizing the DUL for following to the letter the wishes of the Detroit Board of Commerce and Associated Charities.[1] Members of the UNIA also questioned the approach of old-guard leaders and their relationships with corporate elite of industrial Detroit. But Garvey's call to action, appealing to numerous black Detroiters, unlike the Good Citizenship League, left a larger footprint on the political landscape of the community.

Identifying the "so-called leading men" of black Detroit as servile, Garveyites focused on the legacy of slavery when articulating how they differed from the approach of the elite. The UNIA claimed the "slave spirit of dependence" caused the black elite "to seek the shelter, leadership, protection and patronage of the 'master.'" Rather than acting as independent spirits, "our modern Uncle Toms take pride in laboring under alien leadership and becoming surprised at the audacity of the Universal Negro Improvement Association in proclaiming for racial liberty and independence."[2] A blue-ribbon interracial committee, appointed by Mayor John Smith in 1925 to study living conditions for blacks in Detroit during the early twenties, concluded the UNIA was second only to the NAACP in terms of addressing and defending the civil rights of African Americans in Detroit. The committee's final report, *The Negro in Detroit* (1926), described the UNIA as more than a "protest" organization, for unlike the NAACP, UNIA tried to "induce the colored people to meet injustices and denial of rights by starting all kinds of enterprises of their own with the purpose in view of finally becoming . . . independent of the white people."[3]

The Detroit chapter of the UNIA was founded in 1920 by A. D. Williams and organized by F. Levi Lord, a native of Barbados. The chapter grew rapidly under the leadership of Alonzo Pettiford, president of the Detroit division in the early twenties and a lawyer with connections to leading institutions of black Detroit. The division purchased a building on Russell Street and established drugstores, restaurants, laundries, theaters, shoeshine parlors, and a gas station, providing a viable infrastructure for spreading its message along with its weekly newspaper, the *Detroit Contender*.[4] Meetings and marches were, at times, attended by close to 15,000 men and women. The size represented the considerable presence of the UNIA in Michigan, not just in Detroit. Manning Marable describes Earl Little, Malcolm X's father, organizing fleets of cars so that Lansing Garveyites could travel to UNIA gatherings in Detroit. Between 1921 and 1933, there were fifteen UNIA chapters in Michigan.[5] Ruth Smith, who had migrated with her parents from Gadsden, Alabama, remembered how the UNIA shaped her early life and ideals. "Instead of going to church on Sunday," Smith recalled, "we would get up early and go to the Detroit division of the UNIA."[6]

The Detroit chapter had strong support from many women, like Smith, but the majority of UNIA members have been described as black industrial workers. Many, according to Judith Stein, were among "the highest-paid blacks, workers in Ford's River Rouge plant."[7] In 1922, membership in Detroit was estimated at 5,000.[8] While industrial workers made up the base, leaders were drawn from the ranks of small businessmen and the professions, a few also holding positions at the Ford Motor Company (FMC).[9] Why would black Ford workers, only recently recognized by Henry Ford and included as equal partners in his new era, be drawn to the UNIA?

Like so much related to black Ford workers, we can only surmise what the answer is, for we have little direct evidence enabling us to assert why so many joined. To get at an answer, we should note that two prominent leaders of Detroit's UNIA chapter worked at the FMC. One was John Charles Zampty, among the first black Detroiters to join. Zampty helped Alonzo Pettiford build the Detroit chapter in 1920. He traveled with Garvey throughout the United States in 1922 as the UNIA's auditor and stayed active in the Detroit chapter all his life. He told one interviewer he "was not in sympathy with the program of the NAACP" or that of the Urban League, "which is asking for . . . handouts." He remained an employee of the FMC until he retired in 1957.[10]

The other, Joseph A. Craigen, who succeeded Pettiford as president of the Detroit UNIA, was a native of British Guiana; he came to the United States during the war as a Spanish interpreter for the Navy Department at Muscle Shoals, Alabama. Shortly after the war, he went to Detroit and worked at the FMC during the 1920s before going to law school in the early thirties. As head of the Detroit chapter in the twenties, Craigen directed black Detroiters to pursue self-improvement through finance and business rather than through the ministry and the spirit. "As a race we have prayed louder and longer than all other races combined," he declared, and yet "[we] have received less of the world's goods than any race." He suggested that "standing erect we may demand, defy, dare and do; in the church, on our knees, we can only confess to the world that we are a race of . . . whimpering slaves who give thanks for stones when we beg for bread."[11]

Black Ford workers who joined the UNIA very likely were drawn by the messages and example that Zampty and Craigen provided. If so, their participation and membership may reflect the contradictions coursing through their lives. They were grateful for having jobs at the FMC and for being included in Henry Ford's industrial enterprise with its progressive racial policies. Nevertheless, after each shift at the factory, they were reminded when they went home to their segregated and overcrowded community that much of the social agenda condoned by white industrialists did not include blacks as equals. As Judith Stein's study of the world of Garveyism argues, though the language of Garvey was racial, "its ideology was bourgeois, asserting that the road to black freedom was the creation of the core institutions of the modern nation-state."[12] Entry into the FMC family represented access to economic security. However, once again, a historical pattern, noted by Ira Berlin as part of the larger African American experience, unfolded: black Detroiters were directed to stay in their place, defined not just as the geographic locale known as Black Bottom but also as a social imperative.[13] Having made a quantum leap in terms of their place within industry, black Ford workers likely explored the UNIA in their search for alternatives to the politics of exclusion they endured in other aspects of their lives. The phenomenon of blacks' participating in the UNIA while sporting the Ford badge of employment suggests that African American loyalty to Henry Ford was complicated.

The period of settlement during the twenties was also one of transition and experimentation for all migrants, a time fraught with tensions as newcomers adjusted to the expectations of the new racial code that regulated their social boundaries. Ford workers in the vanguard of unprecedented possibilities may have viewed UNIA membership as a complement to their Ford badges.[14] Both represented explorations on new frontiers. What part of the broad UNIA message resonated with the majority of Ford workers will probably remain a mystery. But this was also the age when African Americans demonstrated a new independence throughout the country. Participation in a local UNIA meeting may have felt like spreading one's wings, reaching out to embrace the new sense of race pride that Garvey invoked in his followers. For many, Garveyism was not about returning to Africa so much as a reminder to stand tall, strong, and independent of white control. As such it was a program of adjustment to city life for those who had recently escaped from life under Jim Crow in the rural South.[15]

At the least, resistance to the social imperative, which membership in the militant UNIA certainly represented, suggests the stirrings of a New Crowd in Detroit. One observer from that time said it was a period when "you had to join the UNIA or NAACP."[16] Members of Detroit's elite or "Talented Tenth," those "exceptional" men and women responsible for moving blacks forward who made up the majority of the NAACP local, found themselves on the defensive. As Kevin Boyle put it, they "had no truck with such newfangled movements" as the UNIA.[17] Neither did Charles S. Smith, the African Methodist Episcopal bishop of Michigan, who alerted the Justice Department about Garvey, describing him as a "Red," pedaling "vicious propaganda" and pushing a fake project. Smith suggested that Garvey be required to "discontinue" the efforts of his movement or "be deported as an undesirable."[18]

Despite the reservations of the majority of the Talented Tenth, many middle-class professionals and businessmen joined black industrial workers to build a strong UNIA division in the twenties and "shape the self-consciousness of blacks" in Detroit.[19] As an educated autoworker, Joseph Craigen fit that profile, as did Charles C. Diggs. Born in 1894 in Mound Bayou, Mississippi, Diggs migrated to Detroit in 1913 and established a successful undertaking business in the early 1920s. His funeral parlor, located close to the Russell Street building that housed the UNIA, soon grew into the largest black funeral establishment in Detroit. Diggs managed local properties for the UNIA. After Garvey was imprisoned and deported and Garveyism fell into decline, both Craigen and Diggs focused their efforts on offering an alternative to the Republican Party, which led to the formation of Democratic Clubs in black Detroit in the early thirties.[20] Their efforts in the thirties grew out of the frustration with life for blacks in Detroit that had drawn them to the UNIA in the twenties. Large UNIA memberships during the early twenties were an expression of that discontent, something acknowledged by the mayor's committee on blacks in Detroit, which included a representative from management at the FMC.[21]

The UNIA challenged the politics of accommodation within the black community, but the black vote had a greater long-term impact on shifting the allegiance of black Detroiters. Initially, it had seemed blacks would rubber-stamp the interests of the industrial elite, especially if those were also the interests of Henry Ford. Such was the case when black Detroiters supported the new charter to reform municipal government in 1918.[22] Another election in 1918, however, was not so reassuring to civic and industrial leaders.

James Couzens, an early partner of Ford and stockholder in the FMC, sought the support of John Dancy and Forrester Washington when he campaigned for mayor in 1918. Dancy and Washington pledged their personal support for Couzens, but nothing more, warning Couzens he should not assume that their support translated into the black vote. Most blacks, Dancy said, favored "some of the other candidates." Couzens's previous affiliation with the FMC stood between him and black voters, who thought "when he was general manager of the Ford Motor Co. he had not given very many jobs to Negroes."[23]

Couzens was elected mayor, but a significant portion of black Detroiters, such as the 5,000 UNIA members, expressed a desire to pick their own leaders. The urge was not unique to Detroit as the black urbanization process unleashed challenges to racial exclusion. Such impulses help explain the most widely circulated black radical publication during the war and the postwar period, the *Messenger*. Published in New York City under the direction of A. Philip Randolph and Chandler Owen, black socialists who spoke as the voice of what they called the new crowd in urban America, the *Messenger* regularly harped on the topic of "old crowd Negroes," especially during the height of the first phase of the Great Migration. It was a theme that resonated in black Detroit as those who chose accommodationist tactics clashed with those who favored charting a course independent from white control. The accommodationists were regarded as the old guard or old crowd; those who, instead, agitated for asserting one's right to self-determination were part of the new crowd. Early in 1920, Randolph and Owen, on a national tour, spoke to a variety of groups in Detroit—the Labor Forum, the Labor Lyceum, and two black churches—under the headings "The Americanism of Tomorrow," "New Education," "New Emancipation," "Socialism and the Negro," and "The Negro and the New Social Order," topics addressing the need for the politics of a new crowd.[24]

The impulse stoked by Randolph, Owen, and others in agreement with the so-called Messenger Crowd must have struck a nerve in Detroit's white community, for Mayor Couzens appealed to John Dancy to keep the socialist editors out of Detroit. When Dancy attempted to close the doors of black churches where Randolph and Owen were scheduled to speak, several ministers refused to bow to his pressure. Among them were the Reverend Robert Bagnall and the Reverend Joseph Gomez, who "opened their churches to let the people hear the truth," an action that met with almost "unanimous approval," according to Randolph and Owen. Neither

Bagnall nor Gomez could be "intimidated or misled by the insidious mis-representations of that time-serving, capitalist tool among Negroes—the Urban League." On this occasion, Bishop Smith, driven by the value he placed on free speech and a free press, publically declared that the editors of the *Messenger* ought to be heard. Although he did not agree with all that the editors had to say, he listened to their message and later said a large part of the message "impressed him favorably."[25]

Randolph and Owen also caught the Reverend Robert L. Bradby's at-tention. Though the trustees of Bradby's church canceled a scheduled meeting to host the firebrand editors of the *Messenger*, Bradby went to hear what they had to say. He liked what he heard, admitting that the *Messenger* editors had been unfairly cast in a poor light. The editors ap-plauded Bradby for his courage and "honesty in admitting how we had been misrepresented to him." To make amends, Bradby invited them back to Detroit to "lecture before his congregation, at his expense." The editors also noted that what Bradby did was rare. "It is so hard for most people to admit a mistake."[26]

By that time, Rev. Bradby was on the payroll of the FMC, in the form of in-kind reimbursement (for example, free coal from the FMC for his church) for services rendered, highlighting the complicated nature of his role in the making of black Detroit. Bradby's public reassessment of Ran-dolph and Owen reflected, no doubt, the large following the *Messenger* Crowd had in Detroit in the early twenties. Bradby may have been in a spe-cial working relationship with Ford, but he also needed to be sensitive to opinions and sentiments resonating within black Detroit. In this respect, his actions reflected tensions that rippled through his career during the next two decades. Ford and Sorensen looked to Bradby as a counselor aid-ing in the hiring of good black men and as a peacemaker when racial prob-lems erupted on the shop floor. His congregation looked to him for firm-ness in protesting racial injustice and discrimination. While discouraging agitation by black Ford workers on the shop floor, he nevertheless advo-cated "full exercise of the rights of citizens." Voting was something he was especially vigilant about, regarding the vote as the only reasonable means for overcoming "the Jim Crowism and segregation heaped upon us."[27]

Some have claimed that Bradby's following was directly related to his association with Henry Ford and Charles Sorensen, that membership at Second Baptist soared after he began making job recommendations for black workers. Richard W. Thomas argues that if blacks desired a job at

Ford—"and just about everybody did"—then they had to attend one of the black churches blessed by Ford. As a result, any church outside the system had "little chance of matching the growth and prosperity" enjoyed by a Ford-sponsored church. "Bradby and the Second Baptist Church," according to Thomas, "became the gates to the kingdom of Ford," a relationship that dramatically increased the church's membership.[28] Aware of such charges, Bradby always claimed that he did not use his connections with Henry Ford to build up his congregation and that church membership was not a prerequisite for a recommendation. When it was suggested otherwise, Bradby bristled, maintaining that of the people he recommended for jobs at Ford only a minority were members of Second Baptist.[29]

While we may not know how many joined Second Baptist hoping to secure a job at Ford, it is clear that Rev. Bradby had his finger on the pulse beating in black Detroit well before he was appointed Ford's de facto black personnel director. In 1917, the *Detroit Tribune* noted that Second Baptist, with an average attendance of nearly 2,000, was so popular that potential worshipers lined up each Sunday morning outside its doors. And still some had to be turned away.[30] The fact that Bradby spent his humble youth working as a farmer herding cattle, laboring in a brick mill, and cooking in a lumber camp may explain the origins of his appeal as a man of the people.[31] No doubt, his Canadian background with its abolitionist heritage also attracted recent migrants from the South. In the late 1890s, when Bradby was twenty, he moved to Chatham, Ontario, where he worked as a butcher. His religious awakening, leading him to the ministry, occurred in Chatham, a symbol of emancipation because of the role it played as a terminus of the Underground Railroad.[32]

At an early phase, Bradby experimented with improving the social as well as the spiritual welfare of the souls under his care. During the first months of his tenure at Second Baptist, Bradby held a series of revivals, hoping to increase membership in his new church. After his arrival, membership grew from 250 in 1910 to over 1,000 in 1915, then 2,000 in 1917. Bradby also walked the streets of Black Bottom, evangelizing in "pool halls, gambling rooms, local bars and even prostitution houses." He was known to preach on "street corners" in an attempt to "transform the 'Red Light' district in which his church was surrounded."[33] His actions created a long-lasting impression on black transplants from the South who came to regard Second Baptist as the "Home of Strangers."[34]

Bradby's theological perspective was connected to his mission to es-

The Reverend Robert L. Bradby Sr., pastor of Second Baptist Church, placed hundreds of African American men in "good" jobs at the Ford Motor Company while supporting Mayor Frank Murphy's "new deal" politics. Image courtesy of the Burton Historical Collection, Detroit Public Library.

tablish the "Kingdom of God" in black Detroit. Such a moment would not arrive until black Detroiters gained voting rights and could take advantage of the "same opportunities for schooling, housing and employment as their white brothers and sisters."[35] Seen through this spiritual lens, Bradby's ministry—his impulse to reform society—represents a continuation of a current central to African American Christian thought.[36] Bradby's sense of "calling" as a minister and his sense of leadership were grounded in the Social Gospel, a liberating theology striving to put faith into practice through progressive, socially responsible measures designed to improve all aspects of people's lives. The Social Gospel influenced Bradby at an early point in his career, but as religious historian Julia Robinson Harmon explains, Bradby "walked a moderate line" in the way he put his progressive Social Gospel beliefs into practice. The practical side of Bradby drew precepts from Booker T. Washington, who believed black self-help agendas needed to be linked to "temporarily accommodating white power structures." Thus Bradby wove together threads from both accommodation and black self-help to form his leadership style.[37]

In his work for Ford and as a leader for civil rights within the larger black community, Bradby navigated the sacred/secular divide.[38] As a result, Bradby was in league with other forward-thinking black clergy of his time, who, Wallace D. Best argues, "put primacy on the material conditions of their congregants" at the center of urban church work.[39] Indeed, Bradby, was heavily influenced by the accomplishments of Reverdy Ransom of Chicago's Institutional Church, founded in 1900. Ransom expounded the principals of the Social Gospel, establishing his church as a "social settle-ment" where he could reach out to newcomers.[40] Drawing from Ransom's model, Bradby expanded Second Baptist to include a large auditorium, a kitchen, and a gymnasium. He organized men's and women's clubs, a nursery, a kindergarten, clubs for boys and girls, concerts, lectures, and classes in sewing and cooking. And, of course, he helped black men secure jobs at the FMC. His institutional expansion allowed Bradby to extend a hand to newcomers, helping them adjust so that they might find their way in the new urban environment. It also provided a material base for new residents and a place to build self-esteem, to keep their backs up in hard times, to keep from caving in to vice and crime, and to learn new ways of coping in their adopted city as they made the transition from a rural to an urban lifestyle. Second Baptist was Bradby's vehicle for shaping how blacks would make a living as well as new lives in Detroit.[41]

But Bradby's larger vision—to establish the Kingdom of God for black Detroiters—was fused to a politics committed to gaining greater control over the quality of life. Harmon argues that Bradby's "call" was the sacred foundation, based on his reading of the scriptures, bolstering his secular fight against racism and for assimilation and black empowerment.[42] The distinction between the sacred and secular aspects of his politics, often blurred, make it difficult to "read" his motives at any one point in time. His mission was not carved in stone when he took over as pastor of Second Baptist. While Bradby shaped black Detroiters—on the shop floor as well as with his preaching of a new social gospel—the needs of his congrega-tion influenced Bradby's mission and the approaches he chose to imple-ment his vision.

THE POLITICS OF COURT REFORM
DURING PROHIBITION

By 1925, it was estimated that more than one-half of the black population in Detroit had arrived since 1920. Nevertheless, blacks had been "advanc-ing politically" at a steady pace, for by the middle of the twenties there were between 25,000 and 30,000 eligible black voters in Detroit. Although most of those voters had little experience with the voting process, having come from states where they could not vote, black Detroiters, nonethe-less, exercised the ballot in a manner that surprised the ruling elite.[43]

Black political skills were tested when the leaders of the Detroit Citizens League (DCL) launched a campaign in the early twenties to unify the city's Police Court and Recorder's Court into one body as a single court with jurisdiction over all criminal cases. Targeting the issue of rampant crime, especially illicit activities involving women of the night and illegal saloons, the league thought widespread concern over crime would provide the necessary spur to reform the court system.[44] Court reform was necessary, according to the DCL, in order to infuse the judicial process with a strong dose of business efficiency, a rationale similar to the one that drove municipal reform in 1918 (discussed in chapter 1). Under the two-tier system in effect in 1919, convictions for prostitution and selling liquor were commonly overturned after they were appealed at the Recorder's Court level. Supporters of the Court Reform Bill argued that merging the two bodies and increasing the number of judges from two to seven would greatly help clear the "clogged court docket," speeding up the administration of justice. "Efficiency" was the operative word when the DCL pressed its case to the public.[45] However, if the league could count on four of the seven judges serving its interests, efficiency would also ensure control over the judicial process.

The members of the DCL, including industrialists, were concerned with Detroit's dramatic increase in crime by the early twenties. In the eyes of industrialists and old Detroiters, it was clear the mass influx of new workers and their families between 1910 and 1920 had introduced sin to the city. By then, Detroit, known as a "wide open town," had captured the imagination of Americans at the national level. No area of Detroit was as closely linked in the public's mind with vice as the black East Side, which, as Victoria Wolcott writes, was known as an "immoral landscape," a new frontier for gamblers, prostitutes, rumrunners, and gangsters. The stereotype associating blacks with criminal activity increasingly defined how the rest of the city viewed all blacks.[46]

The DCL got what it campaigned for when, in the spring of 1920, Detroiters approved a statute abolishing the Police Court, retaining Recorder's Court, increasing the number of judges in Recorder's Court from two to seven, and granting judges the right to elect a presiding judge for a one-year term.[47] But the election in 1920 to select the judges for the expanded Recorder's Court did not go as smoothly as the industrial fathers intended, foreshadowing challenges to the league's power that lay ahead. The DCL ran ads highlighting the candidates they deemed to be "eminently qualified," four judges the newspapers ultimately referred to as the "Big 4 Bloc."

The DCL believed support for its favored four judges would guarantee, with their election, majority control over the seven judges on Recorder's Court.[48] Although the DCL's favored four won in November 1920, the election results caught industrial leaders by surprise.

The DCL assumed black Detroiters would support Henry Ford's interests and vote accordingly. To achieve that end, in the months before the election, the FMC distributed tens of thousands of issues of the *Civic Searchlight* to its employees, suggesting exactly how its employees ought to vote.[49] The effort by Ford was not entirely successful. Election results revealed a black population more independent and politically engaged in 1920 than was commonly thought.[50] In a clear reference to the voting patterns of African Americans (as well as white ethnics), the DCL's newsletter, the *Civic Searchlight*, referred to the "ruthless and unscrupulous" efforts of enemies of the reformed court system, which had tried and failed to overthrow the judges approved by the league. Among the "outstanding" features of a campaign that the *Searchlight* described as "unusual," "riveting [sic] popular attention," was the "registration of negroes [sic] who, in many cases, never had voted before."[51] Black Detroiters voted against William Heston, characterized by the UNIA's *Detroit Contender*, as a "hireling of the Citizens League." The *Contender* mentioned Judge Heston's deep prejudice against African Americans, his harsh sentences against "common people," and his tolerance for racial slurs that went unchecked in his courtroom.[52] The message was clear: African Americans did not need the DCL to determine who was a worthy candidate. Although Heston won overall, he did poorly in Detroit's black ward, finishing eighth in Ward 3 and ninth in Ward 5. Ward 3 had 9,140 blacks, which was 22.2 percent of the ward; Ward 5 had 10,449, or 19.1 percent of the ward's population in 1920.[53]

WRESTLING CONTROL FROM THE DETROIT CITIZENS LEAGUE

By the time of the 1923 municipal election of Recorder's Court judges, African Americans were involved in municipal politics, campaigning for candidates and making their voices heard and their votes count. At least two factors contributed to the increased activism. One was the ongoing issue of racial profiling. The black community felt that both the police department and the criminal justice system assumed all African Americans were criminals, a problem no doubt reinforced by the actions of the Recorder's Court, particularly since the election of Heston as presiding judge of the court in 1922.[54]

The other pressing problem was the enormous increase in membership in the Ku Klux Klan. The KKK entered Detroit in the early twenties on the wings of the Americanization campaign that after the war had stressed the threat of "un-American" influences. The Klan's influence increased in tandem with growth in the populations of hyphenated Americans and African Americans. The twentieth-century reincarnation of the KKK, while a close relative to its nineteenth-century ancestor, defined who was an American more narrowly. While the first Klan welcomed white men from any background and grew out of sectional strife, the second Klan fused antiblack sentiments with Anglo-Saxon nationalism and admitted only native-born Protestant whites.[55] In some respects, as John Higham points out, "Klan propaganda echoed the Ford attack on the Jewish banker-Bolshevik," with an additional focus on the full spectrum of urban sins—bootlegging, gambling, jazz, cabarets, and prostitution.[56] All were considered crimes propagated by the loose morals of immigrant Catholics, other foreign elements, and blacks.

The KKK platform honored principles once held dear by the Anti-Saloon League Protestants who carried their campaign forward against the vices associated with Prohibition. In a particularly candid essay written for *North American Review*, Hiram Wesley Evans, the Klan's Imperial Wizard and Emperor, explained the relationship between the Klan's resurgence and the decline of rural Protestant America. Evans suggested that "the Klan . . . has now come to speak for the great mass of Americans of the old pioneer stock." The last generation of that stock, "Nordic Americans," had "found themselves increasingly uncomfortable, and finally deeply distressed." A "moral breakdown," Evans wrote, was unfolding. "One by one all our traditional moral standards went by the boards or were so disregarded that they ceased to be binding. The sacredness of our Sabbath, of our homes, of chastity, and finally even of our right to teach our own children in our own schools fundamental facts and truths were torn away from us." In addition, there had been mounting economic distress and little "assurance for the future of our children." Control of industries and urban areas had been "taken over by strangers, who stacked the cards of success and prosperity against us. Shortly they came to dominate our government." Evans maintained that three basic principles or "racial instincts" were necessary to assure the continuation of "an America which shall fulfill the aspirations and justify the heroism of the men who made the nation." They could be "condensed into the Klan slogan: 'Native, white, Protestant supremacy.'"[57]

The Klan resonated best with lower- and middle-income natives, white factory workers who felt threatened economically by the competition from newcomers to Detroit and America. These factory workers also resented their diminishing social status as the pace of transition within neighborhoods accelerated; areas once white changed complexion, Protestant turned Catholic, and German became Italian.[58] The Klan grew in Detroit as resentment increased among native-born whites toward white ethnics and blacks, who, in turn, fought the Klan and its notions of native, white, Protestant supremacy.[59]

While Detroit was representative of changes taking place throughout the country as more Americans—according to the 1920 census—lived in urban areas than rural areas, they were often more dramatic in the Motor City.[60] The automotive industry was the magnet that drew an unprecedented number of newcomers in a short period of time.[61] Beginning with the outbreak of World War I and continuing with the passage of the Immigration Acts of 1921 and 1924, large numbers of southern whites were among the newcomers.[62] Meanwhile, although black migration decreased briefly during the recession of 1919–21, it surged again in 1922 and 1923.

Demographics give one an insight into the rising tensions between 1920 and 1925: as Detroit's black population increased 100 percent (from 40,838 in 1920 to 81,831), its white population increased only 21.7 percent. The ratio of whites to blacks dropped from 80.1 whites to 1 black in 1910, 23.3 whites to 1 black in 1920, and only 13 whites for every African American by 1925.[63] In addition to the waves of black migrants seeking work in industry, large numbers of professional and business people left the South for Detroit in the early twenties. Doctors, ministers, small businessmen and women, often following their patients, parishioners, and customers, journeyed north.[64]

The Klan, with approximately 3,000 members in the fall of 1921, boasted of having more than 22,000 in 1924. This impressive increase in such a short period encouraged the Klan to come out from behind closed doors and demonstrate in public, burning crosses close to public buildings several times in 1923. On the night of elections in November 1923, the Klansmen set a cross on fire just as officials began to count ballots.

On Christmas Eve, a six-foot cross lit up on the steps of the county building, followed by a Klan rally in Cadillac Square: between 4,000 and 25,000 (depending on the source) watched a masked Santa Claus lead them in the Lord's Prayer.[65]

Although individual members of the DCL supported the Klan, the DCL never officially gave organizational support to the KKK and on several occasions used its prominent position to shore up resistance to Klan demonstrations. For example, the DCL aided African Americans when they took the initiative to protest the Klan's first attempt to gain a foothold in Detroit in 1921. Black Detroiters called for an investigation of the Klan by the U.S. district attorney after the Detroit branch of the Klan publicly invited "white Protestant citizens to membership in the Invisible Empire." John C. Lodge, a DCL member and president of Detroit's Common Council, responded by advising the police department that demonstrations by the KKK disturbed the peace and should be forbidden. As a result, the Klan canceled a scheduled Thanksgiving Day parade.[66]

As social tensions increased, the campaign for judges on the Recorder's Court during the spring of 1923 turned into a referendum on the hegemony of the DCL over the direction of Detroit politics. The league dug in its heels, insisting, as it had previously, on maintaining control over the direction of the Recorder's Court by putting four of its own candidates— as a bloc—on the court. Raymond Fragnoli's reading of the DCL's strategy shows members counting on its "voter's league" to disseminate information in support of approved candidates. As in the past, the league anchored its campaign to the need to stand up to crime, criminals, and corruption, but the municipal election of 1923 turned out to be about much more than which judges ought to be seated on the Recorder's Court for the next six years.[67] The bigger issue was how would democracy be defined and practiced in Detroit, the fourth largest urban area in the United States, as the multiethnic mix of registered voters threatened to tip the political balance of power away from the Anglo-Saxon elite.

Frank Murphy, who made democracy the centerpiece of his campaign for judge, challenged the Big 4 Bloc with its exclusive ties to the DCL. A young lawyer, an Irish Catholic, and a Democratic Party activist, Murphy appealed to black and foreign-born voters who had been targeted by the league reformers in their crackdown on crime.[68] Although he favored the reorganized court system and many of the reforms it had introduced, he thought the bloc-of-four system was nothing short of a miscarriage of justice and the sentences handed down much too severe. Those who had felt left out of the political process jumped on board Murphy's campaign.[69]

While it is important to remember that the DCL was not in direct league with the KKK, the actions the league took to counter the weight of Frank Murphy's campaign, and the others challenging the bloc-of-four concept, fueled resentment within the black communities and among foreign-born Detroiters. At the same time, the KKK's harangues against all things black, foreign, and Catholic fed the fears smoldering among native-born, working-class whites against the intrusion of blacks and foreign-born Catholics. When the DCL took its campaign against Murphy and the three other anti-bloc candidates to the establishment press, the Council of Churches, and the pulpits of leading Protestant congregations, all the ingredients for the perfect political storm fell into place.[70]

The *Detroit News* and the *Detroit Free Press* called opposition to the Citizens League candidates the work of the "underworld." According to the *News*, the struggle was between the better element of the city and the "evil forces of society" that make it a "business" to "destroy the recent strong policy of the municipal court of Detroit."[71] Of particular concern to the "good citizens" was the "rush of registrants from the Negro underworld." New registrations, with addresses linked to poolrooms and "flop houses," must be fraudulent, the *News* assumed, for men did not live in such places "long enough to provide a voting residence."[72]

Capitalizing on these fears, the *News* and the *Free Press* announced that "hundreds of Negroes" were herded to "City Hall under the guidance of underworld characters who have openly boasted that they will deliver 20,000 Negro votes" in order to "smash" the Big 4 Bloc.[73] The front page of the *Detroit News* featured the faces of several black men—along with extensive police records—describing the lineup as the "political henchmen" out to "steal" the election. The not-so-subtle suggestion was that the black underworld wanted to overthrow the favored four because they were the judges that put the "political henchmen" behind bars in the first place. The registration process often took place in poolrooms, barbershops, restaurants, and even in "disorderly houses" (a reference to houses of prostitution) in order to sign up black women.[74] The *News* sensationalized the salacious strain when it trotted out the names of a couple of black Detroit's "disorderly" women. A picture of Hattie Miller, described as "Detroit's most notorious underworld character," was featured on the front page along with her police record, which included an arrest for keeping a "resort." Miller was quoted as a supporter of the anti-bloc campaign movement.[75]

Oakley E. Distin, secretary of the city election commission heeded the call of the *Detroit News* and the *Free Press* for investigations into the dramatic increase in registrations, especially Wards 3, 5, and 7, all heavily African American.[76] W. Hayes McKinney, president of the Detroit chapter of the NAACP, rejected charges of fraud by declaring that the press had cast a "malicious aspersion" on the morality and integrity of 20,000 black voters.[77] Despite allegations that a high percentage of new black registrations were fake, the *News* and *Free Press* charges turned out to be false and were a ploy to scare the "decent citizenry of Detroit" to vote for the Big 4 Bloc, endorsed by the DCL, and against the black "underground." Registrations for this election set a new record. According to the *News*, the "contest for control of the courts that deal with the underworld and the criminal element" aroused public interest in a way that "not even a Presidential election" had.[78] The city's investigation of 18,808 registrations found only sixty-nine worthy for challenge. City Clerk Richard Lindsay concluded that his investigation confirmed his original contention that the registration "scandal" was purely imaginary and was concocted to "stampede the voters." It was a case of "lots of smoke and no fire."[79]

Although the scandal was revealed for what it was, the extensive exposure by the two major newspapers damaged greater Detroit's image of black citizens by equating African Americans with the words "underground" and "underworld." "Concerned good citizens" were those who favored the Big 4 Bloc.[80] The DCL kept a certain distance from the registration scandal by not playing the race card along with the *News* and *Free Press*, but its reputation in black and foreign-born neighborhoods was more negative than ever after the scandal broke.[81]

Murphy, tapping into resentment generated by the scandal, played the class card and called his opponents arrogant men of wealth. "They may have great industries; they may have the powerful molders of public opinion on their side, but we are stronger because we are right and they are wrong." Murphy soon turned his campaign into a mission and saw his supporters as the "young in heart, young in mind, young in soul" who were going to "take up the standard of . . . righteousness" to free the city from "a government un-American."[82]

The fight to "free Detroit from intolerance, from narrowness, from autocracy, from invisible government" was just beginning, he told one audience.[83] Rather than sidestepping the criminal issues highlighted by the DCL, Murphy used them to appeal to black and foreign-born residents. Claiming that he, too, knew something about crime, Murphy noted, "There are two kinds of criminals." The "group of men gloating and boasting over the little criminals," even as they forget to add a word about the "big criminals." "I say they are unfit."[84] The "little criminals," Murphy said, are the "dregs of humanity. They are our weaker sisters and brothers, spewed up from social conditions that the upper crust largely cause." The "underworld would be less if there was a better upper world amongst these church people and some other people."[85] The "big criminals," by contrast, were "men of wealth, men of influence, men who have had the blessings of home, men who have had the comforts of education." They are unfit because of their "selfishness," their absence of "heart," their "depravity," Murphy told a cheering crowd.[86] He named specifically the DCL and ministers who used the pulpit to advocate for a "controlled court."[87]

Acknowledging that "every criminal ought to be punished properly,"[88] he declared the court system unfit for putting all its attention on "little criminals." He pledged to reform the system to make the community a better place for everyone to live in by freeing the court from monopoly control. Murphy declared he would make it into a "temple of justice, not a butcher shop."[89]

The day before the election—Easter Sunday—the DCL called on all Protestant clergy, many of whom had been steadfast allies of the league for years, to address the "moral importance" of the election in their sermons. Thousands of copies of the *Searchlight*, the DCL's newsletter, along with campaign posters, were dropped off at churches. Ministers were asked to "personally circulate" the materials either during the church service or "as people leave the church." One circular drew on the spirit of the occasion by reminding ministers that Easter Sunday was a "wonderful opportunity to impress on your people that as citizens they should 'live the resurrection life' by not failing to cast their ballots." The message from the DCL had consistently mentioned that the election was about "vital issues affecting Christian people." It was clear in context that the Christians referred to were Protestant, not Catholic. The executive board of the Council of Churches gave its tacit consent for such activities when it unanimously endorsed the Big 4 candidates.[90] On election day, the front page of the *Detroit News* reminded its readers that they were "voting heavily in tenderloin districts—can you do less as a citizen?" The paper added that the penalty for shirking one's civic duty would be letting the underworld chose the judges on the Recorder's Court.[91]

The racist, antiforeign charges hurled by the DCL mobilized the black and foreign-born vote and broke the Big 4 Bloc by returning only two of the favored four to the court. All four candidates who had campaigned to overthrow a controlled court system won. Frank Murphy won the largest number of votes. While his appeal was fairly broad throughout the city, he did best in wards with high percentages of African Americans, immigrants, and Catholics.[92]

The DCL had clearly understood that it was in "as hot a fight" as it ever had been, but in advance of election day its members felt they had the "edge on the opposition with a good chance to win, provided we can get out the vote."[93] Thus, the results must have shocked Henry Ford and his lieutenants, the Board of Commerce, and the DCL. William P. Lovett called it the "first serious defeat which the League has suffered in all its history." Members, reflecting on the severity of the setback, wondered how the "the unexpected . . . happened," given the fact that the league's "campaign was most thoroughly organized from every angle,"[94] and referred to the fact that "we are passing out of one epoch and into another."[95] Trying to cheer up the secretary of the DCL, one associate wrote that "we must not allow ourselves to take democracy too seriously I suppose."[96] Lovett of the DCL perhaps best captured what had been lost: "The old Detroit . . . is disappearing and a new Detroit is arising. What it will be, nobody knows." Lovett's summation to a colleague was prophetic: "There is an entirely new deal in the court."[97]

The election also marked a new, brighter deal for black Detroit. Murphy's winning combination relied on a political coalition seldom seen, especially in the urban North: black and foreign-born working people joining together in opposition to the KKK and the power of the Anglo-Saxon elite. Although the election was nonpartisan, the fact that Murphy was widely known as a Democrat presaged changes not yet on the horizon because African Americans viewed the Democratic Party as the political home of white supremacists.[98] Nine years before the election of Franklin D. Roosevelt, African Americans by the thousands went to the polls to overturn tradition and the preferences of leading employers, including Henry Ford. In doing so, they made history, having seized the opportunity presented by the candidacy of Murphy, who, as Kevin Boyle points out, rallied blacks, immigrants, and Catholics into a coalition that served as a model for Roosevelt in 1933.[99] The foot soldiers in Murphy's coalition helped usher in a new kind of politics even as they shaped a better deal for themselves in the process.

THE NEW POLITICS was not a magic bullet. It did not overturn old accommodating approaches that had worked for old-guard black leaders, nor did it lead to black inclusion in civic affairs on an equal footing with whites. But it did plow new ground by opening up the political terrain to include African Americans. Within a year, networks in the black community were mobilized again when a special election was called to elect a replacement for the one remaining year in the term of Mayor Frank E. Doremus, who resigned in 1924.[100] The election grabbed everyone's attention because one of the candidates, Charles S. Bowles, was the pick of the KKK.

By the time of the primary in September, the KKK presence had grown. In February, Hiram Wesley Evans drew 8,000 Klan Knights to the Armory in Detroit, making it the largest indoor gathering of the Klan ever held in the city. New staff arrived to manage membership drives, increasing the Detroit Klan's strength to 32,000 during the year. By then, the increasingly elaborate public demonstrations included refreshments, bands, and even dramatic fireworks displays. Fifteen thousand attended one such display in May.[101] With such numbers, the Detroit Klan felt confident enough to test its strength by supporting Bowles in the primary. Bowles came in third, which normally would have ended his candidacy since only the top two winners in the primary were certified to appear on the general election ballot. Bowles ran as a "sticker candidate" (a write-in candidate) in November in order to continue his run for mayor. Between September and November, the Klan held rallies where they pasted Bowles stickers on public places. It is not clear whether Bowles attended the largest rally of Klansmen in Detroit history, which took place the Saturday before the election in Dearborn Township, home to Henry and Clara Ford. But Bowles stickers, which bore the image of a little red schoolhouse, harking back to simpler times, were prominent on the thousands of automobiles gathered for the event. It was estimated that between 25,000 and 50,000 people attended.[102]

On the ballot was John Smith, a Polish Catholic with a fourth-grade education, a solid pro-labor record as deputy state labor commissioner, a steamfitter and trade union activist, a veteran (of forays into Cuba and the Philippines), and a wet. The shriller the Klan crusade against what it regarded as the anti-Americanism embedded in the DNA of Catholics, the foreign-born, and African Americans, the sweeter the results for Smith. A product of Detroit's East Side working-class neighborhoods, Smith was a fighter who seemed to relish the challenge the Klan presented. He pitched his appeal largely to the new coalition shaped by Frank Murphy's run for Recorder's Court, but deepened the coalition with the backing of the black elite, who had been less enthusiastic than the black working class about Murphy's election a year earlier. As the Klan lit up the skies with flaming crosses and broadcast its message of hate and fear, Smith worked the Catholic parishes, black churches, and Jewish synagogues, reminding his supporters of the lynchings, torture, and burnings carried out by the Klan against minority groups.[103] He also promised to hire black police officers and campaigned heavily for the black vote, for which he was richly rewarded.[104]

The vote for mayor, the heaviest in Detroit history and ultimately a victory for John Smith, was contested because election officials discarded 17,263 votes, most of which were misspellings in voters' attempts to write "Charles Bowles." Ballots marked with "Charley Bowles," "Charles Boles," and "Charles Bowls" were discarded. Had those ballots been honored, Charles Bowles would have been mayor of Detroit in 1924.[105] Henry Leland resigned from the executive board of the DCL after the election because he thought the league should have endorsed Bowles.[106]

Smith's landslide victory in Wards 3, 5, and 7 (with majority black precincts) was more impressive than Murphy's electoral success of a year earlier. Lower East Side black and Catholic working-class districts went for Smith with majorities of over 90 percent. In the St. Antoine Street precincts of Black Bottom, along and near the present Chrysler Freeway, Smith was the overwhelming favorite, sometimes winning 99 percent of the black vote. In the fourth precinct of Ward 3, Smith won 699 votes; Bowles received 0. In the third precinct of Ward 5 (the Adelaide and Hastings Street area), the vote was 792 to 1; in the fourth precinct, Smith gained 806 to Bowles's single vote; the fifth precinct (the area of Rivard and Livingston) yielded 718 votes for Smith and 2 for Bowles. In the Russell and Watson Street region, the vote was 806 to 1; at Medbury and DuBois, 578 to 0. The pattern held for the second precinct of Ward 7, where Smith obtained 762 votes and Bowles only 3.[107] Black Detroiters clearly influenced the outcome.

When Smith ran for a full two-year term in 1925, Bowles opposed him again with the Klan's support, while five Klan-backed candidates stood for alderman. Smith and Bowles were the only two candidates for mayor. Although the DCL did not endorse either mayoral candidate, Bowles's candidacy was discussed, and several executive board members wanted to endorse him. But the shock of the Klan almost winning in 1924 pushed unlikely allies into Smith's camp. Noteworthy in this regard was Henry Ford, who endorsed Smith, perhaps more to allay rumors of his financial backing of the Klan (and even alleged membership) than out of an interest in backing a pro-labor mayor.[108]

Once again, Smith sought and received enormous support from black precincts and neighborhoods. The Klan tried to smear Smith with charges that he had packed the police and fire departments with African Americans, which only reinforced the support he already had within black Detroit.[109] Reinhold Niebuhr, pastor of the West Side's Bethel Evangelical Church who preached a Social Gospel theology, looked favorably on Smith for his advanced attitude toward African Americans. Summing up this period of Detroit's history, Niebuhr wrote that he wished "the good church people who hate our mayor so much because he doesn't conform to their rules and standards could appreciate how superior his attitudes and viewpoints on race relations are to those held by most church people."[110]

IN 1920, industrial interests assumed black Detroit would do the bidding of Henry Ford at the ballot box. Yet when Detroiters voted for a new slate of judges to serve on the reformed court system, black voters turned their backs on Henry Ford and much of the advice offered by the DCL's "voter's league." Rather than support candidates who had won the stamp of approval of the league, black Detroiters split the bloc of four, asserting their judgment of character and ability and pursuing their own agenda. That election turned out to be a dress rehearsal for the political independence demonstrated during the 1923 election for Recorder's Court judges when the votes of black Detroiters helped lay the foundation for a new Detroit. While no one knew what the new Detroit would look like, it was clear, as Lovett noted, there was a "new deal" in the court system.

Part of the agenda endorsed by the political coalition supporting Judge Murphy and Mayor Smith appeared to hold promise for expanding opportunities for African Americans. Black Detroiters were no longer regarded as part of the "problem." Their numbers and participation in Detroit politics made them players in the solution, shaping the city's direction as it moved into the future. Their participation in politics and independence at the voting booth also contributed to increasing tensions with Henry Ford in the years ahead. In the short run, however, the new political coalition proved to be less than blacks hoped for.

Although Mayor Smith had gone to bat for black citizens, opening up opportunities for them in the fire and police departments, by the summer of 1925 racial rage sorely tested the limits of the new coalition politics created by Murphy and carried forward by Smith. That was the year when the issue of discrimination in housing blew up with the Ossian Sweet case, revealing the limits of the politics of inclusion.

CHAPTER FOUR

Drawing the Color Line in Housing, 1915–1930

A man who is living aright will do his work aright.

—HENRY FORD

THE CITY THAT THE town fathers once hoped would be a model for clean and decent living—a master plan for municipal reform in an industrial setting—began to split open at the seams in the early twenties. Although Detroit had escaped the large-scale riots that had broken out in other cities, such as in East Saint Louis in 1917 or Washington, D.C., and Chicago in 1919, racial tolerance on the streets of Detroit reached a low by 1925 as white mobs vented their rage over the black "invasion" of "their" neighborhoods.[1] Detroit police shot fifty-five blacks between January and 1 September. At least some of these deaths resulted from execution-style slaughter by the police, according to 1925 Homicide Squad reports.[2] Walter White, assistant secretary of the NAACP, claimed that the Ku Klux Klan actively recruited members among police officers (and court employees), but how successful the effort was is not clear. Police actions, however, often reinforced the mission of the KKK to keep African Americans confined to a racially segregated area of the city.[3]

The city hailed as Mecca for opening up economic opportunity for African Americans severely restricted opportunities in housing in the 1920s, underscoring the limits of inclusion.[4] What had been a critical housing shortage throughout Detroit during World War I for white and black residents alike turned into an acute crisis for African Americans in the postwar years. By 1925, citywide practices restricted black newcomers to all-black blocks, creating an urban landscape shaped and bounded by race. While this demographic construct was not unique in American history—earlier forms included reservations for Native Americans and "Chinatowns" for Chinese immigrants in places like San Francisco—the rise of the black ghetto was a twentieth-century urban innovation.[5] The black ghetto marked a new phase in residential restrictions by limiting where American citizens could live. Henry Ford's penchant for social engineering did not, during the twenties, extend to open housing, leaving black Ford workers and their families to sort out ways to cope with the rising tide of exclusion that forced them to spend their Ford wages on inferior housing. The experience in housing diminished hopes for realizing the American dream even as it created an urban area whose very restrictions provided conditions for nurturing self-reliance and self-determination within the generation of black migrants who came of age during the twenties in Detroit.

The doubling of Detroit's black population to more than 80,000 between 1920 and 1925, discussed earlier, meant more people and less available space within the ghetto. Black business and professional men sought housing outside proscribed boundaries, igniting a series of aggressive attacks by white mobs. The racially volatile climate, as Kenneth Jackson points out, was stoked by the Detroit Klan, who seized the issue of neighborhood segregation as a means of breathing "new life into the secret order."[6] Ossian Sweet, a physician, and his wife, Gladys, were two of a small number of African Americans who tested the racial waters in 1925. When the Sweets did so and defended their new home with guns, a man from the white mob circling their house was killed. The Sweets were promptly arrested and charged with murder. Politics and housing discrimination intersected in the landmark Ossian Sweet case. Bonds of communal solidarity took root as black Detroiters from all backgrounds realized the depth of white resolve to keep blacks in their place and the need to rely on their own resources to challenge the racial status quo. If 1923 was the year when new coalition politics challenged the balance of power in the courts, and 1924 the year when a new order took the reins of city government, then 1925 was the year when the issue of Detroit's restrictive racial housing market was tested by black Detroiters.

HOUSING PATTERNS: SOUTH VERSUS NORTH

What was new in Detroit, along with other northern cities during the Great Migration, was the construction of a ghetto for housing blacks, a feature in sharp contrast with patterns established in the nineteenth-century South. Housing was the one area in the South largely beyond the otherwise all-encompassing reach of Jim Crow. The layout of southern towns and cities, in combination with the weight played by racial tradition, trumped concentrated residential segregation in the latter part of the nineteenth century. In older southern cities with large black populations—like Atlanta, Richmond, and Charleston, South Carolina—there is little to suggest the modern, twentieth-century concept of a black ghetto.[7] The industrial era had still not reached most of the South, and the ability to restrict black residents to one or two black belts was limited by technological, economic, and spatial constraints.[8] Prevailing social relations were tied to the needs of economies that required close contacts within a hierarchical framework. As Arnold Hirsch argues, "Social—not spatial— distance governed relationships across the southern color line."[9]

Before the Great Migration, Detroit's small black elite was interspersed throughout the city, living a world apart from the majority of African Americans on the near East Side. They were well-educated professionals, public servants, and entrepreneurs who served white clients and interacted socially with whites on a regular basis. Living in an integrated world, the black elite and white professionals have been described as having "cordial, and often intimate," relations. Composed of approximately seventy families, the black elite was known, at least on occasion, to worship in white churches.[10]

Even within neighborhoods on the East Side where the majority of blacks resided, Olivier Zunz found no exclusive racial concentration. Around the start of the twentieth century, when blacks represented only 1.5 percent of Detroit's population, they clustered into neighborhoods with working-class, native white Americans, Germans, and French Canadians. One cluster was in a German section of the old East Side; another was shared with Russian Jews. Indeed, it was not uncommon to see black families living among Germans and Russians.[11] The East Side had been the port of entry for many immigrant families and served the same purpose for working-class black migrants.[12] Many black residents—barbers, servants, and waiters—rented or even owned a basic house. Perhaps a majority of black East Side Detroiters lived in small one- and two-family houses in the crowded old sections, inhabited by Jews, French Canadians, Italians, and Germans. Typically these dwellings, which appeared to be one-family cottages from the street, housed two or three families.[13]

A vast restructuring of the entire Detroit metropolis took shape between 1915 and the twenties, a period when the spatial arrangements defining where all Detroiters would live were in flux and boundaries defining where African Americans could live were being mapped out. Many of the old-guard black elite continued to live scattered throughout the city as they always had. George Haynes, a black sociologist who studied black settlement patterns in Detroit in 1917, located six different areas where African Americans resided. While the majority lived in the crowded East Side neighborhoods, the area known as Black Bottom, there was still flexibility in housing, especially on the West Side.[14] When Forrester Washington conducted his own survey of areas of black settlement and concentration in 1920, the black East Side district had tripled its size in area from what it was 1917. But, by then, two of the West Side black neighborhoods identified by Haynes had disappeared, demonstrating the instability that characterized the settlement process during the war years.[15]

While the demographic transformation reconfiguring the social map of the city was shaped by war, industrial expansion, and the population explosion, the force driving settlement patterns was the increase in demand for housing by black newcomers, combined with growing white intolerance for black neighbors. The war fueled an economic boom that sent land values soaring in the downtown commercial district, an area that included old residential properties, housing for the wealthy near the city center. The white elite, who had once loved living near the downtown commercial district, fled when the nearby neighborhoods, east of the commercial area, became overcrowded with black newcomers. Black expansion toward the city center, however, was not a threat. The market easily prohibited such activity by valuing downtown property in the millions during the boom period.[16]

The boundaries of black neighborhoods expanded by pushing eastward into what became known as the East Side Colored District. And by the twenties the emerging ghetto was spreading northward.[17] Forrester Washington reported on the activities of both black and white "real estate sharks," who preyed on "homeless colored people" in order to make substantial profits as they enlarged the area zoned black. Black newcomers, for example, would move into a house previously occupied by a Jewish family that vacated when the rent was raised to $38.00 a month. Because the newcomers were black, the rent was increased to $50.00 a month.[18]

As the stream of black migrants increased in 1916, the quality and quantity of available housing units decreased. The city's total population increased by more than 100 percent between 1910 and 1920.[19] Under the best of circumstances, with so many newcomers moving into a fixed geographic area during such a short period of time, keeping up with new housing demand would have been a challenge. Housing stock was particularly strained because production for the war effort took precedence over construction of private housing stock. The number of newly constructed buildings, which reached as high as 16,489 units in 1916, decreased to 12,109 in 1917 and 7,011 in 1918.[20] High demand and short supply allowed all those who made their living by managing, buying, or selling property to prosper. With the unprecedented growth of the population, landlords let the laws of the market drive rents up to very high levels. While this trend was observed throughout the urban North during this era, New York and Detroit had the highest rental increases.[21] In 1917, Forrester Washington found average rent for an unfurnished room in Detroit was $4.60 per week, higher than the rent for a similar room in New York City.[22] To pay the rent, families doubled up and conditions deteriorated. John Dancy, the director of the Detroit Urban League (DUL), recalled an apartment renting for $50 a month over a store at Hastings and Clinton Streets where the occupants had to climb a ladder and cross a roof to get into their home.[23]

Every year between 1915 and 1919, general conditions of overcrowding and blight, exacerbated by expansion of the downtown, increased, and the City of Detroit reported a growing shortage of dwelling places. The city estimated that between 1918 and 1919, while total population increased over 100,000, the housing stock should have increased by 20,002 units. Instead 13,928 new dwellings were built, leaving a shortage of over 30,000 units when the backlog from earlier deficits was included.[24]

RESPONSES TO OVERCROWDING

By the time Henry Ford began hiring African Americans in large numbers in 1919, the housing crunch for blacks had assumed crisis proportions. During the height of his Five Dollar Day, Profit-Sharing Plan, Ford's proclamations warning about the evils of crowded housing did not lead him to challenge the rising walls of the ghetto. The major focus of Ford's attention—and that of other industrialists—was the city's new industrial order, which they hoped would stabilize conditions by overturning the power of ward-centered politics and putting decision making back in their hands. Detroit's industrialists overhauled municipal politics and overturned the ward system in 1918, but perhaps the most important measure they introduced for addressing the housing crisis was to pack the City Council with real estate brokers.[25]

Mainstream newspapers kept the populace current about conditions in the overcrowded Black Bottom neighborhood. The *Detroit Free Press* noted in 1917 that the housing situation in Detroit was more acute "than in any other Northern Center of Population, because Detroit's unexampled prosperity is the lodestone that is attracting thousands of Negroes, who are flocking here from southern points just as fast as they can accumulate carfare." Once they made it to Detroit, living conditions were "unspeakably vile." The journalist described "tumbledown shacks whose outward evidences of dilapidation are only a suggestion of the decay to be found within." The shacks "fairly bulge with their human population, herded into stuffy quarters without proper light or ventilation, eating, living and sleeping in a single room." Behind the decay was the problem: "Negroes are not welcome in every neighborhood. A European . . . can find localities where it is possible for him to rent or buy a home on easy terms. In the same district a Negro would be turned away, however worthy he might be."[26]

The *Detroiter Magazine*, an official publication of the Board of Commerce widely distributed among industrialists, called the "Negro problem" in housing "different in every respect from [the problem] of any other racial group, for in Detroit it is impossible for a Negro man or woman to secure decent quarters for self or family. His presence as a resident is not tolerated in many sections of the city. He is compelled to live in the slum districts."[27]

Descriptions of overcrowding echo the classic conditions Ford portrayed as unacceptable for foreign-born, white ethnic workers who wanted to partake in his profit-sharing plan. The major action Ford took was to tell his investigators from the Sociological Department to be lenient when discovering a black Ford family was taking in lodgers to help pay the rent. According to Samuel S. Marquis, Ford's director of the Education (formerly Sociological) Department, he was forced to soften his disapproval of undesirable housing, realizing that it would be better to let his black workers stay in condemned housing than have them be out on the street.[28] Donald Marshall, one of Ford's personnel directors, was a member of the Inter-racial Committee that produced the study *The Negro in Detroit* (1926), which indicated that valuable firsthand knowledge of the housing situation was available to Henry Ford. Nonetheless, Ford avoided housing issues during this period. That he did so rankled the Reverend Reinhold Niebuhr, chairman of the Inter-racial Committee and its investigation of African American living conditions in Detroit.

Niebuhr thought the situation for black Detroiters looked truly grim after he spent months investigating their living conditions. "The situation which the colored people of the city face is really a desperate one," he wrote. Blacks were "hampered," and "the hostility of a white world" makes it a "desperate fight to keep body and soul together, to say nothing of developing those amenities which raise life above the brute level." The culprit was a city "built around a productive process" that gave "only casual thought and incidental attention to its human problems." The result, he believed, was "a kind of hell." While thousands "in this town are really living in torment," the "rest of us eat, drink and make merry. What a civilization!" he declared.[29] Niebuhr's investigation of living conditions for black Detroiters and his analysis of Henry Ford's role in shaping the fortunes of his workers were published in the *Christian Century*, a journal with a national circulation. Ford's secretary read Niebuhr's critique in the *Christian Century*, which he characterized as a "vicious anti-Ford" outlet, and wrote to the board of Niebuhr's church asking its members to lean on the pastor to make amends for behavior that had so offended the Ford Motor Company (FMC). Niebuhr offered to correct any inaccuracies, but he never received a reply, suggesting that his offense lay with his impudent attitude, not his facts.[30]

Niebuhr noted that while "Mr. Ford is celebrated throughout the nation as the most benevolent of employers," he uses human material "with a ruthlessness and a disregard of ultimate effects which may be matched, but is not surpassed, by any industry." Niebuhr was prompted to question whether "Mr. Ford is simply a shrewd exploiter of a gullible public in his humanitarian pretensions, or whether he suffers from self-deception." The pastor was inclined to suppose that Ford was "at least as naïve as he is shrewd" and did not "think profoundly on the social implications of his industrial policies."[31] Had Ford's genius included the insight to do so in the twenties, he might have retained the allegiance and loyalty of black Detroiters longer than he did.

Although Henry Ford liked to point out that the man who is "living aright will work aright," apparently he did not think he was responsible for Detroit's housing problems. Samuel Marquis tried to persuade him otherwise as early as 1916, calling attention to the housing crisis unfolding around them. Ford did not heed his warning. Nor did he act to check the rise of the ghetto, even as he located his factories—first, the Highland Park plant where the Model T was born and, second, the River Rouge— outside Detroit's city limits, creating distance from Detroit's taxes and its urban blight. Operating as the largest taxpayer in suburban sites assured that Ford interests dominated politics, including "civic" policies designed to keep watch over unionization efforts.[32] Marquis may have had the last word on Ford's response to the housing crisis in Black Bottom: "In the end we reap what we sow."[33]

RACIAL COVENANTS AND THE RISE OF THE GHETTO

When Oscar Lee, born in 1902 in Alabama, hopped a train for Detroit in 1919, he had little idea where he would land once he arrived in the city. Like so many before him, Lee was directed to the East Side. That was the one section of the city where Lee and some 30,000 other African Americans who arrived during the war were welcomed.[34] While it was often by chance that black migrants, like Lee, were guided to Black Bottom by the Traveler's Aid Society, it was not by choice that they stayed in that area.[35] Choice was increasingly not an option as the policies and practices of city officials and real estate agents were utilized to concentrate black migrants in one part of town.

Before the war, municipalities could legally separate sections of cities according to race, but this tool was discarded when the U.S. Supreme Court declared the practice unconstitutional in 1917 in *Buchanan v. Warley*. The ruling prohibiting municipalities from carving residential areas into racially segregated zones inspired other means to achieve the same end. The practice adopted in Detroit and other urban areas relied on conveying in perpetuity racial exclusion in regard to the use and sale of property by adding restrictions to property deeds with an instrument called a racial covenant. By the early twenties, developers, on the advice of the real estate industry, frequently wrote racially restrictive covenants into deeds for the new housing tracts rimming the city in order to keep black Detroiters from jumping the color line.[36] The inclusion of racial covenants soon became part of a real estate agent's sales pitch. Advertisements, featuring new housing developments with racial covenants, stressed the freedom awaiting homeowners surrounded by "congenial neighbors"—that is, neighbors who will be "the kind of people you would be glad to have next door."[37]

Among the reasons whites did not want blacks as neighbors was property devaluation. Profiteering real estate agents contributed to racial hostilities by preying on latent white fears and black vulnerability. Declaring that an "invasion" of black homeowners was imminent, the real estate industry scared white residents into selling their property for less than market value. The house that was bought low from the white homeowner would then be sold high to a black newcomer, who felt grateful for a chance to secure a scarce commodity, a house. For the real estate industry, it was a win-win situation. The process created the perception held by whites that blacks depreciated property values.[38] Of course, blacks did not depreciate property values. Rather, as one black real estate dealer explained, "White hysteria and mania cause the loss in value when a Negro moves into a white neighborhood. Real Estate men often profit by this psychological condition."[39] Real estate interests had much to gain by exploiting misunderstandings in a market driven by perceptions. As the myth persisted and gathered power, it was a small step for real estate agents to use the issue of sustaining property values to justify racism.[40]

According to the Mayor's Inter-racial Committee report on the "Negro in Detroit," the misperception that blacks lowered property values was "one of the most important factors in the 'the race problem.'"[41] As a representative of the board of directors of the Detroit Real Estate Board explained it, "When a Negro moves into a district which is entirely white it is disturbing to the peace of mind of the white residents which often results in a neighborhood disturbance causing property damage." If a disturbance does not decrease property values, then the fact that African Americans want to move into the neighborhood results in "decreasing the property value." It followed, according to the Real Estate Board, that "the Negro who moves into a strictly white neighborhood is regarded as undesirable."[42]

Once the restrictive covenant was part of recommended procedure, its inclusion in real estate transactions became a standard business practice, one that white clients expected. That expectation was fed by the real estate industry, whose agents developed special code words and phrases to convey whether blacks would be allowed to purchase property in certain areas. One advertisement for a new development boasted that "Concrete Drive," known as Seven Mile Boulevard, connected the subdivision with Grosse Pointe, an area favored by industrialists, pointing out that "lots restricted and only sold to a desirable class of people." By highlighting the new development's proximity to Grosse Pointe, an established "white" suburb for the elite, this advertising message assured buyers that dwellings in both the new subdivision and its surroundings could not be purchased by people deemed undesirable. The "desirable class," unlike African Americans, would not deflate property values.[43] B. E. Taylor, a very successful real estate agent and developer in Detroit, was more direct in his advertising circulars. Taylor's informative brochure describing his Kenmoor Subdivision said that "premises shall not be sold or leased to or occupied by any person other than of the Caucasian race."[44]

PUSHING BEYOND BLACK BOTTOM

By the early twenties, the black population pushed the boundaries of Black Bottom beyond the old border of St. Antoine Street, creating an area known as Paradise Valley where the "cream of the crop" began to settle. Though the area was still part of the ghetto, its name reflected the promise of a destination linked with hope for the tens of thousands of black migrants who journeyed there to begin a new life.[45] More promising were suburban developments that opened up during this time. John Dancy was responsible for at least one suburban area. With the help of a white real estate developer, "Mr. Packard," a former friend of Dancy's father, he collaborated in the acquisition of land outside the city that was sold in small lots to African Americans. Mr. Packard made the initial contacts with the landowners, Milo Butler and Edward Baker, and purchased from them a large (140-acre) parcel near 14-Mile Road and Michigan Road in what would later constitute the southwest quarter of the village of Inkster. This property has long been associated with Henry Ford, who, it is said, first developed this area for his black workers. That he did not do. What actually happened in Inkster is a far more complicated story.[46]

Inkster was named after Robert Inkster, who was born on 27 March 1828 in Lerwick, Shetland, and immigrated to the United States with his mother in 1848. He made his way to Detroit and in 1855 purchased a steam-powered sawmill for $500 on what became Inkster Road, near the railroad. A post office, established in 1857 under the name "Moulin Rouge," was renamed "Inkster" in 1863, and Robert Inkster served as its postmaster from 1866 to 1868. Inkster also dealt widely in real estate.[47] The first permanent black settler in Inkster was Charles Lawrence, who in 1918 purchased an eight-room house on four acres in the southwest section of the village. In 1919, another black family, the De Baptistes, moved to Inkster.[48]

Several black families fleeing congestion in Black Bottom during the 1920s bought lots in Inkster through Mr. Packard. At the time, the village was little more than a name on a map; it had no sewers, no central water system, no street lights, and few streets. Despite the negatives, black Inkster pioneers seized the opportunity to escape the ghetto even when it entailed a move that was some seventeen miles from Black Bottom. Inkster was attractive because it was relatively close to Ford's River Rouge plant and had a stop on an interurban rail line that extended from Detroit to Novi along Michigan Avenue. The journey from the Inkster stop to the gate for River Rouge on Miller Road was approximately 7.7 miles.[49]

Like other black suburban pioneers, those who made the move to Inkster did so seeking the American Dream of homeownership. Most of the black families, headed by an employee of the FMC, took what resources they had and built shacks of scrap wood, sheet metal, and tar paper, assuming, all the while, that these jerry-built, shoddy shelters were only a temporary measure until enough money could be saved to construct a proper home. Many of these temporary structures were the only dwellings that black families had throughout the twenties.[50]

Ford may not have developed Inkster in the twenties or done much to shore up good housing for his employees, but he offered to build a high school in Inkster and initiated an ambitious effort to enhance property in the city of Dearborn, where he lived, by developing a new subdivision. His goal was to sell developed land for construction of a "high-class residential section" consisting of 3,500 acres of property along Oakwood Boulevard. Unlike Inkster, Ford's proposed suburban retreat included parks, sewers, and well-lighted streets. To ensure the quality of residents and retain the area for single-family homes, the FMC reserved the right to "buy out" speculators or any other purchasers who "became undesirable because of any reason."[51]

The area was open to anyone with enough money and a "reputation for square dealing," and purchasers were not limited to FMC employees. Henry Ford did not want to build houses, nor did he plan to make one penny on the enterprise, according to his publicists. His objective was to develop the "vast acreage lying idle" west of the city and within a few miles of Inkster, turning it into desirable home sites.[52] It is curious that Ford chose this moment, when black families were staking a claim in an area just to the west of Ford's development, to build up property in Dearborn. Was he concerned that suburban blight and squatters might cross over into open areas in Dearborn? Ford was aware of the increasing black presence in Inkster by the early twenties as news of racial tensions over schools and recreation facilities captured headlines in local newspapers.[53] Part of Inkster Village overlapped Dearborn Township.

POSTWAR RECESSION AND HOUSING

Rising racial tension was rooted in more than competition for scarce housing. Industrial violence broke out during the spring of 1919 as stiff competition between black and white workers erupted. A series of strikes during the postwar recession resulted in violence at the factory gates of several Detroit plants as black strikebreakers were hired into coveted industrial positions. Violence over black strikebreakers resulted in at least one black fatality.[54] The fact that some of the strikebreakers were provided by the DUL probably increased the anger of white workers struggling to gain a measure of industrial democracy in the aftermath of the war. In one particularly bold gesture, John Dancy provided 150 black strikebreakers during a strike against the Timkin Company by a metal trades union in 1921 and marched with the strikebreakers past the pickets who were apparently afraid to attack so large a group. White workers feared black strikebreakers because they undercut unionization and were willing to take jobs for less pay than whites would. On the other hand, black leaders believed that unions had done little to earn the allegiance of the black community. An example of poor relations between unions and blacks cited by the black community concerned the Street Railway Men's Union, which in 1920 convinced the Detroit United Railway to cease employing black workers.[55]

During the depth of the recession, when unemployment reached its peak in the winter of 1920–21, there was a measure of racial peace over housing as Detroiters from all backgrounds dealt with the poor economy. That winter more than 55,000 men at the FMC's Highland Park and River

Rouge plants lost their wages for several months.[56] As the recession receded and the FMC and other companies began hiring again in February 1921, the proportion of African Americans on the payroll increased dramatically. It is hard to imagine that white workers did not notice this shift in hiring policies.

Ford was not the only enterprise hiring black men for relatively well-paying positions. According to statistics gathered by the Mayor's Inter-racial Committee, by 1925 16.4 percent of the total workforce employed by the U.S. Post Office were African American, 10 percent of the total workforce at Studebaker Corporation were black, and more than 50 percent of the workers at both U.S. Aluminum Company and Detroit Steel Casting Company were black. Except for work at the post office, these were the hot, dirty, dangerous jobs in the foundry. Nevertheless, the jobs represented upward mobility for black workers who preferred factory work to digging ditches or janitorial service work.[57] Postal work for African Americans was not breaking new ground like a job at the FMC, for blacks had held post office positions since the end of the Civil War.[58] But the relative scarcity of workers hired for postal work—secure, clean, and steady—put it high on the list of positions coveted by black and white men. Employment of black postal workers had a long history marked by white resentment and violence.[59] Use of black employees by the post office no doubt continued to provoke the white working class while the job market was tight.[60]

Resentment between black and white workers was even apparent in some Detroit foundries. In one plant, a black man working in a large automobile foundry rose to the rank of "virtual foreman." Although he supervised a large group of blacks, he was never made foreman, was not called foreman, did not attend the foremen meetings, "but was paid 1 cent an hour more than the highest paid workers in his group." The superintendent of the plant explained: "We can't have Negro foremen." While acknowledging that the situation was not fair for black men, he could not alter the situation for two reasons. One was the fear that black workers—brought to his plant "to do the dirty, hard, unskilled work"—might not stay in their place. "If we let him rise, all of them will want better jobs." The other was keeping a lid on dissatisfaction among white workers, who might not "keep up the competitive pace" if black workers were foremen. Yet another superintendent said simply, "We can't have Negroes supervising white men."[61]

Economic competition between black and white workers and competition for scarce housing were linked. White workers may not have had much control over the hiring policies of the FMC and other enterprises, but they could take action to keep their neighborhoods segregated. What they lost in competition with African Americans over wages and jobs they tried to regain by maintaining the value of their property, an endeavor that strengthened the resolve of white residents to keep blacks out of their neighborhoods.

THE OSSIAN SWEET CASE: CONTESTING THE COLOR LINE

With the adoption of Article 34 by the Detroit Real Estate Board in June 1924, the city's real estate industry officially codified behavior routinely practiced by that time. The article declared a "Realtor should never be instrumental in introducing into a neighborhood . . . members of any race or nationality, or any individuals whose presence will clearly be detrimental to property values in that neighborhood."[62] Article 34 followed a ruling in 1923 by the Michigan Supreme Court that threw the full weight of the law behind racially restrictive housing policies with a ruling that supported restrictive covenants.[63]

One year later, several black Detroiters tested the racial waters by moving into neighborhoods claimed by whites. When they did, political, economic, and social factors that had gathered strength for several years converged, spilling blood on the streets. Several cases of violence broke out as whites, operating through organized efforts in neighborhood associations, forcefully kept African Americans from moving near or into "white areas." Increasingly, black Detroit fought back. The rise in racial violence coincided with increased interest in the KKK and the formation of white neighborhood associations whose purpose was to keep blacks out. It was within the context of the heightened anxiety over the place of blacks in Detroit that Mayor John Smith ran for reelection in 1925 against Charles Bowles, the candidate championed by the KKK.

Violence flared in June and July. There was the case of Dr. Alexander Turner, head of surgery at Dunbar Memorial Hospital, who attempted to move into the Tireman Avenue area in late June. His efforts failed as over a thousand enraged white protesters gathered outside his home, smashed windows, and threw rocks.[64] Vollington Bristol was more successful. He fought for three successive evenings in July—from the 7th through the

9th—as white mobs of up to 2,000 people demonstrated in front of his house with rifles, shotguns, and revolvers. Armed blacks also appeared on the scene. Hundreds of shots were fired, and nineteen whites and twenty-four blacks were arrested. After the violence ended on the third night, the KKK burned a cross in a vacant lot not far from Bristol's home, and Bristol remained in his home.[65] The following evening, Friday the 10th, Tireman Neighborhood Association attacked John Fletcher and his family, who had just moved into the area. When Fletcher called the police, the responding seven cops did nothing except talk with whites who were trying to drive the Fletchers out of their house. The mob succeeded, but not before someone from Fletcher's house shot and injured a fifteen-year-old white boy. Fletcher moved out on 11 July.[66]

Calm was restored along Tireman Avenue that Saturday night but not in the hearts of some 10,000 people attending a KKK rally in another part of the city. The KKK had been drumming up agitation by placing throughout the neighborhood placards inviting "every free-minded citizen of Detroit" to the mass rally. With a backdrop of a huge cross in flames, the KKK's main speaker for the evening denounced the black invasion into white neighborhoods and called on the audience to demand that African Americans be forbidden from living anywhere except the ghetto.[67]

On Sunday, Detroit's newspapers carried Mayor Smith's response to the violence of July. Acknowledging the parallel between recent events in Detroit and those that faced East St. Louis, Chicago, and Washington, D.C., some time before, Smith voiced his concern that history might be repeating itself and "injure this city beyond repair." He reminded his audience that "the law recognizes no distinction in color or race." But, in the end, he revealed his hand when he admonished black leaders to accept the color line as it was presently constructed and to end their struggle for equal access to housing stock for the sake of peace and order. It appeared that Mayor Smith, having taken the political temperature of his constituents, sensed his bid for reelection in November 1925 might be tougher than he anticipated. The rising popularity of the KKK and the outbreaks of violence threatened to break the alliance that put Smith into power a year before. In 1925 Bowles was not a write-in candidate, as he had been in 1924; he was Smith's only opponent; five Klan-backed candidates were running for City Council seats. The Klan's obvious appeal to thousands could not be ignored.[68]

Smith's concerns proved well founded when Ossian and Gladys Sweet moved into their bungalow at 2905 Garland Avenue in early September. The neighborhood, inhabited by lower-middle-class whites who were a hair's breadth beyond working-class status, was, as Kevin Boyle reminds us, socially far removed from Detroit's upscale West Side. "By working-class standards, the people who lived in Garland were to be envied and just a little feared." Among the Sweets' new neighbors were "carpenters, steamfitters, and electricians who roamed the factories as if they owned them, skilled men standing proudly above the mass of common laborers." And they were bound to keep it that way. Their greatest fear, given the mortgages that the Garland Avenue neighbors held, was to have their property values plummet.[69]

Crowds gathered on Garland Avenue the night the Sweets moved their furniture into their new home, maintaining a vigil until well after midnight. No violence occurred until the second night, 9 September, when an unruly mob threw rocks through the windows of the Sweet residence. When the mob grew increasingly hostile, shots were fired from inside the Sweet household injuring one white man and killing another. As Kevin Boyle's exemplary narrative of the case shows, when Clarence Darrow took on the defense of the eleven African Americans charged with murder of a white man, the prospective Sweet trial became part of the nation's conversation on housing and race.[70] Associated Negro Press, the wire service based in Chicago that fed copy to hundreds of weekly black newspapers across the country, went into action immediately, making sure the plight of the eleven defendants was known by everyone. The case, as some of the defendants put it, "boldly" challenged "the liberties, the hopes, and the aspirations of fifteen million colored Americans." James Weldon Johnson, secretary of the national NAACP, similarly connected the Detroit case to the welfare of all African Americans: If blacks in Detroit were not able to defend their homes, "then no decent Negro home anywhere in the United States will be safe." Alternatively, if the defendants were freed, those denying "peaceable and law-abiding colored citizens" their rights were at peril.[71]

The morning after the shooting, white Detroiters were consumed with fear fed by rumors that blacks were on the march. The Waterworks Association, formed to protect white homeowners from black neighbors, held a meeting attended by a thousand people, which was followed by a Klan rally.[72] Smith attempted to soothe concerns raised by the shooting with a letter to the commissioner of police, published for all to see in the Sunday morning newspapers. The letter held the KKK accountable for the heightened racial tensions that contributed to the murder of a white man. But Smith also placed considerable blame on Detroit's blacks, citing in particular the leadership class, for contributing to the violence by acting out of racial pride. It was not always wise, Smith wrote, for a "man to demand to its fullest the right which the law gives him." Such an act could inflict irremediable harm on others. "I believe that any colored person who endangers life and property, simply to gratify his personal pride, is an enemy of his race as well as an inciter of riot and murder. . . . I feel that it lies with the real leaders of the colored race in Detroit to dissipate this murderous pride. This seems to exist chiefly in a very few colored persons who are unwilling to live in sections of the city where members of their race predominate, but who are willing to rely on the natural racial pride of the rest of their people to protect them when they move into districts where their presence may be resented."[73]

By criticizing racial pride in the context of seeking improved housing, the mayor upheld racial segregation as a social good for keeping a lid on potential violence. The letter exposed the nature of racial tensions within the city and put Detroit's major power brokers between the black and white communities—Rev. Bradby and DUL director John Dancy—on alert: what did this backtracking by a trusted white progressive signal? And how should black leaders, heavy with obligations to their patrons among the white elite, respond? Rev. Bradby, appointed by the national office to head what it regarded as an anemic Detroit NAACP branch in March 1925, went on the offensive immediately, calling a meeting at his church to organize strong support of the Sweet defendants for the Sunday following the shooting. His leadership during the Sweet case revived the local. He talked about the civil rights of black Americans from the pulpit, challenging the racialized American dream of homeownership.[74]

John Dancy played a significant role in the Sweet trial, debunking the myth that black homeowners decreased property values in testimony before Judge Frank Murphy's court. Clarence Darrow highly regarded Dancy's testimony, which was so solid and presented with such clarity and precision that even the prosecuting attorney applauded the delivery.[75] By the beginning of October, however, whatever disappointment Bradby and Dancy harbored against Mayor Smith for suggesting that pursuit of civil rights was a threat to peace was trumped when KKK candidates for City Council won majorities in the primary.[76]

With the specter of the Invisible Empire's dragons taking over the reins of power, the city's progressive forces rallied their troops and turned the election into a referendum on keeping Detroit an American city by ridding its streets of the KKK. The Reverend Reinhold Niebuhr took wherever he could his message against prejudice and intolerance, which had uprooted the American ideals of brotherhood, justice, and goodwill. Smith told a crowd that they had to "kill forever this unholy, un-American thing—the Ku Klux Klan"—by voting against Charles Bowles.[77] Four days before the election, Henry Ford came out in support of Mayor Smith, declaring he did not support such movements.[78] While it is not clear why he arrived at that conclusion, it was not good for business to be suspected of supporting a candidate backed by the Klan when Ford depended so highly on the continued allegiance of his black workers.

IN THE SHADOWS OF THE COLOR LINE

On one level, the outcome of the Sweet case and the mayoral election appeared promising for black Detroiters. Mayor Smith was reelected with more than 30,000 votes over Bowles's total.[79] The juries in the first of two trials, both conducted by Judge Frank Murphy, could not reach a full verdict, but in the second trial in June 1926 the jury acquitted the only defendant who had admitted having fired a gun. In 1927 the cases against the remaining ten defendants were dismissed.[80] Black Detroiters had pulled together as a community, and, thanks to the considerable legal resources of Clarence Darrow and Judge Murphy, a stunning decision was on the books declaring that blacks, too, had the right to defend their homes.

Finally, the relationships that developed during and after the trial between Frank Murphy and black Detroiters enhanced the future for Murphy and African Americans. As presiding judge of Recorder's Court, Murphy assigned the Sweet trial to himself. There is little doubt that Murphy understood the potential importance of the case for advancing his career. His insight launched him on a path that took him all the way to a seat on the U.S. Supreme Court in 1940.[81] But the trial, its outcome, and relationships with Murphy also advanced the progress of African Americans for years to come. At the national level, the NAACP's Legal Defense Fund was formed as a result of the campaign to raise money for the Sweet case. From that base, attorneys litigated for the next two decades, slowly tripping up Jim Crow on the path to *Brown v. Board of Education*, which crippled the legal segregation of schools.[82] At the local level, Murphy had won the hearts and minds of black Detroit. With victory in the Sweet case, the black community became part of a political alliance that gave it experience using the tools of democracy to open up opportunities.

Mayor Smith, hoping to dampen the flames of racism stoked by the Klan, won his reelection by gathering his coalition under the banner of inclusion and tolerance during the last six weeks of his campaign. Thus, the question of Americanization—not race—mobilized white ethnics for Smith and against the interests of the Klan. It was good politics, and it worked to restore a semblance of order for a time. The coalition rallied behind Mayor Smith with the cry "Keep Detroit an American city!"[83] Most likely, the strategy worked because, as in the case of a Rorschach test, voters read into the slogan their hopes and dreams, not their fears. If so, the strategy revealed two distinct visions of the promise of America.

The vision of whites, those who harbored hostility toward African Americans crossing neighborhood color lines, was grounded in the market and linked to their presumed right to protect the value of their property. Ultimately, Smith blamed the KKK for the unrest and violence that had erupted in Detroit. But it was not the KKK who laid the foundation for racial segregation in housing. The Klan rode to town to exploit a volatile situation set in motion by real estate agents who used scare tactics to convince whites that if blacks moved in, property values would plummet.

The other American vision, grounded in the Constitution, granted African Americans the right to the same opportunities available to other Americans. Perhaps John Dancy captured the sentiment best. As blacks "become stronger," he explained, "there is a desire to live in better quarters than those found in any of the so-called 'Negro Colonies.'" "A twenty-thousand dollar a year man wants to live in a house commensurate with his salary." Besides, a move to a better neighborhood was what this country was all about. As Dancy put it, "Freedom to purchase wherever they please ought to be advocated in a country whose constitution allows for liberty and freedom and for the pursuit of happiness." Dancy acknowledged that many white people "sometimes resent Negroes coming into their neighborhoods." The reason usually given was that blacks depreciate property values. But, he insisted in a report to the DUL, "Negroes have not wanted to go into white neighborhoods in order to be associated with the whites living in the neighborhoods." The impulse was not to be closer to whites; it was to live in a safer, more secure neighborhood.[84]

For all that was positive in the outcome of both the Sweet case and the mayoral election of 1925, the year marked a shift in relationships between black and white Detroiters. Despite Darrow's moving and brilliant summation and the fact none of the eleven defendants had been convicted, the color line in housing that had been emerging for the good part of a decade did not vanish. Black Detroiters had asserted the right of African Americans to buy and occupy a home on Garland Avenue just like other people, and Judge Murphy concurred with that view in his comments to the jury: "Under the law a man's home is his castle. It is his castle whether he is white or black, and no man has the right to assail or invade it."[85] Despite a trial that the Nation declared was "probably the fairest ever" for black Americans, the power of white racism canceled the law, not for the first or the last time.[86] Freedom of opportunity for all was no match against the power of the marketplace.

Most white Detroiters did not care that it was citizenship rights that led black Detroiters to try to live where they pleased. What they cared about was protecting the value of their hearth and home underwritten by a mortgage. The residents of Garland Avenue had risen in the ranks, Kevin Boyle reminds us, "because they weren't . . . Negroes." By the time they assumed positions as skilled laborers or foremen, they felt they had earned the right to a home in a safe neighborhood. Their upward mobility was tied to keeping property values up, maintaining a good, steady job, and meeting loan payments. Meeting the loan schedule was no easy task during a decade when the government did not back loans and banks were left to shoulder the risk. For white workers whose margin between solvency and insolvency was razor thin, the inclusion of black workers in decent industrial jobs threatened their economic security in a tight labor market. Allowing blacks to move into "white" neighborhoods was certain, they believed, to devalue their property and with it their version of the American Dream.[87]

Exclusion of black Detroiters from social interaction outside designated areas created a city within a city, where blacks mingled in a cross-class commune. John Dancy, reflecting on this period, described black Detroiters as being at a "crossroads," in a time of "transition." The African American, according to Dancy, had "been . . . experimenting here and there in an effort to find himself." While for many years leaders had felt that the "panacea" that would take care of every ill was education, he realized that now there arose the question "What are these educated folks going to do?" As he looked out at the ghetto walls, he sought solace in black business, which he hoped would grow and "merit our patronage and our boasting." In the end, he acknowledged, "we are a new city and have not yet found ourselves."[88]

For the next several years, black Detroiters turned their confinement into a source of empowerment. They took ownership of Black Bottom and Paradise Valley, developing businesses, clubs, newspapers, theaters, and churches strictly meant to serve blacks. Residents developed a new assertiveness out of the experience of living in the lacuna between the rhetoric and reality of the Promised Land. Concentrated as never before within a small geographic area, black voices of protest found audiences on street corners and in churches, women's clubs, neighborhood associations, and barbershops. Independence from white control within black Detroit reinforced leanings toward black self-determination. Physical proximity also nurtured a new style of politics as "New Negroes" expressed the desire to demand full rights of citizenship. As a new crowd formed, the old guard experimented with ways to navigate around the hurdles on the new terrain.[89]

The situation cultivated what Thomas Sugrue calls a "separatist impulse," which ran "like a black thread" through rapidly growing black northern neighborhoods between the wars. Physical racial exclusion and separation were met with mixed emotions. Separation from whites provided a retreat, a kind of refuge from the storm. Sometimes it was welcomed; at other times not.[90] As the reality of confinement set in, there were times when Dancy and Rev. Bradby may have felt, as James Weldon Johnson, secretary of the NAACP, put it, pessimistic. "There is in us all a stronger tendency toward isolation than we may be aware of," Johnson confessed. There are "times when the most persistent integrationist becomes an isolationist, when he curses the white world and consigns it to hell." It was a tendency that bubbled up from what Johnson called a "deep-seated, natural desire . . . for respite from the unremitting, grueling struggle; for a place in which refuge might be taken." Though often "dormant," that desire was "ever present."[91]

BLACK DETROITERS did not live in Black Bottom and Paradise Valley solely by choice in 1925, nor did they think a "black metropolis" should be the last stop on the road to full rights of citizenship. Although the urbanization process for African Americans was structurally different from that experienced by previous groups of migrants to Detroit, the walls keeping all black Detroiters confined to a narrow geographic area could not contain their aspirations to participate as equals. If black Detroit became, at times, the kind of refuge James Weldon Johnson spoke of, it also served, at other times, as a laboratory for ideas that not only kept the dream alive but also transformed the generation of Detroiters who came of age during the 1920s into a self-reliant group determined to keep moving forward.

By the mid-twenties, the promise of America planted by Henry Ford had burrowed its roots deep in the soil of Black Bottom. Between 1925 and 1930, black Detroiters did what they had to do to keep their jobs at the FMC even as they built coalitions and networks that ultimately strengthened their drive for inclusion. The wrenching events linking politics and housing and the Sweet case served to clarify both the limits and the possibilities the city held for African Americans, a process that provided an invaluable education for negotiating the way forward. How blacks worked the soil during the next several years with the resources available to them shaped the promise and the place they ultimately created for themselves.

Like so many others in the North during this time, Dancy and Bradby may have viewed racial solidarity and separation as necessary preconditions for attaining racial equality. Dancy, Bradby, and others did not repudiate the goal of racial integration so much as suggest that they understood the way forward to their ultimate goal would not be straight.[92] Bradby reflected the general leaning of black Detroiters in transition and at a crossroads. Allegiance to the FMC, still high, probably rose after the Sweet trial as demand for the Model T began to drop and unemployment threatened all Ford workers. While the black ghetto represented a step backward in terms of citizenship rights and the walls of residential segregation grew stronger, the principles upheld by Judge Murphy in the Sweet case empowered black Detroiters.

A new assertiveness is apparent in the following incident. Late in December 1926, three black men drove to a Dearborn restaurant for a meal. Seeing them in the restaurant, a police officer "ordered them out saying they did not have any black faces in Dearborn." The men heeded the order, left the establishment, and drove away. Soon, however, the officer "overtook them, got in their car, and ordered them to turn around and go back to the police station," commanding the driver to break the speed limit. When the driver did so, he was charged with reckless driving and speeding.[93] Rev. Bradby used his position as president of the Detroit NAACP to demand answers from the chief of the Dearborn Police Department.

By doing so, Bradby also challenged the racial etiquette in Henry Ford's hometown, noted for the control Ford had over the township, including the police department.[94] Was Bradby accommodating to the wishes of Henry Ford on such an occasion?

The impulse to challenge prevailing racial conventions also spurred the formation of new groups and the expansion of old networks. The purpose of the Colored Civic Pride League, whose mission was defending the right of African Americans to live wherever they wanted, grew out of events of 1925, especially the cases of Bristol, Dr. Turner, and Dr. Sweet.[95] Black Detroiters also did not forget Mayor Smith's "cowardly fear to do his plain duty to the Negro as a citizen" when he blamed blacks for insisting on their constitutional rights in 1925. Colored Civic Pride and other organizations helped defeat Smith when he ran for reelection in 1927.[96] Other new groups included the Detroit Civic and Political Club, the New Citizens League, the Knights of Ethiopia, and the United Voters League.[97] All-black institutions and venues served as incubators, cultivating new strategies and approaches to overcome barriers to opportunity, which, in turn, helped shape the next round in the ongoing struggle during the early years of the Great Depression.

CHAPTER FIVE

The Politics of Unemployment in Depression-Era Detroit, 1927–1931

There is a crack in everything. That's how the light gets in.
—LEONARD COHEN, "Anthem" (1992)

THE OSSIAN SWEET case made a hero out of Frank Murphy within the black community by reinforcing African Americans' push for inclusion and broadening their political horizons. At the same time allegiance to Henry Ford, the other anchor of black Detroit's American plan for full participation, remained high in 1926 and 1927 as competition within the auto industry put Ford jobs at risk. By the time of the Great Depression, however, the balance shifted as black Detroiters threw their allegiance strongly behind the political campaigns of Frank Murphy, Ford's nemesis.

The Great Depression exposed the fault lines in Henry Ford's seemingly flawless approach to mass production. During the first phase of the Depression, 1929–31, black Detroiters, struggling to make headway, participated in Mayor Murphy's campaign to deal with rising unemployment. They also took part in the Unemployed Councils' acts of civil disobedience to avoid evictions, acts that were led by the communists. Through these activities, old networks grew and new ones formed as underemployed and unemployed joined forces, demonstrating against injustice and unequal distribution of scare resources during a time of mass economic distress. Remedies worked out by African Americans for dealing with social upheaval were increasingly independent of Henry Ford's control. It was during this time that ties to the Ford mystique began to unravel as Henry Ford failed to come to terms with the crisis in employment and consumption unleashed by the crash of 1929. Impatience with Ford's responses to the

Great Depression was linked to the uncertainty created when sales of the Model T fell in 1927, a period that served as a dress rehearsal for the crash.

DRESS REHEARSAL FOR THE CRASH:
CRISIS OF CONSUMPTION HITS THE FLIVVER

During the twenties, American consumerism came of age. Washing machines, refrigerators, radios, telephones, cars, canned foods, and motion pictures were among the popular products produced and distributed widely during this decade of prosperity.[1] If the automobile was the most revolutionary item, then the leader in terms of production and consumer purchases was the Flivver, Ford's Model T. It was thanks to the Model T, argues historian Douglas Brinkley, that the automobile age arrived on America's doorstep at least a decade before it might otherwise have. The millions of Model T's spurred construction of an infrastructure—"roads, parking lots, traffic signals, service stations"— that made all cars more attractive. "The Model T . . . did not just proliferate—it begat other cars as well."[2] As other cars proliferated, consumers turned their backs on the all-black—and only black—utilitarian Flivver, choosing, instead, colorful, stylish alternatives produced by General Motors. By 1926, the Flivver was no longer king, and the Ford Motor Company (FMC) showed the first signs of economic trouble, leading to worker layoffs, reduced workweeks, and terminations.[3]

By the middle of the decade, Chevrolet, the major competitor, had cut into Ford's dominance of the market. Rather than altering the Model T, Henry Ford responded by defending it, rebuking all who dared to suggest the Flivver was no longer sovereign, especially his son, Edsel.[4] Some who presented plans for retooling and updating the T were even fired.[5] In Ford's mind, the Model T remained the most perfect car in the world. Why change it?

Alfred Sloan, who took over the presidency of General Motors in 1923, tapped into what he described as a craving for a bit of class expressed by car buyers in the mid-1920s. With the incentive of installment buying initiated by the General Motors Acceptance Corporation, consumers flocked to the stylish Chevrolet. Understanding the culture of consumption driving the market during the twenties, General Motors gave its customers a choice of bright colors in DuPont's Duco paint on Chevrolets that also featured four-wheel hydraulic brakes, balloon tires, shock absorbers, and a gearshift transmission. Chevrolets were more expensive than Ford's Model T, but the installment plan made customers think they could afford a more expensive car.[6] Throughout 1926, Chevrolet continued to eat away at Ford's market share. Still Ford held fast.

When Chevrolet finally surged ahead of Model T sales early in 1927, Ford reluctantly began planning for a replacement.[7] At the beginning of May, the fifteen-millionth Ford Model T was driven out of the Rouge. Shortly thereafter Ford announced the end of the Model T and laid off 60,000 workers as the FMC came to terms with the passing of the Tin Lizzie, with no replacement in sight.[8] Design, testing, retooling of plants, machines, and equipment took months. The majority of workers were not back at work until October, and production did not begin until November 1927.[9]

When the FMC sneezed, all Detroit felt a chill. The five-month shutdown at Ford cost the company some $250 million, but the cost to Detroit and Detroiters was considerably greater. Years later, Frank Angelo, a reporter for the *Detroit News* during the thirties, pointed out "what people don't understand is that the so-called big depression had started in Detroit about two years before when the Ford Motor Company shut down . . . to end the production of the Model T."[10] Economic interdependence dealt a heavy blow to the fortunes of those dependent on Ford jobs for their well-being. When Ford closed down to change models, the city's automobile production fell by approximately 25 percent. Estimates of total unemployment ran as high as 100,000 as hundreds of Ford suppliers also shut down for the duration of the model change. The economic blow hit small stores, real estate businesses, and all the banks holding mortgages on homes. Even so, banks overlooked, for the duration, overdue payments, landlords allowed rent to go into arrears, and merchants extended credit until they had to close. All that slack did not eliminate evictions for families whose monthly mortgage payments were more than their salaries. Children were separated from parents and placed in homes; many had to be housed and fed at public expense.[11]

Hard times landed on the doorsteps of Ford workers well before the shutdown for the model change, as Ford addressed the need to lower production by initiating a five-day workweek in 1926, largely a device for concealing the dislocation of the market. Reduced employment at the Ford plants in Detroit was evident by 1926. On 1 November 1925, 122,215 workers were employed at the Rouge and Highland Park plants combined. By the first half of 1927, employment at the Rouge and Highland Park averaged only 75,000, and it went down from there.[12]

What employment figures disguise is the fact that the majority of those counted as employed were working less than a full week by the fall of 1926. Since at least November 1926, few workers at the FMC enjoyed the chance to work a five-day week. The average was four days, and many had been reduced to three-day workweeks. The result was considerably less than "normal" earnings. Thousands of Ford workers, black and white, some with four, five, or six dependents, had to rely on public or private charity to sustain themselves and their families. By the summer of 1927, declared Reinhold Niebuhr, Ford workers were the heaviest charge on Detroit charities of any single class of citizens, with some charities reporting that more than 50 percent of their beneficiaries were Ford workers.[13]

Detroit's Department of Public Welfare (DPW), considered at the time one of the very best of its kind in the country, believed public relief and family welfare service ought to be its mission. The DPW was not only efficient; it was progressive, delivering relief "ungrudgingly" when needed and without unnecessary embarrassment to the recipients. When the slump overwhelmed the FMC and either put thousands out of work or left them with too little work, the DPW stepped in to bridge the gap.[14]

A few examples illustrate the nature of the severe recession experienced during 1926–27 by employed Ford workers. A Ford worker with a wife and five children averaged three days of work per week, not nearly enough to make $60 per month in mortgage payments. His wife went to work at $15 per week to help cover the house payments. Another worker, who had labored for ten years at Ford, found himself with only three days work per week. In his case, hours had been cut because younger men in his department, considered more efficient, got an extra day's work per week. Another worker, unable to keep up payments on the home he purchased, first received a loan from a charitable organization to meet delinquent payments. Failing to come up with the interest for the first loan because of the cutbacks at Ford, he then took out a second loan to help pay back the first loan. These were some of the circumstances that increased the caseload of the DPW from a low of 757 in 1923 to a high of 3,977 in 1927.[15]

With the recession of 1926–27 at the FMC, a basic tenet of Henry Ford's philosophy, the belief that an adequate wage trumped handouts or philanthropy, began to unravel as Ford workers struggled to keep the wolf from the door. Every social worker in Detroit, Reinhold Niebuhr argued at the time, "knows that the Ford wage places Ford workers in the ranks of social liabilities."[16] As a minister, Niebuhr had been an observer of the upper stratum of Detroit's social order for years. What concerned him were the poorly developed social consciences among Detroit's power brokers, men who had acquired vast wealth in a relatively short period of time.[17] Aiming his fire directly at Henry Ford, Niebuhr contended that Ford represented a fundamental flaw in the nation's ascendancy, that of an America "which has risen almost in a generation from an agrarian to an industrial economic order and now applies the social intelligence of a country village to the most complex industrial life the world has ever known."[18]

A CRISIS OF PRODUCTION

Like so many businessmen, Henry Ford did not see the big crash coming. Just days before, Ford unveiled his version of the progress at the heart of the American experience by opening his museum at Greenfield Village in Dearborn, Michigan.[19] The museum celebrated the art, culture, and way of life that characterized nineteenth-century America. One exhibit was a reconstruction of William H. McGuffey's birthplace. Ford revered the *McGuffey Eclectic Reader*, popular in the nineteenth century, for its lessons in morality and industry and committed many of its maxims to memory.[20] The occasion also honored Thomas Edison, a close friend of Henry Ford, for his invention of the incandescent light. Calling the celebration "Light's Golden Jubilee," Ford regarded Edison's invention as exemplifying the idea that history is the story of technological progress.[21]

The opening of Greenfield Village and the crash of 1929 capture the thinking of Henry Ford on the eve of the Great Depression. His village and museum—with horse-drawn wagons, village blacksmith shops, cooper shops, slave cabins, and covered bridges—embodied the simple virtues, work ethic, and morality taught in the *McGuffey Readers*. But Ford hoped to convey more than a sentimental gaze through the rearview mirror with his emphasis on an era when the world was simpler. The village was an expression of Ford's conviction that history was not just "bunk," an often-quoted remark of his taken out of its original context.[22]

Rather, Ford believed that when history is linked to technological developments, it serves as a record of progress. That was in fact an article of faith inscribed in *Looking Forward through the Past* (1935), a handbook given to visitors of Greenfield Village: "No one can truly appreciate the present, or even dimly picture the future, who is insensitive to the past and to the advances men have made."[23] Ford, however, was never entirely successful in reconciling the comfort he derived from the mores and aspirations of the past with the life his revolutionary endeavors did so much to create.

The road to progress built by Ford's new-age tools of mass production had been carved out of the bedrock of mass consumption. Mass production required mass consumption; without consumer buying power, a crisis in overproduction would result. The nation had traveled a great distance from the sentiments enshrined at Greenfield Village, and much more was needed than evoking the work ethic and simplicity of bygone years. With the collapse of consumer spending, an entirely new way of thinking about how to move forward would have to be developed. But Ford's genius as a businessman and innovative engineer—the very traits that did so much to create modern consumer society—faltered when presented with the crisis in production that threw the nation into severe economic decline in the early 1930s.

Like many others, Ford clung to a tried-and-true formula to overcome the crisis, relying on the power of public relations and wage increases. In reality, rising unemployment at the FMC exerted a downward pressure on aggregate real wages even while individual wages rose. As sales fell and the production of new cars slowed, Ford cut employment drastically, even though Ford officials proclaimed that the company would escape the fallout. But Henry and Edsel Ford were not alone in their optimism. Within days of the historic October crash, the Fords joined other business leaders—among them John D. Rockefeller and J. P. Morgan Jr.—in claiming complete confidence in the American economy. "Every indication," Edsel Ford said, "is that the general business condition will remain prosperous."[24]

THE GREAT DEPRESSION IN DETROIT

We do not have any comprehensive measure of unemployment in Detroit during the first eight months of 1930.[25] We do know from the Census Bureau that 13.3 percent of the labor force (76,018 workers) were unemployed in April 1930, while an additional 15,479 Detroiters had been laid off without pay, giving Detroit the highest level of unemployment among the nation's largest cities. The city's Board of Commerce and the Employers'

Association suggested that factory employment fell 37 percent between January and August 1930.[26] Observers noted the despair. When Helen Hall, director of Philadelphia's University Settlement, arrived in Detroit in January 1930, she declared that she had "never confronted such misery."[27] *Detroit Saturday Night* reported that "sullen and despondent knots of men gathered about the doorways or congregated in the streets."[28]

Initially, workers at the FMC fared better than those at most other firms during the year of the crash because Ford production and sales in 1929 were relatively good. Sales increased by 138 percent as Model A's outsold Chevrolets 1.5 million to 950,000. On closer inspection, it was clear that Henry Ford once again, as he had in 1921, pumped up sales by pressuring his dealers to take price reductions out of their commissions. Employment at Ford, which was 122,680 in March 1929, tumbled to 100,500 by December. While there was no growth in Ford sales during 1930, the fact that the company was not in a slump was considered, given the circumstances, a success. Henry and Edsel Ford continued to issue optimistic press releases, highlighting Ford's faith in rising above the damage caused by a severely depressed auto market.[29]

The full force of the depression hit the FMC early in 1931, shattering the fiction that Ford was exceptional. During the three worst years of the Depression, 1931–33, Ford lost more than $125,000,000.[30] Henry and Edsel Ford's optimism notwithstanding, Detroiters, employed and unemployed, probably found 1930 tolerable only in hindsight, for 1931 through 1933 was a vastly worse period of time. When the federal government studied Ford workers in the Detroit area in 1930, they found that average annual earnings for heads of families were $1,694, while average annual household expenditure was $1,719. The gap between earnings and expenditures was closed by dipping into personal savings, assuming debt, or from financial assistance provided by relatives. To close the gap, 59 percent of the Ford families made purchases on installment plans.[31]

Ford workers had tightened their belts during the dress rehearsal for the Great Depression. Many had been laid off during that period and later rehired. But at the end of the day, Ford workers—especially those who had been employed for years by Henry Ford—generally believed there was a tacit, personal covenant between Ford and his employees assuring steady employment to good, faithful workers. It grew out of the multiple ways that Ford personalized his image at the company. Unlike General Motors, for example, there was no chain of command, no managerial chart detailing who should report to whom. Henry Ford was the Ford Motor Company, and his word was gospel. When Ford's actions went against his words, when Ford workers who had been faithful employees for many years were fired, many felt betrayed by more than just the grim times that gripped the nation. They felt Henry Ford had personally betrayed them.[32]

As late as April 1931, Ford was claiming he would not cut wages.[33] Yet he did just that year after year between 1929 and 1933. After the workforce was cut drastically, attempts were made to equalize work. Instead of employing a man for a week, the company might use one man for two days and another for three. But that situation led to fierce competition and jealousy and reinforced favoritism from the foremen. Moreover, Ford's promises not to cut wages were broadcast widely, increasing the numbers of unemployed who rushed to Detroit seeking a mythical $7 a day wage, which only made matters worse.[34]

Thousands were unemployed in Detroit. Schoolteachers, lawyers, mechanics, production line workers, foundry workers, engineers, architects, toolmakers, maids, and journalists stood in the breadlines together, without regard for the color line.[35] The impact on Detroit was apparent in the caseload of the DPW, which increased from 3,380 in October 1929 to 21,759 in April 1930, with unemployment (as opposed to old age, sickness, and desertion) accounting for more than 80 percent of the cases.[36] The monthly expenditures of the Detroit DPW increased from $115,759 in February 1929 to $500,000 in December 1929 to $1,581,981 for February 1931, while the family caseload grew from 3,160 to 47,312 families in this period.[37]

Detroit entered the Great Depression under the political leadership of the KKK's favorite candidate, Charles Bowles, whose third attempt for the post was successful. Prominent leaders of the Detroit Citizens League (DCL) enthusiastically supported Bowles and viewed his election as a victory for "decency, law and order."[38] William Lovett, executive member of the DCL, explained that he was confident that Bowles would deliver on his promise for more law enforcement because "all the drys, church forces, Masons, KKKs, and many other good citizens on a strict law enforcement platform" supported him.[39] Within a few short months, however, Lovett regretted his misplaced confidence, joining a citizens committee to recall Mayor Bowles. Unbridled lawlessness triggered the recall and enlisted 111,270 signatures, more than enough to force an election. On 22 July Bowles was unseated by a vote of 120,862 to 89,907. But even though the

DCL initiated the recall, he was still strongly endorsed by the majority of Protestant churches.[40]

In a confidential memo to leaders of the DCL, Lovett said he opposed Bowles because he "was not running the city government," which had fallen into the hands of a "gambling organization." The graft was once isolated in the police department under the supervision of Harold H. Emmons, who was a DCL member, a lawyer for Henry Ford, and a former president of the Detroit Board of Commerce, but it had spread "through the political underworld" and was "increasing daily with tremendous financial profits to operators."[41] Bowles's alliance with organized crime kept Detroit high on the list of America's most venal and dangerous cities.[42] A cursory read through Detroit newspapers revealed details of violent crimes. The KKK, most noted for its prominence in the early twenties, was still alive and well by the late twenties and had many fanatical followers, some of whom were known to work inside the Ford plants.[43] Moreover, ethnic and racial antagonisms continued, adding yet another element to an already explosive situation.

Shortly after the crash, James Couzens, former mayor and former executive of the FMC, warned members of the Michigan Manufacturers' Association, "If you do not solve" the problems of low aggregate wages, seasonal unemployment, and unfair treatment of unions, "government will step in and solve them for you" and "that will be just too bad."[44] Couzens was giving voice to concerns that coursed just below the surface in management's mind: Would the Depression lead to radicalism in the politics of Detroit? How, wondered the industrialists, would the ethnically diverse population deal with unemployment, underemployment, and scarcity?

It was not long before radicals took advantage of the economic debacle and Bowles's political incompetence to pitch their message to the unemployed. When Detroit's Communist Party (CP) held a demonstration for the unemployed on 6 March 1930, they were, reportedly, as surprised as anyone with the huge turnout. Thousands demonstrated despite repressive police tactics. Within the year, fifteen Unemployed Councils had organized along neighborhood lines, seeking to bridge racial and ethnic divisions, uniting people to protest and rally for government assistance, and helping evicted families reclaim their homes.[45]

The CP had tried to spread its vision of interracial unionism among foreign-born men and women as well as among black workers between

1924 and 1930. Though their numbers were small, the communists managed to take control of the Auto Workers Union (AWU) from the Socialist Party. Walter Hardin, Paul Kirk, Joseph Billups, and William Nowell were among the first wave of African Americans who joined the CP before the Depression. Black communists worked with both the AWU and the League of Struggle for Negro Rights, hoping to introduce revolutionary and nationalist ideas within the political discourse.[46] But before 1930 most black Detroiters knew very little about the communists.

The Unemployed Councils and the Depression changed that. Because African Americans, for all their progress, were still most likely the first fired by the majority of employers, their unemployment rate, according to Sidney Fine, was double that of whites.[47] Thus, Unemployed Councils held great appeal for black Detroiters, especially the practice of organizing neighborhoods around the issue of opposing evictions. Joseph Billups, a black Ford worker, remembered "when people were evicted we would place them back in their houses." He had "seen times when we would have four or five evictions in one block."[48] Unemployed Council meetings rallied forces for demonstrations and educated ordinary Detroiters about the failures of the American economic system and about democratic rights. Massive participation in Unemployed Council demonstrations and meetings by African Americans reflected not so much belief in the gospel of the communists as broad support for increased political activism and the rise of protest networks, a trend originating in the twenties.

By the early months of the Depression, as the strain on resources severely restricted the ability of established, traditional organizations within the black community to deliver help, grassroots organizations were formed to address the community's multiple problems. Besides participating in the Unemployed Councils, black Detroiters worked on several fronts with organizations bringing together people from different points on the ideological spectrum. For example, members of the Booker T. Washington Trade Association (BTWTA) and its Housewives' League shared the goals of Marcus Garvey and the Universal Negro Improvement Association (UNIA), believing that only through the development of robust business and industry within the black community could African Americans gain economic independence. Garveyism drew on a network that included many ministers and their wives, but its activities also overlapped with others dedicated to self-determination within black Detroit.[49]

Marshals standing on the steps of City Hall in Detroit before leading a march to Lansing, the state capital, to protest unemployment. 25 May 1931. Image courtesy of the Walter P. Reuther Library, Wayne State University.

After the recall of Mayor Bowles, ethnics, blacks, and organized labor gathered 73,000 signatures to recruit Frank Murphy to run for mayor of Detroit for the remainder of the Bowles term.[50] Black organizations and networks, many initiated during the organizing days of the Sweet case, immediately went to work as volunteers for Frank Murphy. In addition to Murphy, the special election, scheduled for early September, included candidates Charles Bowles, encouraged by strong support from white Protestants; John Smith, the former mayor; and George Engel, a businessman supported by the DCL.[51]

During Murphy's two-week campaign run by volunteers, he set himself and his vision apart from politics as usual, demonstrating remarkable oratorical talent as he championed the unemployed and the weary. He grasped before other candidates did that the election would turn on the issue of unemployment, attacking what he called the "conspiracy of silence" about the dire economic conditions gripping Detroiters and the nation.[52] In the speech that opened his campaign at the Fort Wayne Hotel, Murphy stressed what he would do if elected mayor. Beginning with a short history of Detroit, Murphy connected bad times in Detroit's past to those of the thirties. Recalling a tragic fire that wiped out 300 homes in the nineteenth century, Murphy reminded his listeners that the experience etched a new motto on the seal of the city: "We hope for better days. It shall arise from its ashes." Detroit was once again, Murphy noted, in "ashes, a political ruin, burned to the ground, by hate, by discord, by selfishness, by government put to corrupt and selfish ends. But, 'it shall arise.'" Underscoring the dire nature of the city's condition, Murphy asked rhetorically, "What is the use in misleading the people?" He then told the crowd, "You plain folks, you men and women upon whose shoulders and bent backs this city rests," Detroit is "dead broke . . . flat broke at this very hour." The bonded debt of Detroit on that day was, according to Murphy, "$378,000,000." Interest on that debt "since four o'clock this afternoon is enough to give the normal citizen a chill."[53]

After identifying several institutions suffering from corruption—the police department, the public transportation system, municipal finances, and the department of public works—Murphy proposed that it was time to "lift our eyes high up to a new dawn. Let us lift our eyes to a more enlightened horizon." He appealed to the "Common Herd," those interested in overthrowing "machine politics." Murphy promised that "Detroit's past should belong to dead yesterday." He promised a "new deal" for the common herd, for "we want something new. We want the dews, the sunshine of a new morning. We want to know that a square deal exists between the people and their government, that preference is not given to a select and fortunate group because of campaign contributions, and as we go forward we will let no one talk us out of our conception of social and progressive justice."[54]

Murphy was passionate as he addressed the problem of unemployment, "of the jobless men and women . . . who, in one month of this year, reached the grand total of 200,000 workmen and work women." The power brokers of old were afraid to tackle the problem. "They avoid Cass Avenue, that tragic street of jobless men and women, where the procession is unending, where hope is shattered, where in the high noon of life, the sweet supplication, 'Give us this day our daily bread' has brought a new significance." Murphy promised that the first part of his new approach would be to "do away with this defeatist psychology, that nothing can be done about it . . . this conspiracy of silence on the part of the press."[55]

The opening speech of Murphy's campaign drew a clear line between the haves and the have-nots, building on his philosophy of a "new deal." "What," asked Murphy, "has brought Detroit to her tragic plight?" The problem lay with the deal that had been struck between the industrial elite and politicians. "In order to be elected Mayor, in order to succeed politically, men have pledged themselves until they are hogtied, shackled and bound by promises." In a time of dire destitution, Murphy declared it is not possible to be a good mayor with such constraints. "In order to succeed, our department of Public Works is traded off with the ease with which some men engage in a horse deal." His proposal promised to sweep away all "old machines," the power brokers, and those who "do not belong in the new deal."[56]

Murphy's campaign was intense, focusing on winning the hearts of African Americans and ethnics, the forgotten ones. Race was one of several threads galvanizing voters. Bowles, in contrast, told a crowd from the twenty-second ward, his Protestant followers, that he did not want the votes of the 100,000 residents of Wards 3, 5, and 7, where blacks and Catholics lived. "I don't want the votes of that kind of people." Rather, Bowles insisted, he wanted votes from "my kind of people." Murphy said he would gladly take those votes, "every one." It was hard to imagine, Murphy acknowledged, "that any mayor would want to be mayor for just one segment of our family."[57]

On 5 September, six of the eleven groups Murphy addressed were black; on the 8th, he spoke at several black churches, including King Solomon Church.[58] Though he was pitched as the candidate of the common herd, within the black community the elite was just as enthusiastic as the masses in supporting Murphy. Beulah Young, the editor of the *Detroit People's News*, a black newspaper, and second vice president of the National Negro Press Association, worked hard to get out the vote for Murphy.[59] Oscar DePriest, the first black member of Congress since 1901 and the first ever from the North, traveled from Chicago to speak in Detroit for Murphy; Walter White, the secretary of the national NAACP, worked from outside Detroit on Murphy's behalf; black professionals and pastors overwhelmingly supported Murphy, including figures like Rev. Bradby and Moses L. Walker, the vice president and treasurer of the Great Lakes Mutual Insurance Company, and John Dancy of the DUL.[60] Rev. Bradby was in the vanguard of black leaders arranging meetings for Murphy within black Detroit; he called Murphy one of the "outstanding men of the day" in his church newsletter, the *Second Baptist Herald*.[61]

The support from volunteers from all walks of life within the black community was significant and historic. Harry Mead, Murphy's campaign manager, was impressed and grateful for what he called the "big support" Murphy got from the "colored boys." The black community went all out for Murphy, according to Mead, "because of the Ossian Sweet trial at which time Mr. Murphy announced from the bench that a man's house was his castle." As a result, "they went wild" supporting Murphy. "I'd say as for one bloc," Mead said, "they did as much as any other one; at that time he wasn't too big with labor." Mead related events that occurred late on an August Sunday afternoon when Murphy spoke at Ebenezer Baptist Church. "We drove up and got out and the sidewalks were packed and that church . . . was packed. You would have thought it was the second coming of Lincoln or second coming of Christ."[62]

Murphy was elected with widespread black support. Within black precincts throughout the city, Murphy won as much as 80 percent of the vote. While Smith ran second to Murphy in black precincts, he was a very distant second. In Ward 3, for example, Murphy won a total of 4,188 votes to Smith's 643. When broken down to the precinct level, the margins are striking. In Ward 3, precinct 6 went 189 for Murphy to 31 for Smith. In

Ward 5, precinct 7 supported Murphy by 277 votes to Smith's 54, and precinct 12 gave Murphy 350 votes and Smith only 54. The total vote count was 106,637 for Murphy, 93,985 for Bowles, and 21,735 for Smith.[63] As Murphy explained to Walter White, "Your people were as faithful and true as any group could be. They went right out on the firing line for me and stood by me almost to a man." But, Murphy added, "the only exception was Dr. Sweet. Can you figure that out?"[64] Murphy also received over 50 percent of the total vote cast in Wards 9, 11, and 13, representing foreign-born voters and their children. His worst showing was in Ward 22 with only 18 percent of the largely native-born, Protestant white vote, a pattern that repeated itself in other wards with large numbers of native-born whites of native-born parentage.[65]

Black support for Murphy was noteworthy for the speed with which community groups hit the ground running. A plethora of organizations rooted in black Detroit immediately took charge and canvassed the community, suggesting the existence of active, organized, political networks with strong foundations.[66] The power and strength of the groups coalescing around the election of Murphy depended on energizing the neighborhoods. The work was voluntary. One political organization, the Allied Political Club, operating as an umbrella organization, listed seventeen different groups within its coalition: the Afro-American Councils, Colored Civic Pride of Michigan, Community Voters League, Cosmopolitan League, Delray Rep. (Republican) Clubs, Encorse Community Clubs, 8 Mi. Rd., Fact Finding Com., Scott M. E. Church, Knights of Ethiopia, Klugs Ryan Rd. Political Club, the North Detroit Civic Pride League, New Citizens League, United Voters League, West Side Community Voters League, Women's Political Club, and the Willing Workers League located in Oakland County.[67]

The Charles A. Young Post of the American Legion, composed of a group of African American war veterans, worked day and night distributing literature, canvassing neighborhoods, and arranging meetings for Murphy during the election campaign. The vets in this post were almost entirely members who were employed in the Sanitary Division of the City of Detroit. They claimed one of their members borrowed $20.00 on his furniture to open a Murphy campaign headquarters at the corner of Adams and Antoine Streets in Black Bottom.[68]

Because black grassroots political networks rose to the occasion to serve Frank Murphy, his campaign did not have to create political groups to serve its interests. The Detroit Civic and Political Club, which had over 1,000 members, stood for and behind Murphy 100 percent. The club, like so many other black organizations, energetically worked for Murphy, arranging speaking engagements within black Detroit. The black representatives of the common herd were active in Murphy's campaign at the precinct level; they got people to the polls and prayed for Murphy's good health. His election inspired an avalanche of correspondence from black Detroiters. Many of the congratulatory messages that Murphy received spoke about the access to the mayor's office that black citizens felt they now had. Many mentioned the "critical time" that had brought Murphy to City Hall and thanked him for his vision and inspiration.[69] Black organizations and leaders did not wait for Mayor Murphy to ask what he could do for the black community. Instead, black leaders petitioned the mayor for positions in municipal departments. One of the more important issues Murphy received advice on was who to hire in the police department in order to make it accountable to the City of Detroit as well as "our group."[70] Beulah Young told Mayor Murphy to "lean" on her for keeping the black community organized, not just for his reelection to the mayor's office, but also to mobilize the state for him when he would run for president.[71] Before the year was out, Young had established her Political Leadership Assembly to organize black neighborhoods into "block assemblies," headed by "captains," much like precinct arrangements favored by major political parties.[72]

Several residents of black Detroit took it upon themselves to be the eyes and ears for the mayor. One black supporter documented the tactics of "the Big Shots" to "split the colored people in two" after Murphy was mayor (as contenders paved the way to challenge Murphy's reelection in the fall of 1931). Harold Emmons, a candidate for mayor the following year, questioned the allegiance of Murphy to black Detroit. Emmons, according to the source, was "going around having a bill printed" in Murphy's name announcing a future meeting within the black community. Since Murphy did not know of the meeting, Emmons would appear instead and "tell the People we knowed he [Murphy] was not coming." Emmons was putting forth the idea that Murphy could not be trusted; after all, he could not even arrive and "make a talk" when he said he would.[73] Such efforts did not seem to fool black Detroiters.

The DCL and interests representing Henry Ford shared concerns about the future direction of the city under Murphy's administration. Lovett, of the DCL, kept an ever-watchful eye on Murphy's actions, planting suggestions about how to seize the high road to gain some ground during the upcoming 1931 mayoral election. "The greatest need of our city government right now," said Lovett, was for a more business-oriented mayor. Lovett's critique of Murphy, he made clear, was not "personal." But while Murphy emphasized "human" qualities, Lovett thought, "problems of administration, finance, taxes, etc. are equally human." Lovett's first desire was to change the city charter yet again, so that city policy would be driven by big business and not the personality of a strong mayor.[74] Murphy felt the undertow from the business-oriented DCL and others, but believed the "social aspects" of city government, especially during the Depression, "loom up above all others."[75]

Murphy's commitment to social justice was both conscious and novel. Government "should penetrate through and past mere business enterprise," according to Murphy, and incorporate the problems of "the multitude of obscure men and women who face eviction and starvation." Looking beyond the mere task of municipal management, he set his sights on what he called the "tragic struggle for social justice."[76] His was a call for a "union of head and heart," the marriage of business efficiency with a commitment to "human understanding and sympathy." For these reasons, Murphy believed that the "great cities of the nation" had "become the battleground for social justice."[77] It was this understanding that set Murphy apart and made him, according to historian Hans Kohn, "the founder of the whole New Deal idea," several years before there was a New Deal.[78]

Long before becoming mayor, Murphy began contemplating unemployment issues. He had converted his Recorder's Court chambers into an unofficial employment agency, which tried to find jobs for the needy. In April 1930, he consulted with Professor William Haber, an economist at Michigan State College, who became one of the nations' first academic experts on the topic of unemployment. From those discussions, Haber developed a plan for Murphy to implement in Detroit.[79] Indeed, the first matter of business for the Murphy administration was unemployment, the issue that was a centerpiece for his election. He formed the Mayor's Unemployment Committee (MUC) on 15 September, within days of his election, to coordinate the city's relief effort, putting the Haber plan into effect.[80] One of the subcommittees established by the MUC was a Colored Advisory

Committee, formed to address issues and concerns related specifically to African Americans, the part of the city's population hardest hit by the Depression. The DUL's director, John Dancy, chaired this committee.[81]

Murphy's efforts were under way none too soon. By the fall of 1930, Detroit's percentage of unemployed had kept the city in front of other major metropolitan areas, such as New York, Chicago, Philadelphia, Cleveland, and Cincinnati. Detroit was hit harder, in part because of its image as the nation's center for industrial workers. As C. C. McGill of the Detroit Board of Commerce explained, Detroit was the "magnet that draws the machine tool operator, the sheet metal worker, the lathe hand." By 1930, many such workers in Detroit were "not Detroiters at all" but were there because unemployment problems elsewhere led them to the last frontier for industrial work.[82]

Murphy appointed G. Hall Roosevelt, brother of Eleanor Roosevelt, as chairman of the MUC, whose membership represented Detroit's diverse population from the boardrooms of the automotive industry to organized labor, middle-class reformers, and black community activists.[83] The Colored Advisory Committee stood apart from other MUC committees because it did not initiate relief programs, monitoring, instead, ongoing programs to make sure they were free from discrimination. John Dancy gave the city high marks for taking good care of citizens, black and white, stating that there were no "barriers of participation." Detroit was also properly responsive to protests from the black community about the attitudes of certain welfare workers toward African Americans. Mayor Murphy personally wrote to the head of public welfare, insisting that there be no discrimination against black Detroiters.[84]

Detroit's employment situation was compounded because the city derived over 95 percent of its relief money from public sources. In most urban areas in 1930 and 1931, approximately 65 percent of monies for general relief came from public sources. Detroit accounted for more than 27 percent of all public relief distributed in the country in 1930, with a caseload that totaled about 27 percent of the total caseload in seventy major urban areas.[85] By the spring of 1931, as unemployment numbers ratcheted up week by week, draining the public coffers and increasing the DPW's caseload, Mayor Murphy and the Welfare Department were put to the test. Business interests put pressure on the mayor to trim the DPW's sails, advising the administration to show as much sympathy for taxpayers as it did for the needy. The DCL, for example, recommended that welfare payments be progressively reduced every month. In a public radio address, the publicity agent for the Detroit Board of Commerce claimed that "the open-handed, come one–come all welfare policy of Detroit" was responsible for the large caseload at the DPW. Moreover, it was Detroit's liberal welfare policy that had attracted "derelicts from all parts of America," who were learning how to live with no effort thanks to Detroit's tax dollars.[86]

By February 1931, the cash-strapped DPW began to reduce the weekly food allowance for welfare families. By April, a family of five received a maximum of $7, down from $11.24 in November. To keep the DPW operating, Murphy secured a $19.3 million bond issue, but only when the city agreed not to apply for another long-term bond until the end of the next fiscal year (1931–32).[87] At that point the mayor attacked the tight-fisted policy of the FMC and its lack of responsibility toward former Ford employees.

W. G. Bergman, organizing secretary of the MUC, charged that Henry Ford, who cared "well for idle machinery," does not mind turning "idle men into the streets to care for themselves as best they may." Bergman claimed that 36 percent of the families receiving care from the City of Detroit were former Ford employees.[88] A DPW report, issued in April, identified 5,061 welfare recipients as former employees of the FMC. Murphy suggested that a major employer like Ford had a responsibility to help with the burden of relief. Because Ford's facilities, with the exception of one Lincoln plant, were located outside Detroit's city limits, the company made only negligible contributions to Detroit's tax base.[89] These charges were leveled while Henry Ford was still proclaiming, despite major layoffs and wage reductions, that there would be "no deflation of labor by the Ford Motor Company."[90]

Spokesmen for the FMC responded by claiming that the city administration was guilty of incompetence and fraud. How could the company be responsible for helping unemployed Ford workers living in Detroit when the Rouge was located outside Detroit in Dearborn, where the company dutifully paid its taxes? The argument did not impress the public. Harry Bennett spoke for the company by declaring there was not a single former employee in dire circumstances that "we are responsible for whom we have not tried in some way to relieve." Out of a list of approximately 4,000 former Ford employees forwarded to it by the DPW, Bennett said that many had never worked for the FMC and that 329 were actually working for Ford even as they drew welfare checks and defrauded the city.[91]

After much back and forth between the FMC and the mayor's office, the *Detroit News* investigated the allegations, finding little evidence to support Bennett's claim of fraud. The *News* reported that the DPW found only thirty-one cases in which current Ford employees were receiving checks from the DPW. The welfare officials took the opportunity to point out that had the FMC complied with the DPW's numerous requests for the work record of every person on relief, as other Detroit industries had, the thirty-one cases would never have arisen in the first place. For months, the other major automotive industries and businesses had worked with city government, screening against fraud by checking lists of welfare applicants against their payrolls. The only large concern refusing to cooperate was the FMC.[92]

By the summer of 1931, the controversy made national headlines for several weeks, as Murphy spoke of Detroit having been "saddled" with a disproportionate number of welfare cases that were really "Ford cases."[93] That fall, the *New Republic* published an editorial on starvation and unemployment in Detroit suggesting approximately four people a day were brought to Receiving Hospital "too far gone from starvation for their lives to be saved."[94] The bitter controversy put Henry Ford on the defensive and exposed the hypocrisy of Ford's claims of being his "brother's keeper." At the national level, the press criticized Ford's laissez-faire approach and expressed sympathy for the plight facing Detroit. Others criticized Murphy for standing up to Henry Ford, and there was even a death threat to the "Irish son of a bitch."[95] But Murphy did not mind the exposure, or the depiction of him as David standing up to Ford, the Goliath.

Murphy was encouraged to challenge Ford by Louis Ward, an assistant to Father Charles E. Coughlin, a popular priest who spread a Catholic brand of social justice and reform over the radio. Father Coughlin discussed the nature of revised Fordism on his radio show. He pointed his finger at the system of integrated production that once distinguished the FMC—ownership and control over raw materials and the chain of production from "mine and forest, through transportation, both water and rail, into . . . fabricating plants . . . to the finished product"—and declared that the Ford system was fragmented. As Ward put it, the days of operating as a vertically integrated entity were past. In its place, he said, were car bodies "made by Briggs—the wheels by Kelsey—the brakes by Bendix—the tires are by Firestone—the clutch assembly is by Continental—the starting, lighting and ignition is by Autolite," thus exposing the Ford myth of a vertical structure. The changed system at the FMC eroded the sacred Ford wage—equated in the public's mind with "living wage" since the $5 a day plan of 1914—subjecting the company and its workers to a daily wage that was often "what the parts manufacturer decides it shall be."[96]

Ward and Father Coughlin felt that a lot of political hay could be harvested from the resentment felt by "the great old army of Ford workers who gloried in being with the greatest industrial institution in the world." Father Coughlin's assistant advised Murphy that the best thing "that can happen to you politically is the active open antagonism to the Ford organization." Murphy replied that he had "read and reread" their letter of advice. "The idea is well set in my mind, and I appreciate its possibilities before the public."[97]

Coughlin's advice had credibility because his star had risen rapidly as a result of his attacks on Henry Ford. During the previous summer, Coughlin, who routinely blasted the communists on his radio show and from his pulpit, had testified before a congressional committee investigating the extent of communist activities in the United States. Much to the committee's surprise, he boldly singled out Henry Ford as the "greatest force in America for the internationalization of labor throughout the world," accusing Ford of forcing men into the CP. For evidence, Coughlin cited ignorance, greed, and the disregard for workers exhibited when a Ford ad printed on the first page of most major newspapers during the winter of 1930 said he needed "30,000 additional workers at his Detroit plants." Coughlin explained that the advertisement encouraged "many more than the 30,000" to flock to Detroit at a time when the temperature was at zero. "There were no jobs for them and the only redress they had was to have the fire hose turned on them."[98]

It is doubtful that Murphy needed Coughlin's political advice. When Murphy fought back, defending his welfare policies in the depth of the Depression, he was drawing from the wellsprings of his moral education. That and his finely tuned political instincts thrust him into a battle in the summer of 1931 that redefined the politics of Detroit. Did Murphy consciously realize he was "opening the door to a public re-examination of Ford's contribution to social progress," as suggested by Josephine Gomon, Murphy's political ears and eyes as well as secretary? Within a decade, Gomon maintained, the brush lit by Murphy's fire led to an "almost complete reversal of public opinion" about Henry Ford.[99] While it may be difficult to gauge just how prescient Murphy was that summer, it is clear he

Two trailblazers, Henry Ford and Mayor Frank Murphy, circa 1931.
Image from box 95 (3,704 photos), folder: Mayor (III), Frank Murphy Papers.
Image courtesy of the Bentley Historical Library, University of Michigan.

understood the stakes of the battle as he drew his sword. His new deal was all about exposing the myth shrouding Henry Ford's reputation as a benevolent industrial giant. The man the world looked to for guidance into a new era of high wages for workers was too tight-fisted to help the City of Detroit feed unemployed Ford workers.

During the showdown between the two Detroit trailblazers—Henry Ford and Frank Murphy—Ford decided to make a short-term loan to the city government; the amount was for $5 million, with a 3.5 percent interest rate (modest for the times). While this loan from Ford, who loathed philanthropy or charity, may seem out of character, Josephine Gomon, explained that "Ford hates the New York bankers worse than he hates us."[100] The money was intended to repair his image, which was badly damaged by the months of invective, and it was, no doubt, put to good use by the

DPW. Whether it gained Ford much in the court of public opinion is not so certain.[101]

By the time Murphy ran for reelection in 1931, as the champion of the common herd, the idea that government relief should aid the needy was directly counter to Henry Ford's opposition to big government. Issues of unemployment, poverty, and rising welfare needs continued to occupy Murphy's administration for the rest of the summer and framed his reelection campaign, turning it into a referendum on the emerging Democratic Party's appeal to African Americans, ethnics, and working-class white voters. Ostensibly, the mayoral election was nonpartisan. In reality, voters saw the candidates as partisan. Murphy, actively involved in the Democratic Party at the state and national levels, did not hide his Democratic roots and affiliations. Certainly, in retrospect, the appointment of Eleanor Roosevelt's brother to head Detroit's MUC looks like a maneuver to expand his options on the larger Democratic stage in the future. When Murphy visited Franklin Roosevelt at his Hype Park estate in June 1931, rumors multiplied about Murphy running as the vice-presidential candidate on a ticket with Roosevelt.[102] Harold H. Emmons, Bowles's former police commissioner, stated that he was the mayoral candidate of the Detroit Republican Party. The other candidates for mayor also let their party affiliations be known.[103] Murphy's campaign pitted his politics of welfare activism against Henry Ford's record. To underscore this dichotomy, Henry Ford endorsed Emmons, a long-time associate of his.

Evidence of Henry Ford's deteriorating public image surfaced at Detroit's annual Labor Day Parade in September 1931, which Josephine Gomon, Murphy's secretary, described as the largest turnout ever witnessed in the city. "But it was the huge placards and banners marching men carried that drew the interest of the tens of thousands of spectators who lined the curbs as deep as the space permitted. Roars of applause rose as slogans came into view where they could be read. WE WANT JOBS. . . . A white banner, so large that it hid all but the feet of the row of men carrying it, was blazoned in giant letters of red paint, WORKERS OF THE WORLD UNITE." Although the Detroit Federation of Labor had organized the parade, as they always had, they were not prepared for the numerous uninvited participants who joined the long procession with their independently organized demonstrations. "It was a parade of angry men with determined steps marching down Woodward Avenue," as Gomon described it. "It was the first time that factory workers—unskilled workers—had ever marched in a Labor Day parade." Big banners represented the workers of Briggs and Dodge, giving "credence to the rumors of a secret labor organization within the big plants." The biggest surprise of the day came at the end of the long formation. A banner read WORKERS OF FORD MOTOR COMPANY. But, in this case, behind the banner marched men with their faces covered with masks. "These were both the employed and the unemployed from the great Rouge and Highland Park plants," said Gomon. "They were greeted with a deafening roar. Ford was presumed to be the invulnerable fortress where unions could make no inroads."[104]

In case there was any doubt that the 1931 mayoral campaign represented a contest between those struck hardest by the Depression and the upper-income, "silk-stocking" districts inhabited by whites of native parentage, the launching of Murphy's reelection campaign removed such uncertainty. To highlight his political priorities, Murphy gave one of the first public speeches of his reelection campaign in a "mammoth mass meeting" held at Rev. Bradby's Second Baptist Church on 14 September. Rev. Bradby opened the meeting by speaking about the "economic, political, and racial crises" confronting black Detroiters, suggesting the "ministry of our group should lead the way" toward relieving "the political and economic distress." In that spirit, he introduced Murphy, someone who "has not just an interest in the Negro but has an interest in humanity," and praised him for his courage as judge during the Sweet trial, which, Bradby said, "freed" black Detroiters "from the stigma of race prejudice." The mayor spoke about government's duty to aid citizens in time of need, reminding the congregation that in a democracy the government is the servant of the people. "In Europe, in the old days, all governments were in the hands of the kings who were the sovereigns, but today, in this country, the citizen becomes the sovereign," intimating a comparison between the monarchs of old and the reign of King Henry over Detroit's black community. Murphy reminded the gathering that the only criticism leveled during his administration was "not for graft for the few, not for spoils for the powerful, but for mistakes made in aiding the masses." For these reasons, he urged the audience to "get behind" his campaign; "meet the social demands of the hour; do the right thing; and organize so that we will not stay in this panic nor have another."[105]

Charles Sorensen, manager of the Rouge and Rev. Bradby's confidant and patron in the executive suite of the FMC, took note of Murphy's speech. He was, apparently, not amused. Sorensen asked Bradby to explain the mayor's appearance at Second Baptist, as he stumped for reelection against Emmons, Henry Ford's candidate. Bradby's reply to Sorensen was revealing for its deferential compliance as well as its subtext of resistance. We hear Bradby, the faithful servant of Henry Ford and Sorensen, remind his benefactor of services he has rendered to the company through the years. Nevertheless, Bradby, who had thrown down the gauntlet by going against the wishes of Henry Ford from within the hallowed halls of "Ford's church," did not renounce his challenge. Emmons desperately needed the black vote to counter the overwhelming support Murphy commanded within the larger Detroit electorate. He would, no doubt, have loved to be invited to speak at a key church in the black community.[106]

Bradby claimed, not very convincingly, it was just a coincidence that Murphy chose his church to deliver a reelection speech. But Bradby also told Sorensen he could not "possibly support Mr. Emmons . . . [because] he is the chairman of an organization that sold me a lot in the cemetery and then compels me because I am a Negro to go in the back gate."[107] Why did Bradby not hide his feelings toward Emmons? Blacks who worked for Ford were expected to support Republican candidates for public office.

Bradby's public support for Murphy suggested that frustration and resentment toward Henry Ford's control over black Ford workers and the black community in general was brewing well before Franklin Roosevelt's New Deal. As the Depression deepened and employment for black Ford workers was cut back to two or three days a week, their situation grew more untenable, and Bradby was thrust into an increasingly difficult position. Although he was perhaps Ford's most important representative within the community at that time, by the early thirties, old guard leaders like Bradby, sensing the temperament of the people, took a stand, showing their support for Murphy. Bradby had also campaigned for Murphy in 1930, which, no doubt, did not please Ford and Sorensen. But the stakes were higher in the 1931 election for several reasons. First, Emmons was anointed by Ford as his candidate, and Ford actively worked to get him elected. Second, unlike the 1930 election to complete the remainder of Bowles's incumbency, the 1931 election was for a full term and the campaign lasted for several months, not two weeks. For Bradby, the risk of offending Ford and Ford's interests was trumped by the right to vote his conscience.

Bradby's response to Sorensen also referred to rumors circulating "around town" about how blacks must "vote the way . . . the Ford Motor

Company dictates" or lose their jobs. "Now I am positive," he continued, "just as positive as if I heard you say it, that you would not drive the Negroes back into such slavery as that. That is not the way to win their cooperation. A man's franchise is his sacred right," something Bradby had long stood for.[108] Bradby felt it was his sacred and secular duty to express not only his beliefs but also those of his congregation, hoping Sorensen might, out of fear of losing the allegiance of the black community, heed the warning. Father Everard Daniel, who ministered the members of the other major "Ford" church, continued to toe the line. Daniel's congregation, however, was smaller and represented many fewer Ford employees.[109] Bradby was clearly apprehensive about his relationship with Sorensen, telling him of "special treatments for nervousness" he was taking. But he never denied supporting Murphy.[110]

The rumor that black Ford workers had to vote the Ford ticket or suffer the consequences grew into a major topic of conversation in the days leading up to the November election. Few could ignore the issue, least of all Charles Sorensen who was forced to take time away from his post as manager of the River Rouge complex to meet with Rev. Bradby. Sorensen and Bradby discussed the political rights of black Ford workers for three hours on 28 September, a few days after Sorensen's rebuke of Bradby for his support of Murphy and a week before the primary on 6 October. As Sorenson had instructed him to do, Bradby gave a report on the meeting at the FMC to a large gathering at his church. He told the crowd he reminded Ford executives that they would face a dangerous situation were they to force black workers to vote their pocketbooks and not their conscience. "I plainly told [Sorensen] he would not want to drive the Negro that far back into slavery." According to Bradby, Sorensen asked him to "tell them [black Ford workers] for me we are not a political organization and we are not seeking to use our influence as a big stick over the heads of anybody." Bradby made it clear that he was, as he put it to his congregation, speaking "not upon the authority of Bradby"; he was speaking that night "upon the authority of two executive heads" (he did not name the second executive), who wanted him to affirm it was a "lie" that the FMC fired those who did not vote the way the company dictated.[111]

Whether Bradby played the role of middleman between Ford executives and black workers to Sorenson's satisfaction is hard to tell. After the meeting, the community continued on its path to reelect Mayor Murphy, an effort that began well before the September primary ballot was finalized. Beulah Young marshaled the power of her newspaper with its tens of thousands of readers to pull people together through her Murphy for Mayor Clubs, formed in July 1931.[112] She drew from her earlier mobilization efforts as president of the Political Leadership Assembly, an organization she formed late in 1930 (perhaps earlier) to build Murphy for Mayor Clubs. Her efforts had created "block assemblies" within neighborhoods, headed by "captains," who led discussions on "Americanization," "Good leadership Politics," "Social ethics," "Parliamentary law," and "other important Community subjects," which presumably might include Murphy's campaign.[113] Once the campaign was under way in September, the Allied Political Club, which included dozens of well-organized groups long active within greater black Detroit, unanimously endorsed Murphy.[114]

The mayor spoke with numerous other community groups and associations such as the Michigan Conference of Bethel A.M.E. Church.[115] Not only was the black presence in Murphy's reelection campaign prominent, black leaders were also known to remind the mayor's office when key representatives were left off certain invitation lists. Young, for example, did just that when black leaders were not included in a breakfast meeting of some 700 during the American Legion convention.[116] She reminded the mayor that blacks, too, had fought in America's wars. A band formed by black workers from the Sanitation Department provided music for several events during the campaign.[117]

Murphy won the primary on 6 October with 55 percent of the vote overall in a field of eight candidates and 80 percent of the vote in black-majority Wards 3, 5, and 7. In black precincts, Murphy won 90 percent or more of the vote. Voter registration was almost as high for blacks (41.7 percent) as it was for whites (42.2 percent) in this election. Despite Murphy's majority in the primary, he faced off with Harold Emmons in the general election on 3 November.[118] During the next month, Murphy spoke repeatedly about the plight of the "forgotten" men and women and the need for a union of "head and heart in the conduct of community affairs." The present time, Murphy declared, was "no hour for cliques, or groups, or classes; this should be the most unselfish hour in our lives."[119]

In desperation, Emmons supporters issued a pamphlet titled "How and Why Are You Voting on November 3rd?" To mobilize white Protestants, the document raised the religious issue, claiming that Catholic men and women would vote their religious preference as a bloc. Although the tract was put out under the aegis of the "Citizens' Fact Finding Committee," the KKK was the suspected source. In its preface, it argued that although Detroit was a predominantly Protestant city, "Catholics dominate its elections only because they show a fidelity to their duties of citizenship second only to their unswerving loyalty to their faith." While this argument appeared to explain the enthusiasm generated by Murphy among working-class voters from southern Europe, it did little to explain the overwhelming preference by Protestant blacks for Catholic Murphy.[120] Ultimately, the pamphlet did little to stop the wave of support for Murphy, who won 64 percent of the votes cast.[121]

Both Bradby and Dancy were part of the "black cabinet" in Murphy's new deal for the forgotten man. John C. Dancy was appointed to the House of Correction Commission, only the second African American to serve on a city commission since the adoption of Detroit's 1918 charter, while Bradby worked largely out of public view with Murphy, who responded to his requests for patronage appointments.[122] While Bradby and Dancy maintained active ties to the industrial elite, they did all they could to open up the public sector for black participation, helping solidify a new politics for black Detroit. It is likely that Bradby imagined himself to be a crucial link between the old politics of Henry Ford and the new politics of Frank Murphy. Despite Sorensen's pledge that black workers at the FMC would not be penalized for voting their conscience, several black Ford workers were fired for their politics. Bradby, however, used his influence with Murphy to expose the dismissal of those workers.[123]

One case in particular—that of the Reverend Arthur Randall—stands out. Randall, a veteran of both the Spanish-American War and World War I, had worked at the FMC for several years with an untarnished record before he was fired "for political views" that disagreed with "those of the Ford Motor Company," meaning that he actively supported Murphy's administration.[124] Several days after Murphy was reelected, Donald Marshall made an example of Randall and others, whom he "turned out" (fired) for making speeches supporting Murphy.[125] Ira W. Jayne, a judge on the Circuit Court in Detroit and an executive board member of the NAACP, shared Bradby's assessment of what had happened to Randall, writing Murphy that the facts were "undisputed." The company had fired Randall "by reason of his support of the administration." Murphy wrote to Harry Bennett, the head of the FMC's Rouge Employment Office, asking that Randall be rehired and reminding Bennett that Randall had a "very fine standing among his people."[126]

DANCY AND BRADBY'S participation in Murphy's coalition suggests that the idea of inclusion was firmly grounded and that black Detroiters in the early thirties expected it to be realized. During the Murphy years, thousands within the black community took part in raising political awareness and nurturing the growth of a new political alignment, one that would offer challenges to Ford and his company later in the thirties. Beulah Young, an active member of the MUC, learned, no doubt, valuable political lessons as she worked with the heads of corporate Detroit and leaders from churches, organized labor, and social-service organizations and played a role in making policy. At the same time, Murphy and his administration exposed the darker side of Henry Ford. Unlike other corporate executives, FMC officials did not participate in the MUC and failed to aid the city during its hour of need until shamed by the mayor.[127] Black activists not only took part in an administration that looks in retrospect like a rehearsal for Roosevelt's New Deal; in many instances they also helped shape the policies and actions of Detroit's municipal government, loosening their ties to Henry Ford.

CHAPTER SIX

Henry Ford at a Crossroads

INKSTER AND THE FORD
HUNGER MARCH

Something has happened to Ford and perhaps through him
to the America he represents.

—ANNE O'HARE MCCORMICK, *New York Times*, 9 May 1932

BY THE END OF 1931, Henry Ford's image was tarnished. Murphy's re-election as mayor of Detroit was not just a win for the forces of a new order, but also a loss for Henry Ford. More was required to clean up Ford's image in terms of his responsibilities toward unemployed Ford workers than the $5 million dollar loan to the city that he underwrote. A few days after Murphy's reelection in November 1931, Henry Ford took over the village of Inkster, adjacent to Dearborn. Ford's rescue of Inkster was in many respects a brilliant move, for he gained much needed positive publicity, locally and nationally. The village was said to be destitute when he intervened, with, reportedly, no electric lights, no police protection, no bank, and no viable shops. Several cases of rickets were discovered among the 500 black families living in Inkster at the time. Almost overnight, the families enjoyed improved city services, housing, and clothing, and Inkster became a model community for black Ford workers. The message was clear: African Americans could count on Henry Ford to protect them from "the worst ravages of depression."[1]

Several months later, Henry Ford sent another message to his workers and the world, but this one delivered bullets instead of bread to thousands of unemployed Ford workers who took part in the Hunger March in the winter of 1932. Again the message was clear: the era when Henry Ford represented the gold standard in personnel policies was gone; new industrial relations had emerged at the Ford Motor Company (FMC). What were black workers to make of these mixed messages?

For those questioning Ford's dedication to his black employees, the Inkster Project restored a measure of confidence. But on the day of the Hunger March, when the company answered the pleas of the unemployed with bullets, a keystone in the arch of Ford's industrial relations cracked. Out of the ruins, a new era in labor relations rose at the FMC.[2] During the second phase of the Great Depression—between 1932 and 1935—black Detroiters focused on surviving economic hardship. Despite the political independence African Americans had gained through alliances with Mayor Murphy's administrations, they welcomed what help they could get from Ford during the economic decline.

INKSTER

The Inkster Project reveals the power of public relations. Good publicity about Inkster repaired Ford's tarnished image nationally, casting him as the benevolent caretaker of black Detroit, leaving a positive public impression of Inkster that remains, decades later, an enigma shrouded in myth. There is the belief that Inkster was an all-black community or village.[3] Inkster was not all black when it was incorporated in October 1927, nor was it all black in 1931 when Ford's experiment in philanthropy began.[4] It is more accurate to think of Inkster as a racially mixed community. The first recorded permanent resident of Inkster who was African American moved into Inkster in June 1918.[5] By the time Inkster village was incorporated in 1927 it was less than 30 percent black.[6] The 1930 Census put Inkster's population at 4,440, of which 1,195 were African American, making the proportions 27 percent black and 73 percent white (one person was listed as "other races").[7]

The Inkster rescued by Ford late in 1931 was portrayed as an enclave of poor blacks living in squalor, a "miserable shantytown" where people got by on the "standard of living of the Dark Ages."[8] Because the overwhelming majority of those assisted by Henry Ford's project were African American, the public perceived Inkster as black. Much is made of the fact that Ford turned on the lights, organized police protection, and established a bank, as though there had never been such amenities previously in Inkster. Few would have questioned the claim that Inkster was suffering by 1931, for many of the accomplishments carried out by civic-minded African American and white residents during the 1920s were falling apart. Inkster was a suburb with no industry and few businesses, and village services operated on a shoestring budget. The first commissioner of police and fire, who assumed his duties in December 1927, was aided by three part-time policemen, one an African American, paid a salary of one dollar a month.[9] Cutbacks in a scanty budget left little or nothing to underwrite the most minimal of services.

Yet an assessment of black churches in Inkster, undertaken by the FMC earlier in 1931, did not mention squalor within the village. The earlier investigation cited the salary of the pastors, the financial condition of the churches, and the approximate number of FMC employees attending the churches. Nearly all church members were present or former FMC employees. Although the report noted that one church was low on fuel, it did not convey an impression of destitution. The end of the report noted that "most of the people are buying property on contract or own their homes and are depending on the Ford Motor Company for work."[10]

A fuller portrayal might have mentioned that African Americans who carved out a life for themselves in Inkster before the Depression were a self-reliant lot. By 1924 the first black student, Bill Heards, enrolled in the local school, which by 1925–26 had so many students that it ran two half-day sessions. African American students were a majority in the school by 1926 as whites were enrolling their children in public schools in neighboring townships.[11] Blacks continued to put down roots in Inkster, and when the village was incorporated, they took an active part in shaping the new local government. The first elected council included one African American, David T. Griffin, among its five members. Griffin, who moved to Inkster via Detroit from Milledgeville, Georgia, was a carpenter and real estate dealer by profession. He prospered by purchasing several lots in Inkster in 1925, building houses on them, and then selling the houses to newcomers. Within a few years, his real estate business was so successful that he opened a grocery store in Inkster.[12]

Griffin, along with one other councilman, was appointed to secure a $10,000 loan from People's State Bank of Inkster to initiate infrastructural services for the residents. The first project was to obtain access to water from Dearborn Township, after which sewers and water mains were installed, giving some residents of Inkster running water for the first time. The council received fire protection from Dearborn Township as well. Griffin was responsible for the installation of lights at several Michigan

Central Railroad crossings and had a fire hydrant placed in front of the Annapolis School. When reelected in 1929, Griffin and his fellow council members struggled to keep the town from sinking hopelessly into debt with the onset of the Great Depression. Most of the men in Inkster were out of work by the middle of 1930; the bank closed; and storekeepers and residents were deeply in debt. The electricity, which the first council had so proudly secured, was shut off, streets went unpaved, and stagnant water filled ditches and low areas. Despair hung in the air.[13]

One can only imagine the relief Inkster residents felt when water was again supplied by Dearborn Township and paid for by Henry Ford, when coal was hauled from the coke ovens at the River Rouge plant and distributed to all who needed it, when clothing appeared, and when Ford took care of utility bills and mortgage payments. Perhaps most important was the work that Ford provided for black residents of Inkster.[14] However, although they were, no doubt, grateful for Ford's assistance, one should not assume that they were waiting for his intervention.

Black Inkster residents spent a good part of the twenties as pioneers organizing the community to further their advancement. By the time of incorporation in 1927, blacks had formed the Inkster Booster Club, a political organization, which merged a couple of years later with the Inkster Civil League. These organizations sought to promote civil and political development for black Inksterites. Robert Simmons was a leading figure in this effort. He arrived in Inkster in 1928 from Sparta, Georgia, with his B.S. degree from Morris Brown College in Atlanta. While at Morris Brown, he was president of the student body and a member of the debate team. In 1929 Simmons presided over the Booster Club and became the second African American elected to the Inkster Council. He continued to represent black residents, helping shape their politics for at least two decades.[15]

Black and white Inksterites spent months trying to keep the wolf from their doors before appealing to the American Red Cross for assistance, doing so only when the township was no longer able to supply even the bare necessities of life to its welfare recipients. Late in October 1931, within days of Mayor Murphy's reelection, the Red Cross asked the FMC for a supply of vegetables, enlisted a number of local women, and opened up a soup kitchen in what was once Inkster's community dance hall. The Red Cross made Henry Ford aware of the bleak situation in Inkster.[16]

The opportunity to engage in a show of lavish philanthropy could not have come at a better time. By virtually shutting down the River Rouge plant in order to retool the factory for the new model Ford, the V-8, the FMC relegated thousands more to the unemployment rolls. And the press kept the showdown between Mayor Murphy and Ford over unemployment, welfare, and Ford's civic responsibility alive throughout Murphy's robust campaign for reelection. Ford's genius was realizing that the Inkster situation could buy positive publicity: while rehabilitating the township, he set out to restore his image as a benevolent employer.

Ford's experiment was not just good public relations; it also paid for itself, something that could not have escaped the notice of black Inkster residents, but was not widely known by outsiders. Hiring unemployed adult males in the village for twelve cents an hour, Ford put black Inksterites to work cleaning streets, repairing homes, and planting gardens. Twelve cents an hour equaled $1 a day, an amount considered sufficient to meet the minimum daily food requirements of a wage earner's family. Rather than paying these men the prevailing $4 wage in effect at the Rouge, Ford paid them $1 and used the remaining $3 to pay for Inkster's rehabilitation. Black Inksterites were also hired for work at the Rouge—when jobs were available—for $1 a day, with the remaining $3 again going into the Inkster revitalization fund or toward paying off debts accumulated by individual workers.[17] Though often portrayed as an example of philanthropy, the Inkster project was actually a loan from Ford to black FMC workers and their families in Inkster.[18] Rather than being made available in cash, the loan arrived in the form of commodities—food at the Ford commissary, coal delivered from the Ford factory, shoes from Ford-owned stores. Black Inkster residents repaid the loan with their labor.

More than a welfare program, Ford's loans were tied to rehabilitating morals and manners as well as material well-being. It was an effort to remake the black community from the foundation up, a clean sweep of bad debt the members of the community had incurred and the bad habits they were practicing. Ford paid off the debts, loans, and charge accounts of village residents. Those living in substandard housing had their homes repaired according to code by Ford-employed carpenters, most of whom were residents of Inkster. Ford company stores at River Rouge provided the materials. Ford addressed residents' health care by opening a medical and dental clinic in July 1932. If a condition needed more specialized treatment, the resident was referred to the Henry Ford Hospital in Detroit.[19]

All necessities of life could be purchased at the Inkster Commissary, which was located in the "heart of the colored settlement of that portion

One of the first African Americans put to work by the Ford Motor Company's Sociological Department to clean up and rebuild Inkster, Michigan. 24 November 1931. From the Collections of The Henry Ford. ID#P.188.5206.

of the village of Inkster located in Nankin Twp." The commissary, opened on 24 December 1931, was modeled after Ford's Highland Park Commissary. Anything required for furnishing a home, feeding a family, or repairing a house could be obtained at the Inkster Commissary. And it could be purchased on credit or an "I.O.U" issued to "each indigent for all material or services rendered through the Commissary." The IOU was to be repaid to the company within six months after the debtor regained employment. Each weekly paycheck from the FMC itemized how much debt remained on a worker's account. Until the debt to Ford was paid in full, the "indigent" would receive $1 a day with the remaining $3 a day paid back to Ford through some form of labor to progressively reduce the amount owed.[20]

The Inkster rehabilitation project attempted to impose Ford's personal code of ethics on the residents. Home investigators surveying Inkster in the 1930s, under assignment from the revived Sociological Department, took notes on the level of crowdedness and cleanliness of living quarters even as they assessed the "financial picture of the assets and liabilities of the applicant."[21] The lives of black Inksterites were measured by Henry Ford's yardstick. Home investigations exposed cases of "gross mismanagement" "in the handling of the family pocketbook." Black families were charged with using "no judgment" if they owned an automobile, radio, or player piano while living in flimsy unpainted shacks that were held together with used lumber and lacked acceptable sanitation, ventilation, or lighting.[22] But more than improving purchasing habits inspired Ford's policies.

The larger message identified Ford as the "patriarch of Inkster," for he knew best how black residents should live their lives.[23] One report issued by the FMC refers to the speed with which the community "caught the spirit of cleanliness" to pick up and haul away "literally hundreds of tons of glass, cast iron, steel, tin and waste." In carrying out this cleanup, the company noted, "volunteer groups of the unemployed were forced to grade roads, to load rubbish trucks and also to sort out the various materials at the dumping ground." Does use of the term "forced" suggest black residents would not have cleaned up the premises on their own? Cooking classes were given for housewives to teach them how to prepare balanced meals from the goods stocked at the Ford Commissary. Shortly afterward, sewing classes, taught by white instructors, were added to teach housewives how to make dresses. These skills were designed to give "every mother . . . that experience so necessary to the successful building of a home."[24]

Beyond feeding black residents, turning the lights back on, and getting water flowing again, Ford's agenda with Inkster's black residents bore a remarkable similarity to his Americanization campaign during the 1910s to teach cleanliness, sobriety, thrift, and domestic harmony to foreign workers. If Americanization was, as convincingly argued by Stephen Meyer, "the social and cultural assimilation of immigrants into the mainstream of American life," then Ford may have intended to help African Americans in Inkster assimilate into the cultural mainstream as model American workers.[25] If so, the model Ford had in mind was tethered to deep allegiance to him and his approach to industrial harmony between workers and management, a decidedly anti-union ideal.

By the early thirties, most black Detroiters lived in Black Bottom and Paradise Valley, areas described by a former resident as "very near to the downtown section but very far removed in terms of being isolated economically and geographically."[26] Perhaps Ford's interest in Inkster was related to the cultural independence and weak allegiance that racial isolation had fostered. Participation in Mayor Murphy's campaigns and administrations combined with challenges related to economic destitution shaped the black perspective and sharpened political skills. The Communist Party's Unemployed Councils grabbed the attention of black Detroiters from all walks of life. While the question of allegiance continued to dominate the calculus of both Henry Ford and black Detroiters, both had reason to reevaluate the relationship: Ford contemplated the place of black workers at the Rouge and worried about unionization; black Detroiters continued to be grateful for Ford's "hand up" and his pivotal role in creating a place for black workers in the industrial house of labor even as they questioned their second-class status in the larger Detroit community.

Regardless of how one rationalizes Ford's objectives in rehabilitating Inkster, it is worth noting that Ernest Gustav Liebold, one of Henry Ford's closest advisers and confidants, suggested Ford did not think blacks were capable of putting their own house in order. According to Liebold, Ford felt "the Negro had not yet developed a sufficient intellect to be able to be on his own." Thus, blacks needed to be "guided and supervised."[27] But before they could be guided and supervised, they needed to be investigated, which was done through the Inkster project.

Although surveillance by the Sociological Department was notorious and is fairly well documented for white workers, the degree to which it extended to the black community is less well known.[28] Reports kept track of individual purchases at the Inkster Commissary as well as monthly totals. One showed that the commissary had sold 3,477 loaves of bread during January 1936 and that 284 families and 881 individuals had been served.[29] Nearly all residents purchased goods through the Ford commissary; thus a profile emerged, including calories consumed per day, Btu's of coal consumed per month, number of postage stamps purchased, and gallons of paint applied to a person's house. One could easily construct a composite of the typical black family's consumption patterns from the data available at the FMC archives on black families in Inkster.[30]

A group of African American women at Fair Lane, home of Henry and Clara Ford. Henry Ford is standing, second from the far right. 9 July 1932. From the Collections of The Henry Ford. ID#P.188.7096.

As was the case with Ford's earlier Five Dollar Day, Profit-Sharing Plan, the Inkster Project was entangled in a web of obligations, requirements, and control. The moral mandate that required Ford families to demonstrate a commitment to sobriety, self-control, thrift, and domesticity was carried forward from the Five Dollar days to Inkster.[31] When families signed an IOU at the Inkster Commissary, they agreed to more than repaying the amount on a piece of paper. There was no dollar value placed on the price of privacy, for example. Yet loss of privacy was part of the cost black families bore to get benefits from a system requiring house visits to evaluate finances, housekeeping practices, and consumption habits. Another cost was self-determination. The Ford plan for Inkster was not open to negotiation. In fact, when residents tried to assert their wishes and vision for repairs and reconstruction of their houses, they were reminded that there was only one way to repair and reconstruct the housing stock: Ford dictated all the terms of the relationship. E. D. Brown, one of the three employees from the Sociological Department responsible for the Inkster Project, noted that the village had failed to enforce an ordinance regulating the "type of buildings to be erected in Inkster." While it is not clear what ultimately happened in this particular case, the lack of enforcement was frowned upon by the company.[32]

Another report by Brown revealed the terms of an unwritten agreement between black residents of Inkster and the company. The Sociological Department conducted detailed checks of every black employee's home in Inkster in order to determine "what is necessary to modernize same." The company also made sure that areas of Inkster restricted "unsightly shoe-shining parlors and noisy garages and other places of business" considered a nuisance from the perspective of Ford's inspectors.[33]

Black Inkster residents had reason to resent the fact that the program withheld pay, a practice closely parallel to that of the system of sharecropping in the rural South. One of the many onerous aspects of daily life that recent migrants from the rural South thought they left behind was debt peonage.[34] The paper trail created by the Inkster Project—linking every purchase at the commissary to an IOU issued in one's family name to the number of hours or work required to pay back the "debt"—could be regarded as holding residents in a state of virtual bondage to the FMC for many years.[35] E. D. Brown was submitting reports in the late thirties on home visits along with all manner of other pieces of information gathered by his staff.[36] And as late as the middle of 1942, the FMC tracked debts

Senior Banquet, Inkster High School, 2 May 1940. Hanging on the rear wall are pictures (left to right) of Henry Ford, Thomas Edison, and Abraham Lincoln. From the Collections of The Henry Ford. ID#P.188.27535.

still owed to the company. One worker—identified by name, badge number, and account number—owed $10.97 as of 31 January 1941. For another outstanding debt of $346.77, the company was seeking payment from the administrator of the deceased worker's estate.[37] In some cases, defaults on Inkster accounts were simply "charged off."[38] Within black Inkster, the similarity to the caste system in the South may have been hard to ignore, especially among those who had done so much to build the village during the twenties. Indeed, the FMC's control over the lives of black Americans in Inkster during the 1930s suggests striking similarities to the "plantation mentality" scholar Laurie B. Green found in her study of black workers in Memphis, Tennessee, during the decades leading up to the 1968 sanitation workers strike, a battle not just for better wages but also for independence from white control. Black Ford workers from the thirties and later often referred to the FMC as "the plantation." By extension, the Inkster Project was considered a product of the plantation mentality.[39]

Ford's Inkster Project received mixed reviews during the thirties: the greater the distance from the project, the more positive the evaluation. Thus at the national level Ford was hailed as the savior of black Inksterites in black newspapers.[40] Within Inkster, the evaluation was less favorable. Charles Lawrence, the first African American to settle in Inkster, had an altogether negative view: he rejected Ford's rehabilitation plan and the "strings attached."[41] Despite the desperate economic situation most black families faced, ambivalence toward Henry Ford surfaced as the FMC assumed greater control over their affairs. Understanding this reality is key if we are to comprehend the shifts in allegiance toward Henry Ford that emerged during the thirties. Although Henry Ford's Inkster Project may have rehabilitated the village and saved many black Ford families from physical destitution, it did not succeed in reestablishing unquestioned loyalty to Ford. The Inkster Project was halted when the UAW-CIO won its union contract at the FMC in 1941. H. S. Abelwhite, a manager at the FMC who moved into the Sociological Department in 1940, observed that the Inkster Commissary was in operation when he arrived in the department, but closed after the union came. "It would appear," Abelwhite said, "as though it were a form of punishment."[42]

THE DEPRESSION DEEPENS

The winter of 1931–32 was hardly a time for biting the hand that fed African Americans in Inkster. There were 223,000 jobless workers in the capital of the automotive industry. By early 1933, approximately 350,000 of Detroit's 689,000 potential wage earners were unemployed; of those counted as employed, many worked only part time.[43] "Brother, can you spare a dime?" was the cry taken up by lawyers, engineers, journalists, and schoolteachers who joined unemployed autoworkers in the bread lines.[44] Employment in the auto industry was barely half of what it had been three years before. Wages were cut, and the payroll plunged to a third of what it had been in 1929, leading to a devastating decline in purchasing power.[45] Losses for the Big Three in 1932 were astounding: General Motors (GM) had a $4,559,000 loss; Chrysler was second hardest hit with a loss of $10,162,307; Ford was the largest at $70,831,153.[46]

While the FMC was in good shape relative to GM and Chrysler in 1929 and outpaced its closest rivals by some 400,000 units, it was overtaken by GM in a race that almost put Chrysler in second place over Ford in 1931.

Ford sales for passenger cars, which were at 1,155,162 in 1930, slipped to 541,615 in 1931, plunged to 287,285 in 1932, rising weakly to 325,506 by 1933.[47] The FMC was caught in a two-front war: it faced the challenges of the Great Depression on one front and the creative marketing and engineering of two rivals on the other. In the midst of the greatest economic slowdown this country had ever seen, GM and Chrysler caught the attention of consumers with new Chevrolet and Plymouth models, addressing their desire for choice and popular options. Ford lost market share and was forced to upgrade the Model A. Ford's choice, installing a V-8 engine, something that had not been accomplished for a low-end car, took time and forced the company to sustain large losses. Deficits, after taxes, for the period 1931–33 reached $120,000,000.[48]

Ford floundered as the ground shifted beneath him during the Great Depression. More than the chassis for his V-8 engine needed to be retooled; he needed to rethink his basic formula for success. When granting interviews to the press, Ford was Janus-faced, at times expressing great concern and at other times feigning indifference, as though the business affairs of his competitors were not of note. Which attitude Ford assumed depended on where he was in the protracted crisis. When *Fortune* magazine interviewed Ford at length at the end of 1933, he declared, "I don't know how many cars Chevrolet sold last year. I don't know how many they're selling this year. I don't know how many they may sell next year. And—I don't care."[49] As we shall see, the truth was more complicated, something Ford well understood.

Ford's reputation for paying exceptionally high wages and benefits, which began with the $5 day in 1914, still had traction at the end of the twenties. During the Depression, he tried to cash in on the moral capital he had accumulated over the years as a different kind of employer, a friend of the worker, someone whose altruism trumped company profits. Critics noted the discrepancy between legend and reality well before the thirties. But, prior to the Great Depression, the gap between fact and fantasy was largely a matter of perspective. When Ford adopted the five-day week in 1926, for example, his daily *rates* of pay continued to be high within the industry, but his workers' weekly *earnings* were not high.[50] Yet, by 1931, the question of responsibility to the unemployed—explored in the previous chapter—exposed rather dramatically the subterfuge behind the myth that Ford's industrial capitalism was more humane than most other forms of it.

It is tempting to read assessments made by Ford about the state of his business during the first years of the Great Depression as the product of an unhinged mind. A more productive approach is to read Ford's declarations during the turbulence as attempts to make sense out of a system adrift, having lost its economic moorings. When Henry Ford proposed a wage increase some weeks after the October 1929 crash, his suggestion was favorably received, but his pronouncements revealed a naïve belief that the economy was fundamentally robust. He blamed unemployment on laziness, claiming that the problem was not work but the unwillingness of people to take the initiative to find it.[51] Although Ford pretended to have the answer to the Depression, the testimony of those close to him suggests otherwise. William Cameron, a spokesman for Ford, said he did not know what Ford's thinking about the Depression was. "He doesn't talk about it much. It's so terrible that I believe he doesn't dare let himself think about it."[52]

In April 1931, just as in 1929, Ford declared that neither the FMC nor any of its suppliers would cut wages. Yet the FMC initiated sweeping wage reductions in October 1931.[53] The massive Rouge complex, which had just under 100,000 hourly workers in 1929, employed 56,264 in 1932 and fewer than 29,000 in 1933, which amounted to a reduction in the work force of nearly 50 percent between 1929 and 1932, and nearly another 50 percent between 1932 and 1933.[54] Missing from this snapshot is the number of hours employees worked, with some hired for only a day or two each week and others hired for three days a week. The lucky ones still could work, but very few worked a full week and made a living wage, challenging the veracity of what Ford's personnel program claimed.

During the twenties, "Ford mules," as black workers were called, demonstrated loyalty to the Ford formula, for which they expected a measure of security, an expectation they shared with most white Ford workers. Indeed, many workers at the FMC believed they labored under a personal covenant with Henry Ford.[55] There was no formal, binding agreement; the informal compact was based on a strongly held belief, which had evolved over the years, linking allegiance to Ford to attaining tenure within the Ford system.

Walter M. Cuningham, who worked for the FMC for five years in production and in the Advertising and Publicity Department, wrote a memoir, *J8: Chronicle of Neglected Truth*, detailing labor relations at the company. He contended that in exchange for the high wages Ford paid, workers relinquished their "personality, individuality and inventive genius." Henry Ford did not care about the identity behind the number on the Ford badge; he expected that "a man's thoughts, no matter how constructive or how valuable . . . [were] the property of the Ford Motor Company." Cuningham's badge number was J8—thus the title of his memoir.[56] Ford workers tolerated such depersonalization because of the benefits Ford employment guaranteed. Especially valued was protection from prolonged unemployment.

THE FORD HUNGER MARCH

On 13 January 1932, Frank Murphy announced to the Common Council that 4,000 children a day were standing in breadlines and that the suicide rate in the city was up 30 percent over the previous five-year average. The *Detroit Times* reported sightings of people unconscious on the streets after eating out of garbage cans. On 6 March, *Detroit News* announced that the Welfare Department would cap recipients of aid at 20,000 families, despite the fact that 27,000 were on its rolls and 30,000 were expected to be by the end of March.[57] When Detroit's director of public welfare, Captain John F. Ballinger, released a report on 31 May 1932 on the impact the Depression was having on America's most prosperous manufacturing community, the details were so disturbing that "every newspaper in the city" suppressed its contents.[58]

Employment at Ford's Detroit area plants, which had reached 128,142 in March 1929, dwindled to 37,000 in August 1931, a drop of 91,000, when Ford shut down the assembly line producing the Model A, keeping it idle for months, except for a brief period in October. At that point, Henry Ford contemplated the peculiar status of his company: he was in the business of making cars but had no concrete plans for the next model.[59] Ford, groping for answers, tried to work out, not by formulation but through experience and instinct, what he called "a sample" of a "better-balanced scheme." The solution proposed was to upgrade the Model A by putting a V-8 engine under the hood, hoping production of the new model would "make the country" what it "needs most—work, jobs."[60]

Jobs were on the minds of thousands of Detroiters, especially the 3,000–5,000 unemployed workers, most laid off by Ford, who marched from Detroit to the employment office of Ford's River Rouge plant in Dearborn to present a list of demands to Henry Ford on 7 March 1932.

The assembly point for the march was located inside Detroit, several hundred yards from the Dearborn border. Unemployed Ford workers arrived in groups from "Ford towns" carrying signs with specifics from their demands: "Give us Work," "We want bread not crumbs," and "All war funds for Unemployed Relief." Included among the fourteen demands the marchers had hoped to present to Ford were "Jobs for all laid-off Ford workers," "immediate payment of 50 percent of full wages," "slowing down of the deadly speed-up," and "no discrimination against Negroes as to jobs, relief, or medical service."[61] Arriving in truckloads from all parts of the city, marchers were unemployed black and white workers, some communists, but the overwhelming majority were noncommunists. When the marchers, still in Detroit, were about to cross the line into Dearborn, one of the march leaders, Albert Goetz, a communist, reminded the crowd, "We don't want any violence." Remember, he shouted, "all we are going to do is to walk to the Ford employment office. No trouble. No fighting. Stay in line. Be orderly."[62]

When the marchers arrived at the Dearborn city limits, approximately fifty Dearborn police offices ordered them to halt, blocking forward movement. Ignoring the command, the crowd marched across the city line, and Dearborn police hurled tear gas canisters at the marchers. When the crowd walked toward Gate 3, the Rouge entrance for job seekers, Dearborn police lobbed more tear gas and the Dearborn fire department poured streams of icy water on the protesters.[63]

A deadly battle ensued at this point as workers threw stones at the police (both Dearborn and Ford Service Department employees), who, in turn, began shooting into the crowd. Two young men were killed, and twenty-two workers were injured. Harry Bennett, chief of the Ford's Service Department, drove out Gate 3, stepped out of his car, and was hit by a piece of brick, which covered his head with blood. Believing Bennett had been shot, Dearborn and FMC police increased the ferocity of the violence unleashed on the crowd. Using pistols, revolvers, and a submachine gun, they shot with abandon. By evening, two more workers were dead. All four killed that day succumbed to bullet wounds in either the head or the chest or both.[64]

Initially, the FMC attempted to blame the communists. While communists were involved in planning the protest through the Unemployed Councils, the march grew out of the desperate conditions created by the Depression in combination with unemployment at Ford. David Moore, a twenty-year-old black worker from South Carolina who would later join the Communist Party, took part in the Ford Hunger March in 1932. Moore blamed the collapsed economic structure for the march. "Saying all these people are CP [Communist Party] is a . . . damn lie." The March was much larger than the communists.[65] It was about getting Ford jobs back.

Henry Ford had declared that "anyone who really wanted a job could find one, if they looked" and "No Ford Worker will starve!" His son, Edsel, had stated, "If any unemployed Ford worker needs relief, he knows where to get it!" According to black labor organizer Christopher Alston, the march was a direct response to these statements. The intent was to test the promises Henry Ford had made to his workers. The response of the FMC on that March day shot holes in the myth that Ford cared about his employees, that he was different from other businessmen.[66]

While the exact numbers of African Americans participating in the Ford Hunger March are unknown, we do know that those who marched were drawn from a broad swath of the unemployed who had worked at the FMC. David Moore recalls significant numbers of black men, white women, and black women joining the ranks, "all pulling together right down Miller Road." Truckloads of marchers came from black neighborhoods in Inkster and Encorse.[67] James Ashford, a young black worker active in the campaign to free the Scottsboro Boys, was among those wounded, falling to the ground with a bullet in his leg.[68] Shelton Tappes, a black Ford worker and later an organizer for the United Auto Workers, remembered seeing numerous blacks taking part in the march.[69] At a large public gathering to honor the four slain workers, Frank Sykes of the Unemployed Negro Workers Council introduced the speakers and chaired the meeting.[70]

For months, public outcry focused on the toxic Ford formula for dealing with the Hunger March. Mainstream Detroit newspapers defended the marchers. The *Detroit News* described the march as having been orderly until Dearborn police turned it into a "bloody battle."[71] At the national level, many who had embraced Henry Ford for his Five Dollar Day turned against him. Upton Sinclair, who had once praised the earlier Ford plan for workers, was one. Another was novelist John Dos Passos, who pilloried Ford in *The Big Money*. When workers marched in Dearborn in "cracked shoes, in frayed trousers, belts tightened over hollow bellies," wrote Dos Passos, "asking for work and the American Plan, all they could think of at Ford's was machine guns."[72]

During the summer, Curtis Williams, a black participant in the Hunger March, died from his wounds. Joseph Billups, a black communist and chairman of the burial committee, wanted Williams buried beside the other four victims. The directors of the Woodmere Cemetery refused, presumably because Williams was black, but agreed that Williams could be cremated at Woodmere. Billups later reflected on the absurdity of the situation: "a man who was killed had no place to be buried." Rather than scattering the ashes at Woodmere, Billups kept the ashes until "things quieted down, then we sprinkled them over the plant [the River Rouge plant]." The company must have learned about the plan to use a plane to scatter the ashes because they kept a plane in the air over the factory for a time to prevent Williams's ashes from falling over the Rouge. When conditions seemed right, Billups "notified the fellows inside the plant that we were going to fly a plane over them and sprinkle the ashes." As they did, hundreds of Rouge workers watched from below.[73]

The Ford Hunger March marked a turning point in the lives of many black Detroiters. Employed or unemployed, black Ford workers who had retained a sincere allegiance toward Henry Ford and his company viewed his benevolence with a more jaundiced eye after the events of March 1932. Although African Americans continued to be grateful for jobs at the FMC during the Depression, increasingly when they hailed Henry Ford as their "friend," it was not the heartfelt sentiment it once was. Bloody Monday (7 March) and the funeral that followed marked the point, according to David Moore, when he and his compatriots began to understand "something had to be done with respect to Ford's." There was a feeling that "we'll get even . . ." Moore refers to the Hunger March as "a turning point in my life, the day I was no longer a boy but a man."[74]

Shelton Tappes, born in 1911 in Omaha, Nebraska, moved to Detroit in 1927 and was among the unemployed shaped by the Hunger March. He did not participate in the march because he got up too late that day. Later that morning, however, curiosity drew him to the Rouge. By the time he got to the plant, "people were coming back." Nevertheless, he "saw people and heard things," things that stuck with him forever. In particular he never forgot that the purpose of the march was to "bring attention to the plight of Ford workers who were out of work." To acknowledge the workers' presence and plight, the company turned on the water hoses, peppered the air with tear gas, and fired their guns at the crowd.[75]

Reflecting on the event many years later, Christopher Alston, just seventeen in 1932, said he "skipped school on the day of the march." He did so with his "father's blessing." His father was a socialist and told him, "If you want to work, you get in that march . . . and you stay there regardless of what happens." Alston, an African American, went off to the march with his friend George Bussell, who was gunned down by the police. Alston said he was "near the front [of the march] because I was a nosey little kid. The shooting started pretty close to the front line." And "they turned the hose on us." When the first shots were fired, he thought they had run into some bees. The "bullets were whizzing by us. And [Bussell] moved forward. That's the last I saw of him." Alston was already "politically charged," but because of the events of that day, he said, "I became a confirmed radical."[76]

Though Harry Bennett clearly was in charge of the FMC's response, the use of submachine gun bullets and fire hoses against Hunger Marchers depleted a good portion of the public relations capital that Henry Ford had gained with his Inkster Project. From the time when he announced his revolutionary Five Dollar Day for workers, Ford had demonstrated a remarkable talent for generating publicity.[77] E. G. Liebold, and others close to Ford, claimed publicity was important to him not just for advertising purposes but also to enhance "his popularity."[78] But the violent response by Bennett and Dearborn and company police robbed workers of their lives and "shredded the legend of high wages, good conditions [and] contented workers."[79]

The Ford Hunger March reflected the degree to which FMC labor policy had been transformed under Harry H. Bennett, whose position of enormous power over personnel, especially from 1928 forward, included acts of "arbitrary brutality previously unknown," according to Allan Nevins and Frank Hill. The carnage of that March day in 1932 emerged from an approach adopted by the FMC to control labor instability as it faced a dramatic decrease in its market share and resulting unemployment. Bennett, as director of Ford's Service Department, was charged with, among other matters, keeping a lid on labor agitation. The idea that workers might create their own sense of community was an anathema to Ford, as it was to most industrialists. The actions of the company's service men during the Hunger March were designed to kill the spirit of community that led to the march.[80]

FORD'S NEW LABOR POLICIES

Seeking more control over workers and a more predictable and efficiently run over-all system, Ford put his trust in Bennett, who became his strong arm in industrial relations. Bennett not only served as Ford's personal private guard; he also protected Ford from the wrath of his workers. But contrary to some perceptions, Bennett did not operate alone. Increasingly, Henry Ford expanded Bennett's power over company operations. One of the chief means for keeping labor in line under the Bennett plan was to instill fear into workers, something that was possible thanks to the more than 3,000 men who made up the Service Department. Service men were the tools Bennett used for investigating, spying, and disciplining company employees, actions that took place both inside the plant and outside in the larger community of Detroit and environs. When the department was fully formed it constituted a network of spies and private police that the *New York Times* once called the largest private quasi-military organization in existence.[81]

Espionage had a long history as an instrument of company policy. During the Red Scare after World War I, "investigators" reported on all manner of political meetings attended by Ford workers during their personal time, outside company property within the larger community. What was new by the early thirties was an increased reliance on spies to shore up control over workers. As activities of union organizers increased, Bennett planted informers, spotters, and stool pigeons wherever Ford workers gathered. Few places were safe for candid conversations regarding working conditions, labor policies, or politics in general.[82] One journalist estimated that 10 percent of Service Department workers were not gangster-style bullies but stool pigeons, spies, and informers. Some worked on the assembly lines trying to "entice a trusting fellow worker to give his opinion of Ford" and the company. The wise worker "keeps his nose to the grindstone and his mouth shut."[83]

Control and efficiency issues were perennial concerns for management at the FMC. These issues inspired the creation of the Five Dollar Day, Profit-Sharing Plan in 1914 as well as its abandonment after World War I, when Ford opened up employment to large numbers of African Americans. At that point, Ford introduced harsh labor polices, the speedup on the production line, and insisted on greater regimentation, uniformity, and control over his workforce. "We expect the men to do what they are told," Ford wrote in 1925. Without the "most rigid discipline we would have the utmost confusion" within an organization that is so highly specialized. Workers cannot "have their own way" in a plant where "one part is so dependent upon another."[84] However, the iron fist of Ford's service men had fallen disproportionately on white workers. Black Ford workers—the Ford mules—were the new kids on the block who, as Warren Whatley and Thomas Mahoney put it, "made the extra effort" to work harder than whites and fit into Ford's system. White workers had alternatives for employment that blacks did not.[85]

All that began to change in 1932 as Ford revised his black labor policies within the Rouge as well as within black Detroit. Increased surveillance was applied to black workers, and a new policy for staffing the foundry emerged when the Rouge plant and foundry reopened after the model change and the Hunger March. According to Whatley, Gavin Wright, and Christopher L. Foote, what had been until the early thirties a department for black and white workers, shifted—as a matter of policy—to a virtually all-black department. Between 1920 and 1932 blacks had made up 20 to 50 percent of foundry employees, depending on the state of the labor market for whites in the rest of the industry. Between 1918 and 1927, nearly 25 percent of new white hires started work at the FMC in the foundry, a unit notorious for hot, dirty, and dangerous working conditions. Quit rates for whites in the foundry during this period were "about the same as elsewhere." A decided aversion to the foundry by white workers became apparent between 1928 and 1932, as 50 percent of newly hired white employees quit within 30 days (most likely as a result of gradual cuts in incentive pay during this period of a depressed market). When the Rouge reopened, the foundry became increasingly a black department as a matter of policy.[86]

From a business perspective, high foundry worker turnover had to be changed. But was this shift in policy entirely a result of the high cost of turnover at the foundry? Or was the all-black policy more a result of a readjustment of wages and working conditions after reassessing opportunities that could attract blacks, who had, unlike white workers, few alternatives? Perhaps the FMC took advantage of the shutdown of 1931 and 1932, to adjust, in the words of Whatley, Wright, and Foote, "the package of wages, working conditions, and promotion possibilities in the foundry to fit the labor supply elasticity of blacks rather than whites." By shifting from a racially open to a racially closed foundry workforce, Henry Ford reduced turnover.[87]

In addition, Ford's new policy eliminated what had been a foundry wage premium, offered in a booming labor market when the department included a substantial number of white workers.[88] Foote, Whatley, and

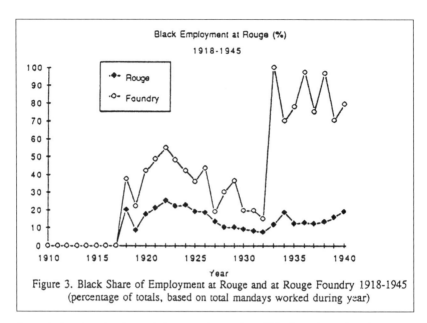

Figure 3. Black Share of Employment at Rouge and at Rouge Foundry 1918-1945 (percentage of totals, based on total mandays worked during year)

A graph showing the dramatic increase in number of black workers placed in the Rouge foundry beginning in 1933. Courtesy of Warren C. Whatley.

Wright argue that Ford's new labor policy for the foundry at the Rouge "exploited racial differences in outside alternatives" for black and white Detroit workers.[89] As is pointed out in chapter 2, Ford was able to take advantage of the fact that work at the FMC was still the best employment opportunity for African Americans. He could draw talented, dedicated, hardworking blacks to work in the foundry, which was described as a "Hell hole."[90] They were less likely to quit; they would work harder than white workers and do so for less. Ford could engage in this strategy because the other automakers still hired very few black workers and unemployment was a major concern for everyone. Since Ford was no longer trying to lure white workers to the foundry, the foundry premium wage was phased out. The savings for Ford were substantial.[91]

Harder to measure was how the shift in labor policy resonated with black workers. Prior to the early thirties, Ford was unique in that, as Lloyd Bailer pointed out, the best opportunity for employment did not segregate black workers from the rest of the labor force. From 1933 onward, labor policies at Ford sent a different message. The most common position blacks could obtain was increasingly the hottest, dirtiest, and most dangerous one in what became a virtually all-black foundry at the Rouge.[92] It was also becoming harder to tell the difference between work at the FMC and work in the foundry of Midland Steel or Bohn Aluminum and Brass located across town. Although other positions for blacks remained opened, the assumption that the foundry had always been an all-black department emerged from this period in the thirties. Allegiance to Henry Ford represented food on the table and money to pay the rent or mortgage, but the new labor policy must have raised questions about Ford's long-term intentions for black workers. In the short run, African Americans gained more positions at the FMC at the expense of white workers. Most firms exhibited a preference for white workers during the Depression by laying off black workers. By contrast, Ford added close to 7,500 blacks to his Rouge workforce during the 1930s, while cutting the number of white workers by over 15,000. By 1940, the FMC employed approximately half of Detroit's black male workers and only 14 percent of the city's white male workers.[93]

After the Hunger March, when the question of unionization of autoworkers was raised, many eyes were on labor conditions at Ford Motor Company. Henry Ford resolutely clung to his condemnation of unions, holding onto the belief that he alone knew best how to look after the welfare of his "fellow workers."[94] To the extent that Ford consciously fortified his company against the rising tide of labor unrest by employing proportionately greater numbers of African Americans, his labor policy was premised on capitalizing on racism within the larger community of white workers who feared competition from African Americans in a tight labor market.[95] Black and white Ford workers noticed the shift in policy. White workers had less contact with their black brethren, raising the bar union organizers had to jump to unite black and white in the fight against the FMC. But, most important, Ford's new labor policy diminished the value of equal opportunity and inclusion that his American Plan had promoted. By transforming the foundry into a virtually all-black department, he made a mockery of the concept of inclusion, the essential principle holding the compact between Ford and his black workers together, and risked losing the loyalty of black Detroiters.

Henry Ford acknowledged some of his concerns as he looked ahead several months after the Hunger March. Harboring "no illusions about the return of the old times," he told Anne McCormick, a *New York Times* reporter, that he was searching for a way to restore balance to a system that was not in equilibrium. The world of his past spectacular success had vanished, and he was "feeling his way toward another order." Henry Ford understood well the sea change a world with too little work had created. As he said, the world was "sadly out of plumb."[96] Although he did not have a clear vision of what the future of industry would look like, he was most concerned with figuring out "how industry as a whole can be adjusted to life without crushing it."[97] In the process of reestablishing balance in the economy, Ford warned, industry will be changed. "The old mold is broken," he asserted, "but people are still thinking backward. That's the reason no one is useful as a leader now whose mind is stuck in the old pattern. You can't make a new model without new tools."[98] But what did the person who supplied "us all with Model T's and a Model T philosophy propose"?[99]

THE *DETROIT INDUSTRY* MURALS:
MAN AND MACHINE AT THE ROUGE

Ford gave little indication he was inventing a new model, but as he was feeling his way forward, he took time to bask in the tribute Diego Rivera, an internationally famous artist, Marxist, and leader of the Mexican Muralist Movement, paid to the River Rouge complex as well as to the architect of the industrial process driving men and machinery. Ford, who had once declared all the art in the world was not worth five cents, found much to value in Rivera's *Detroit Industry* murals. Though Rivera was a known radical and recently a member of the Communist Party, he and Ford developed a mutual admiration. Ford appreciated Rivera's passion for mechanics, and Rivera was awed by the "amiable genius." Rivera later wrote that Ford engaged him in "one of the most intelligent, clever, and lively conversations I have ever enjoyed."[100] Rivera also honored Ford's multiracial work force and took pride in utilizing his talents to bring workers of color out of the shadows and into the limelight.[101]

A month after the Ford Hunger March, Diego Rivera arrived in Detroit. Edsel Ford, Henry's son and a trustee of the Detroit Institute of Arts, commissioned Rivera to cover the walls of the museum's central Garden Court with his murals, leaving the subject matter "entirely" up to the artist.[102] Rivera spent more than a month observing operations at the Rouge, making hundreds of sketches of machinery, stamping presses, conveyor belts, blast furnaces, talking with hundreds of workers, and generally getting a grasp of the Rouge from both a macro and a micro perspective. Rivera wrote that his "childhood passion for mechanical toys" was transmuted into "a delight in machinery for its own sake" as well as "its meaning to man—his self-fulfillment and liberation from drudgery and poverty," a large part of the reason he decided to depict the interaction between man and machine.[103]

Rivera's frescos, rooted in his understanding of ancient Mexican history and mythology, did not just portray men toiling at the Rouge on the production line. He conveyed the flow, the interconnection, and the interrelationships between men and machines.[104] Rivera's rendering was a tribute to the revolutionary process Henry Ford had wrought, especially the phenomenal collective power generated when organized human effort, acting in concert with machines, yielded a product of a greater magnitude than the energy expended by any individual part.[105]

Scholar Linda Downs suggests that Rivera's eureka moment came when he realized how the production processes at the Rouge corresponded to ancient archeological sites he knew from Mexican history. The result was an artistic allegory of the interdependence between man and machine created by Ford's industrial processes at the Rouge.[106] A key component of Rivera's understanding of "ancient religious concepts included the idea of a compact between Aztec Indians and their gods." The message conveyed by Rivera's murals captures this spirit of interdependence embedded in Ford's industrial process. Modern industry, not unlike the Aztec notion of the universe, is a system larger than the sum of its component parts. Ford's industrial system, fueled by the sacrifice of human individuality and energy, produced a product in an efficient manner, presumably for the collective good of all.[107]

At first glance, it may appear, as Robert Lacey suggests, that the Rouge was a place enslaving "the men who worked there, and Rivera's murals were . . . the story of that slavery." Yet, even though Rivera's workers may appear faceless, on closer scrutiny one can see in their resolve an expression of grit, stamina, and even self-reliance that reveals them to be men who know they can do anything, having withstood working conditions at the Rouge.[108] One of Rivera's artistic challenges in the *Detroit Industry* project was to portray the struggle, the sweat, and the sacrifice from the perspective of Rouge workers. The time he spent on the shop floor talking with laborers before he began to paint helped him understand the degree to which work at the Rouge robbed workers of their identity and

North Wall, *Detroit Industry*. The mural portrays black workers in the vanguard of the production of the engine and transmission for the Ford V-8, which was launched in 1932. Image courtesy of Detroit Institute of Arts, Gift of Edsel B. Ford. Artist: Diego Rivera (1886–1957), Mexican fresco painter.

individuality.[109] Rivera's rendering evokes the solemn strength and dignity coursing through the muscles of black Rouge workers, who may have been silent but were not victims.

Rivera considered the *Detroit Industry* murals the finest work of his entire career. He felt this way in part because he thought they exemplified the spirit of the Mexican Mural Movement, integrating politics and art for the working class along with promoting a greater understanding of workers' contribution to industry.[110] In his autobiography, Rivera noted the enthusiastic approval he received from approximately 200 factory workers, who felt his murals had been "created exclusively for the pleasure of the workers of this city." He was "deeply touched by this tribute" from Detroit's working class, the group he "wanted so much to impress."[111]

To grasp what Rivera achieved on behalf of black Ford employees, imagine, for a moment, that there were no black workers in his *Detroit Industry* murals. That they are included in Rivera's masterpiece depicting the revolutionary contributions of Fordism is a mark of African American progress. While much is made of the individuality lost by workers in mass production industry, black workers at the Rouge were not so much robbed of their individuality as transformed into a *critical* cog in the wheel of production at the most revolutionary industrial factory in the world. Black Ford workers were critical because they were willing to endure more hardship than white workers, who had other alternatives for employment. Ford understood the value of the extra effort he could expect from his black workforce. Given where black workers were in the industrial hierarchy in 1910, work at the Rouge was a giant step forward, one that allowed them to advance beyond the factory gates.

While Rivera may not have appreciated the distance black Ford workers had traveled, he understood that the effort they expended was not ordinary. They had been transformed by sweat and energy through synchronized actions to produce for Henry Ford and his company. It is easy to imagine that, having traveled so far, African Americans had no intention of sliding backward. As they moved forward in the ensuing years, they were able to operate from a more powerful position than a decade earlier. By the thirties, black Ford workers were armed with the knowledge they had gained from Henry Ford about the power of organization and the experience of laboring at the Rouge, lessons they were to put to good use in the future.

CHAPTER SEVEN

Behind the Mask of Civility

BLACK POLITICS IN DETROIT,
1932–1935

Indirectly, though, while it brought on the demise of many good men, the Depression also gave life to Black Bottom. The social and economic conditions, brutal and unpitying as they were, animated the neighborhood over matters like housing and unions and communism and the Ford Motor Company. For answers—for salvation—people turned to church and politics. In many cases, the two were symbiotic. Every pastor had a political position, and every address had multiple purposes. Maben's barbershop was a left-wing caucus in the afternoon, and the nights were for meetings held in private houses behind drawn curtains. It was a climate very conducive to the nurturing of young radicals.

—COLEMAN YOUNG

AS THE DEPRESSION DEEPENED, political and material circumstances inspired black Detroiters to look in new directions for a way out of their second-class status. On one level, the black community appeared to be much the same as it had been in the late twenties. African American men lucky enough to have a job at the Ford Motor Company (FMC) continued to make an extra effort at the Rouge, grateful for the chance to work amid widespread unemployment. The largesse distributed by Ford to black Detroit and African Americans within Inkster Village was welcomed.

At a deeper level, a strong current of frustration with the racial status quo and the slow pace of change raged throughout the black community. Behind the mask of civility, black Detroiters from all persuasions came together to exercise their rights as citizens. Social forces and challenges arising out of the Depression opened the community to progressive politics, inspiring citizens to embrace a more aggressive agenda. Some members of the army of African Americans who put Frank Murphy in the mayor's office in 1930 and again in 1931 were part of diverse networks of organizations and clubs committed to carrying the struggle forward. These networks, which included political clubs, the New Citizens League, community clubs situated in various black neighborhoods, women's clubs, and black veterans groups, had canvassed neighborhoods to get out the vote for Frank Murphy's new deal. Others were connected to the Nation of Islam, linked to the lingering presence of the Universal Negro Improvement Association (UNIA) or Garvey movement.[1] Still others found messages that resonated as they listened to communists on soapboxes at Grand Circus Park or participated in actions organized by the Unemployed Councils.

Black men and women from all walks of life wrestled with the experience of unemployment and economic deprivation even as they crafted new approaches to secure a more inclusive place for themselves within the larger body politic. Proposals, agendas, and politics representing many voices emerged from gatherings in churches, pool halls, barbershops, beauty parlors, lodges, and parks. Self-reliance, a unifying theme, was woven through a patchwork of persuasions, whose larger design addressed the abiding quest for human dignity and black advancement.

As Coleman Young observed, during the Depression social and economic conditions "animated" the neighborhoods over "matters like housing and unions and communism and the Ford Motor Company," nurturing new approaches to old problems.[2] Some of the defining conditions were local, and others were national. Politics took a dramatic turn as the community welcomed the support and efforts of communists who were fighting for the lives of the nine black youths charged in the Scottsboro case. Black Detroit found new allies in their fight for inclusion, and activities inspired by the Scottsboro case challenged traditional approaches for overcoming racial inequality even as it softened the image of the communists. When Franklin D. Roosevelt voiced concerns for the "forgotten man" and the underdog in his campaign speeches, black Detroiters heard the language of Frank Murphy and felt included. Roosevelt's National Industrial Recovery Act (NIRA) may have sent mixed messages to black America, but it pushed black leaders—locally and nationally—to reconsider their position with respect to unions. At the same time, at the local level a new organization, the Detroit Civic Rights Committee (CRC), revitalized community organizing by demanding jobs for African Americans. Before Franklin Roosevelt was swept into office for a second term, African Americans in Detroit were engaged in advancing their own economic interests through the protest politics of a new crowd.

Henry Ford may well have been aware of the turn black Detroiters took during this period, for he made an extra effort to win their hearts and minds. He devoted additional resources to his patron-client relationship and brought nationally acclaimed African American leaders in the arts to Detroit for performances in the community. Clara Ford, Henry's wife, entertained black clubwomen and church groups at teas and luncheons at the Ford estate in Dearborn.[3] At the same time, however, Ford beefed up his Service Department in order to increase surveillance of the black community.

Donald Marshall, the black policeman employed by Harry Bennett for the Ford Service Department in the early twenties, was widely known as the unofficial "mayor" of black Detroit—the eyes and ears for Henry Ford. In 1935 another African American was hired by Bennett to assist Marshall as he kept watch over black workers, especially monitoring their interest in union activities. Unlike Marshall, Willis Ward was debonair, educated, and widely known as a track star and football hero from the University of Michigan. Ward seemed to be a perfect spokesman for Ford interests in black Detroit because the community was so proud of his accomplishments.[4]

Ford gave Harry Bennett's Service Department an even larger role in curbing signs of radicalism and discontent at the Rouge. One source related that Ford service men were constantly on guard searching for labor "agitators." By 1933, according to Allan Nevins and Frank Hill, the question circulated as to whether Bennett or Hitler first conceived the idea of the Gestapo. With the implementation of Franklin Roosevelt's NIRA in June 1933, organized labor had an ally in the White House and the era of the "open shop" was threatened. As labor agitation increased, Ford responded by relying even more on Bennett's services.[5] At the same time, Ford hoped support from his black workers would offset the growing interest in labor unions.[6]

Henry Ford continued searching for an exit strategy out of the Depression. He was determined to find an alternative to Roosevelt's New Deal, a "planned economy" fueled by big government policies. Ford, the individualist, wanted to show through his example that ingenuity, effort, and a free market were the means for putting the economy back on track. He resisted demonstrating public support for Roosevelt's NIRA. While most businessmen displayed the Blue Eagle, emblem of the NIRA, as a sign of their patriotism, Ford flatly refused to do so, calling the Blue Eagle, "Roosevelt's Buzzard."[7] Following his own drummer, Ford turned the Rouge around financially and put thousands of men back to work. By January 1935 employment at Rouge was almost 70,000, more than double the 30,000 workers employed there late in 1932. This remarkable feat was due to Ford's expenditures on plant and equipment inside the Rouge. He clung to his long-standing aversion to organized labor, totally dismissing Roosevelt's New Deal for workers and their right to organize. Jobs at the Rouge kept African Americans in line and in the foundry during the dark days of the Depression, even as Ford's policies planted doubts about much that once had been seen as positive in his American Plan for African Americans.[8]

Toward the end of Roosevelt's first administration, black Detroiters from diverse perspectives embraced collective action in order to open up economic opportunity. They did so from within Detroit-based organizations shaped by local social and economic conditions as well as the influence of a national conversation about expanding rights for African Americans. Conventional political stripes—designating right, left, or center—faded as the contours of a united front came into focus and demands were made challenging the racial status quo.

THE SCOTTSBORO BOYS WIN THE
HEARTS AND MINDS OF BLACK DETROIT

In March 1931, nine young black men and two white women, who had been traveling south on a freight train from Chattanooga, were forced off the train near Scottsboro, Alabama, by the local sheriff. The nine men were arrested and charged with raping the two white women. Within two weeks, an all-white grand jury indicted the nine black men for forcible rape. They were subsequently convicted, and all but the youngest were sentenced to death in the electric chair. The case and the defendants were rescued by the actions of the International Labor Defense (ILD), the legal arm of the Communist Party, which wasted little time in turning the case into an international cause célèbre. From the standpoint of the communists, the cause was not just fighting for the lives of the Scottsboro Boys, but equally to prove the value of mass-based, protest tactics in the struggle against Jim Crow.[9]

The NAACP, dragging its feet when the case broke, expressed interest after the conviction and challenged the communists' right to represent the nine boys. The ensuing public debate—not just for control over the case but to win "the hearts and minds of the black public"—made headlines in African American newspapers across the country for the good part of a year.[10] The NAACP argued that a "fair" and successful case for the defense required using local lawyers and minimizing demonstrations that might upset public opinion in Alabama. According to Walter White, secretary of the NAACP, it was important to maintain "proper conduct of the defense." Proper conduct was the problem, argued the communists, who steadfastly believed "there can be no such thing as a 'fair trial' of a Negro boy accused of rape in an Alabama court." By January, the ILD completely controlled the case, and the NAACP ceased its attempts to challenge the legal defense of the Scottsboro Boys.[11]

In Detroit, as elsewhere, the question raised by the ILD approach further undermined the NAACP at a time when the association was particularly vulnerable to sagging membership contributions. Branch memberships, considered the lifeline of the organization and its chief source of funding, had dropped considerably by the beginning of the Depression. In Detroit, the NAACP branch suffered when the Depression hit large donors—such as Edsel Ford—who had to limit their financial support.[12]

Competition for limited sources of funds grew intense as the NAACP and the ILD attempted to draw support from similar bases, even holding fund-raising events for the Scottsboro fund on the same day and at the same time in Detroit.[13] While choosing which organization to support may have been difficult, the *Detroit Tribune*, often considered a "conservative" newspaper, supported the ILD more consistently than the NAACP.[14] The key issue was the lives of the "nine innocent Negro boys," which were "hanging in the balance. They are our boys." For that reason, while the newspaper "heartily" endorsed all efforts—including those of the NAACP—on behalf of the Scottsboro Boys, its editorials applauded the ILD's efforts for putting the "spotlight" on the case through mass meetings held throughout the country. "The facts must be made so luminous that the whole world can see and judge for itself that the young men are innocent." Samuel Liebowitz, chief counsel for the Scottsboro defendants, was held in high esteem because, according to the *Tribune*, he understood what it meant to be "identified by birth with a persecuted race." Liebowitz "protests against injustice to Negroes, just as we condemn and abhor the outrageous treatment now being inflicted upon the Jews in Germany."[15]

The ILD approach also struck a chord with a population the NAACP in Detroit had not been able to reach, inspiring activism across the political spectrum. As Rose Billups, wife of Joseph Billups, a local black activist in the ILD, observed, the Scottsboro case "aroused the interest of all Negroes. There wasn't any question of left, right, or middle. It was a question to save the boys, and it was a Negro problem." When the ILD took on the defense of Angelo Herndon, a black communist who faced the death penalty in Atlanta for "inciting Negroes to insurrection" under an antebellum provision in Georgia's slave codes, Detroiters added the Herndon case to causes it supported financially in the mid-thirties.[16]

Observing the widespread interest black Americans had in the ILD "together with other Communistic efforts to secure equal justice and living wages for Negroes and white workers," the editors of the *Tribune* found it interesting to see the "alarm among certain classes of white Americans and Government officials, not only in the South, but in all sections of the country." The editors explained that many found it difficult to understand why blacks, who had always been "loyal to the nation despite the many injustices suffered," should turn a "sympathetic ear to the voice of Communism, which is so dreaded in this country." The answer, they believed, was clear: black "students and workers, like students and workers of other racial groups, are beginning to think for themselves." The present situation was ushering in a new era, according to the editors, because the "Capitalistic system in this country has broken down." As a result, other philosophies of government were flourishing—communism and socialism were mentioned—which "might prove helpful in bringing about the 'New Deal' that the American people are determined to get."[17]

Communists had not won large numbers of converts for the party among black Detroiters, but their militant approach raised questions about appropriate strategies for challenging racial inequities in a system embedded in a racist social context.[18] Protest activities sponsored by the ILD brought Detroiters together across the political spectrum, initiating a process of cross-fertilization that strengthened networks formed during earlier periods of political activism. Those earlier struggles, in turn, prepared the way for the ILD's campaign. The ILD's reception in Detroit may not have been so smooth had black Detroiters not taken part in the political struggles of the twenties and the campaigns that ushered in Frank Murphy's version of a new deal. Blacks also reaped the benefit of piggy-backing on the ILD's infrastructure as they pushed their larger agenda forward, strengthening their indigenous networks and empowering participants in those networks.

The richness of the political times was reflected in the transformation within the Booker T. Washington Trade Association (BTWTA), led by the Reverend William Peck, minister of Detroit's second oldest and second largest black church, Bethel A.M.E., between the early and mid-thirties. The BTWTA, made up of businessmen whose prosperity depended on the paychecks of black Ford workers, was founded in 1930 with the intention of addressing the effects of the economic system on Detroit's black business community. Believing in economic nationalism, the BTWTA promoted buying black as the way to boost black businesses and gain economic justice, drawing from black nationalism and race pride impulses promoted during the Garvey movement.[19]

Fannie Peck, the wife of Rev. Peck, formed a "sister" organization, the Detroit Housewives' League, at the same time, to educate the community about black-made products sold in black-run stores. "Sustaining small businesses owned and run by African Americans" would create employment, it was believed.[20] Housewife League boosters went door-to-door disseminating the message of black economic self-help, raising consciousness toward activism within black neighborhoods, and reinforcing the work and mission of the BTWTA.[21] By including poorer black women in the boosting process, Peck's strategy encouraged alliances between working class and middle-class clubwomen who no longer valued "respectability" so highly. As Victoria Wolcott notes, the "cross-class effort" marked "a crucial shift in Detroit's black community" of women. By the spring of 1934, the Detroit Housewives' League, some ten thousand members strong, greatly strengthened racial unity behind the walls of segregation.[22]

Initially, these organizations focused on building black capitalism, leaving it to others to reform the larger system of discrimination. The BTWTA was regarded as not only conservative, according to Meier and Rudwick, but "frankly open shop in their sympathies."[23] Yet, by 1933, BTWTA's founder, Rev. Peck, helped Snow F. Grigsby form the Detroit CRC, which pushed economic rights for black Detroiters by utilizing aggressive, confrontational tactics to challenge discriminatory hiring in the public sector and questioning the racial politics of the larger system. The Rev. Peck–

Snow Grigsby alliance hitched its agenda to political changes in Detroit and the nation, which intersected and reinforced each other.

THE EMERGENCE OF BLACK DEMOCRATS

The formation of a black Democratic Club in April 1932 marked the turning of political tides. Black female Democrats reached out to the larger community by forming the "Democratic Whip," an explicitly "women's organization." Mary Belle Rhodes, vice chairmen of the parent black Democrats, headed up the women's "auxiliary" to the officially titled Michigan Democratic League, Inc. Rhodes and the precinct captains in the Democratic Whip hoped to be ready to "open their campaign in full by the first of August."[24] By that time, Franklin Delano Roosevelt's Democratic campaign for president had drawn the interest and participation of large numbers of black Detroiters. Black supporters of Frank Murphy had developed a positive image of the Democratic Party at the local level for several years. Although the positions Murphy held in local politics were ostensibly nonpartisan—judge on the Recorder's Court and mayor—he entered politics as a Democratic activist and remained so throughout his career. Indeed, it is likely that the black Democratic club was built on the foundation laid through earlier political mobilizing for Frank Murphy. Beulah Young, the dynamic member of Murphy's administration who had organized districts within the black community for Murphy's campaigns, apparently drew on the talents of one of her precinct "captains" to foster development of the Democratic club.[25] Blacks' participation in Murphy's political campaigns since 1923 placed them in the position of being not just observers of a broadening of the Democratic Party's base, but also members of the new coalition of voters expanding that base.

Until 1931, Mayor Murphy largely kept his partisan politics out of the public arena. All pretense of municipal nonpartisanship was dropped when Mayor Murphy publically declared his admiration for Roosevelt and played an active part in the Democratic Party at the state and national levels. Hall Roosevelt, Franklin Roosevelt's brother-in-law and chair of Mayor Murphy's Unemployment Committee, introduced Murphy and his politics to Franklin Roosevelt, suggesting that his success reflected voter dissatisfaction with the politics of an "old crowd." Murphy, a delegate to the National Democratic Convention, delivered a passionate speech to more than 100,000 people who turned out when Roosevelt campaigned in Detroit on 2 October 1932.[26]

Murphy's command of the black vote trumped efforts by others, including Henry Ford, to dilute his influence. As the black Democratic club established its footing in 1932, Henry Ford made no secret of just how he wanted his workers to vote in the national election. Plastered throughout Ford plants were political notices that read: "To prevent times from getting worse and to help them get better, President Hoover must be re-elected." Ford was personally upset when voters swept Hoover into the history books and Roosevelt into the White House.[27]

Mayor Murphy did more than appear in public with candidate Roosevelt. In his speeches for the Democratic presidential contender, Murphy focused on unemployment, and attacked the Hoover record as one of "brutal, cold, un-American indifference to the welfare of our government and our people."[28] In addition, Murphy formed a Non-Coercion League to counteract the pressure that employers, like Henry Ford, were putting on employees to vote Republican in the presidential election. Murphy took this action following a radio address by Henry Ford praising Hoover and his record. When President Hoover came to Detroit to campaign, it was Henry Ford who supplied a company limousine to drive Hoover around the city.[29]

Although the majority of black votes went for Republicans in Detroit in 1932, a dramatic shift toward the Democrats occurred in black wards. In 1930 the black Democratic vote was 19.5 percent of the total in black wards; in 1932 the black Democratic vote rose to 36.7 percent, an 88 percent increase, indicating that more than a few black "Ford" families may have voted against the wishes of Henry Ford in 1932, just as they had in 1931 when they voted for Mayor Murphy.[30] Given Ford's attempt to control black Detroit, the 1932 presidential election and the birth of the black Democratic Party were about more than party realignment. The electoral shift also represented a loosening of Ford's grip over black Detroit.

The organizers of the Democratic League were three black Detroit politicians—Charles C. Diggs, Joseph A. Craigen, and Harold Bledsoe—who were in the vanguard of new-crowd activists emerging from the turmoil of the Great Depression and the political dynamics of the migration and black urbanization process. Diggs began his political career as a Republican during the twenties, the period when he was heavily involved in Garvey's UNIA (as discussed earlier), but switched to the Democratic Party in 1932. Four years later, Diggs became the first black Democrat to be elected to the Michigan Senate. He represented a district composed of black and Polish residents, with Poles in the majority.[31]

Craigen, whom we also met in an earlier chapter, worked for the FMC and was executive secretary of the Detroit chapter of the UNIA during the twenties. In 1931 he was elected constable from Ward 7, the first black to hold that position. In 1932, while a freshman at Detroit College of Law, he helped form the Democratic League and became its executive secretary. Craigen, noted for his oratorical skills, was appointed clerk to Circuit Judge Guy A. Miller while he studied law. He graduated summa cum laude in 1936, passed the Michigan bar exam, and practiced law.[32] In 1937 Governor Frank Murphy appointed Craigen to the Michigan Workmen's Compensation Commission, a position he held until his death in 1962.[33]

Harold Bledsoe, a lawyer and a partner in the firm Stowers, Bledsoe, and Dent, chaired the Democratic League in 1932. He was known for his courtroom skills, especially his success in the early thirties defending a black man wrongly accused of murdering a white man.[34] He was the first black presidential elector in Michigan's history, a position he won in 1936. Bledsoe, and his wife, Geraldine, were members of the educated elite and had a reputation as mavericks, taking detours that led them away from the straight and narrow.[35]

In the case of Diggs and Craigen, the Garvey movement most likely shaped their new-crowd agenda with its emphasis on self-reliance, self-determination, and independence from white control. Traditionally, black leaders of the old guard—such as the Reverend Robert L. Bradby—had operated within black Detroit as power brokers between the black and white communities. Craigen, Diggs, and Bledsoe represented the voices of a new crowd committed to making demands for rights long overdue. They came from diverse backgrounds and age groups. What united new-crowd activists were approaches, strategies, and tactics that, when taken together, signaled a waning of the deference to the racial etiquette prescribed by white society.

Diggs was a friend of the labor movement in the Michigan legislature. As the Congress for Industrial Organization (CIO) took off, Senator Diggs supported the right to organize, encouraged black workers to join unions, monitored activities of the unions, and reprimanded unionists who did not respect the rights of African Americans, demanding that they put their own house in order before appealing to black workers. By the late thirties, Diggs wrote a regular column for the *United Automobile Worker*, the union's newspaper.[36] He also strengthened the state's Civil Rights Law. Public Act 117, known as "Diggs Law," made it a misdemeanor to discriminate on the basis of race, color, or creed when delivering public service in public places.[37]

Henry Ford "bridled," as Steven Watts put it, at President Roosevelt's emphasis on massive use of big government to overcome the Depression.[38] Although his objections to Roosevelt's New Deal were well known, they did nothing to stop black leaders from publically expressing support for the new president. Rev. Bradby, for example, endorsed the work and achievements of President Roosevelt in an opinion piece for the local newspaper.[39] Frank Murphy linked his politics to the new president's agenda at a farewell event, organized by the NAACP, to honor the departing mayor who had just been appointed governor general of the Philippines by Roosevelt. In thanking the black community for their steadfast support for him, Murphy cited the importance of Roosevelt's collective approach for carrying the struggle forward.[40] Rev. Bradby and Rev. Peck, among others, used the occasion to applaud all the mayor stood for, suggesting it was the legacy that the black community must uphold.[41] While Bradby was not solidly in the camp of the new crowd, his support of both Roosevelt and Murphy suggests the degree to which local politics was moving on a path independent from the dictates of Henry Ford. Bradby's support for Roosevelt suggests as well the ease with which blacks in Detroit were able to turn their backs on the Republican Party and vote for a Democrat for president.

SNOW GRIGSBY AND THE DETROIT CIVIC RIGHTS COMMITTEE

The tribute to the parting mayor was a success, one of the few the Detroit NAACP enjoyed as the stature it gained during the height of the Sweet case in the mid-twenties crumbled. The black working class, riveted by the question of jobs, felt little connection to the NAACP. The local branch, often mired in factional disputes, had lost the vitality and relevance it enjoyed under the leadership of Rev. Bradby in the mid-1920s. Snow F. Grigsby, who once struggled to revitalize the local, concluded that his efforts for reform fell on deaf ears, and formed the Detroit CRC as an alternative organization in 1933.[42]

Initially, Grigsby's goal for the CRC was to put pressure on the city to hire more African Americans.[43] Rev. Peck's collaboration and assistance in the launching of the CRC helped fuse the common interests of the nationalistic Booker T. Washington alliance with Grigsby's decidedly more confrontational approach. Grigsby intentionally named the organization the "civic" rights committee, not the "civil" rights committee, to signal its intent to challenge discriminatory hiring in the public sector. Grigsby and Peck agreed that black Detroiters had to gain economic rights in order to acquire a measure of power and regarded equal opportunity in public sector jobs as a route to obtaining greater economic stability.[44] These black leaders were not alone, but they were clearly in the vanguard during the 1930s in opening up channels for the inclusion of black Detroiters as municipal employees in the urban North.[45] While their advocacy resonated during the Depression, the CRC's success depended on having trusted leaders who could inspire a following.

Rev. Peck brought to the new organization his prestige as head of black Detroit's second largest and second oldest church, Bethel A.M.E. Church, as well as his role as founder of the BTWTA. While both Peck and Grigsby organized the CRC, Grigsby's influence was decisive in shaping the organization's direction and character. His vision for the CRC grew out of his experience as a postal worker and active member of the National Alliance of Postal and Federal Employees (NAPFE), the historically black postal workers' union, known as the National Alliance, or "the Alliance." The National Alliance had struggled for years to gain greater access for black workers in federal positions in the post office. By the late twenties, Grigsby cut his teeth on confrontational politics in the local branch of the NAPFE. In 1940 he was elected editor of the NAPFE's national monthly journal.[46] Known as a strong, principled veteran of the black freedom struggle, Grigsby was eulogized at his funeral as "one of a kind," referring to his life-long fight for economic rights of citizenship as well as to his rather unusual name. It snowed on the day he was born in Chappelle, South Carolina, in 1899, leading his mother to name her newborn, Snow Flake, in honor of the unusual weather that marked his birth.[47] He moved to Detroit in 1923 after graduating from Harbison College in Irmo, South Carolina. One of his first racial confrontations was with the administrators of Detroit Institute of Technology, where he was studying pharmacy. To graduate, students had to take a course in physical education, which white students did at the white YMCA gym. Black students were told that had to go to the black YMCA, something Grigsby refused to do. With the help of a lawyer, Grigsby

Snow F. Grigsby, who co-founded the Detroit Civic Rights Committee in 1933, established the National Negro Congress's local in Detroit in 1935, and became editor of the *Postal Alliance*, the national monthly journal of the National Alliance of Postal and Federal Employees, in 1940. Image courtesy of the Burton Historical Collection, Detroit Public Library.

changed the policy, an experience, he later said, that taught him the importance of arming oneself with all the "facts and figures" when challenging the racial status quo.[48]

After graduating from the Detroit Institute of Technology in 1927, Grigsby learned another lesson about inequality when no one would hire him as a pharmacist. He responded by doing what many educated black men did when locked out of jobs in their specialty: he took a position at the U.S. Post Office. Once hired, Grigsby challenged the policy preventing black postal workers from selling stamps. The postmaster claimed white people would not buy stamps from African Americans. Grigsby asked the postmaster where white people were going to buy stamps if not at the post office, since that was the only place they were sold. With that, black postal workers in Detroit started selling stamps.[49]

Grigsby's economic focus grew out of his belief that "it's not worth anything to be able to go in one of your finest places and sit down to eat, if you don't have the price of a meal. We figure the first thing is to have the job, and other things will automatically follow."[50] Although the CRC targeted access to public sector jobs, the organization had a decidedly educational mission as well. Grigsby spoke of his group as an instrument to awaken the black community, to teach them what they could do if they just pulled their efforts together. His double purpose was to confront the members of the black community—shame them if necessary—and then confront public sector employers.[51] We can in fact track the CRC's battle against discrimination in various institutions throughout the thirties. In the fall of 1933, the CRC took on discrimination in health and hospital care, exposing the "Jim Crow set up" at Receiving Hospital, a major Detroit hospital for white patients, while African Americans had to go to Dunbar Memorial, the "black" hospital. Grigsby charged the city with denying black doctors and nurses their constitutional rights.[52] To press its case, the CRC presented claims of discriminatory practices to the Public Welfare Commission and charged Receiving Hospital with "premeditated unfairness" to black doctors, interns, nurses, and auxiliary employees.[53] It is not clear how successful that campaign was in terms of opening up jobs for black doctors and nurses. Another effort at the end of the 1930s opened up jobs at Detroit Edison, a campaign discussed in chapter 9.

The spirit of the CRC's educational mission inspired a collaboration with the Pastor's Brotherhood in February 1934 to set aside one Sunday for ministers to use their pulpits to discuss explicitly "economic, industrial and political rights" for black Detroiters.[54] Another example of political education took the form of a ten-page booklet, "An X-Ray Picture of Detroit," which analyzed activism at the ground level and the "unequal distribution of jobs in departments maintained by public funds."[55] The cover, no doubt designed to provoke, depicted the silence of three groups Grigsby hoped to awaken: black politicians and the Urban League, the local branch of the NAACP, and civic and Christian leadership. Each was represented by one of the classic three monkeys who do not hear, speak, or see any evil.[56]

The booklet aroused the entire community when it landed on doorsteps, porches, and pews in December. Charles Perkins, an attorney, used the booklet to teach his adult Sunday school class at New Bethel Church.[57] The *Detroit Tribune* featured the pamphlet on its editorial page under the headline, "Grigsby Goes Gunning." Calling it a "sizzling hot pamphlet," with its caricature of local group leaders and organizations "as being 'deaf, blind, and dumb' to the evil conditions suffered by Negro masses in Detroit." Despite "controversial issues" raised by the pamphlet, the editors nonetheless felt that "it contains much that will furnish the people of Detroit food for thought."[58]

Grigsby exposed what he called the lax behavior of black "political leaders, ministers, and particularly our Local Branch of the N.A.A.C.P.," who, he said, should "bow their heads in shame" for neglecting to put forward a strong program "for the advancement of the Negro masses." He called on the local branch to "become militant, if we are to get the people's support."

But new tactics would only emerge when "our Negro leaders quit being so selfish, and stop using organizations for personal and private business advancement, but use them for the welfare of the masses."[59]

For decades, Grigsby would play the role of agent provocateur within black Detroit, the thorn in the side of both white and black upholders of the status quo. He headed the Detroit CRC between 1933 and 1939, until the Hatch Act, prohibiting federal employees from taking part in "political activity," forced Grigsby to retire from his position as CRC chair. Grigsby continued working as a postal worker and serving as a watchdog over the direction of local politics, but his colleague, the Reverend Charles Hill, took over as leader of the CRC, which remained active until after World War II.[60] Grigsby continued his lifetime crusade for the rights of African Americans in the workplace until his death at the age of 82.[61]

Grigsby targeted black middle-class professionals he considered too comfortable with a politics of negotiation and unwilling to confront whites with demands. Yet black professionals gradually began adopting the aggressive tactics of the CRC. Within a few years, the effectiveness of the CRC broke down resistance within the middle class, drawing support from a broad spectrum of black Detroit, ultimately providing a bridge to interracial unionization efforts in the late thirties. But the politics of Roosevelt's New Deal also reinforced and validated the thrust of the CRC's efforts in black Detroit.

NRA CODES: A CATALYST FOR NEW TACTICS

Discussion of Roosevelt's NIRA between 1933 and 1935 provided a means for decoding whether the president's New Deal meant much in terms of economic opportunity for African Americans. The overarching purpose of the NIRA was, according to Roosevelt, "to put millions of men back in their regular jobs" and to pay a "living wage" for their labor. Yet that simple directive was fraught with confusion and complexity, especially for African Americans, as the National Recovery Administration (NRA) implemented the act.[62] Two aspects of the NIRA captured the attention of black Americans. One was the industrial code; the other was the implication of the act's section 7a. The industrial codes regulating wages, intended to apply equally to all, led many employers to change job classifications to exclude coverage for positions held by African Americans or simply to displace black workers and hire white workers.[63] Black Detroiters suffered less from NRA policies than African Americans in most regions of the country since so many black men were employed at the FMC, which hired proportionately more blacks than whites during the Depression. Nevertheless, African Americans in Detroit scrutinized the rhetoric of the NRA's reform agenda and the reality of its implementation. In this respect they were in step with others throughout black America.[64]

The local black newspaper tracked the loss of jobs in Detroit and the ramifications of the NRA for African Americans.[65] Critiquing the politics of the recovery plan was a means for exploring the way forward. When John P. Davis, a young Harvard-trained lawyer, spoke in Detroit in March 1934 as part of a national tour, his twelve-page booklet, "The Negro Faces the New Deal," received a positive review in the *Detroit Tribune Independent* (a short-lived change in the name for the *Detroit Tribune*) and within the community. Davis, whose political sympathies during the Roosevelt era were transformed from Republican to a close relationship with the Communist Party by the late 1930s, had been investigating racial implications embedded in the NRA as an employee of the NAACP.[66] But Davis also used NRA codes to arrive at a crucial insight about the new politics represented by the NRA.

Looking at the New Deal plan for recovery, Davis argued Roosevelt's political operations presented a new opportunity for black America. The president adopted new methods to exercise power, Davis noted. Rather than relying on "cumbersome legislative action" to jumpstart the economy, Roosevelt took control of all resources at his command. In order to respond to the new "mode of attack," Davis suggested that black American organizations adopt "a different set of tactics." He proposed a pooling of organizational strength in order to carry the "fight" on "all fronts at the same time." In a phrase, a "united front."[67]

The *Detroit Tribune*, connecting the national conversation to local conditions, advised that the time was ripe for "economic self-defense." The NRA's wage scale caused "certain firms to let their colored employees go rather than keep them at the wage rate demanded by the NRA," something the editors observed in Detroit as well. A "grim economic struggle" had emerged because millions were out of work and there were not enough jobs. "The weaker individuals and racial groups are being shoved aside and trampled upon by the strong ones who grab the jobs." The time had come, the editors advised, "for us to think and act."[68] African Americans were living through what the *Tribune* described as "one of the most critical and momentous periods that this nation has experienced since the days of the Civil War and the Reconstruction era." Despite economic hardships, "the Negro masses" were hopeful that the "new social, economic, and political order" that was "being slowly and painfully born" would open up new opportunities.[69] These concerns were part of the larger discussion within black Detroit over Roosevelt's definition of the New Deal. Was the New Deal "Myth or Reality?" asked Theodore R. Barnes, a local journalist. "To our group," Barnes suggested, "a new deal could mean only one thing, and that is a greater opportunity to share in the benefits of our Country."[70]

In Detroit, African Americans linked the New Deal to the "forgotten man," a phrase used heavily during the Democratic presidential campaign. The phrase resonated with black Detroiters. Mayor Murphy evoked the concept in a radio address, "The Procession of Forgotten Men," which he gave on the eve of the 1932 presidential election to encourage Detroiters to vote for Franklin Roosevelt. Promising that "the forgotten Man will be remembered; Roosevelt's election will fall like a benediction upon him," Murphy evoked the missionary spirit that had won the allegiance of black Detroiters a decade earlier. Just as Murphy had appealed to the little people, those in the shadows and on the margins of society, when he launched his political career in 1923, he connected the "Forgotten Man" in 1932 to the biblical beatitudes, "Blessed are the poor, the meek ... those that thirst after justice." Roosevelt was presented as the one who would voice "the needs of the people in the nation."[71] The address may not have yielded the endorsement of Roosevelt by a majority of African Americans in 1932, but it shaped expectations. According to the *Detroit Tribune*, it was not that Detroiters expected a lot from Roosevelt's New Deal. But they did expect "that which he through his own ingenuity and conquest can bring to pass in his favor." Given that the new administration had opened a door, there was reason to hope. Where that door would lead, no one knew. But as one writer put it, "The way is open; let's take every advantage. They say a new deal—let's see if they mean it."[72]

Even as black newspapers led the community in a discussion of what Roosevelt intended with his New Deal, Detroit's CRC offered one interpretation of what such a deal might look like at the local level with its attacks on discrimination in health and hospital care discussed earlier. The CRC's efforts assumed greater prominence when the *Detroit Tribune Independent* revealed, late in the winter, that it not only supported the Detroit CRC but had been a silent partner of the organization, cooperating with its effort to probe the facts. It was committed to uncovering the truth about "a studied policy of discrimination and civic injustice toward Negroes, especially in the allotment of tax supported jobs." The editors added just how morally bankrupt they regarded the municipally financed institutions. "If the 100,000 colored people of Detroit were lined up and mowed down with machine guns," the editors noted, "Christian citizens of the community and the entire country" would protest such a "murderous outrage." But what is the difference, they asked, between murder and killing blacks "economically by denying us a fair share of jobs, food, clothing, and shelter? It is no worse to murder men and women with machine guns, than to starve them to death."[73]

By the spring of 1934, many black leaders had removed the mask of civility traditionally tying them to patronage politics and the racial etiquette espoused by the white elite. Rev. Bradby, who had earlier clashed with Grigsby over the integration of a swimming pool, worked alongside Grigsby and Rev. Peck, addressing a "mass meeting" sponsored by the CRC under the rubric of "The Greatest Need of the Negro in Detroit"; that need was to unite as a group for "common action."[74] Bradby said, "There is no room for selfish interest." Rather, "this is the time to work for the good of the whole." He pleaded for "unity" and "mass consciousness" in order to secure racial survival.[75]

While it is not clear what Bradby meant by mass consciousness, his alliance with the CRC suggests that the era of individual brokering between the black and white community was fading. Bradby never was a fellow in new-crowd circles, but the bold stands he took on occasion reveal how the community was changing politically. Bradby made it clear when he embraced Murphy's candidacy for mayor that he thought of himself as more than just a power broker for the FMC. His interest in enlarging the sphere of civil rights enjoyed by African Americans guided his actions as well. As the tide turned in Detroit, Bradby wanted to be responsive to change and not left standing high and dry. Through the rest of the thirties, he walked a tightrope between what would be regarded as obsequious behavior by new-crowd activists and what the FMC would regard as aggressive, militant behavior, the kind that could sever his relationship with the company.

By the early thirties, Donald Marshall, Ford's point man for surveillance within black Detroit, tried to diminish Bradby's stature at the FMC.[76] Throughout the long relationship involving Rev. Bradby, Father Daniel, and Ford officials, it was always Bradby who was the loose canon from the company's perspective. Daniel ministered to his exclusive flock, making little attempt to deal with conditions for black workers within the plant.[77] When Bradby had Frank Murphy speak from his church at the beginning of his 1931 campaign for mayor, Bradby received several letters warning him of efforts by both Donald Marshall and Father Daniel to silence him. One Detroiter, reporting a discussion of Bradby at St. Mathews, wrote "I am shure [sic] that you know that there has been a movement or underhand methods going on for some years now, to kill you at the Ford Motor Companys Plant, by D. Marshall and his pastor, Father Daniel."[78] Rev. Bradby clearly complicated Donald Marshall's work as an employee of Ford's Service Department. Marshall's job, under Harry Bennett, was to spy on black workers, monitoring any pro-union tendencies or lack of allegiance to Henry Ford within black Detroit. With time, Marshall gradually tried to assume many of Bradby's responsibilities at Ford. When Marshall assumed a role Bradby had played, the latter's response was simply to go over Marshall's head to Sorensen. Bradby's independence was at the root of the schism between the two. But, by the late thirties, Marshall had effectively marginalized Bradby.[79]

"IN UNION THERE IS STRENGTH": SECTION 7A OF THE NIRA

The NRA also forced a discussion about organized labor, opening up the torturous history of relations between black Americans and white labor unions. Section 7a encouraged workers to exercise their "right to organize and bargain collectively through representatives of their own choosing."[80] Lester B. Granger, secretary of the Workers' Bureau of the National Urban League (NUL), put the dilemma directly: would blacks be "friend or foe of organized labor?" The question was really about loyalty. Should a black worker's loyalty be given to fellow workers who toil "side by side with him," Granger asked, "or his employer who hires and pays him, sometimes against the wishes of white labor?" Behind the question lay decades of discrimination against black workers by white unions, which had, "so often kicked them [black workers] in the face."[81]

At least a century of distrust between black and white workers had to be set aside to make room for the rise of the new union movement in the

1930s. It was not that the policy and practice of organized labor had always been one of excluding African Americans or segregating them in Jim Crow locals. Exceptional examples of black-white unity, such as the Knights of Labor, grace the idealism of industrial brother- and sisterhood.[82] But the overwhelming pattern of exclusion practiced by organized labor poisoned the relationship, making a "vicious circle" out of attempts to locate an exit from the conundrum. Black leaders who traditionally argued that the interests of African Americans lay with employers supported strikebreaking as a legitimate tactic for expanding economic opportunity. Strikebreaking, in turn, cast black workers as "scabs" in the eyes of the white labor movement; the discriminatory policies and attitudes of white men's unions created the image of white workers as more racist than white employers.[83] As a result, by 1930, no fewer than twenty-four national and international unions, ten of which were affiliated with the American Federation of Labor (AFL), excluded African Americans from membership through their constitution or rituals.[84]

The policies that shaped the NRA forced reconsideration of the organized labor conundrum. Woven into those policies was the complicated wage-code issue. Although Roosevelt insisted his wage code was color-blind, there was a push to write into the wage code "differentials" reflecting the reality that equal pay would lead to less employment for blacks.[85] Why, asked white employers (especially, but by no means exclusively, from the South), would one hire a black at the same wage you pay a white worker?[86] The push for wage differentials presented black leaders with a dilemma. They had to choose support for racial differentials or support for writing equality of economic opportunity into NRA codes.[87] The NUL drafted a long-term outlook, one that was not just about keeping jobs during the present crisis but also about pushing African Americans closer to inclusion as equals in the economic marketplace. Did black leaders really want to support differentials, thereby reinforcing African Americans' second-class citizenship? The cost, according to Robert Weaver, an African American economist advising cabinet member Harold Ickes, would destroy "any possibility of ever forming a strong and effective labor movement in the nation." Robert Russa Moton, the former president of Tuskegee Institute, agreed.[88] On the wage differential question, delegates at the NUL Convention of 1933 resolved that they were "unalterably opposed" to wage codes "based on the color of a worker's skin." But there were qualifications. The

NUL delegates also concluded that the "cause of the Negro worker" could not be "honestly and sincerely" considered "without recognizing the importance of collective bargaining."[89]

But still unresolved for the NUL was the question of supporting organized labor. It was difficult to bury the hatchet while the AFL continued to reject offers by the NUL to assist the labor organization by reaching out to black workers. As Touré Reed notes, the AFL's dismissal of NUL's overtures of conciliation "reflected the Federation's enduring indifference to black labor." In addition, there was more than anecdotal evidence linking the NRA with increasing the strength and status of the AFL to the detriment of black workers.[90]

At the local level in Detroit, sentiment was growing among a great many middle-class black leaders that the time had come for black workers to organize. John Dancy, whose strong anti-union position led him to march 150 black strikebreakers through a picket line in the twenties (mentioned in chapter 4), reassessed his position in the thirties. In a 1934 address to the Lucy Thurman branch of the YWCA titled "The Economic Life of the Negro," Dancy explained that opposition to unions did not take into account how conditions had changed. With Roosevelt in the White House and the AFL holding more power than at any time in the past (if in fact the NRA accorded greater status to the AFL), he felt "it was urgent that the colored worker join the unions." The audience at the "Y" discussed Donald Marshall's recent warning that the black community should be wary of the AFL's intentions. But Dancy, at least on this occasion, left no doubt as to where he stood on the question of the necessity for black labor to unionize.[91]

Dancy also appeared to be in the vanguard of national efforts within the NUL to form Negro Workers Councils in cities across the country, including Detroit.[92] Although often portrayed as anti-union throughout the thirties, Dancy's position was more nuanced.[93] His positions shifted according to how he assessed the value of jobs gained through accommodation with the white power structure against what might be achieved through collective resistance. But his public statement of having previously been against unions, printed in the local black newspaper in 1934, was a confession he did not, no doubt, make lightly.

Years later, Christopher Alston, a leader in the effort to organize black workers at the FMC, recalled that his father, a Garveyite and Debs socialist, took him to meet John Dancy in 1933, when Alston was a young man. Dancy "took me under his wing right then and there," advising Alston to stay in school, advice he did not take. Alston joined the Young Communist League and worked for it in Richmond, Virginia, and Alabama before returning to Detroit to play an active role organizing for the United Auto Workers in the late thirties. Despite the different political paths the two followed, Alston had enormous respect for Dancy, who, he claimed, was not opposed to unions on principle, just on grounds of practicality.[94] When circumstances changed so did Dancy's approach.

Dancy was joined by Charles Diggs, Rev. Hill, and Harold Bledsoe, among others, all part of a new offensive pushing the idea of organized labor for black workers. When the Workers Councils of the NUL under the direction of Lester B. Granger were established, the labor-oriented perspective was reinforced.[95] For many, it was a matter of acknowledging, as the *Detroit Tribune Independent* put it, "the world is being made over," with "old political and economic systems . . . being replaced by new ones." Once that realization took hold, it was easy to argue, as the newspaper did, those who "cannot or will not adjust themselves to the changing conditions, will perish." Reflections on the NRA helped leaders at the local level better understand the nature of the new world and its governing philosophy, which led the editors to place their bets on the power of collective organization of black workers.[96]

"The time has come," the newspaper editors declared, "when we must follow the example of those races who have gained power through unity." One example they cited was that of Mahatma Gandhi's struggle against the British Empire. Thus, they declared, "every Negro organization, every politician, and civic worker in the race, should unite in a concerted and sustained effort to organize the masses of Negro workers into Negro labor unions, for economic protection and defense." This new approach was necessary for self-preservation in the new era. "Whether Negro workers join the American Federation of Labor or not, self-preservation demands that we organize and learn to bargain collectively." It was thought to be the only way to shore up a strong economic foundation, "upon which the race might stand." Creating black worker solidarity was not just for the benefit of the working classes. It would be "beneficial to our churches, business and professional folk, politicians, and other leaders who are supported by the masses." With that analysis, the editors concluded with an appeal to every black leader and organization in "Greater Detroit" to "get together and smoke the pipe of peace, and then unite in a determined effort to organize Negro Labor. In union there is strength."[97]

Black Americans who tracked actual applications of NRA policies may have observed that the much-heralded New Deal was just a variant of the raw deal with which black America was only too familiar.[98] But in the process of establishing industry wage codes and applying NRA polices, another message also emerged, catching the attention of Dancy and others. For all its negative features in terms of maintaining the racial status quo, the NRA process demonstrated how the new Democrats understood government and power. To negotiate with Roosevelt's big government, black America should unite around single issues and marshal the power of collective action.[99] That understanding helped redirect the course many black leaders took after 1933. Rather than seek alms, they joined the cry demanding opportunity and helped it grow louder. The same impulse led to the creation of the Workers Councils, under the tutelage of the NUL. The councils grew out of the realization that collective or interest group agitation was the key to economic progress.[100] "Building a New Road," an NUL pamphlet distributed in Detroit in 1934, planted a seed for establishing a Workers Council in the city. In October 1935, Lester G. Granger came to Detroit to promote and organize a chapter of the NUL's Workers Councils. The favorable reaction to "Building a New Road" in 1934 seemed to indicate that a robust chapter might be formed in the city. A chapter was formed, but it never developed much momentum, dissolving under the weight of opposition from the FMC and the efforts of Harry Bennett.[101]

By 1934 fifteen men and women were listed on the masthead of the Detroit CRC. Rev. Hill, minister of Hartford Avenue Baptist Church, was listed along with Grigsby and Peck and others. Although Hill was a member of BTWTA as well, he seemed to find the activism of the CRC more to his liking. His membership in both organizations, which was quite common, exemplified what historian Angela Dillard calls the "holistic approach toward Black social advancement."[102] By the mid-thirties an increasing number of black Detroiters joined networks that organized around such a holistic approach, embracing concerns of middle-class professionals as well as of the working class and pushing the struggle toward an economically based civil rights agenda. The alliances forged between groups seemingly supporting disparate goals requires the reader to put aside categories— such as left, right, center—traditionally used to portray motivations and behavior. It was a time when black Detroiters' quest to remove barriers to equal opportunity increasingly broke down political boundaries that once gave definition to left, right, and center.

As Rev. Hill and so many others joined the CRC, they became part of an effort to awaken black Detroiters to the economic grievances shared by all. But the CRC also aspired to introduce a new style of protest tactics, meant to promote a collective response to second-class citizenship. In addition to being instigators, CRC activists were educators, who hoped shared sentiments might "crystallize" in black Detroiters' minds as they protested against the racial status quo. To assist the process of what they called "crystallization," the committee issued educational materials to further an understanding of the common cause uniting the black community. By the beginning of World War II, twenty-four "lessons" were issued, printed in batches of 60,000 to 75,000 and distributed through churches, clubs, and special public meetings of the CRC.[103] The CRC also published broadsides, pamphlets, and the *Civic Rights Bulletin*, a newsletter. They all focused on claims for economic rights, placing the protest against economic exclusion within the larger context of overcoming second-class citizenship. An example appears in an excerpt from Langston Hughes's poem "Flag," which was published in its entirety by the CRC and distributed as a broadside throughout Detroit.

> But, Mr. Editor,
> I've been loyal to my country
> A long time, don't you see,
> Now how about my country
> Being loyal to me.
>
> So when I pledge allegiance
> To our flag so fair,
> I keep looking at the stars and
> Stripes a-waving there,
> And I'm wishing every star
> Would really be a star for me,
> And not just half a star
> Like Jim Crow Tennessee—[104]

Langston Hughes captured the public sentiment that Grigsby, Rev. Peck, Rev. Hill, and others in the CRC believed defined their crusade, inclusion as full citizens in the American social contract: that "every star would really be a star for me, and not just half a star like Jim Crow Tennessee." As the CRC put it, their objective as an organization was to be an "integral part of American civilization" and included in "the same opportunities as other racial citizens" so that African Americans could play their part in the functioning of government at the "City, County, State and National" levels.[105] Consistent with its original objective, to act as a "spur" to get organized groups moving and taking the "lead, when necessary," as a social movement for the betterment of black Detroit, the CRC unleashed a new era of protest politics.[106]

By 1935, Detroit networks connecting activities of the CRC overlapped with those supporting the ILD and the Scottsboro case as well as the interests of black workers through Workers Economic Conferences and the Workers Councils of the NUL. But perhaps the best example of the cross-fertilization that fed new-crowd politics was Maurice Sugar's campaign for Recorder's Court and the Detroit Common Council in 1935. In both campaigns, Sugar won enormous support from the black community. The CRC helped publicize the many qualities that Sugar offered as a white lawyer, a fellow traveler of the Communist Party, and a friend of organized labor. Grigsby and Rev. Peck allotted space in the *Civic Rights Bulletin* to promote Sugar's record, especially the fact that he had represented several black defendants, without taking a fee for the service.[107]

Sugar was the only candidate for the Common Council who replied to a series of questions sent to candidates by the CRC, asking them about their plans to advance interests of black Detroiters.[108] The CRC reminded the contenders that the black community was aware of discrimination perpetuated by the Common Council, wondering why it ignored black citizens yet sought their "support every two years, with the promise to see that everyone gets a square deal."[109] Since Sugar "fights for the Negro People," then the black community "*must* elect him." The list of supporters from black Detroit included the head of the NAACP local, L. C. Blount, and four ministers, including the Reverend R. L. Bradby and Dr. O. H. Sweet. Rev. Bradby sent a mass mailing to "my Friends, as Citizens of Detroit & Wayne County," reminding the community to get out and vote. "As a group," he wrote, "we would manifest the basest ingratitude were we not unanimous and enthusiastic in favoring his [Sugar's] election."[110] Sugar lost both elections, but his campaign drew upon several new-crowd networks, demonstrating the reach of black protest politics by the middle of the thirties.

By then, the direction of politics in black Detroit had shifted from one based on accommodating to the interests of the industrial elite to demanding equal participation in economic and civic affairs. In order to expand the opportunities for all, black Detroiters needed to utilize the power of collective action. Embracing collective action as an organizing concept and tool for bringing about change did not close the era of accommodationist politics, but it marked the beginning of its end. New-crowd protest politics reinforced the impulse, shared by most of black Detroit, toward self-determination. By using the tool of collective action, black Detroiters were able to negotiate with whites on a more equal footing and thus had more power to determine the outcome of events. Collective action also raised the bar in terms of the demands made by black Detroit: rather than settling for the advancement of a couple of black Detroiters, the goal of new-crowd politics was to advance the interests of all black Detroit.

And that was the rub. Every challenge hurled against the city's hiring practices by the CRC validated the suspicion that racial inequities were systemic. Over time, the CRC's demands escalated. By anchoring the politics of black Detroit in collective action, addressing hot-button issues that spoke to all, the community's demands assumed an aggressive, militant quality as the frustrations of more than a decade were voiced.

Even Rev. Peck shifted, in a period of a few years in the early thirties, from a Garveyite position of black nationalism to advocacy of a united attack on the larger system of discrimination. Through his actions, he exemplified the dynamic transformation of an old-crowd to new-crowd leader. He began his political education by working for reform within the boundaries of black Detroit. By working with Grigsby in the formation of the CRC and learning about the nature of economic inequality in the municipal sector, Peck realized that black Detroiters had to do more than unite behind ghetto walls. They also had to confront the injustices forced on them by challenging systemic inequality.

The characteristics of the new leadership style that had emerged by the mid-thirties were apparent in Rev. Bradby's and Rev. Peck's responses to Maurice Sugar's campaign for judge of Recorder's Court and membership on the Detroit City Council in 1935. The fact that Sugar publically endorsed known communists was trumped by his commitment to fighting for the interests of black Detroiters. John Dancy, another old-crowd leader, endorsed participation of black workers in organized labor during this time.

Negro Ministers of Detroit Back Maurice Sugar; Urge Members of Race to Vote for Labor Nominee

Letters Tell Why They Support Sugar

To My Friends as Citizens of Detroit:

I think that Mr. Sugar's record is too well known for it to be necessary for me to recall it to your attention. As a group we would manifest the basest ingratitude were we not unanimous and enthusiastic in favoring his election.

I hope that each of us will not only vote ourselves, but do everything we can to pile up for him a comfortable majority in this race.

REV. R. L. BRADBY,
Second Baptist Church.

* * *

Maurice Sugar has generally been the champion of the rights of the underprivileged. His attitude on issues which have come up between capital and Labor has always expressed itself in a constructive policy.

We need men on the bench who are faithful to their sworn pledge to sustain the constitutional rights of all citizens, rich and poor alike, and to guarantee to us all the privilege of the fullest expansion of human personality. Maurice Sugar seems to be that kind of man.

Rev. Alfred C. Williams,
Metropolitan Baptist Church.

* * *

The Honorable Maurice Sugar has a record in his practice of law in Wayne County that appeals to every citizen that believes in justice.

The fact that he has frequently appeared as the attorney for the laboring man, the foreign-born, and the Negro, in cases where it was evident that the defendants were without money but not without evidence to prove their innocence, should make every Negro think.

In the Crawford and Victory cases he was our only great defender; and success in both of these cases, where he served without fee, should convince us all with the necessity of giving him a vote for Judge of the Recorder's Court.

Rev. William H. Peck,
Greater Bethel A. M. E. Church.

Letters by Rev. R. L. Bradby and Rev. William H. Peck to a Detroit newspaper supporting Maurice Sugar, a lawyer and well-known champion of workers' rights, for a seat on the city's Common Council, 1935. Clipping from the newspaper *It's about Time*, 1 April 1935, 2, box 10, folder 17, Maurice Sugar Papers. Courtesy of the Walter P. Reuther Library, Wayne State University.

Historian Harvard Sitkoff argues that black America "received no new deal from the first Roosevelt Administration."[111] While that may have been the case nationally, it did not stop black Detroiters from laying the foundation for a new era of their own making. Drawing on political experiences gained in the twenties and early Depression years, black Detroiters began the process of pushing back barriers to equal opportunity by making demands that challenged the very structures shaping the racial status quo.

CHAPTER EIGHT

Charting a New Course for Black Workers

The Negro will never take his place as a respectable citizen
until he learns to serve notice on everyone that he is willing
to fight for his rightful place in the sun.

—SNOW F. GRIGSBY, *White Hypocrisy and Black Lethargy*

AS ACCOMMODATIONIST POLITICS began to fade and the protest politics
of a new crowd took center stage, the Detroit Civic Rights Committee
(CRC) broadened its agenda. What began as an effort to challenge the exclusion of African Americans from municipal jobs expanded into a larger
crusade for jobs in the private sector as well. To take its challenge to the
next level, the CRC, utilizing its diverse network, helped launch in 1935 a
local chapter of the National Negro Congress (NNC), which strengthened
its demands for private sector jobs for African Americans.

Under Snow F. Grigsby's guidance, the CRC charted a course connecting local challenges to the racial status quo to larger national efforts unleashed in black America. The CRC's crusade to broaden the economic
horizons of black Detroiters and its mission to expand the scope of civil
rights framed the discussion as activists in the mid-thirties sketched the
contours of their progressive agenda. But it was not until the rise of the
NNC in 1935 that the CRC began concentrating its resources on creating a
place for black workers within the house of labor. Through the collaboration of the CRC and the local NNC chapter in Detroit, we can trace the
footsteps of black Detroiters as they walked down this path, charting a
new course for black workers.

The task was huge, the obstacles were many, and the probability for
success was not at all certain. It was five years before the efforts undertaken by the alliance between the CRC and the NNC local bore fruit with

the strike at the Ford Motor Company (FMC), culminating in the historic labor contract signed in June 1941, between the United Auto Workers–Congress of Industrial Organizations (UAW-CIO) and the FMC.

The trail leading African Americans into the UAW-CIO was blazed by the black vanguard in three stages. In the first stage, the CRC further strengthened its position within the community by gaining new allies, broadening its base, and staking out the coordinates for its new relationship with organized labor as it formed the Detroit chapter of the NNC. The CRC and the NNC local used the issue of equal opportunity to cultivate the reception of a labor-oriented, civil rights agenda. In the second stage, the NNC local reached out to the newly formed UAW-CIO by seeking a favorable position within the union for black Ford workers, who remained in the shadows during this period. The dearth of information documenting the response of black Ford workers to the drama unfolding between Henry Ford's open shop, anti-union crusade and the UAW's closed shop in the late thirties, while frustrating, may also be suggestive. Three factors contributed to the silence: the recession of 1937–38 raised the specter of unemployment; plain-clothed Ford Service Department workers stalked the factory floors and black neighborhoods looking for signs of union activity; and factionalism within the UAW indicated the union needed stable leadership before it could adequately address specific concerns of black workers. The view from the ground level within black Detroit suggests that the benefits of membership in the UAW-CIO were not obvious. Of greater concern was the penalty waiting for black Ford workers and their families if one of the FMC's "stoolies" or snitches, as they were called, reported disloyal behavior to Ford managers. The third stage in charting a new course for black labor developed after the UAW shifted its direction and began courting black workers and the community in 1939 and 1940. The climax of the process took place during the winter and spring of 1941. When black Ford workers finally gave their support to the UAW-CIO, they were not passive players in the outcome.

The initial stage in the process of changing the status quo for black workers emerged toward the end of Roosevelt's first administration. As black Detroiters debated whether Roosevelt represented a New Deal for African Americans, the general consensus was that the glass was half full, rather than half empty. While black Detroiters may not have agreed with the way Roosevelt's policies were implemented at the local level, they could relate to Roosevelt's party as an extension of the new Democratic politics ushered in by Mayor Frank Murphy. In 1936 the black Democratic vote in Detroit increased by 114 percent over what it was in 1932, which was, in turn, 88 percent over what it had been in 1930. The Democratic vote for Roosevelt in the black districts of Detroit in 1936 was 66.2 percent, while citywide it was 65.4 percent.[1] As African Americans threw their support overwhelmingly for Roosevelt, the surge of activism aimed at reconstructing Detroit's racial status quo increased.

Snow Grigsby, the Reverend William Peck, the Reverend Charles Hill, C. LeBron Simmons, Malcolm Dade, Geraldine Bledsoe, Louis C. Blount, and hundreds of others mounted aggressive campaigns against racial exclusion embedded within Detroit's body politic, chipping away at entrenched social relations.[2] The CRC became a vehicle for introducing alternative approaches, including new ways of reflecting on the state of the black community and how to expand opportunity. When Carter Woodson addressed a standing-room-only crowd about his new book, *The Miseducation of the Negro*, claiming African American minds were "enslaved" even though their bodies were liberated, Thomas R. Solomon, active in both the CRC and the National Alliance for Postal Workers, disagreed. Solomon thought Woodson's message was dated, for Detroit's black community was no longer willing to tolerate leaders who "dare not speak against the 'status quo' . . . and special privileges."[3] While that assessment may have been self-serving, it does suggest progressive Detroiters felt great strides had been made by turning traditional leaders in a new direction. Nevertheless, in the late thirties, several black leaders took a step backward to appease Ford management.

THE DETROIT LOCAL OF THE
NATIONAL NEGRO CONGRESS

In the summer of 1935, the CRC used its networks as a platform to launch the NNC local in collaboration with the national organization. Economic issues drew black Americans to the NNC along with its pledge to shake up black America by challenging old-guard social relations.[4] The NNC hung its hopes on activism from within black communities, not the New Deal, for relief from racial inequities.[5] John P. Davis, the secretary of the NNC, and A. Philip Randolph, the organization's president, anchored the NNC's success on the power of collective action. Randolph advised blacks to reject the old-guard approach, seeking redress for grievances by placing "their problems for solution down at the feet of their white sympathetic allies."[6] The NNC's agenda was all about pulling together under one umbrella the efforts of existing organizations within black communities across the country, providing protection and direction in the common struggle against economic and social oppression.[7] The collaboration that unfolded in Detroit worked to the advantage of both organizations. The CRC's star grew brighter with its link to the national collective headed by both Randolph and Davis. The NNC benefited by tapping into a locally based network organized around the protest politics of a new crowd.

John Davis outlined the NNC's program during the summer of 1935 for the editorial board of the *Detroit Tribune Independent*. Although we possess only the *Tribune Independent* accounts, Davis probably visited all of the other local news outlets. He likely stopped at the office of the *Detroit People's News*, whose editor, Beulah Young, had been a significant voice for more aggressive, new-crowd politics since the twenties.[8] The editor of the *Detroit Tribune Independent* enthusiastically endorsed the NNC, describing Davis as a "brilliant young attorney of Washington, D.C.," and portraying the NNC as an organization "seeking to enlist all the leading Negro organizations in the country in a united drive to improve the economic status" of blacks.[9]

Davis sought the help of Snow Grigsby to organize the Detroit chapter. Utilizing the broad-based CRC network, Grigsby began organizing a local chapter and making plans for a local NNC conference during the fall. Aiding Grigsby were the Reverend William H. Peck, the Reverend G. W. Baber, Rabbi Leon Fram, and Thomas R. Solomon.[10] Although Grigsby was not known for his diplomacy and was clearly a thorn in the side of traditional leaders like the Reverend Robert Bradby, by the mid-thirties he had found his voice, packing public facilities when he spoke. His provocative style helped open up jobs, and he was known for throwing municipal officials off balance.[11] In collaboration with the *Detroit Tribune Independent*, the CRC showcased the NNC local at an economic conference held at Rev. Peck's Bethel A.M.E. Church in October. John Davis and Lester Granger, the director of the National Urban League's Labor Bureau, were the featured speakers. Granger, combining his efforts to form Workers Councils with his support for the NNC, highlighted the protection against arbitrary unemployment built into union contracts. The issue was aimed, no doubt, at black Ford workers who understood the power that Donald Marshall and the Ford Service Department held over their jobs.[12]

The conference also signaled the NNC's broader social vision with a panel, "Ethiopia and Negro People at the Cross Roads in World Affairs," followed by a discussion of the occupation of Ethiopia by the Italians.[13] The FMC, apparently sensitive to the interests of black Detroiters, announced, one week after the conference, that it was stopping all shipments of trucks to Italians in Ethiopia. Was Ford responding, in part, to the activist community's mood reflected by the approximately 3,000 black Detroiters who attended this conference? It was, at the least, a convenient moment for Ford to withdraw aid that helped the enemy of Ethiopia.[14]

Davis, calling the Detroit NNC a success, suggested New York City model its local chapter on the Michigan pattern.[15] At several "mammoth mass meetings" held at the YWCA and the Brewster Center on Detroit's East Side, participants discussed using the power of collective effort to help black Detroiters take their "place as . . . respectable citizens."[16] Grigsby joined the 8,000 from throughout the United States who traveled to Chicago in February 1936 to attend the first NNC convention; his address, "How Civic Associations Can Attack Jim Crow Practices," drew from his efforts to open up jobs in Detroit's public sector to all candidates.[17]

Detroit's youth division infused the NNC local with energy and vigor as young people, acting as foot soldiers, visited the services of every black church in Detroit, selling NNC literature and postage stamp–like publicity stickers, a chief means for raising revenue for the chapter.[18] C. LeBron Simmons, tapped as chairman of the youth division in 1935, worked with the local for several years and became its president in 1937.[19] Though a graduate of the University of Michigan Law School and a member of the Detroit Intercollegiate Club for the young, educated elite, Simmons was motivated by the same preoccupation with the plight of the black working class that galvanized the efforts of his less-educated colleagues in the NNC crusade.[20]

Activists from diverse backgrounds were drawn to the NNC local. Simmons's background and experience, resembling that of Geraldine Bledsoe and John Davis in terms of intellectual pedigree, contrasted with the education and experience of Coleman Young, Snow Grigsby, or Paul Kirk, a crane operator at Michigan Steel Casting Company.[21] Philosophical differences existed among ecclesiastical activists, which included the Reverends Charles Hill; John Miles, Hill's assistant pastor at Harford Avenue Baptist Church; William Peck, pastor of Bethel A.M.E. Church; George W. Barber, pastor of Ebenezer A.M.E. Church; Horace White, pastor of Plymouth

Congregational Church; and Father Malcolm Dade, minister of St. Cyprian's Episcopal Church. Others who added to the diversity were UAW trade unionists such as Christopher C. Alston, Veal Clough, Arthur McPhaul, Hodges Mason, John Conyers Sr., and Joseph Billups. Female activists such as Rose Billups and Vera Vanderberg worked alongside politician Charles Diggs Sr. and Robert J. Evans, an attorney and the secretary of the Detroit branch of the NAACP. Yet, for all the differences in background, a common commitment to inclusion and social justice cemented the alliance.[22]

A radical, Social Gospel tradition—a tradition of applying Christian principles to social conditions—was responsible for the unusually "strong religious underpinnings" that grounded the Detroit local.[23] A leaning toward Marxism or the Communist Party (CP) on the part of a member was not—by itself—a sufficient condition to drive a wedge in the common struggle for social justice that united the network.[24] To some degree, then, NNC activists were mavericks who had been pushed aside from playing major roles in mainstream black improvement organizations such as the NAACP. Davis's prior career with the NAACP at the national level, for example, resembled that of Grigsby's at the local level: both had threatened the old-guard, black status quo, whose adherents continued to embrace more traditional approaches.

While scholars have noted the dissatisfaction many black churchmen had with the NNC at the national level, feeling that its grounding was too left-wing, religion and politics were not points of contention in the Detroit NNC chapter.[25] Snow Grigsby and Rev. Peck had developed strong relationships with the clergy of black Detroit during the early years of the CRC. Grigsby's approach to opening up municipal jobs to black Detroiters was endorsed by many clerical leaders, and most of them would probably have agreed with Grigsby when he wrote that "all racial discrimination is sinful as well as wicked." Early meetings of the CRC were held at St. John's United Presbyterian, where Grigsby was an active member. Grigsby's politics grew out of his personal belief that it was a "sin to deprive men of an opportunity for their own growth and development."[26] Grigsby carried his personal beliefs and those of many of Detroit's black clergy into the NNC local as he reached out to broaden its appeal. He and Peck were, no doubt, acutely aware of the loyalty the FMC cultivated in certain black ministers, and they wanted to put down a welcome mat for those who severed ties to Ford's paternalism.[27]

Over the years, much has been made of the communist influence on the NNC, some even claiming that communists formed the Detroit local.[28] Reports circulated suggesting that "the Communist Party [was] vainly trying to run the show," as Jeannette Worlds, a Detroit CRC staff member put it in a note to Davis. "But don't worry about the last remark," Worlds added, because "you and I both know Snow F. Grigsby," referring to Grigsby's reputation for intolerance of outside domination. Davis did not want the NNC local to be regarded as a tool of the communists, which was, most likely, why he favored building the Detroit local on the CRC foundation.[29] At the other extreme, the reported linking of communists with the NNC has led some to dismiss the organization and its influence within the black community. August Meier and Elliott Rudwick, for example, view the NNC local as largely a "paper organization," discounting the vitality, independence, and deep-seated commitment to overcoming racial discrimination that drove the local and grounded its efforts.[30]

Rather than taking Meier and Rudwick's view of the NNC as an organization that "operated on the periphery of black community organizations" before World War II, we would do better to try to understand how the NNC at the local level tapped into the robust, broad-based activism of those dedicated to racial progress and social justice. Within new-crowd circles in black Detroit, the burning issue was not whether an activist was a communist. The important question was whether an activist was committed to advancing civil rights and economic opportunity for black Detroiters. In the minds of several leaders within the Detroit local, such as Rev. Hill, these issues had little to do with one's position on an abstract political spectrum. Hill's theology, anchored in the prophetic tradition of African American Christianity and the idealism of the Social Gospel, mandated reforming society and bringing it in line with Christian ethics. Hill believed that within the industrial unionization movement lay the opportunity to reconstruct the social order, "fulfilling the promise of economic, and by extension racial, democracy." The struggle within black Detroit, in the view of many in the NNC fold, did not belong to the communists or the socialists or the Democrats in the New Deal. It grew out of centuries of injustice toward black Americans, and, for that reason, as Ruth Needleman points out, black people fighting for their freedom and equality were not driven by radicalism so much as by "a powerful sense of righteousness."[31]

The organizational reach of the Detroit NNC chapter expanded throughout 1936, enlarging the network committed to its agenda. A River Rouge Local Council was formed, and efforts were under way for satel-

The Reverend Charles A. Hill,
pastor of Hartford Avenue Baptist
Church, played a major role in
shaping the labor-oriented civil
rights agenda that emerged from
coalition building during the 1930s
in Detroit. Image courtesy of
the Burton Historical Collection,
Detroit Public Library.

lite outlets in Inkster and Ecorse, Michigan, neighborhoods housing black Ford workers and their families. The River Rouge council included participants affiliated with Triumph Baptist Church, the River Rouge West Side Community Club, and Young Valois Palmer Post No. 84 American Legion Department of Michigan. Dred Scott Neusom, a lawyer who lived in River Rouge, organized the council. Having the local organized and directed by Neusom, rather than an employee of the FMC, provided protection for members who worked at Ford, helping keep union persuasions hidden from Ford stool pigeons. To what extent black Ford workers were active behind Dred Scott Neusom's cover is difficult to say.[32] By the late fall, more of the day-to-day operation of the Detroit chapter was in the hands of Robert Evans as Grigsby became a member of the National Executive Council of the NNC. Evans managed daily operations for the NNC chapter while acting as secretary of the local NAACP.[33]

The NNC chapter launched its activist agenda as the sea change in labor relations opened up new possibilities for black workers. Roosevelt's landslide reelection, the formation of the Committee for Industrial Organization (CIO) in 1935, and the passage that year of the National Labor Relations Act by Congress boosted the confidence of workers across industrial America because they saw these events as the beginning of an era of aggressive union organizing.[34] C. LeBron Simmons recalled the time as a moment to build the NNC as an alternative to the NAACP, which was primarily, he thought, interested in "professionals as far as civil rights were concerned," not workers' rights.[35]

Beginning in 1936, the Detroit NNC focused on helping the UAW organize black workers, and its leaders recommended that an African American be appointed a full-time UAW organizer for black autoworkers. The suggestion was not taken up until the spring of 1937, after the successful wave of sit-down strikes led General Motors and Chrysler to sign labor contracts with the UAW.[36] Minimal participation by blacks in the sit-down strikes raised questions within the union about black allegiance to the FMC, the UAW's next target. Roy Wilkins, the assistant secretary of the NAACP, investigated union sentiment at the time of the sit-down strikes; he noted that "while some Negro workers in General Motors plants . . . joined" the UAW, and while others took part in the sit-down strikes in Flint, "many more [were] hanging back, asking the usual question: 'Will the union give us a square deal and a chance at some of the good jobs?'"[37] Black workers were "still reluctant to cast their lot with the union," for the UAW had not demonstrated "membership in the unions [would] bring them any benefits."[38]

With the FMC in the union's crosshairs, the UAW appointed its first salaried black organizer, Paul Silas Kirk, in April 1937.[39] Kirk, son of an Alabama preacher, was born in Talladega, Alabama. After graduating from high school in Alabama, he moved to Detroit in 1929. Before becoming a union organizer, he worked as a crane operator with the Michigan Steel Casting Company, joined the UAW in 1936, was elected recording secretary of UAW Local 281, and was actively involved in the local NNC chapter when he was tapped by Homer Martin, president of the UAW. The union used its announcement of Kirk's appointment to highlight its constitutionally mandated policy of nondiscrimination.[40]

Soon after Kirk was hired, the UAW created a nonsalaried "Sub-Committee for Organization of Negro Workers," led by Samuel Fanroy, a black worker who participated in the sit-down strike at Chrysler. By the fall of 1937, the black staff included two additional full-time organizers and three part-time organizers. Nearly all of the members of this committee, including Fanroy, were active members of the NNC local. An African American woman was hired to assist with research and publicity.[41] Although these appointments were promising—and the Detroit NNC spoke highly of the UAW in public venues—problems emerged.

Social extensions of a new relationship between black and white workers in the UAW measured the sincerity of the union's rhetoric. White union workers' refusal to let African Americans join them in UAW-sponsored dances and picnics led, at first, to the cancellations of several events. During the summer of 1937, protests by the NNC local highlighted the issue of social exclusion and yielded some positive results. A picnic planned by a Chevrolet plant for 21 August led to a revolt by the "racial reactionaries," who opposed an interracial event. After several meetings, the UAW "went on record against any discrimination." Several black UAW members were placed on the Picnic Committee, and others were chosen to sell tickets to social events.[42] Yet, a few months later the race question flared up again when UAW Local 235 at Chevrolet Gear and Axle refused to let its black members take part in a dance at Book Cadillac Hotel. The *Detroit Tribune* featured the story with a large bold headline that read: "UAW JIM CROWS WORKERS." Once again, the local branch of the NNC protested. The executive committee of the UAW local subsequently met and drew up a statement reiterating the union's commitment to no discrimination "whatsoever, regardless of religion, race, creed, color, political affiliation or nationality."[43]

As much as black autoworkers may have wanted to believe that statement, hoping that this time the UAW really meant what it said, the UAW's policies did not match many of its practices. During the mid- to late 1930s, as St. Clair Drake and Horace R. Cayton maintained, African Americans used social events as a litmus test to measure the sincerity of white union members.[44] Memory of the long history of union racism practiced by the AFL (discussed in the previous chapter) reinforced the fear that unions sought only to promote the interests of white workers.[45] In the eyes of many black Detroiters, the UAW would remain guilty of racism until it could prove itself innocent through new practices. Thus, despite the fact that the UAW officially affiliated with the CIO in August of 1936, it was regarded by many in the black community as a part of the CIO in name only.[46]

As the alliance between the CRC and the NNC strengthened, new-crowd activists drawn to this network often found themselves swimming upstream in their efforts to enlist support for the UAW. They could not count on the UAW. Union organizing during the economic recession of 1937–38 was particularly challenging as the FMC increased its surveillance of black Detroit, creating a bunker mentality within the community. While espionage, carried out on the shop floor by hired agents or through contracts with professional detective agencies, was commonly practiced by management throughout the auto industry after 1933, the spy system at the FMC, according to Walter Galenson, "reached its acme of perfection."[47] Often isolated by the UAW, NNC activists learned to depend on their own resources within the black community, clearing a way forward over uncharted territory.

HENRY FORD AND THE REIGN
OF TERROR IN DETROIT

As labor's challenge drew closer to Dearborn, home of the River Rouge, Henry Ford struggled to gain control over the direction of events. He watched the unprecedented upheaval in the traditionally anti-union city known as Mecca for the open shop and calculated the enormous losses suffered by General Motors and Chrysler when sit-down strikes stopped production at his competitors' factories.[48] "We'll never recognize the United Automobile Workers Union or any other union," Ford declared.[49]

After the union organizing campaigns began, Charles Sorensen, chief of production at the River Rouge plant, recalled, "there never was a happy moment in it for either Ford." Recognizing that a new era had emerged, Edsel favored bargaining with the union. Henry was fiercely opposed.[50] His hostility to both the Roosevelt administration and the UAW "knew no bounds."[51] Sorensen remembered the split between father and son reaching a fever pitch in late fall and winter, a time marked by "long, heated wrangles." "I found it best to avoid my visits when they were together." The feud continued for the next several years.[52]

To buy time, Henry Ford resorted to tactics he had utilized in the past to maintain order. Always known as a mercurial figure with a complex personality, Ford had his dark and light sides. But during the Depression years the dark side overshadowed the moments when he let the light in. Steven Watts suggests that Ford, like many people who become fabulously successful by relying on their own wit and wisdom, was so "utterly confident in his view of the world" that he could not appreciate and fathom what he did not know. Edwin G. Pipp offered another theory. As the first editor of the *Dearborn Independent*, Pipp had worked closely with Ford in the early twenties. After being associated with Ford over a period of years, Pipp observed, he "would learn of things in the Ford organization that I would have believed impossible in a civilized country." What troubled him was Ford's inclination to "use the lash of his power more and more on those who resisted or opposed him."[53] Ford was known to put labor unions and strikes in the same category he reserved for financiers of Wall Street.

He once expressed his thoughts on labor unions in his pocket notebook this way: "all wars, labor unions, strikes, by an insidious conspiracy group of war mongers and mongrelds [original spelling]."[54]

The Ford Service Department, locally known as a police force, had long relied on a large contingent of prizefighters and ex-convicts to carry out specified and unspecified tasks, keeping watch and control over company employees, whether at work or at home. The domain of Harry Bennett since the late teens, the latitude and responsibilities assumed by Bennett had expanded manyfold by the mid-thirties. By then Bennett was re-ported to have 3,000 street fighters, underworld characters, and athletes on Ford's payroll and under his control.[55] While much is made of Bennett's fierce tactics that kept him abreast at all times of the faces, names, and whereabouts of radical organizers, his power increased immensely on 12 April 1937 when the Supreme Court upheld the constitutionality of the Wagner Act, supporting collective bargaining and the right of workers to organize labor unions.[56]

Ford exploded when he heard the outcome of the Supreme Court deci-sion and told a reporter that he would resist it with his last dollar.[57] He responded by announcing to the two top people in his company—his son, Edsel, and his River Rouge production manager, Charles Sorensen—that Bennett would henceforth direct the company's position toward labor. "The elder Ford," according to Sorensen, decided to give full power to "a strong, aggressive man who can take care of himself in an argument," someone who also had the elder's "full confidence." When announcing this decision, Henry turned to his son and chief production manager and said, "And I want to be sure that you, Edsel, and you, Charlie, will support him."[58] With no more fanfare, Henry Ford anointed Bennett as second in command of the FMC.

Ford's plan to obstruct the Wagner Act was not well disguised. Mem-bers of the National Labor Relations Board (NLRB) observed the compa-ny's refusal to change its policies and work culture to accommodate the new deal in labor relations. The NLRB declared that the company "sought to defy the law by formulating and sanctioning a highly integrated and amazingly far-reaching program of interference, restraint, and coercion" in areas where, Congress had ruled, employees were "entitled to enjoy un-hampered freedom."[59]

Emboldened by the Supreme Court's decision, the UAW initiated its first campaign to organize workers at the FMC. On 26 May 1937, Harry Ben-

Black and white labor organizers distributing UAW newspapers in 1937, just outside the gates to the River Rouge plant of the Ford Motor Company. From the Collections of The Henry Ford. ID#P.833.69369.Q.

nett's forces clashed with Walter Reuther and Richard Frankensteen, UAW-CIO leaders, in the Battle of the Overpass. Reuther and Frankensteen's plan to pass out UAW literature during a shift-change at the River Rouge, a standard method for reaching employees with a union's message, back-fired. Aware that the company might resist and hoping to forestall physical assaults on those distributing leaflets, Reuther brought along ministers, reporters, photographers, and staff members from Senator Robert La Follette's Civil Liberties Subcommittee. Bennett's men were not impressed or intimidated by the eyes of the public. When Reuther and Frankensteen climbed to the top of the Miller Road Overpass, forty Ford Service Workers confronted them. The group of service employees—including Angelo Caruso, boss of the Down River gang in Detroit; Warshon Sarkisien and Ted Greis, professional wrestlers; and Oscar Jones, a boxer—that greeted Reuther and Frankensteen proceeded to slug the union leaders systematically and mercilessly, and even viciously kicked some of the women.

The violence was fully reported, complete with pictures, in the national media.[60]

With the Battle of the Overpass, the UAW lost the first round of its offensive, and Henry Ford lost much of what respect he still commanded in the public arena around the country. Nevertheless, Ford, more concerned with the larger war he was waging against organized labor, thought he was on the offensive by late summer. As factional fighting sapped the UAW's offensive against Ford, the FMC battened down its hatches to keep intact the open shop and sustain its control over black workers. The company fired around 4,000 actual or suspected union organizers over the next four years, beefed up its surveillance at every level, and created such a reign of Ford Terror, an atmosphere of dread and intimidation, that Edmund Wilson was led to refer to the elder Ford as "the despot of Dearborn."[61]

Benjamin Stolberg, a journalist who wrote primarily about labor issues, described Ford's new culture of work by comparing it to living and working conditions in Nazi Germany. He claimed there were some 800 underworld characters under Bennett's command whose function was to "keep order" within the "plant community through terror." Another 8,000–9,000 regular "authentic workers" operated as "spies and stool-pigeons" for this "industrial mafia," according to Stolberg.[62] Was it a coincidence that in July 1938 Ford was awarded the "Order of the Grand Cross of the German Eagle," the highest honor bestowed on a foreigner by the Third Reich, in a ceremony held in his Dearborn office that included a personal message from Adolf Hitler?[63]

In addition to underworld characters, Bennett also relied on the good graces and quid pro quo arrangements he had established with J. Edgar Hoover, director of the Federal Bureau of Investigation (FBI). John Bugas, head of the FBI's Detroit operations, called Bennett a "very valuable friend of this office." One scholar has suggested that in exchange for looking sideways when Bennett operated outside the law, the bureau obtained from Bennett information from the company's vast files on communist labor agitators.[64] This may explain the FBI raids on twelve people in the early hours of 6 February 1940 in Detroit. All but one were connected with the CP, the UAW, and/or the International Brigade in Spain, a CP organization.[65]

Ford also increased his surveillance of African Americans in Detroit. In 1935, the reader will recall, Willis Ward, a former track and football star for the University of Michigan and the first black football player on the team since 1898, was hired to assist Donald Marshall's surveillance and public relations work within the community. Both reported to Bennett. Ward welcomed the job at Ford when he graduated from the university because times were tough and he liked the idea of being part of an effort to enhance Ford's public image within black Detroit. When he was hired, Ward noted, it was "a good time for me or someone like myself to . . . build up the public relations aspect" of the company. As a model for what black youth could accomplish, Ward could make an assessment of the benevolent side of Ford's policy toward African Americans that would be noticed.[66]

Ward's remembrances of his public relations job for Henry Ford differed from the recollections of many of the black employees whose activities were scrutinized and criticized by Ward and Marshall during the late thirties. Outside the plant, ministers, even some who were pro-union in their hearts, bowed to the pressure of doing what Henry Ford wanted in order to protect their access to his patronage for their church members. Despite the fact that Wilbur C. Woodson, the secretary of the St. Antoine YMCA, was pro-union and had acted on his beliefs on several occasions, he changed course and refused to allow R. J. Thomas, the president of the UAW-CIO, to use the Y in 1940. He rationalized the denial of use by pointing out that had he allowed a labor meeting to take place in his facility, "the next day Ward and Marshall would have been down here to know why." The end result, according to Woodson, would have meant that he could not "recommend any more men to Ford's. I've got to be an opportunist. I've got to do what is best for the largest number."[67]

Ford also began, as early as January 1937, recruiting black employees for temporary duty in the Service Department. Bennett preferred large, strong men, especially former athletes. They were armed with blackjacks and other weapons for their patrols of the factory, either cruising in cars or standing guard at plant gates. Temporary black Service Department employees represented those Ford workers who believed, as Ford management reminded its black workforce, that the triumph of the UAW would lead to the loss of the superior position African Americans enjoyed at the Rouge.[68]

During this period it was, likely, not so much loyalty to Henry Ford that kept black Ford workers from signing up with the UAW as keeping the gains they had made. Although many African Americans throughout the country complained about the fact that whites had taken so-called Negro

A foundry worker at the River Rouge Plant pours hot metal into molds. 1934. From the Collections of The Henry Ford. ID#P.833.59567.

jobs from blacks as a way out of unemployment, African Americans at the FMC were hired in proportionately greater numbers than whites during the critical 1933–39 period (see chapter 6). The FMC employed 9,825 black men at the Rouge plant in 1937, a critical year of the recession within the Great Depression.[69] The majority of the jobs were positions in the foundry at the Rouge, ironically turning the foundry job into the "black job" at the

Rouge. Shelton Tappes, an NNC organizer and black foundry worker who became recording secretary and later president of production foundry for UAW Local 600, "vividly" remembered that in the early thirties there were "so few Negroes in the foundry.... So few, in fact, they were outnumbered about two to one. And there were some jobs [in the foundry] with no Negroes at all." Tappes worked a short while, was fired, and not rehired again until March 1937. By then, the foundry was overwhelmingly black.[70]

Although African Americans were fortunate to be hired in large numbers during such hard economic times, making the foundry job "blacker" suggests Ford may have squandered an opportunity to improve his relationship with black employees. Working conditions in the foundry deteriorated during this time. As it became "blacker," it was the site of more intense speedups in the late thirties than had been the case earlier. Finding themselves in what was called a "madhouse," open-hearth foundry workers were previously expected to dismantle 130 cars a day for scrap and now had their quotas raised to 190 and more.[71] Ford continued to offer a small number of entry-level black workers access to the Ford Trade School, and he even made available to blacks a few slots as tool-and-dye workers, the aristocrats of automotive labor. Quill Pettway, an African American who graduated from Northwest High School in Detroit and was trained as a tool-and-dye worker in the Ford Trade School, was hired at Ford on the eve of the strike that took place in 1941.[72] The odds, however, were less favorable that such an opportunity awaited young black men in the mid- and late 1930s.

During these years, Ford was not just preoccupied—one might argue obsessed—with the threat labor unions posed to his control over Ford workers. He also was focused on several other projects, including his ongoing research on soybeans, his renewed passion for tractors, his reconstruction of an antebellum plantation, Richmond Hill, located about twenty miles south of Savannah, Georgia, and his attempt to run a rubber plantation in the heart of the Amazon.[73] As a result, by 1937 Harry Bennett not only oversaw labor issues, but he also put his heavy stamp on many day-to-day decisions, such as vouchers for trips, transfers, and expense accounts. Even Charles Sorensen was "coldly checked" when he attempted to speak against Bennett to Ford.[74] It is possible that Henry Ford could not successfully control such a far ranging industrial empire. In July 1938 Ford had a mild stroke.[75]

THE UAW ALTERNATIVE

As the summer of 1937 wore on, black autoworkers, generally, maintained a "wait and see" stance toward the UAW. Black Ford workers and the community were well aware that the economic downturn was not a propitious moment to challenge Henry Ford and his security forces. Just as important, the fledging union raised more questions than it answered in the minds of black autoworkers. Would UAW seniority clauses be manipulated to the disadvantage of blacks with the first layoffs for industry retooling? Would the union fight white racism when it came to integrating black workers into higher-level positions?[76] Hopes that may have been raised with the hiring of Paul Kirk, the first black paid organizer for the UAW, were dashed by the early fall as the union's position on sensitive issues left black activists uncertain about the UAW's intentions with respect to black auto workers.

Events of the summer resembled a three-ring circus in terms of the number of factions angling for attention. The national NAACP annual convention, held in Detroit in June 1937, highlighted the schisms within labor as well as mixed perceptions harbored by black Detroiters toward the UAW. A speech by UAW president Homer Martin served as a lightening rod because it reinforced the view that Martin was more a grandstander than a stable personality who might inspire trust. Before Martin arrived for the conference, Henry Ford's most prominent black ministers—Father Daniel and Rev. Bradby—threatened to boycott the event if Martin spoke, guaranteeing packed audiences for Martin's speech.[77]

Homer Martin did not begin work in the auto industry until 1932, after a career as a Baptist minister in Missouri. He was known as a gifted speaker, delivering his message with otherworldly fervor, using language colored by biblical phrases. It was said that he made men feel "that in organizing a union they were going forth to battle for righteousness and the word of God."[78] His talents, however, backfired at the NAACP convention when Martin compared himself to Jesus by saying that he came "representing the poor, the oppressed and exploited people, both colored and white." His words did not ring true. Most heard the comparison as the self-regard of an arrogant egotist. He lost a chance to win the confidence of African Americans. Those inclined to support the FMC over the union made sure Martin's comparison to Jesus was repeated over and over in the press and from the pulpit.[79]

Black workers, suggests historian Richard W. Thomas, held another view of the labor union. A black member of the UAW was frustrated, Thomas notes, with both the traditional NAACP leaders, who did not necessarily know what black workers wanted, and the UAW, which tended to depend for support on "ready-made, bandwagon-conscious Negro national and community leaders" rather than black autoworkers, "who after all really know what they want." While the idea that black autoworkers all knew what they wanted is, most likely, overstated, Thomas's reflections remind us that black Ford workers may not have been so much anti-union in 1937 as not pro-UAW.[80]

The majority of NAACP officers at the local level were still suspicious of the union, yet the youth division of the NAACP chapter tended to support the union. Old-guard black leaders, local and national, debated for two long days whether to endorse the UAW-CIO. The final NAACP resolution, though not a rejection of the UAW, was also not a ringing endorsement. After advising black workers not to go blindly into any labor organization, the NAACP leaders reminded them that they must bear responsibility for making a labor union movement "more just."[81]

To further complicate matters, factional disputes within the UAW divided the union into two groups that summer. The Progressive Caucus, headed by Homer Martin, and the Unity Caucus, led by Wyndham Mortimer, Ed Hall, and Walter Reuther, struggled for control over the direction of the UAW. President Martin, engaged in a crusade against what he viewed as a "Communist conspiracy," shuffled black personnel on the UAW's salaried and unsalaried staff to cleanse his operation of communists. Paul Kirk's recommendation for a second salaried black organizer, Lonnie Williams, was rejected because of his CP membership, and Walter Hardin, an ex-communist, was chosen instead. Kirk was let go, presumably for his communist affiliation, and Hardin rose to the top black salaried position under Martin. But the NNC local retained connections to the union even after Kirk was fired, for many UAW members were also active in the NNC. One of NNC's links was Joseph Billups, a known communist, whom Martin added to his black organizing staff after firing Kirk, presumably to benefit from Billups's following among poor black Detroiters. Martin's policies were not always consistent with his rhetoric. Thus Martin's phobia about communists nurtured self-reliance in black Detroiters and turned the NNC local into a center for organizing black Ford workers.[82]

Factional politics drove a wedge into the UAW's plans, keeping the union from making much forward progress in its proposed campaign against Ford. As Carl Haessler, a labor activist, observed, the "UAW at the beginning was a wild scramble of largely inexperienced unionists trying to organize themselves into a functioning union with a number of groups struggling for control."[83] As the fledging union made an effort to define itself, its origins within the AFL continued to haunt the organization. Shelton Tappes knew it would take much more than mere affiliation with the CIO for black Americans to overcome wariness of a link to the AFL, the organization in which "14 international unions . . . either by ritual or constitutional provision excluded Negroes from the union." Tappes had no doubt that "many Negroes that had experiences with those unions were very bitter about it."[84]

Questions about the UAW troubled black Americans far beyond Detroit in 1937. "We would like to know from Mr. Homer Martin," declared an editorial in the *Pittsburgh Courier*, "whether the policy of his union, if it is successful, will be that of the A.F. of L. or the C.I.O. toward Negro workers." The larger black community, the *Courier* claimed, regarded the CIO as the natural heir of the Knights of Labor and the Industrial Workers of the World because of its stated policy to organize "ALL workers in an industry regardless of color, skill or wages." The CIO's biggest supporter, the United Mine Workers, had been "conspicuously and continually fair to Negro workers," according to the *Courier*. If the UAW plans to follow in the footsteps of the Knights of Labor, the IWW and the UMW, "then its victory will be a great boon to Negro labor. If not, then as desirable as an automobile industrial union seems to be, the Negro will have to continue his policy of watchful waiting."[85]

The black community was aware, especially through black newspapers, that an alternative CIO model existed, one that made reaching out to black workers a top priority. But the UAW was born under the AFL tent, not formed initially as an "irrevocable break with the AFL" as was the case with the Steel Workers Organizing Committee-CIO (SWOC-CIO). Unlike SWOC, which was, as Robert Zieger points out, created "from top to bottom [as] a direct creature of John L. Lewis and the CIO," the UAW was formed by leaders from within the auto industry.[86] From the start the UAW was largely self-financing, only receiving aid from other CIO unions during sit-down strikes in 1937 and later during the Ford Organizing period. Until the late 1930s, CIO influence on internal affairs was limited to working out compromises among factions within the UAW, unlike the situation in steel and mines where CIO officials were at the helm. However much the UAW may have valued its independence, the auto union's disconnect from CIO control did not help reassure black Detroiters, and its factionalism took valuable time away from addressing the interests of black workers.[87]

Considerable attention in the *United Automobile Worker*, the union's official organ, was focused on black workers, but two issues sometimes made the union's views seem ambiguous. One was assuming black workers were the problem in achieving solidarity, as though the racism endemic within organized labor had vanished. For example, the UAW Ford Organizing Committee pitched its message in terms of educating workers on the "vital necessity of solidarity regardless of race," begging the question of how the union planned to deal with decades of white racism that had become part of the air many members breathed.[88]

The other issue was a condescending tone invoked to remind black workers that—as Walter Hardin, a black UAW organizer, put it—Ford's "exceptionally liberal policy" toward his black workers was "an illusion."[89] Perhaps many black workers still subscribed to the illusion of a liberal Ford policy. But the UAW—as workers reflected years later—had not demonstrated that its policy toward blacks was also not illusory.[90] Another UAW article adopted a quasi-missionary tone, warning "You Negro workers" that "King Henry is merely fattening you for the slaughter" by buying up loyalty.[91] Yet, as Paul Boatin, the recording secretary of UAW Local 600 in 1943, observed, while there was the semblance of loyalty among Ford workers, such demonstrations "should not be misunderstood, because workers were playing safe because there were spies all around." Hanging a picture of Henry Ford in a prominent place, where one would expect to see a picture of Abraham Lincoln, might indicate more about the pragmatism of workers than their loyalty quotient. The worker who displayed Ford paraphernalia, Boatin said, "was a thinking individual who was merely trying to protect his job security because he knew how dangerous it was to do otherwise."[92]

August Meier and Elliott Rudwick argue that despite the effort to win the allegiance of the black community with a "persistent propaganda campaign," the leaders of the UAW were "well aware that much more was needed."[93] If that were true, why did John Davis, the NNC's national secretary, meet so much resistance from Homer Martin and the UAW when he attempted to promote organizing efforts among black autoworkers?[94] Was Davis's and the NNC's cozy relationship with known communists the reason? Or was there more to the turbulent relations between Martin, John Davis, and Detroit's chapter of the NNC? While John Davis and NNC connections with the CIO in steel and tobacco industries were positive, the NNC won little cooperation from the UAW, particularly between 1937 and the end of 1939.

By 1937, when the NNC local was poised to pave the way for the UAW within black Detroit, Martin focused on consolidating his power within the Progressive caucus after the successful spring sit-down strikes at General Motors and Chrysler. Martin's power base was particularly strong with older Anglo-Americans and such workers as white southern migrants raised on racism, who journeyed to Detroit in the twenties and thirties. Steve Fraser suggests that the unionists Martin counted on felt little kinship with the secular, racially mixed, often anticlerical crowd represented in the Unity caucus by the socialist Reuther brothers or the communist-leaning caucus, and he calls the civil war that erupted between Homer Martin and those allied with the socialists and communists "fratricidal." He also points out that the divisions were symptomatic of social anxieties and fissures brought about by the rise of the New Deal and the CIO, which generated powerful countercurrents within the working class. Fraser's argument, then, supports the idea that anticommunistic rhetoric resonated with workers feeling alienated by the policies of CIO leaders and their allies, including the CIO effort to integrate blacks into its industrial and political coalition.[95]

The NNC local in Detroit, and John Davis at the national level, regarded organizing black Ford workers for the UAW as their mission, something they thought they were well equipped to do, having achieved success with the NNC-SWOC model in other parts of the Midwest. Thus, leaders within the NNC local assumed that Homer Martin would welcome their assistance in giving him entre into the black community.[96] Perplexed, Davis asked Walter Hardin about the "anti-Negro attitude" of the UAW. How, Davis asked Hardin, could the union not be concerned about "the need for the closest cooperation between the auto workers and the Congress," as it moved forward to organize Ford and its 10,000 black workers?[97] After several failed attempts to get Martin to work with the NNC, a frustrated Davis told John L. Lewis, chairman of the CIO, that "our relationships with Brother Homer Martin have not been as cooperative as we would have liked."[98] However, the Detroit local did get cooperation from the UAW for a statewide conference featuring A. Philip Randolph as its speaker. At the time, Randolph was within a few days of successfully negotiating a path-breaking contract between the Pullman Company and the Brotherhood of Sleeping Car Porters (BSCP), a union of black workers Randolph headed. For that reason, he drew an especially large crowd to the conference.[99]

There was a "terrible fight to get the church" to hold the conference, LeBron Simmons, head of the NNC local, later recalled. Donald Marshall and Willis Ward pressured Simmons to keep Randolph's message from reaching the black community. Marshall warned Rev. Peck that if Randolph spoke at his church, members who worked at Ford would be fired. Peck stuck to his principles, and Marshall stuck to his, dismissing many of Peck's church members.[100]

From the pulpit of Peck's church, one of the largest black facilities, Randolph launched the conference with an attack on the FMC. In most circles, his speech was well received. The headline in the *Detroit Tribune* urged that "Workers Stay with Labor instead of Capital." He "assailed" all elements within the community opposed to the "forward march of labor," stressing that "the time has come when the Negro has to decide between organized labor and organized capital." Finally, he emphasized the fact that black workers were in many respects a pivot around which the larger labor movement would turn; thus, they held a significant position in the ongoing industrial scheme.[101]

Not everyone appreciated Randolph's point of view. A week later, Father Everard W. Daniel, pastor of the St. Mathews Episcopal Church, and Donald Marshall, a member of Daniel's congregation, went on a counterattack praising Ford's attitude toward the "Negro." Father Daniel challenged anyone to "show him an industrialist who has done more for colored labor than Henry Ford." Rev. Bradby was also supporting Ford's policies during this time.[102]

The contrast between Daniel's assessment and Randolph's was stark. Black Detroiters—like most black Americans—focused their attention on Randolph and the BSCP. The long struggle of black Pullman porters, sustained by the grit of black self-reliance, was almost over. Could the BSCP actually get officials of the Pullman Company to sit down with black Pullman porters to negotiate a labor contract? On 25 August 1937, within a week after the conference at Rev. Peck's church, Randolph and the BSCP signed their historic labor contract with the Pullman Company. The *Chicago Defender*, widely circulated in black Detroit, applauded the contract because the BSCP had succeeded without "begging"; by negotiating as "upstanding fighters for justice, the porters have pointed the way." As a result, continued the *Defender*, "race men have broken with a long established trait."[103] Winning the contract with Pullman undoubtedly boosted the overall esteem of black America—at this juncture, Randolph and the BSCP could do little wrong. Nonetheless, the reality of mixed messages from the UAW did little to encourage black Ford workers to sign up with the auto union in the midst of a worsening labor market. Embracing the UAW did not necessarily follow from a belief in a labor-oriented civil rights agenda.

EFFORTS OF THE CRC and the NNC local between 1935 and the end of 1937 paved the way within black Detroit for a new relationship between labor unions, black workers, and the black community. The agenda launched through progressive networks promoted labor unions as a vehicle for expanding economic opportunities and civil rights. With the UAW increasingly consumed by its internal struggles, the NNC-CRC alliance became stronger, more self-reliant, and more secure within black Detroit. Black workers at the FMC may have continued making the "extra effort" to fulfill demands for speedups in the foundry, but they likely felt there was little to motivate them to join the UAW's cause. Although this period has been portrayed as a time of waiting, activity within the NNC local shows new-crowd activists sketching the contours of a new course for black workers with unions. The final stage would be the effort to transform the UAW and its organizing campaign into a cause addressing the larger interests of black Detroiters.

CHAPTER NINE

Black Workers Change Tactics, 1937–1941

We just didn't trust the UAW.

—DAVID MOORE

Black workers "figured they would be used—used by white people, and then kicked out."

—JOSEPH BILLUPS

THE SECOND NATIONAL CONVENTION of the National Negro Congress (NNC), held in Philadelphia in October 1937, followed closely in Detroit by those listening to a live radio broadcast, emphasized the role black self-reliance must play in gaining an equal place in America.[1] As A. Philip Randolph, president of the NNC, said, "The task of realizing full citizenship for the Negro people is largely in the hands of the Negro people themselves."[2] The NNC's message seemed tailor-made for the Detroit local, reinforcing the self-reliance promoted and practiced by the Civic Rights Committee (CRC) and the NNC local. With little support from the NAACP local, much resistance from the UAW, and hostility from old-guard leadership of black Detroit, the CRC-NNC alliance continued organizing the black community around a labor-oriented civil rights agenda, often beyond the purview of forces outside the ghetto walls. As the NNC concentrated its efforts on expanding economic and social opportunities, its Trade Union Committee became the epicenter for efforts to organize black workers. Volunteer labor activists met in the privacy of workers' homes, "in the shadows" of black Detroit, to discuss labor union issues. The CRC and NNC sponsored other, more visible activities and events, often carried out jointly with other organizations, to oppose the racial status quo. For example, the Reverend William Peck and Snow F. Grigsby organized the CRC, with support from the NNC, to remove employment barriers at Detroit Edison, the electrical utility company, and the fire department.[3] The International Labor Defense, the Detroit Scottsboro Defense Committee, and the NNC worked together to bring two of the Scottsboro boys to Detroit.[4] But in terms of constructing a bridgehead within black Detroit for the labor offensive against the Ford Motor Company (FMC), it was mobilization outside United Auto Workers (UAW) union halls, within a black Detroit under neighborhood surveillance, that laid the foundation for the second Ford Organizing Drive in 1940.

LABOR ORGANIZING IN THE SHADOWS OF BLACK DETROIT

LeBron Simmons, the president of the Detroit chapter of the NNC, remembered organizing workers at home meetings in the black district starting in 1937. The approach was necessary because so few African Americans were hired as organizers by the UAW, compared to whites. Though the UAW launched a formal Ford Organizing Drive in 1937, Zygmund Dobrzynski, who directed mass meetings for the UAW at its Detroit headquarters in the Hofmann Building on Woodward Avenue, purposefully "advised the Negroes to stay away," according to Simmons.[5] Shelton Tappes, a Ford foundry worker who was active in the NNC and belonged to the UAW, had a slightly different memory of the summer of 1937. He recalled working as a volunteer with UAW organizers, visiting workers in their homes as the UAW made "an extremely hard effort to get Ford organized" that summer.[6] Support for the union was "favorable" at the Rouge, Tappes noted, as workers reacted to deteriorating conditions there and to the beatings of union organizers by Ford Service workers during the Battle of the Overpass in May.[7] The oral histories available to us, while sometimes containing recollections from different perspectives, offer a window on some of the circumstances that led the Trade Union Committee of the NNC to form a volunteer organizers' group.[8]

The system of volunteer organizing carried the momentum for organizing black Ford workers forward through the dormant period when the union was mired in factional disputes.[9] The basic strategy was to work behind the scenes in people's homes and to safeguard the effort by periodically flushing out stool pigeons. Shelton Tappes recalled that he did not attend union meetings much from 1937 through 1939, but he still talked with fellow autoworkers about unions wherever and whenever he could.

He said you might make contact with a fellow while "eating a sandwich on a street car, talking to a fellow about how tired you are, and talking about what you need in the shop." Then you might drop an example of what General Motors (GM) and Chrysler were doing in terms of safe-guarding workers' rights. "If a guy responded favorably you go so far as to develop a friendship with him and when you get a strong personal acquaintanceship you can talk." Usually in those days, not much was said on Ford company property.[10]

Attendance at regular meetings was slim because workers were "always afraid of spies and things like that," recalled Tappes. An elaborate surveillance system was established to make sure intruders were kept at a minimum. At secret meetings, members had to submit a numbered card, which was then triple-checked by Bill McKie, an unpaid white communist UAW organizer who worked with members in the NNC local chapter and with other underground leaders.[11] Extreme secrecy meant not having a clue in most cases as to who, among your fellow workers, might also be a union member. Tappes remembered Ford Service workers coming through the foundry right after lunch to pick out "big fellows" to work for them at quitting time. Harry Bennett's men would load all the "fellows up in cars . . . and have them parked at certain spots near the entrance of the plant." The idea was that the chosen men would rush out and "beat up the CIO guys" as they were leaving the plant. When one of his co-workers was chosen to perform this service, the man told Tappes, Bennett was "crazy" if he thought he was going to "beat up anybody that's coming out here to help me." But the man chose to go because it got him off his shift early. His plan was to go out to the car, remain seated, and stay there. Whether this strategy was successful was not clear, but Tappes made a note of the fact that the man seemed favorably inclined toward the union.[12]

Volunteer organizers from black neighborhoods—many employed, some not—worked the streets, often under the dark of night for added protection from Donald Marshall and Ford's vigilant Service Department. They met in groups of five and ten or three and four in those ragtag houses that looked "too poor for the attention of the police." Entire families were complicit in the conspiracy that developed to camouflage the "independent" union-building process. The need to make organizing activities blend in with one's daily routine must have cultivated a bunker mentality in families, including children. Women were instrumental in covering up indiscretions that might otherwise have revealed their husband's work.[13]

Rose Billups was part of the volunteer network of organizers, which included many women, who laid the foundation for what became Local 600 of the UAW-CIO. Billups, whose husband was a UAW organizer at the time, brought black women into the organization because often the wives, too, were afraid of the repercussions attached to going against the wishes of Henry Ford. "So we had to go in, individually," Billups said. Eventually, Billups organized the women, formed an auxiliary for Local 600, and was the auxiliary's first chair. The most important part of her job, as she told it, was to dispel fear of losing a job at the FMC. She promised the wives and female family members that the union would be responsible for making sure their husbands kept their jobs. She also pointed out how a union would improve working conditions and see to it that their husbands would not be coming home drunk or sick, issues important to wives and mothers.[14]

Billups met one-on-one in saloons and alleys to collect memberships. Her guarantee was that "no one would know but myself," she recalled. The women would bring the dues for their husbands to Rose Billups, and she then took the money, by the fall of 1940, to Mike Widman, a Ford organizer for the CIO. Before the UAW was organized at the FMC, this "secret underground organization," as Billups described her volunteer work for the NNC local's organizing campaign, became a force within the community.[15]

Meetings were often held on Saturday and Sunday mornings or at night, with women watching the streets for suspicious characters from the Ford Service Department. The issue of flushing out spies was always on the minds of activists. One favorite story involved a meeting called to shake out a suspected stool pigeon. When organizers gathered around a table in someone's home, a particularly large NNC volunteer, Dave Perkins, accused the suspect of ratting on them, telling Ford foremen about those who were trying to organize the union, and showing NNC handbills to top management. The man was so scared he jumped out the window.[16]

At least one minister held "underground" union meetings. The Reverend Charles Hill of Hartford Avenue Baptist, worried about the broad reach of the FMC's security forces, was inspired to lead special prayer meetings at his church, which served as a cover for clandestine union meetings. Were black Ford workers to meet in a union hall, Hill pointed out, "some of the spies from Ford would take their automobile license numbers and . . . [they would lose] their jobs." He felt that by holding meetings in a church, "it would be difficult for them to prove we were just discussing union matters."[17]

Veal Clough, one the most successful black organizers during the many months when the issue of organizing black Ford workers remained on the UAW's back burner, began his active union career as a Pullman porter. He worked with A. Philip Randolph in the early days of the Brotherhood of Sleeping Car Porters, from 1925 until 1933, when he was fired from the Pullman Company for his union activities. In 1934, after he landed a job at the FMC, working in the foundry at the River Rouge, he began organizing again, until he was fired by the FMC, again for union activities. Unemployed for the next several years, he joined the volunteer services under the auspices of the NNC in 1937, working along with Percy Llewellyn, a white UAW organizer, and others.[18]

The severity of the recession and internal conflict wreaked havoc on the union. Support for the UAW waned, and members stopped paying dues.[19] The year 1938 was the most inactive in terms of UAW initiatives to reach out to black workers as widespread unemployment took its toll. Volunteer organizer Tappes, laid off in December from the FMC and without work all of 1938, joined the Works Progress Administration (WPA). His WPA union card, which cost 25 cents a month, allowed Tappes to keep his membership alive in the UAW during his many months of unemployment. While Tappes did not think the WPA union was very effective, he used it to continue talking up the union to Ford workers, both on the WPA project to which he was assigned and within the black community. On his project, when it was 100 degrees in the shade, his labor committee would ask for more rest periods and more "boys" to supply drinking water. It was, Tappes explained, a way to demonstrate to "Ford people," who came from a nonunion experience, "how a union worked, the effectiveness of having representation."[20]

The bottom fell out of the automobile market, cutting output drastically. General Motors reported its sharpest monthly drop in auto sales in its history in December 1937. The UAW estimated at the end of January 1938 that out of 517,000 production workers in the industry, 320,000 were jobless and another 196,000 were barely getting by on short-time status. By March, as membership dues dropped substantially, the UAW had little money. To keep it going, the union was bailed out by a $100,000 loan from the International Ladies Garment Workers' Union. The first Ford Drive, which never really got off the ground, collapsed.[21]

Realizing the Ford Organizing Drive had sunk to the bottom of the UAW's list of priorities, John Davis resolved to hold the 1938 national convention of the NNC in Detroit in order to put "some fire in the Ford Drive by centering our attention upon the problem of organizing the tens of thousands of Negro autoworkers in the Henry Ford plant." Although extensive plans were made to carry out this goal, support from the UAW was so minimal that the plans were put on hold and never executed.[22]

"WHO OWNS THE NEGRO CHURCHES?"

Fears inspired by unemployment during the economic recession triggered a clash in 1938 between ministers when the West Side Improvement Association (WSIA), an organization of black workers, tried to get a church to hold its annual New Year's Day emancipation program. The Reverend Robert H. Pittman, the minister of the Tabernacle Baptist Church, refused to allow the Reverend Horace A. White, the minister of Plymouth Congregational Church, to speak in his church.[23] Pittman was afraid that foremen at the FMC would fire members of his church if he gave WSIA and Rev. White permission to use his facility. Rev. White, an NNC member and an outspoken union supporter, subscribed to a theology reflecting the Social Gospel education he had received at the Oberlin College Divinity School. From the time he took over as minister at Plymouth Congregation in 1936, the church had earned a reputation of being liberal on social issues.[24]

Though locked out of Tabernacle Baptist, Rev. White delivered his message via radio, and a transcript of the broadcast was printed in its entirety a week later in the *Detroit Tribune*.[25] In early February, White responded to Rev. Pittman, the Tabernacle Baptist Church, and old-guard black Detroiters in an essay published in the *Christian Century*. "Who Owns the Negro Churches?" White asked in the title of the piece. "Something important" had taken place in Detroit, he claimed, "something nobody expected." Black labor had "waked up." How accurate this statement was at the time is difficult to determine, but it could have reflected White's knowledge of the work carried out through the Trade Union Committee of the NNC. The pro-union inclination that had taken hold in Detroit was "alarming" to any minister who, as White explained, had "preached all his life that the hope of the Negro rests in the generosity of the rich people." But, White observed, the one organization through which a black person "ought to feel free to express his hopes and to work out his economic salvation cannot help" because Detroit's black churches were often "the property of the big white industrialists."[26]

A week later, Snow Grigsby captured the spotlight by inviting Dr. Mordecai Johnson, the president of Howard University, to speak in Detroit. In February 1937 Dr. Johnson had endorsed labor unions for black workers at Rev. Peck's Bethel A.M.E. Church, inspiring Donald Marshall's first censorship of speakers at Bethel. Several months later, the reader will recall, Peck ignored Marshall and offered his facilities to Randolph and the NNC. On that occasion several church members were dismissed from the FMC and were told by Ford officials, in no uncertain terms, it was because Rev. Peck did not show proper loyalty to Ford's policies. When Johnson was invited back in 1938, Peck finally caved in to pressure from the FMC and would not allow Dr. Johnson to speak at his church.[27]

As a long-time ally of Grigsby and co-founder of the CRC, Peck did not make this decision lightly. During an interview several years later, Peck said many of the members of his church who worked for Ford approached the board of his church and said "they were afraid they would lose their jobs if Johnson spoke . . . [at Peck's church] a second time. The Board did not feel it could jeopardize the jobs of our members in that way."[28] Snow secured the Brewster Community Center for Dr. Johnson's talk.[29] Some 3,000 people turned out to hear Dr. Johnson speak about "Our Government and Our Liberty." The current struggle, Johnson said, was not just for civil liberty or "economic liberty." It was for basic human rights and democratic equality.[30] The editorial staff of the *Detroit Tribune* used these incidents to expose Donald Marshall's tactics and shame him for the surveillance he carried out on behalf of the FMC. Those in the "employ of the Ford plant" who do not "wish to run the risk of losing their jobs" were forced to refrain from "directly or indirectly affiliating with the advocates of unionism," wrote the editors.[31]

George S. Schuyler, a well-known black journalist, also exposed Henry Ford's labor policies in an article published in the *United Automobile Worker*, the UAW's newspaper. Schuyler depicted in gripping terms the cozy relationship between Detroit's old crowd and Henry Ford that sustained Ford's "industrial plantation." The "well-regimented and policed" Rouge was, according to Schuyler, a "modern version" of the world portrayed in Harriet Beecher Stowe's *Uncle Tom's Cabin, or Life among the Lowly*. Black supporters of Henry Ford reminded him of the sycophantic relations present under slavery between the slave master and the "me, too, Massa" slave. "Since every Uncle Tom's Cabin must of course have an Uncle Tom, it need occasion no surprise that there are any number of

Uncle Toms in the Ford setup." Nor, he added, should we be surprised to learn that the "Uncle Toms" were not above selling out "their people for filthy lucre." Castigating those who propagated the Ford party line against the unionization of workers, he said the "Uncle Tom" figures would "do anything that will antagonize white and colored workers." Wondering where the present labor drive would lead, Schuyler speculated that if all white workers got organized, and blacks stayed out, then perhaps the FMC would "continue being run like a Georgia plantation," perhaps a reference to Henry Ford's Richmond Hill Plantation near Savannah, Georgia. The alternative that Schuyler suggested was for black Ford workers to look out for "their own interests," becoming "masters of their own fate."[32]

Schuyler's provocative article, published when the UAW organization effort was "stymied," received a lot of attention.[33] Homer Martin and his assistants continued to resist cooperating with the NNC local. The UAW would not cooperate on antilynching campaigns, which could have demonstrated the union's interest in civil rights issues. When the Detroit NNC local held a citywide conference on economic issues, the UAW chose to hold a competing banquet on that same evening. Despite these frustrations, the NNC, along with its diverse membership drawn from ministers, businessmen, professional women, autoworkers, and trade unionists, continued to publicly advocate labor unions as a viable alternative to black Ford workers.[34]

By the summer of 1938, eighteen organizations were listed among the affiliates of the NNC.[35] The count would have been higher had the NAACP, for example, listed itself as an affiliate. Prominent officers in the NAACP were actively engaged in forming alliances with the NNC local on many issues and at numerous events. It was no secret that Robert J. Evans, Louis C. Blount, the Reverend Malcolm Dade, and the Reverend Charles Hill, all officers of the NAACP local, either served as officers or were actively involved in the NNC local. Although the local branch of the National Postal Alliance played an energetic role within the NNC, it was also not officially considered an affiliate. Theodore T. Jones, the president of the local chapter of the Postal Alliance, was state director of the NNC in Michigan.[36] Dr. J. J. McClenden, the president of the Detroit NAACP, worked with Wilbur C. Woodson, the secretary of the YMCA, on a key NNC committee.[37]

Communications between LeBron Simmons, leader of the NNC local, and Davis show that a concerted effort took place to draw in "leading people of Detroit" or those described as the Talented Tenth. The NNC conducted meetings at the YMCA right after YMCA forums held every Sunday afternoon, a move encouraging attendance from "people who had heretofore been lukewarm toward the congress."[38] Simmons hoped to build a cross-class group in Detroit, one that was not "top heavy with trade unions"; he sought to attract a wide range of "other social, cultural, and political organizations of Negroes."[39] What did nonmembers think about the Communist Party (CP) members in the NNC network?

One clue comes from an undated—but likely March or April 1938—handwritten letter from LeBron Simmons to John Davis. William Nowell, one of the black UAW organizers hired by Homer Martin for his "Negro Department," had "injected the red scare," fear of communist infiltration, into a conversation with several local NNC members. According to Simmons, local members not affiliated with the CP had no problem with those who were, so long as there was no "question of dominating." Domination was often the Achilles' heel in relationships between black Detroit and groups from the outside. The NNC local, just like the CRC and many other organizations, attracted supporters because it was committed to advancing an inclusive agenda for black Detroit, one shaped by black Detroiters.[40]

During the period of the Popular Front from 1935 to 1939, communists supported cross-class black unity and democratic coalition politics.[41] Short of occasional references in the correspondence about monitoring the issue of domination, the question of radicalism did not consume much attention.[42] Communists had earned their wings as credible allies with their work on the Scottsboro and Angelo Herndon cases, as discussed earlier, because they had, as St. Clair Drake and Horace Cayton put it in *Black Metropolis*, fought for "Negroes *as* Negroes." African Americans who found it easy to work with known or suspected communists did so not because they dreamed of a socialist society, but because they dreamed of an America where all black Americans had rights that white Americans were bound to respect.[43]

Consensus among African Americans on the "red" issue explains why the *Detroit Tribune Independent* pointed out that the "lynch law is worse than communism,"[44] the *Chicago Defender* published an editorial titled "Why We Cannot Hate Reds,"[45] and Carl Murphy, editor of the *Baltimore Afro-American*, declared that "the Communists are going our way, for which Allah be praised."[46] Black activists had no quarrel with the support of communists—white or black—so long as they believed in the equality of black people. It was the color of one's politics, not the color of one's skin, that mattered as black Detroit forged alliances.[47]

Harry Bennett and Henry Ford took advantage of the UAW's administrative disorganization by attempting to split the union. As Charles Sorensen noted in his memoirs, when Bennett assured Henry Ford in 1937 that he could handle the UAW, Bennett did so, in part, because he enjoyed a cozy relationship with Martin, who, he said, "held uneasy sway" over the faction-ridden UAW.[48] Sketchy evidence suggests that, in the fall of 1938, Bennett tried to gain control over Martin's faction through a verbal agreement between the two. If Martin withdrew the UAW from the CIO and canceled the UAW cases before the National Labor Relations Board (NLRB), Ford would recognize the UAW as a bargaining agent for its own members, allow the wearing of union buttons, and reinstate union activists who had been fired. Henry Ford and Bennett would condone bringing Ford workers into a UAW-AFL union headed by Martin, but with Ford forces in control. As Nevins and Hill suggest, even though a lack of concrete evidence may keep us from knowing the full nature of the deal Martin and Bennett brokered, Martin "made a reprehensible mistake in accepting personal favors from Bennett and writing him an effusive note of thanks."[49] After this, it did not take long for several members of the UAW executive board to threaten to impeach Martin, at which point he officially resigned from the UAW-CIO.[50]

REORGANIZATION OF THE UAW-CIO

With the overthrow of Martin in early 1939, the protracted fighting within the UAW entered its final phase as both factions angled for control of the union's administrative apparatus. A special convention for the pro-Martin forces was held in Detroit on 4 March; the CIO held a special convention in Cleveland on 27 March to formally reorganize leadership of the UAW-CIO, having thrown Martin out.[51]

Although it was months before the drive to organize the FMC would be actively under way again, the concerns of black workers were raised and discussed at the special CIO convention in March. The list of issues presented at the Cleveland convention was the result of three meetings held by black UAW members in the weeks leading up to the larger convention. The first meeting, initiated by the Trade Union Committee of the NNC local, took place early in February at the Brewster Center; the committee discussed with Tracy M. Doll, a member of the International Executive Board of the UAW, the role that black workers could play in the reorganization of the UAW. The NNC local pressured Doll to put the organization of black Ford workers higher on the union's agenda and demonstrate its commitment to civil rights issues. LeBron Simmons pushed for a black seat on the executive board, and Christopher Alston, back in Detroit after organizing for the Southern Youth Conference, stressed placing blacks "in advanced positions of responsibility" as a way to draw more black workers into the UAW. Tracy Doll agreed with both Simmons and Alston but cautioned that such action could not precede the need to "carry on an intensive campaign of education among the white workers in order to break down the prejudices which many of them still have."[52]

The final list of demands for the convention included adding blacks to the organizing staff; giving black women the right to work in the offices of the locals and the international as well as on the production line in factories; giving blacks the same access that whites had to apprenticeships, promotion, training, and advancement; mandating that there be at least one black on the International Executive Board; and establishing a department of black and white workers to monitor problems of national minorities. Finally, union officials were singled out for compounding a bad situation when they did "not understand that the problems of the Negroes must be dealt with as such, apart from the regular problems of the whole membership."[53]

At the convention, Henry Clark, a black delegate and the executive secretary of the NNC local chapter in Flint, attempted to get the union to discuss including an African American on the board, but he was ruled out of order. R. J. Thomas, the UAW president, kept the issue from reaching the floor of the convention, standing firmly against attaching, as he phrased it, a "'Jim Crow' car" to the International Union. Clark presented, in addition, resolutions calling for an antidiscrimination clause for apprenticeships and promotions. Both measures died before reaching the floor.[54]

The UAW executives did, however, recommend black organizers for the "permanent" organizing staff, especially encouraging their presence on the Ford Organizing Committee. Walter Hardin was brought back to serve on the revived UAW staff as "General Negro Organizer."[55] Several weeks later, Thomas and Hardin, along with George Addes, secretary-treasurer for the UAW-CIO, met with black leaders at the Lucy Thurman YWCA. Both Addes and Thomas admitted there was discrimination in the auto industry and that unions had a lot of work to do to educate their own membership about the need for the unity of labor "with no exceptions because of race."[56]

While these measures were welcomed, more was needed to convince the rank and file that African Americans were owed the rights of labor. The fault lines of a new division were discernible—even after Martin's departure from the UAW-CIO—which contributed to the wait-and-see attitude taken by black workers. One faction was led by Walter Reuther, the other by George Addes. By 1939, the Reuther faction identified with the Association of Catholic Trade Unionists, which spoke to the interests of anticommunists, white southerners, and ethnics. The Addes faction was left-leaning and included some Communist Party members.[57] Hodges Mason, an African American activist in UAW Local 208 at Bohn Aluminum in Detroit, thought black workers evaluated the two factions in terms of what Reuther—thought by many to have "no use for Negroes in any shape or form, except as he can use them"—did not bring to the table, rather than what Addes and Thomas offered. Mason claimed, years later, that at the time of the UAW's reorganization, black workers were "left-wingers." But, he noted, "when we say left-wingers, we mean anti-Reutherites."[58]

Years of organizing by volunteers centered in the NNC's Trade Union Committee probably gave Veal Clough and Shelton Tappes an advantage, for they had built a trust that thrust them into leadership roles as the organizing process proceeded. Efforts initiated and shaped by the volunteering organizing campaign reinforced practical, grassroots tactics, often placing NNC organizers like Tappes at odds with UAW-CIO international officials. Meanwhile, the strategy devised by the leadership of the revamped auto union to win back UAW members pushed the UAW-CIO down a path relying less on shop-floor democracy and more on order and discipline from above.

As director of the UAW General Motors Department, Walter Reuther played a key role in the union's revival. First he went after GM workers, the single largest bloc of union members and key to the survival of the UAW-CIO. In May 1939 only 6 percent, or 12,000 of the 200,000 GM workers, were paying dues to the UAW-CIO.[59] Reuther turned the situation around with an approach that took some of the bite out of shop-floor bargaining. Called "power under control," Reuther's strategy demonstrated to management that the reorganized union was, according to Nelson Lichtenstein, "a disciplined, responsible organization," not one riddled with the chaotic militancy of the Martin years. For that reason, Reuther issued a warning against "individuals taking things into their own hands and causing a stoppage."[60] Reuther's tactics placed grievance arbitration under a permanent "umpire," an industrial supreme court that could rule on disputes. As Lichtenstein argues, the very nature of the "orderly system of industrial jurisprudence," maintained with a "web of rules" that regularized and limited management power, also shifted the "balance of class power into management's hands." Reuther's pact with GM was so order driven that sit-down strikes and wildcat strikes, tactics that created "disorder" for the purpose of increasing workers' leverage over capital's control, were not allowed.[61]

Next, the UAW focused on winning back workers at Chrysler.[62] A strike was called after negotiations over line speeds, quotas, and wages broke down between the union and Chrysler in the fall of 1939. Management locked out 24,000 workers—including 1,700 African Americans—from the Dodge Main Foundry and organized a back-to-work movement among its black employees.[63] A broad-based group of twenty-five prominent black professionals, ministers, and businessmen joined black autoworkers in opposition to the back-to-work movement.[64]

Senator Charles Diggs and Rev. White led the effort, organized by the NNC local chapter and its affiliated organizations, to rally the community against a corporation that, they said, was so callous it was willing to risk the lives of its black workers. White and Diggs were joined by, among others, Father Malcolm Dade, Rev. Hill, attorney Charles H. Mahoney, Rev. Peck, Wilbur Woodson, Louis Martin, Walter Hardin, and Percy Keyes. The group was united in opposition to using black workers as scabs. As the *Michigan Chronicle,* a black weekly based in Detroit, said, "No labor dispute should be permitted to result in a racial clash." Prejudice and racial discrimination "must be eliminated before our democracy can really work." In conclusion, the editors suggested that the "time has come when all the world should know that there is a New Negro in America." No longer can a "scab army" be recruited from the black community and be tricked "into pulling other people's chestnuts out of the fire."[65]

With the success of the united front against the back-to-work movement, the NNC local's alliance of civic leaders and union organizers gained steady support for the UAW-CIO.[66] Would the UAW-CIO utilize this opening to further an alliance between the union and blacks? While the union was grateful for the support of black leaders in exposing and then derailing the back-to-work movement, black workers still had questions about wage differentials, for example, between blacks and whites doing the same job. For all of the *United Automobile Worker*'s rhetoric proclaiming the UAW's race sensitivity, the union was remarkably silent when it came to how it would go about upgrading black workers in the new era. The thorn in the union's claw had not been extracted: how to resolve the conundrum of convincing black workers that a new day in labor relations would begin with the UAW-CIO without losing support from whites, especially southern white autoworkers.[67]

Reflecting on labor and the race question, Frank Winn, a UAW staff member and publicity agent for Reuther, noted that the officers of the UAW-CIO "do not deceive themselves that when a white worker signs an application card he automatically sloughs off the race prejudice which has been most probably instilled in him since he was a child, even though the union's constitution says it will not tolerate discrimination." Experience taught union officers that appeals to the unity and bonds of brotherhood were lost on many white workers.[68]

The international leadership of the UAW-CIO, however, did not have a unified approach for resolving racial discrimination issues. William Baltimore, elected as a union steward in 1937 in the Dodge Main Foundry and chairman of a black group within the plant called the "antidiscrimination group," recalled how frustrated black workers were in the mid- to late thirties because "the white elements within the Dodge plant refused to accept the Negro brothers and sisters as equals."[69] As black foundry organizer Joseph Billups put it, black workers "just didn't trust the union. They figured they would be used—used by white people, and then kicked out."[70] Were black Ford workers so naïve they took comfort in a UAW poster that proclaimed, "Organized Negroes always have the protection of their Union"?[71]

Problems continued to erupt over interracial social events, increasing black skepticism. Challenges that presumably were resolved in 1937 resurfaced in Local 235 a year later when a black member attended a picnic with a white woman, raising resentment among white members to a fever pitch. Locals with a large proportion of southern whites often were the most resistant to the full participation of black members. Within the city of Detroit, many entertainment establishments frequented by the white rank and file refused to accept black patrons, exacerbating any efforts by the international to enforce its written social policy. Until the UAW International took control over social issues away from the locals, issues of racial discrimination would continue to keep union members divided.[72] Perhaps this explains why some black Ford workers continued attending the Loyal Workers Club of the FMC to hear Donald Marshall talk and the Ford Dixie Eight, a choral group of black Ford workers sponsored by Henry Ford, perform.[73]

Union officials also had to consider to what extent a racially inclusive policy might alienate white supporters, which could harden rather than weaken the divide between black and white.[74] Lloyd Bailer suggested such a possibility after interviewing a white Packard worker and minor official in the union local in early 1940. The white unionist estimated that at Packard at that time about 40 percent of the workers were Polish and a large number of southern whites were employed there as well. He claimed "both of them are very prejudiced." The Packard worker explained that a "rumor got out not long ago that Negroes were going to start working in the trim department—where I work. Most of the men there are southern whites. They said, 'I'll be goddamned if I'm going to work with a goddamn black nigger.'"[75]

Race friction accompanying the advancement of black workers to higher positions within Detroit industry was so common by the late thirties and early forties that it was almost expected. Although Quill Pettway, a black graduate of the Ford Trade School, expected hostility from whites when he gained employment as a tool-and-dye maker at the FMC, he deeply resented having to negotiate his way through the thickets of his unit's work culture for months with no assistance from his fellow workers.[76]

While the UAW-CIO gained its footing as a revitalized labor union, the CRC and the NNC addressed interests outside the automotive industry, strongly pressing the theme of inclusion. One successful challenge was aimed at Detroit Edison, a campaign that led Daisy Lampkin, regional field secretary for the national NAACP, to ride the CRC's coattails as she appealed to Detroiters in the annual membership drive of the association. Lampkin hoped her alliance with Grigsby's group would project a new image of the local NAACP, overturning its depiction as a haven for the black elite. Grigsby's aim with this campaign involved two objectives. The broad theme was to use the challenge as yet another lesson in what black Detroiters needed to do to "take charge." More narrowly, the objective was to gain 800 new jobs for African Americans at the Detroit Edison.[77]

High school students went door-to-door throughout black Detroit collecting data on how much black Detroiters paid for their light bills.

Grigsby approached Detroit Edison, citing the forty jobs held by blacks at that time in relation to the amount the community paid the utility company. The spokesman for Edison noted that Grigsby did not have "access to our books" and asked how he could know how much blacks pay. At that point, Grigsby said, "We have the other side of your ledger-sheet," and then proceeded to "walk" thirty-two feet of adding-machine tape across the room to dramatize how much black Detroiters paid in just one day. The CRC/NAACP collaboration led to a significant number of new jobs at Detroit Edison for blacks. Lampkin's efforts paid off in another way: there was an impressive jump in memberships in the Detroit branch of the NAACP, from 3,283 to over 6,000 in 1938–39. By trying out new-crowd tactics and working with the CRC, the NAACP local chapter revitalized its base, suggesting the traction such tactics had at that time.[78]

The UAW missed opportunities during this period to join efforts initiated within the black community as a way to reach out to African Americans. Practices of the CIO in other regions of the Midwest—its campaigns to organize steel workers in Gary and South Bend, Indiana, and its efforts with packinghouse workers in Chicago—demonstrated an understanding of what Lizabeth Cohen calls a CIO "culture of unity," with its stress on gaining workers' loyalty. By paying attention to the social and cultural experiences that shaped workers' lives inside and outside the workplace, the CIO in many areas was able to motivate workers from diverse backgrounds to find common ground. The approach assumed that workers must change to overcome divisions that had pitted them against each other in the past.[79] It was instructive that the UAW-CIO did not take the initiative to do the same.

THE SECOND FORD ORGANIZING DRIVE, 1940–1941

Along with their white allies, African American trade unionists—many working as volunteers under the auspices of the NNC local—advanced the union cause months before the second union drive to organize the FMC and its black workers. By the early 1940s, organizers for the NNC effort included black activists Shelton Tappes, Veal Clough, David Moore, Paul Kirk, Joseph Billups, Percy Llewellyn, Norman Smith, Nelson Davis, Coleman Young, William Johnson, Art McPhaul, Horace Sheffield, Percy Keyes, and Christopher Alston. Bill McKie, a white communist, was a trusted and important ally.[80]

Black UAW-CIO organizers planning their successful campaign to organize the Ford Motor Company. From left to right: Joseph Billups, organizer; Walter Hardin, international representative; Christopher Alston (standing), publicity director; Veal Clough, organizer; Clarence Bowman (standing), organizer; Leon Bates, organizer; John Conyers Sr., organizer. 5 April 1941. Image courtesy of the Walter P. Reuther Library, Wayne State University.

The UAW paid some organizers; some were volunteers; others worked sometimes as volunteers and sometimes as paid staff. Veal Clough was paid by the UAW to organize at the Ford foundry by the late winter of 1939. David Moore worked as a volunteer in and outside the FMC, signing workers up for the UAW-CIO.[81] Art McPhaul, who was first hired by the FMC in 1928 and worked in the Pressed Steel department, regarded himself as a union activist from the early days of the Depression. He was for the union as soon as it emerged because he was "always anti-boss." Though not a member until after the strike in 1941, he "worked to help to support the union long before that, to organize, that sort of thing."[82]

Joseph Billups, who was on the first black staff developed by Homer Martin (see chapter 8), recalled transferring both his membership lists and cash over to the CIO after Martin was ousted in 1939. When the UAW was revamped, Billups was assigned to organize at the Rouge.[83] Although he worked at Ford, he took special measures to escape detection of his union activities by Ford service workers. "I got fired from the Rouge Plant for union activity and every time I got hired under different names . . . [until] they would find out and put me out of the plant." He finally resorted to joining the UAW through another local. Billups chose UAW Local 174 for his cover, pretending to be a worker at Murray Body, to fool the spies at the FMC.[84] Billups's story shows how one devoted black organizer plotted a path intended to keep him under management's radar. His struggle to keep up his organizing for the UAW illustrates why it is difficult to document precisely the role played by black Detroiters in the day-to-day, week-by-week maneuvers carried out during the period between 1938 and 1941. Throughout, Billups remained active within the NNC local.[85]

Sometime after the Cleveland convention, Veal Clough became a member of the Executive Board of the reconstituted UAW Local 600. With that promotion, Clough was able to draw from the "pin-money" available in the expense account of the Ford Drive to pay for his gas while organizing.[86] He was reinstated at Ford once the union successfully appealed Ford's anti-union behavior in the NLRB case in February 1941.[87]

Clough's role in the Ford Drive was significant. He had, according to Tappes, a tremendous following within the rank and file. "He was so sincere" that everyone believed in him. Blacks apparently loved him, but so did whites.[88] With a background like his, he became the perfect model for making workers understand the patience required to combat a corporate giant like the FMC. It took A. Philip Randolph and the Brotherhood of Sleeping Car Porters (BSCP) twelve years to get the Pullman Company to sign a labor contract. During that protracted struggle, company paternalism raised issues similar to those involved in Ford's unwritten agreement with the black community in Detroit. Clough "was not a learned man," in that he had not finished grammar school, Tappes observed, but as an organizer for the BSCP he was, no doubt, steeped in African American history, which Randolph and his union drew on heavily to break down resistance to the BSCP. Specifically, Randolph's campaign to organize the Pullman porters was aimed at breaking the old-guard strategy of politely asking the dominant culture for rights that should have already belonged to black Americans. According to Randolph, the way this etiquette of civility structured relations between blacks and whites left almost no room for collective self-assertion and independence.[89]

Shelton Tappes, who met Clough in 1937, recalled gravitating toward him because of the social vision that grounded his labor orientation. They became "very good friends," visited "back and forth with our wives in each other's home and discussed the ways and means by which we could make a better contribution to the organizing of Ford."[90] A devoted lieutenant to Randolph and his philosophy, Clough always made it his business to see Randolph whenever he could and built on the BSCP's strategy of winning the allegiance of proud black men who weighed their options in the late thirties with the larger history of African Americans' oppression in mind.[91]

Tappes, too, was inspired by Randolph's success in securing the BSCP contract with the Pullman Company in August 1937 and by Randolph's approach in "man-to-man organizing efforts." It was for this reason, re-called Tappes, that his pitch to whites was basically in terms of economics, whereas his appeal to blacks was "special," based on social equality and aimed at a chance to advance and to move out from under the dominance of whites.[92] From two different organizing approaches or appeals, two different sets of expectations emerged out of the Ford Organizing Drive. The tactic that appealed to black workers, cultivated by organizers like Veal Clough and Shelton Tappes, planted the union in the larger struggle for social justice. It was this vision that bolstered union support from people such as Rev. Hill, who firmly believed that industrial unions offered an opportunity to realize the promise of economic and, by extension, racial democracy.[93]

The Detroit Labor Day Parade in 1940 signaled that a new day had dawned for workers at the FMC. Ford workers marched under the banner of the FMC without their masks and sported union buttons. They also displayed a new float with an old Ford car up on a strut and Bill McKie at the wheel. The sign read: "As ancient as Hank's labor policies." (Within workers' circles Henry Ford was commonly referred to as "Hank.")[94] This was a sure indication that a new era was unfolding at the FMC. Shortly thereafter, the CIO, impatient with the UAW's foot-dragging, took partial charge of the Ford unionization drive.

Michael Widman, a CIO official from the United Mine Workers union, was sent to oversee the campaign to organize the FMC in the fall of 1940.[95] According to David Moore, Rev. Hill, who was head of the CRC and part of the NNC's Trade Union Committee at the time, told Mike Widman, during a meeting in the winter of 1940–41, that if the union relied on the same tactics used during earlier organizing campaigns at GM and Chrysler, "you're not going to organize Ford." By "the same tactics," Hill had in mind the fact that the UAW did not reach out to black workers and ignored black concerns about social issues.[96] Word soon spread within black Detroit that

Widman was listening to volunteer organizers who were working through the NNC's Trade Union Committee in the black community. Widman was not interested in red baiting; his attitude was simply "as long as you build the union, that's all I ask."[97] "He listened to us," remembered Moore.[98] As Tappes suggested, Widman's strategy marked a turning point because the black community felt that the UAW was finally sporting CIO colors.[99]

The transition in black Detroit from the volunteer network of NNC organizers to a focused Ford Organizing Drive was smooth. Widman piggybacked on the enormous underground alliance that had connected and sustained the "rump" Local 600 for months.[100] The transition worked, according to Tappes, because the officers of the River Rouge foundry's UAW Local 600 surrendered their positions and "turned the Local over to the International." Widman wanted this shift in order to take control out of the UAW local "so that no factionalism would interfere with getting the job done." Widman and John L. Lewis were, most likely, doubly motivated, realizing that if they could win a contract with Ford, they would gain a huge number of workers. Whoever controlled Local 600 at the Rouge would be a power bloc within the UAW-CIO.[101] Because aggressive union organizers in Local 600 connected the revised UAW-CIO to an agenda grounded in civil rights, the union won more support from black Ford workers.

In February 1941, when the Supreme Court ruled that the FMC was guilty of unfair labor practices, the UAW-CIO's Ford organizing campaign got a tremendous boost. One of the issues in dispute was the right to distribute pamphlets and literature outside the Rouge facility, the issue that had led to bloodshed in the Battle of the Overpass in 1937. Another involved Ford's discharging workers for union activity. After those two hurdles were removed, change came swiftly: union protesters greeted workers during a shift change with pamphlets; fired UAW organizers like Veal Clough were rehired in the foundry; and members sported union buttons openly at the Rouge.[102]

In fact, the proliferation of buttons and even caps that had the union logo on them within the foundry led to an almost carnival atmosphere, according to a Ford foreman. Workers smiled, they talked freely with each other, and they even laughed, right there on the shop floor. Some recalled, most likely, that not long before, John Gallo, a young rank-and-file organizer, was fired for laughing on the shop floor of the Rouge.[103] Al Smith, superintendent of the motor building, said the coming-out party for the union within the Rouge "just popped up all at once." Regular men who had been working at the FMC for years started signing up fellow workers for union membership. A man whom no one "even suspected because he was an old employee" suddenly went union. Lots of men wore union buttons, and "if Bennett's force tore them off, [the men] pinned them right on again." In this climate, as Nevins and Hill point out, "Bennett could no longer crack the whip."[104] The Ford unionization drive was finally out of the closet, in high gear.

During the critical 1940–41 period, the NNC played a key role in helping to break down lingering fears among black Ford workers. One successful method was demonstrating the broad-based support black Ford workers had within the community. Hesitant Ford workers were introduced to civic supporters behind the NNC alliance—people like Rev. Hill, Geraldine Bledsoe, Harold Bledsoe, and Vera Vandenberg—who then opened up discussions about basic fears like "being spotted."[105]

Within the foundry, starting in January 1941, Billups, Tappes, and Clough, all then on the staff and payroll of the UAW-CIO, along with many others, carried out several successful strategies to promote the union. Shelton Tappes recalled relying on the same strategy of independence and self-reliance that grew out of the volunteer organizing spirit engendered within the NNC local. Although Walter Reuther had hoped to control the Ford effort, once the national CIO took charge of the Ford campaign much of the forward momentum came from actions taken by shop-floor activists, such as Tappes and Clough.[106] Tappes was fond of saying that the foundry, during the period between January and March, "initiated a lot of things."[107] One of the more successful approaches, according to Tappes, was built around a grassroots steward system. When UAW officials "heard we had established a steward system they almost went to pieces," Tappes claimed. "They were sure we were premature . . . putting people on the spot to be fired and very vulnerable for attack from the company." Tappes and his colleagues stood their ground by insisting that since these activities were the "doings of Ford workers themselves, why should the Ford Organizing Committee stop it?"[108] Later, Tappes claimed that the grassroots steward system was wildly successful at the Rouge, bringing into the UAW-CIO hundreds of additional workers between January and the end of March.[109] He also recalled organizing a mini-sit-in with some of the more militant foundry unionists to demand a raise to 95 cents an hour. This action, too, was unauthorized by the union bureaucracy. Everyone who was earning less than 95 cents an hour received the raise. Tappes estimated

Shelton Tappes, seated in the first row, third from the right, as part of the first Ford UAW delegation at a Michigan CIO convention held in Jackson, Michigan, May 1941. Image courtesy the Walter P. Reuther Library, Wayne State University.

that this amounted to about 6,000 of the 13,000 foundry workers, but it is difficult to determine how accurate that figure was.[110]

From his plantation in Georgia, Henry Ford again promised he would "never submit to any union."[111] Nonetheless, concessions made by Bennett and his forces at times amounted to de facto recognition; at other times, clashes between the workers and management resulted in more men being fired. While workers were making progress on the shop floor, top officers within the UAW remained convinced that more time was needed for better organization before negotiating with the FMC and calling for a union vote. They were particularly concerned about whether the loyalty of the thousands of black workers could be counted on. Reuther had declared all unauthorized activities by groups of workers unacceptable, the very sort of actions that took place in the late winter and early spring of 1941 inside the Rouge. Soon union officials would realize the futility of trying to stop a moving train.[112] Meanwhile, workers barged into Widman's office pressuring him to call a strike to shut the plant down.[113] While Widman may have been sympathetic to such pleas and wanted to act, he also paid attention to the wishes of UAW officials. That all changed at the beginning of April.

Late on the afternoon of 1 April, after Bennett fired eight men, including the union leader in the rolling mill, thousands of workers shut down the River Rouge plant. The action was a wildcat strike, unauthorized by union officials of the UAW.[114] All the uncertainty about the loyalties of black workers was answered on that April Fools' Day. For those intensely involved in organizing black Ford workers during the previous several years, there was little doubt that the moment was right. It was several hours, however, before UAW officials—Addes, Thomas, Reuther, and Frankensteen—knew what to make of the rumors flying through Detroit broadcasting the fact that "Ford's Down."[115] While union officials debated, thousands of workers—black and white—carried out the first stage of the strike by moving from the rolling mill through the Rouge complex, shutting down every department in their path.[116] Black UAW-CIO union organizers inside the plant took measures to prevent any incidents between the races.[117] In the gear and axle plant, six rank-and-file union members, including David Moore, pulled the switch to shut down their section.[118] UAW leaders sanctioned the workers' initiative, officially calling a strike against Ford at 12:15 A.M. on 2 April. When they did, they yielded to the actions of shop-floor workers, allowing the tail to wag the dog.[119]

Most of the black workers who walked and joined whites on the picket lines outside the factory were veterans from the foundry and did not return until after the strike.[120] The action they took was not so much impulsive as it was opportune. Veteran black Ford workers had finely tuned networks keeping them abreast of actions on the shop floor. Of those black workers who stayed in the plant, most were new to Detroit and the FMC, recently recruited by Harry Bennett, who paid them at least a dollar an hour.[121] The company, hoping that large numbers of black workers would fight the union, began hiring blacks in unusually large numbers on 11 February 1941. The hiring continued for two weeks and then slacked off for a month. About ten days before the strike, the massive hiring of unemployed black workers began again. By the end of March, Ford had its largest black workforce ever at the Rouge, some 14,000 to 16,000 men, well in excess of the average of between 10,000 and 12,000. The foundry was so crowded that many of the workers did little more than loll about.[122]

Walter White, secretary of the NAACP, flew to Detroit to add his support to the strike and talk strikebreakers out of the plant. He took a gamble, knowing that if the UAW did not deliver on its promise to put an end to discrimination against black Americans, the "NAACP and I are going to be on the spot." He took the chance because he realized that the Ford strike went beyond just union representation. It represented the "new order of things" in "the eyes" of African Americans in Detroit and the nation.[123] The Reverends Charles Hill, Horace White, and Malcolm Dade, as well as John Dancy and Horace Sheffield of the NAACP's Youth Council, made appeals to black strikebreakers to leave the Rouge. Once the UAW assured their safety, over 1,000 left by 4 April. The black workers who stayed inside the plant, Hill argued, did not understand "what it was all about."[124] They were not part of the larger black community in Detroit and its two-decade-long relationship with the FMC, which had led to the transfer of allegiance from Henry Ford to the UAW.

Those who did walk out did much more than demonstrate their solidarity with white Ford workers. By acting as they did, black Ford workers turned not only against labor relations rooted in Ford's paternalism and against dependency on the goodwill of powerful whites, but also against what was once considered a revolutionary plan for including African Americans in jobs across the occupational spectrum at the FMC. They voted with their feet for independence from domination and control by Henry Ford over the way they made a living and a life. But they did so in a way that sustained the momentum of self-determination cultivated by volunteer organizers and others actively engaged in challenges carried out under the auspices of the CRC and the NNC local. Walking out was not about exchanging one form of domination for another. Black Ford workers let it be known that until the UAW's organizing campaign recognized them as equal partners and addressed their special concerns, the UAW was not going to get their support. Decades later, David Moore, who for months organized for the UAW in the shadows of black Detroit without pay and without recognition, remembered UAW's leaders acting as though they just did not care about black workers at the Rouge.[125] The decision to turn against Henry Ford and his labor policies was not arrived at overnight. It emerged after years of toil at the FMC and years of struggle to expand and build upon the opportunities first opened up by Henry Ford.

When African Americans turned the corner to support the UAW, they did so for many reasons. Chief among them was the determination to advance the ongoing black freedom struggle, the issue motivating NNC

Strike leaders confer on strategy during the Ford Organizing Campaign, April 1941. From left to right: Walter Hardin, James Morgan, Arthur Johnson, Hosea Young (Local 208 hat), and Joe Billups (Local 600 hat). Image courtesy of the Walter P. Reuther Library, Wayne State University.

leader Rev. Hill and many others. Whether one worked at the FMC or not, the company's influence reached far and wide within black Detroit. By 1941 approximately half of Detroit's black male wage earners were employees of the FMC.[126] For many, the FMC was the battleground not just for jobs, but also for justice. Veal Clough's success as an organizer was related to the fact that he connected the larger black freedom struggle to support for the UAW. The new order envisioned by Clough was to use the union as a vehicle for advancing racial democracy. Shelton Tappes also imagined a UAW-CIO embracing social unionism, with the union serving as a base for expanding civil rights for the entire community.[127]

When black Ford workers turned against Henry Ford and joined the union cause, they did not act alone. The effort represented a sea change within black Detroit, as the progressive forces within the community forged a new approach to gaining democratic rights. Not all black Detroiters joined in celebrating the new contract with the UAW. Serious differences existed among the leadership class and within the clergy. Before the NLRB vote on the union, the Baptist Ministers Conference went on record twice in endorsing Henry Ford and his company. Forty ministers signed the statement of support for an anti-union position. Rev. Bradby, however, was not one of them.[128] Did his silence mean support for the union and the beginning of another chapter in the long struggle for equality? Perhaps. Bradby's great success as a minister, after all, was linked to his ability to keep his finger on the pulse of the people.

Henry Ford, too, was at least partially responsible for the larger role black Ford workers expected from the new union. By including black workers in his American Plan, Ford raised their expectations about gaining a more equal place in America. He inspired newly arrived African Americans in Detroit to view work at the Rouge in terms larger than making a living wage. Black Ford workers "made the extra effort" to demonstrate that they could outperform other workers across the occupational spectrum. Labor relations at the FMC had always been about much more than just what one did at work. They involved how one voted, whether one was thrifty, what car one drove, how clean one's house was, and the nature of community institutions, most notably the churches.[129]

Loyalty to Henry Ford and the FMC was complicated, but it was never as one-dimensional as outsiders suspected. However, Ford's revised labor policies of the 1930s—particularly turning the foundry into a virtually all-black department—tarnished the social compact that had kept many black workers loyal. Perhaps Ford's foundry policy encouraged the atrophying of black workers' allegiance. With the transformation of the foundry's workforce, Ford introduced a politics of racial exclusion, reinforcing the notion that better jobs were for white men only. What were black Ford workers who had made the extra effort for all those years to think? Had they just come full circle?

By the time Ford took off his gloves, black Detroit had expanded its expectations well beyond economic opportunity. The labor-oriented civil rights agenda endorsed by the CRC and the NNC local grew out of black Detroiters' experiences during a two-decade-long settlement process. The agenda, infused by the Social Gospel tendencies present within activist community networks, was carried forward through the revolution at the Rouge and continued to shape black workers' expectations for the union well into the 1940s. In time, UAW officials understood that even though they had succeeded in conquering the open shop at the FMC, the larger war for unity and stability going forward might be more of a challenge than they originally bargained for. The breakthrough at Ford complicated UAW politics for many years as unauthorized shop-floor conflicts continued, much to the frustration of union officials. The Rouge workers' UAW Local 600 became known as the most militant union local in the country.

For over a decade it remained, as Nelson Lichtenstein noted, a "cockpit of factionalism" and the elusive prize sought by Walter Reuther and his union rivals.[130]

During April and May 1941, *Ford Facts* distributed the writings of black organizers at the FMC and the testimonials of national black leaders like Paul Robeson who endorsed the efforts to vote for the UAW-CIO. Christopher Alston's pamphlet *Henry Ford and the Negro People* was widely distributed.[131] Michael Widman, the CIO official overseeing the Ford unionization campaign, brought Robeson to Detroit for a concert two days before the historic union vote at Ford, boosting black support for the UAW-CIO after the successful strike. An estimated 60,000 people heard Robeson sing "Ballad for Americans" in Cadillac Square. One line declared, "Our country's strong, our country's young, and her greatest songs are still unsung."[132] The sweeping victory of the UAW-CIO in the union election of 21 May 1941 yielded more than a victory for the UAW, for the UAW accord also signaled the beginning of a new day for African Americans. Black Detroiters carried the chords of another song—"still unsung"—locked in their resolve to make their new relationship with organized labor a model for civil rights unionism. With the UAW contract, black Detroiters took a giant step toward fuller inclusion in the promise of America. Years later, Geraldine Bledsoe, addressing what the NNC local had taught the black community through its labor organizing process, said they learned "that they could make their way in this democratic society, and that they had to be vigorous and uncompromising and demanding in order to find their place."[133] It was a lesson they did not soon forget.

EPILOGUE

HENRY FORD transformed the United States and the world by revolution-izing the way we make things. But the man so responsible for reconstruct-ing industrial production also transformed human relations. As he ob-served, "Power and machinery, money and goods, are useful only as they set us free to live. They are but means to an end." He hoped the success of the FMC would demonstrate the soundness of his approach, which "looks toward making this world a better place in which to live."[1] When Ford invited African American men to work for the FMC, he looked to them as good strike insurance, but he also envisioned his revolutionary policies for hiring black workers as a way to "do some good." He hoped to transform their lives in positive ways, just as he had changed the lives of many oth-ers. As he told Samuel S. Marquis, the head of his Sociological Depart-ment, "All that man needs is an opportunity that has some hope in it, some promise for the years to come."[2]

African Americans took the keys Ford offered, opened the door to eco-nomic opportunity at the FMC, and walked into a new era. The right to walk through that door on an equal basis with whites had eluded black Americans since Emancipation. When Henry Ford rejected the notion that better jobs were for white men only, he raised black expectations about what was possible in America. Black workers in the twenties held positions at the FMC as electricians, bricklayers, crane operators, diamond cutters, and tool-and-die makers. They were included in apprenticeship programs at the Ford Trade School. Henry Ford's American Plan for black workers, incorporating them into his open-shop movement on an equal basis, was their best deal in American industry at the time. And black Ford workers, their families, and the black community were grateful. A corner had been turned in the larger, ongoing black freedom struggle.

The initial bond between Henry Ford, black Ford workers, and the black community was tied to their mutual aspirations. Ford expected loyalty and allegiance from his black workers as well as the larger community, thus reducing the threat of unionism. African Americans were anxious to prove that they were worthy of inclusion in Henry Ford's new-age industrial jobs, demonstrating their allegiance to both Ford and the American way. The work for most was hard. As speedups increased during the twenties, the Rouge became a hellhole. White workers who could often quit to pursue less arduous employment, but the racially restrictive polices at other auto companies left black workers with few alternatives. Black Ford workers, noted for making the extra effort, allowed the FMC to capitalize on the broader industry's restrictive racial policies and hire the best black workers. A key consideration for Ford was the high incidence of marriage among his black workforce, an important guarantee of stability and loyalty.

Black Ford workers bore the direct, physical costs required to fulfill their part of the arrangement. Known as "Ford mules," they had high rates of tuberculosis, pneumonia, and general ill health. But the benefits of work at the FMC were also personal and political. Ford wages took black workers and their families to a higher level of status, and the prosperity of black Detroit was yoked to the circulation of Ford dollars. Black workers made the extra effort without complaint not just because employment at the FMC was the best job in town. A Ford badge was worn with pride for the milestone it represented and the respect it garnered from the black community.

But a job at the FMC was only a first step on the road to fuller inclusion. A second step was made when, in 1923, black Detroiters turned out in large numbers to support Frank Murphy for judge on Detroit's Recorder's Court. African Americans were drawn to Murphy because he championed the rights of excluded blacks and Catholic immigrants and invited them to participate in the political process. The election not only demonstrated the willingness of black Detroiters to exercise their democratic rights as citizens; it also initiated a long-term, mutually beneficial relationship between Frank Murphy and the black community. For the next decade, participation in Frank Murphy's "new deal" coalition greatly expanded black expectations for equal treatment. The experience provided an opportunity for African Americans to use the tools of democracy to push back restrictions and open up opportunity. Valuable networks formed during the twenties provided staging grounds for political action during the thirties.

The developing relationship with Murphy revealed, however, a basic incompatibility between Ford's American Plan for his black workers and black Detroiters' new aspirations. Ford's plan, tied to his desire for control extending well beyond the shop floor and factory gates, was based on the creation of a grateful black community united in its support for Ford's political candidates, his ideas of how blacks ought to live their private lives, and his opposition to organized labor. African Americans, on the other hand, subscribed to a more expansive view that included their right to self-determination. Ford's American Plan for black workers was fraught with frustration as black Detroiters tried to balance issues of inclusion versus those of control.

These issues came to a head when Frank Murphy ran for mayor of Detroit against Henry Ford's candidate in the early thirties. The support that the Reverend Robert L. Bradby gave to Frank Murphy during this campaign showed just how complicated the question of allegiance had become. By the time of the Depression, loyalty to Henry Ford was bound up with gratitude for a job during hard times, even as loyalty to Frank Murphy and his politics increased. From this point forward, two factors—one economic and one political—drove the relationships between Henry Ford, black Ford workers, and black Detroiters as the community turned from a pro-Ford to a pro-union position.

The Depression took its toll on Detroit. Black Detroiters suffered disproportionately, but the decreased demand for automobiles created a crisis for Henry Ford as well. His response to the Depression at the local level revealed his dark side, one seldom publically seen in the past. The Rouge, closed for part of 1932, was the destination for a peaceful march of several thousand unemployed autoworkers, largely Ford employees, in March of that year. The workers, greeted by agents of the FMC's private police force with bullets, not bread, were turned away after four were killed. When the Rouge resumed operations in 1933, Henry Ford's black labor policy was more restrictive and exclusive than before, transforming the foundry from an integrated department into one that was virtually all black. The shift was hard to ignore. Transforming the foundry into a "black" job represented a giant step back to the place where black workers started when they left the South.

In addition, Ford, obsessed with keeping unions out of his company, ramped up surveillance over both white and black workers at the Rouge as well as within their respective communities. It can be argued that Ford's fixation on unions may not have served him well, at least with regard to his black workers. Initially, he had little to fear from the UAW, as the various factions within its leadership jockeyed for power. At the least, Ford's response to the new unionization movement supported by New Deal policies suggested that he was no longer an innovative industrial genius.

Two local organizations—the Detroit Civic Rights Committee and the Detroit branch of the National Negro Congress (NNC)—cultivated interest in the new union movement sanctioned by the New Deal. New-crowd activists marshaled support for the idea that a union could serve as a base for initiating social change. Volunteer labor organizing, under the direction of the Trade Union Committee of the NNC local, focused on enlisting support for labor unions from diverse elements within the community—black Ford workers, professionals, clergy, and others. From these efforts and others, a labor-oriented civil rights agenda emerged within black Detroit. By the time the UAW-CIO launched its Ford Organizing Drive of 1940, the mobilization by progressive forces within black Detroit served as a bridgehead for the UAW's campaign.

At the end of the thirties, a cost-benefit analysis of the union option by black workers might have revealed more indecision than clear direction. At the River Rouge, while black workers still could be found throughout the plant, their increasing concentration in foundry jobs was a cause for concern. In addition, the equal pay between black and white workers, once expected at Ford, was diluted with the introduction in the foundry of a de facto racial pay differential. Finally, Henry Ford's image as a benevolent industrialist was in shambles for many reasons, but the Reign of Terror carried out by Harry Bennett's army of thugs was particularly repugnant. The question remained: would black workers be used by the union to get their votes and then pushed aside and ignored?

Much of the gratitude the black community had traditionally felt toward Ford had been replaced by fear. By suppressing disobedient black ministers who allowed A. Philip Randolph and Dr. Mordecai Johnson to speak from their pulpits and firing black workers who did not vote for Ford's candidates, the Ford system for controlling behavior in black Detroit rose to a new level. The job security that had been a hallmark for all workers, particularly blacks, at Ford eroded during the Great Depression with layoffs, pay cuts, part-time work, and the transformation of the foundry into a largely black unit. When workers tried to protest with their feet—as they did during the Hunger March and the Battle of the Overpass—Ford responded with violence. But how did the UAW propose to overcome the prejudice of white unionists who resisted job promotions for African Americans?

As the thirties turned into the forties and all eyes in Detroit were on the FMC, black workers and the community weighed the advantages and disadvantages of Henry Ford's open shop versus the UAW. In assessing the situation, several questions loom large: (1) Did black Detroiters turn their backs on Henry Ford because they enthusiastically embraced the UAW? (2) Did they choose the UAW because it was the least offensive alternative? (3) Were black workers pushed to act by an ungrateful Henry Ford, whose policies increasingly narrowed their economic opportunities? Wherever the truth may lie, it does seem that when black Ford workers removed their masks of loyalty, they were standing up not so much *to* Henry Ford as *for* the contract that appeared most likely to keep the door to equal economic opportunity open.

The new-crowd organizing within the black community focused on the need to view labor unions as a means to expand the range of opportunities opened to African Americans. The collaboration of communists and communist sympathizers provided important support, as did the participation of several activist ministers who were led by spiritual principles grounded in the Social Gospel. For several years, while black Ford workers and the black community appeared to take a "wait and see" approach to the UAW, the black community moved forward to develop its own version of civil rights unionism. The agenda adopted by labor and civil rights activists in Detroit grew out of experiences shaping that particular community during the two-decade settlement period between World War I and World War II. The "wait and see" phase of the late thirties was about much more than simply embracing a pro-union position, on the one hand, or remaining loyal to Henry Ford, on the other. It reflected a deep-seated desire to take another giant step toward full inclusion in the promise of America, but not until the opportune moment arrived.

When that moment arrived, black Detroiters were prepared to help shape the historic Ford-UAW labor contract, hailed by the *Michigan Chronicle* as a model agreement. For the black community, it was nothing less. A key feature was the unprecedented nondiscrimination clause: "Provisions of this contract shall apply to all employees covered by this agreement, without discrimination on account of race, color, national origin or creed." Clause No. 78, the antidiscrimination clause, was the handiwork of Shelton Tappes, a member of the union's negotiating team and chairman of the Ford foundry. In the mid-forties, Tappes continued his efforts to expand the UAW's work for social and economic equality as recording secretary of the 60,000-member Local 600.[3]

With the labor agreement, Rouge Local 600 turned into a power block of historic proportions. It was the largest union local in the United States. But it was historic not just for its size or even for the large proportion of African Americans in its ranks. The black workers at Ford had successfully negotiated their way through the hills and valleys of Henry Ford's new era for African American labor. They came to Detroit anxious to work at Ford in order to be included in the remarkable experiment Henry Ford unleashed in the early twenties. He was able to hire married, committed workers who made the extra effort, driven by the power of raised expectations. Since the early twenties, they had demonstrated in countless ways throughout the vast River Rouge factory their ability to handle highly skilled jobs, manage construction projects, oversee nonblack workers as foremen, and take the heat in the foundry. They did not approach the UAW with hat in hand.

The marriage that ultimately took place between black Ford workers and the UAW, it could be argued, united a reluctant groom and an anxious bride. While that may be, it is important to note that the groom held a few aces. For when black Ford workers joined the UAW, they did so not out of desperation but, rather, in the hope of fulfilling the economic expectations raised by opportunities at the FMC and their political participation during the 1920s and 1930s. Economic and political inclusion boosted the resolve of black Detroiters to advance, still further, the promise of democracy and racial equality in America. Black Ford workers joined the new compact uniting autoworkers at the FMC, hoping the relationship would be a model for greater economic democracy and social citizenship. With the alliance, black Detroiters began writing another chapter in the unfinished struggle for racial and economic justice, carrying expectations raised by Henry Ford to a higher level even as they divorced themselves from his control.

NOTES

ABBREVIATIONS

In addition to the abbreviations found in the text, the following abbreviations are used in notes.

ACDP Americanization Committtee of Detroit Papers, Bentley Historical Library, University of Michigan, Ann Arbor

ACTUC Association of Catholic Trade Unionists Collection, Archives of Labor and Urban Affairs, Walter P. Reuther Library, Wayne State University, Detroit

ALUA Archives of Labor and Urban Affairs, Walter P. Reuther Library, Wayne State University, Detroit

BHC Burton Historical Collection, Detroit Public Library, Detroit

BHL Bentley Historical Library, University of Michigan, Ann Arbor

BFRC Benson Ford Research Center, The Henry Ford, Dearborn, Michigan

BLM Black Labor Movement Oral Histories, Archives of Labor and Urban Affairs, Walter P. Reuther Library, Wayne State University, Detroit

CMAP Chris and Marti Alston Papers, Archives of Labor and Urban Affairs, Walter P. Reuther Library, Wayne State University, Detroit

DCLP Detroit Citizens League Papers, Burton Historical Collection, Detroit Public Library, Detroit

DULP Detroit Urban League Papers, Bentley Historical Library, University of Michigan, Ann Arbor

FMP Frank Murphy Papers, Bentley Historical Library, University of Michigan, Ann Arbor

JGP Josephine Gomon Papers, Bentley Historical Library, University of Michigan, Ann Arbor

MHC Michigan Historical Collections, Bentley Historical Library, University of Michigan, Ann Arbor

MKP Milton Kemnitz Papers, Bentley Historical Library, University of Michigan, Ann Arbor

MOR Mayor's Office Records, Burton Historical Collection, Detroit Public Library, Detroit

MSP Maurice Sugar Papers, Archives of Labor and Urban Affairs, Walter P. Reuther Library, Wayne State University, Detroit

NAACPP   National Association for the Advancement of Colored People,
          Papers, Library of Congress, Washington, D.C.
NGC   Nat Ganley Collection, Archives of Labor and Urban Affairs,
          Walter P. Reuther Library, Wayne State University, Detroit
NNC Papers National Negro Congress Papers, Microfilm, Schomburg Center
          for Research on Black Culture, New York Public Library, New York,
          and Library of Congress, Washington, D.C.
SBCP   Second Baptist Church Papers, Bentley Historical Library,
          University of Michigan, Ann Arbor
TU-OH   Talking Union, Oral Histories, Archives of Labor and Urban
          Affairs, Walter P. Reuther Library, Wayne State University, Detroit
UAW-OH   UAW Oral Histories, Archives of Labor and Urban Affairs,
          Walter P. Reuther Library, Wayne State University, Detroit
UM-HS   University of Michigan, History Seminars, Department of History,
          Bentley Historical Library, University of Michigan, Ann Arbor

INTRODUCTION

1. Henry Ford quoted in Nye, *Henry Ford*, 71.

2. Garet Garrett, "The World That Henry Ford Made," *Look*, 25 March 1952, 35, cited in Brinkley, *Wheels for the World*, 113. For changes in social behavior inspired by the automobile, see Bailey, *From Front Porch to Back Seat*.

3. Watts, *People's Tycoon*, x.

4. The links between black Detroit and Henry Ford and his industrial policies mark the boundary line for the treatment that follows. Life for black workers at other auto plants is not part of this study.

5. Litwack, *Trouble in Mind*; Hahn, *Nation under Our Feet*.

6. Eric Foner, *Free Soil, Free Labor, Free Men*, xxvii–xxix.

7. Eric Foner, *Story of American Freedom*, 185–93.

8. *Dearborn Independent*, "Ford's Page," 17 June, 6 and 21 October 1922, 5.

9. Nevins and Hill, *Ford: Expansion*, 111–13, 145, 159.

10. Carlson, "The Negro in the Industries of Detroit," 61. Henry Ford's desire for maintaining control in the aftermath of World War I drove him to adopt what Steven Meyer calls a more "hard-nosed, pragmatic, and tough" stand, a variant of the American Plan, "which typified the more recalcitrant employer attitudes of the twenties." Nevertheless, it was a big step forward for black workers. See Meyer, *Five Dollar Day*, 169.

11. Litwack, *Trouble in Mind*, 492. This study is intended to extend the conversation exploring the Great Migration as a grassroots social movement between World War I and World War II. As such, it builds on an extensive scholarship that includes, but is not limited to, Chad Williams, *Torchbearers of Democracy*; Reich, "Great War, Black Workers, and the Rise and Fall of the NAACP in the South" and *Encyclopedia of the Great Black Migration*; Trotter, *Black Milwaukee* and *Great Migration in Historical Perspective*; Grossman, *Land of Hope*; Gottlieb, *Making Their Own Way*; Phillips, *AlabamaNorth*; Lemke-Santangelo, *Abiding Courage*; Arnesen, *Black Protest and the Great Migration* and

Brotherhoods of Color; Bates, *Pullman Porters and the Rise of Protest Politics*; Jordan, *Black Newspapers and America's War for Democracy*; Nikki Brown, *Private Politics and Public Voices*; Gregory, *Southern Diaspora*.

12. Meier and Rudwick, *Black Detroit*, 5.

13. For black leaders as conservatives, see ibid., 32; Christopher Johnson, *Maurice Sugar*.

14. Craig, "Automobiles and Labor," 90.

15. Boyle, *Arc of Justice*; Zunz, *Changing Face of Inequality*; Fragnoli, *Transformation of Reform*; Fine, *Frank Murphy*; Levine, *Internal Combustion*; Richard Thomas, *Life for Us Is What We Make It*; Wolcott, *Remaking Respectability*; Dillard, *Faith in the City*; Babson et al., *Working Detroit*.

16. This study builds on the growing scholarship investigating civil rights unionism in the thirties and later. See, especially, Feurer, "William Sentner, the UE, and Civic Unionism in St. Louis"; Honey, *Black Workers Remember*, esp. 237–85, and *Going Down Jericho Road*; Korstad, *Civil Rights Unionism*; Rubio, *There's Always Work at the Post Office*, 9–11. This project also hopes to add to the larger conversation exploring the long civil rights movement by linking the struggle for jobs with that for freedom. Works that have enriched that discussion include, in addition to the above, Zieger, *For Jobs and Freedom*; de Jong, *A Different Day*; Halpern, *Down on the Killing Floor*; Horowitz, *Negro and White, Unite and Fight*; Honey, *Going Down Jericho Road*; Minchin, *Hiring the Black Worker* and *Color of Work*; Thompson, *Whose Detroit?*; Needleman, *Black Freedom Fighters in Steel*; Cayton and Mitchell, *Black Workers and the New Unions*; Eric Foner, *Nothing but Freedom*.

17. Korstad and Lichtenstein, "Opportunities Found and Lost," 787.

18. Literature on civil rights activism in the urban North and West has greatly extended the discussion of the larger black freedom struggle. A short list of relevant studies includes Sugrue, *Sweet Land of Liberty*; Countryman, *Up South*; Quintard Taylor, "Civil Rights Movement in the American West"; Theoharis and Woodard, *Freedom North*; Rhonda Williams, *Politics of Public Housing*; Needleman, *Black Freedom Fighters in Steel*; Biondi, *To Stand and Fight*; Dillard, *Faith in the City*; Self, *American Babylon*; Thompson, *Whose Detroit?*; Woodard, *A Nation within a Nation*; Ralph, *Northern Protest*; Phillips, *AlabamaNorth*; Richard Thomas, *Life for Us Is What We Make It*; Kurashige, *Shifting Grounds of Race*. This study was influenced as well by several southern and community studies focusing on the importance of following the trail blazed by local community activists who sought a path through the thickets of local racial domination. Pertinent works include Morris, *Origins of the Civil Rights Movement*; Payne, *I've Got the Light of Freedom*; Chafe, *Civilities and Civil Rights*; Dittmer, *Local People*; Kelley, *Hammer and Hoe*.

19. Reich, *Encyclopedia of the Great Black Migration*, 1:xxxv; Jacquelyn Hall, "Long Civil Rights Movement," 1239; see also Self and Sugrue, "Power of Place," 20.

20. Studies on the Great Migration include Grossman, *Land of Hope*; Gregory, *Southern Diaspora*; Reich, "Great Migration and the Literary Imagination," and *Encyclopedia of the Great Black Migration*; Arnesen, *Black Protest and the Great Migration*; Wilkerson,

Warmth of Other Suns; Berlin, *Making of African America*; Wright, *Black Boy*; Earl Lewis, *In Their Own Interests*; Gottlieb, *Making Their Own Way*; Trotter, *Great Migration in Historical Perspective*. Studies on black religion include Dillard, *Faith in the City*; Best, *Passionately Human, No Less Divine*; Cynthia Taylor, *A. Philip Randolph*; Clarence Taylor, *Black Religious Intellectuals*; Luker, *Social Gospel in Black and White*; Ronald White, *Liberty and Justice for All*; Sernett, *Bound for the Promised Land*. Studies on the role of New Deal politics include Sitkoff, *New Deal for Blacks*; Sullivan, *Days of Hope*; Alan Brinkley, *Liberalism and Its Discontents*; Fraser and Gerstle, *Rise and Fall of the New Deal Order*; Jackson, *Crabgrass Frontier*; Lieberman, *Shifting the Color Line*; Poole, *Segregated Origins of Social Security*.

21. Young, with Wheeler, *Hard Stuff*, 45.

CHAPTER ONE

1. Strauss, *Images of the American City*, 25, cited in Tichnor, "Motor City," 135; Zunz, *Changing Face of Inequality*, 16–17.

2. Between 1904 and 1909, Detroit's industrial production increased 97 percent; between 1914 and 1919, it increased 357 percent. For statistics, see Kocher, *Economic and Physical Growth of Detroit*, 60–61, MHC. See also Zunz, *Changing Face of Inequality*, 286; Tichnor, "Motor City," 136–41.

3. Nevins and Hill, *Ford: Expansion*, 9; Chandler, *Giant Enterprise*, 3.

4. Zunz, *Changing Face of Inequality*, 286–88; Bureau of the Census, *Abstract of Thirteenth Census*, 1910, 95; *Abstract of the Fourteenth Census, 1920*, 108–9; *Abstract of the Fifteenth Census, 1930*, 98–99; Akers and Kemnitz, "Southern White Migration," 24–33, box 3, MKP; Tichnor, "Motor City," 168.

5. Tichnor, "Motor City," 168, 171, 173; Chicago Commission on Race Relations, *Negro in Chicago*, 80; Fusfeld and Bates, *Political Economy of the Urban Ghetto*, 25.

6. During the first week in May 1920, Washington counted 1,809 blacks arriving from the South. Washington, *Negro in Detroit* (1920), chap. 5, part A, "The Historical Background of the Negro in Detroit from 1800–1920," BHC. For the post–World War I downturn, see John C. Dancy, "Report on Migration of Negroes to Detroit since 1920," 18 August 1926, response to request of Charles S. Johnson, 16 August 1926, box 1, folder 18, DULP; Peterson, "Black Automobile Workers in Detroit," 177; Marks, *Farewell*, 1, 122; Martin, *Detroit and the Great Migration*, 1, 4.

7. Young, *Hard Stuff*, 15; "Negroes in Michigan," John C. Dancy, 1933, 19, box 74, folder: "Negroes in Michigan," DULP; Washington, *Negro in Detroit* (1920), chap. 5, "Migration," BHC.

8. Scott, *Negro Migration during the War*, 22–25.

9. Young, *Hard Stuff*, 15.

10. Ibid., 15; Young's analysis is similar to that of Leon F. Litwack, who argues that "rather than cite a specific grievance, many prospective migrants ascribed their decision to the totality of their experience in the South." See Litwack, *Trouble in Mind*, 490; compare with Marks, *Farewell*, 166–70.

11. Anderson, *A. Philip Randolph*, 53.

12. A. Philip Randolph, "The Indictment," *Messenger*, April 1926, 114. Bates, *Pullman Porters and the Rise of Protest Politics*, 3–4.

13. Wilkerson, *Warmth of Other Suns*, 160; Litwack, *Trouble in Mind*, 477. For more on the politics of black southern resistance to Jim Crow, see Higginbotham, *Righteous Discontent*; Paula Giddings, *When and Where I Enter*; Hunter, *To 'Joy My Freedom*; Woodruff, "African-American Struggles for Citizenship in the Deltas"; Salem, *To Better Our World*; Painter, *Exodusters*; Wells-Barnett, "A Red Record"; Norrell, *Reaping the Whirlwind*; Rosengarten, *All God's Dangers*; Kelley, *Hammer and Hoe*; Kelley, "'We Are Not What We Seem'"; Trotter, *Coal, Class, and Color*; Arnesen, *Waterfront Workers of New Orleans*; McMillen, *Dark Journey*; Hahn, *A Nation under Our Feet*.

14. Grossman, *Land of Hope*, 13; Litwack, *Trouble in Mind*, 493–94; Scott, *Negro Migration during the War*, 24.

15. Washington, *Negro in Detroit* (1920), chap. 5, "Migration," BHC. Washington viewed his survey as a contribution because it examined the "causes for migration as given by Negroes after having arrived in the North and discussed these causes based on information given to Negro investigators." The black migrant, "feeling secure in the northern environment and talking to one of his own race, has been more frank in giving the real reason" for his migration than he would discussing causes while still in the South or with white investigators.

16. Grossman, *Land of Hope*, 13; Fusfeld and Bates, *Political Economy of the Urban Ghetto*, 25; Wilkerson, *Warmth of Other Suns*, 160–61. For total immigration figures, U.S. Bureau of Immigration, *Annual Report of the Commissioner-General of Immigration, 1922*, 108, cited in Spear, *Black Chicago*, 131.

17. Berlin, *Making of African America*, 154–58; Grossman, *Land of Hope*, 13–14; Alexander, "Demographic Patterns of the Great Black Migration," 237; Marks, *Farewell*, 1. Labor agents played a relatively minor role in bringing African Americans to Detroit. Forrester Washington found that less than 1 percent of the black migrants who went to Detroit after 1916 had their way paid by labor agents. See Washington, *Negro in Detroit* (1920), "Migration," BHC.

18. Litwack, *Trouble in Mind*, 489–94.

19. Work, *Negro Year Book*, 9, quoted in Sernett, *Bound for the Promised Land*, 60; ibid., 3 ("Second Emancipation").

20. Reich, "Soldiers of Democracy," 1504 (quote); Grossman, *Land of Hope*, 13.

21. Scott, *Negro Migration during the War*, 6; Eric Foner, *Story of American Freedom*, 173–74. James Grossman points out that "'pushes' and 'pulls' might be abstractly separable, but they operated together in the minds of black southerners comparing one place to another." *Land of Hope*, 37.

22. Young, *Hard Stuff*, 13–14.

23. David Moore, interview by author, 10 December 2007.

24. C. J. Young, cited in Litwack, *Trouble in Mind*, 491. Statements by the Alabamian, the Georgian, and the Floridian quoted in Scott, "Additional Letters of Negro Migrants," 439–43.

25. Wells, *Crusade for Justice*, 47, 64.

26. *Congressional Record*, 56th Cong., 1st sess., 2242–45, cited in Logan, *Betrayal of the Negro*, 91.

27. Wilkerson, *Warmth of Other Suns*, 43–44.

28. Scott, "Additional Letters of Negro Migrants," 444. For black men and women at that time, the appeals to "beaing a man," though couched in gendered language, meant exercising humanity.

29. Mary Shadd quote on Harper from Boyd, *Discarded Legacy*, 45; Conot, *American Odyssey*, 75–76; Katzman, *Before the Ghetto*, 12–16; 42–44.

30. Wright, *Black Boy*, 309, 308.

31. Zunz, *Changing Face of Inequality*, 286.

32. Higham, *Strangers in the Land*, 244–45; quote from Zunz, *Changing Face of Inequality*, 323.

33. Douglas Brinkley, *Wheels for the World*, xxii, 155–56; Lee, "So-Called Profit Sharing System in the Ford Plant," 299.

34. Ford, *My Life and Work*, 103.

35. Ibid., 129–30; Zunz, *Changing Face of Inequality*, 311; Sward, *Legend of Henry Ford*, 49; Meyer, "Adapting the Immigrant to the Line," 69.

36. Zunz, *Changing Face of Inequality*, 312; Schwartz, "Henry Ford's Melting Pot," 192; Meyer, *Five Dollar Day*, 77–78; and Meyer, "Adapting the Immigrant to the Line," 69–71.

37. For Americanizing the FMC workforce, see Meyer, *The Five Dollar Day*, 5.

38. Press Release, "Five Dollar Day," typed from original, 5 January 1914, accession #940, box 16, folder: Ford Motor Company, BFRC; Ford, *My Life and Work*, 127; Douglas Brinkley, *Wheels for the World*, 162–63; Meyer, *The Five Dollar Day*, 109.

39. Meyer, *The Five Dollar Day*, 6, 109–12; Levin, "Ford Profit Sharing, 1914–1920," 76; Lacey, *Ford*, 126.

40. Ford Motor Company, "Helpful Hints and Advice to Employees to Help Them Grasp the Opportunities Which Are Presented to Them by the Ford Profit Sharing Plan" (Detroit, 1915), 9, and Fitch, "Making the Job Worthwhile," 88; both cited in Meyer, *Five Dollar Day*, 111; Levin, "Ford Profit Sharing," 80; Lacey, *Ford*, 131.

41. For quotes on living habits, see Meyer, "Adapting the Immigrant to the Line," 70; for checking personal documents, see Zunz, *Changing Face of Inequality*, 312–13; for gaining counseling from the Sociological Department, see FMC, "Helpful Hints" (Ontario, Canada, version), 5–9; "Squalid Homes Banned by Ford," *New York Times*, 9 April 1914, section 1, 12.

42. FMC, "Helpful Hints" (Ontario, Canada, version), 5–6.

43. Douglas Brinkley, *Wheels for the World*, 172.

44. FMC, "Helpful Hints" (Ontario, Canada, version), 5–6.

45. Henry Ford quoted in Marquis, *Henry Ford*, 153–54; Watts, *People's Tycoon*, 208.

46. Nevins and Hill, *Ford: Expansion*, 5.

47. For Henry Ford's foreshadowing of John Maynard Keynes, see Lacey, *Ford*, 139. See also Grandin, *Fordlandia*, 37–40, 73n, 74n; Douglas Brinkley, *Wheels for the World*, 135.

48. Henry Ford quoted in Marquis, *Henry Ford*, 154.

49. Ibid., 34–35; Nye, *Henry Ford*, 71; Douglas Brinkley, *Wheels for the World*, 173; Meyer, *Five Dollar Day*, 171–73.

50. Meyer, *Five Dollar Day*, 111–14; Douglas Brinkley, *Wheels for the World*, 172–75.

51. Henry Ford interview, *New York Times*, 9 April 1914, sec. 1, 12.

52. Meyer, "Adapting the Immigrant to the Line," 70; statement addressed to branch manager from Letter to Omaha, 29 January 1914, accession #683, BFRC, cited in Meyer, 70.

53. Copy of Testimony, before U.S. Senate's Commission on Industrial Relations, 22 January 1915, 2–3, accession #1, box 178, BFRC.

54. Douglas Brinkley, *Wheels for the World*, 174.

55. Zunz, *Changing Face of Inequality*, 311.

56. Marquis, "The Ford Idea in Education," in National Education Association, *Addresses and Proceedings . . . 1916*, 910–17, quote on 915, cited in Meyer, "Adapting the Immigrant to the Line," 76.

57. Meyer, "Adapting the Immigrant to the Line," 74–75; Marquis, "Address Delivered, 17 May 1916, Convention of the National Conference of Charities and Corrections, YMCA," 11, accession #63, box 1, BFRC.

58. Marquis, "Address, Convention of the National Conference," 11–12.

59. Schwartz, "Henry Ford's Melting Pot," 193; Meyer, *Five Dollar Day*, 160–61.

60. Higham, *Strangers in the Land*, 235, 237 (first quote), 238 (second quote).

61. Ibid., 244.

62. Ibid.; letter to Oscar Marx, 15 July 1915, 2–3, ACD Papers, BHL.

63. Zunz, *Changing Face of Inequality*, 313; Minutes of ACD Meeting, 31 August 1915, 1–3, ACDP, box 1, BHL.

64. Higham, *Strangers in the Land*, 244.

65. Eric Foner, *Story of American Freedom*, 187.

66. Ibid., 172–73; Reich, "Soldiers of Democracy," 1483.

67. W. E. B. Du Bois, "World War and the Color Line," *Crisis*, November 1914, 28–30, reprinted in Aptheker, *Writings in Periodicals Edited by Du Bois*, 84.

68. Grossman, "Blowing the Trumpet," 86.

69. Wright, *12 Million Black Voices*, 146; Marks, *Farewell*, 155.

70. Zunz, *Changing Face of Inequality*, 309.

71. Ibid., 286.

72. Ibid., 319.

73. Murage, "Making Migrants an Asset," 1–2 (electronic pagination).

74. Zunz, *Changing Face of Inequality*, 318–19.

75. Monthly Report, Forrester Washington to the Joint Committee, 16 October 1916, box 11, DULP; Murage, "Making Migrants an Asset," 2–3.

76. Horace H. Rackham, one of FMC's lawyers, represented the company on the board. Given the overlapping networks formed by industrialists, the key organization promoting the activities of the DUL was the Detroit Board of Commerce, which also had an active Ford presence. Levine, *Internal Combustion*, 77.

77. Correspondence and Reports, July–December 1916, box 3, United Community Services Collection, ALUA, as discussed in Murage, "Making Migrants an Asset," 2 (electronic pagination).

78. Levine, *Internal Combustion*, 85.

79. Ibid., 71–86; Meier and Rudwick, *Black Detroit*, 18–19; Carlson, "The Negro in the Industries of Detroit," 189; Bailer, "Negro Labor in the Automobile Industry," 31; George W. Grant, secretary of the Employers' Association of Detroit, to Forrester Washington, 3 December 1917, box 1, DULP; Martin, *Detroit and the Great Migration*, 12; Murage, "Making Migrants an Asset," 3.

80. Forrester Washington, "A Program of Work for the Assimilation of Negro Migrants into Northern Cities," 17 December 1917, 1, 19, box 10, folder 8, DULP.

81. Wolcott, *Remaking Respectability*, 53–54 (quote on 53).

82. Murage, "Making Migrants an Asset," 2; for remaining nonmilitant, see interview of John C. Dancy, 1946, transcript, box 11, DULP.

83. Monthly Report, Washington to the Joint Committee, 16 October 1916, box 11, DULP; Murage, "Making Migrants an Asset," 3; for housing, see Washington, *Negro in Detroit* (1920), "Housing of the Negro in Detroit" (no chapter designation), BHC.

84. Murage, "Making Migrants an Asset," 3.

85. Washington, *Negro in Detroit* (1920), chap. 6, "Social Life of the Negro in the Factories," BHC.

86. Ibid., part, "Housing," in section, "Housing of the Negro in Detroit."

87. Kocher, *Economic and Physical Growth of Detroit*, 77, MHC.

88. Conot, *American Odyssey*, 299; Boyle, *Arc of Justice*, 11.

89. Zunz, *Changing Face of Inequality*, 373–77; Mayor's Inter-racial Committee, *Negro in Detroit* (1926), sec. 5, 1–5, 10.

90. Haynes, *Negro Newcomers in Detroit, Michigan*, 8–9, 21–23.

91. Zunz, *Changing Face of Inequality*, 377; Mayor's Inter-racial Committee, *Negro in Detroit* (1926), sec. 5, 10.

92. Zunz, *Changing Face of Inequality*, 353.

93. Washington, *Negro in Detroit* (1920), parts, "rents" and "comparison of rents paid by Negroes and population in general," section, "Housing of the Negro in Detroit," BHC; Martin, *Detroit and the Great Migration*, 27.

94. "Annual Report of the Americanization Committee," 31 March 1920, folder: Correspondence/minutes, 1918–1921, 3–4, ACDP.

95. Fragnoli, *Transformation of Reform*, 20–32; Fine, *Frank Murphy*, 25, 91; Levine, *Internal Combustion*, 132–33.

96. Fragnoli, *Transformation of Reform*, 20–32; Fine, *Frank Murphy*, 91–92, 96; Zunz, *Changing Face of Inequality*, 323.

97. Fragnoli, *Transformation of Reform*, 45, 94; Marsh to McGregor (undated) Correspondence 2, DCLP.

98. Fine, *Frank Murphy*, 96; Lovell to Reinhold Niebuhr, 13 October 1927, DCLP.

99. Fragnoli, *Transformation of Reform*, 139–41, 165.

100. Rabbi A. M. Hershman to Congregation (composed by Lovett), 28 May 1918,

Correspondence 4, DCLP, cited in Fragnoli, *Transformation of Reform*, 162–63; see also *Civic Searchlight*, February 1918, 3, for abolishing ward-aldermanic system.

101. Ramsey, "Some Aspects of Non-Partisan Government in Detroit," 94–95.

102. Fragnoli, *Transformation of Reform*, 184.

103. Wik, *Henry Ford and Grass-roots America*, 4.

CHAPTER TWO

1. Jones, *Blues People*, 97, 98 (quote). See also remembrances of Quill Pettway, interview by Duncan, Lindberg, and author, 22 January 2002, and remembrances of General G. Baker, interview by author, 17 February 2004.

2. Washington, *Negro in Detroit* (1920), part 2, 5, BHC; for Ford's job equality, see Northrup, *Negro Employment in Basic Industry*, 57.

3. Meyer, *Five Dollar Day*, 168–71.

4. Lacey, *Ford*, 139.

5. Meyer, *Five Dollar Day*, 170; quote from Kazin and McCartin, *Americanism*, 5.

6. Meyer, *Five Dollar Day*, 173–89; for workers wanting a voice in labor policies, see 186.

7. David Levering Lewis, *When Harlem Was in Vogue*, 15 (Du Bois), 23 (Woodson).

8. David L. Lewis, "History of Negro Employment in Detroit Area Plants," 1; Searle, "Reminiscences," 37, BFRC; David L. Lewis, "Working Side by Side," 25–30.

9. Watts, *People's Tycoon*, 490; David L. Lewis, "History of Negro Employment in Detroit Area Plants," 7–8.

10. Washington, *Negro in Detroit* (1920), part 2, 5, BHC; David L. Lewis, "History of Negro Employment in Detroit Area Plants," 12–13.

11. David L. Lewis, "History of Negro Employment in Detroit Area Plants," 8; Bailer, "Negro Labor in the Automobile Industry," 71.

12. Bailer, "Negro Labor in the Automobile Industry," 69; Nevins and Hill, *Ford: Expansion*, 540.

13. Bailer, "Negro Labor in the Automobile Industry," 70–71; Meier and Rudwick, *Black Detroit*, 8–9.

14. Zunz, *Changing Face of Inequality*, 324; Kocher, *Economic and Physical Growth of Detroit*, 81, MHC; Klug, "Employers' Strategies in the Detroit Labor Market," 63; Maloney and Whatley, "Making the Effort," 470.

15. Nevins and Hill, *Ford: Expansion*, 149–52.

16. Ibid., 210.

17. Unemployment data from "Scope of Unemployment," *New York Times*, 11 February 1921, 21.

18. Kocher, *Economic and Physical Growth of Detroit*, 81, MHC; "Married Men Shift Formed in Ford Plant," *New York Times*, 11 February 1921, 23.

19. David L. Lewis, "Working Side by Side," 27.

20. Bailer, "Negro Labor in the Automobile Industry," 139–40; Meier and Rudwick, *Black Detroit*, 11–12; Douglas Brinkley, *Wheels for the World*, 384; Nevins and Hill, *Ford: Expansion*, 539–40.

21. Marquis, *Henry Ford*, 110, 111, 112. See also Meier and Rudwick, *Black Detroit*, 11; David L. Lewis, "History of Negro Employment in Detroit Area Plants," 9–10; Nevins and Hill, *Ford: Decline*, 407.

22. Maloney and Whatley, "Making the Effort," 469–70.

23. H. S. Ablewhite, accession #65, box 77, folder: Oral history, 4, BFRC.

24. Henry Ford quoted in Douglas Brinkley, *Wheels for the World*, 250.

25. Nevins and Hill, *Ford: Expansion*, 111–13, 159, 210.

26. Ibid., 111–13, 159.

27. Ibid., 111–13, 145, 159, 210.

28. *New York Times*, 21 January 1921, 1, 11 January 1921; "Ford Tells How He Foiled Wall Street," *New York Times*, 23 July 1921, 23; Nevins and Hill, *Ford: Expansion*, 160–63.

29. Henry Ford, *My Life and Work*, 177.

30. Ibid., 170; Douglas Brinkley, *Wheels for the World*, 268–69.

31. "Ford Tells How He Foiled Wall Street," *New York Times*, 23 July 1921, 23; Sorensen, *My Forty Years with Ford*, 167–68; Nevins and Hill, *Ford: Expansion*, 163.

32. Watts, *The People's Tycoon*, 59, 382; Nevin and Hill, *Ford: Expansion*, 311–12; Douglas Brinkley, *Wheels for the World*, 259.

33. Selected issues of *Dearborn Independent*, 29 March 1919, 7; 10 May 1919, 14; 31 May 1919, 3; 22 May 1920, 1–3 ("The International Jew: The World's Problem"); 5 June 1920, 2 (The Jew in the United States"); 10 July 1920, 8 ("Does a Jewish World Program Exist?"); 6 November 1920, 9; 13 November 1920, 8 ("The Struggle for Jewish Supremacy in the American Financial World"), microfilm, BFRC; *Detroit Free Press*, 7 August 1922.

34. Henry Ford, *My Life and Work*, 129; Sward, *Legend of Henry Ford*, 51–52, 56; Meyer, *Five Dollar Day*, 150.

35. Henry Ford, *My Life and Work*, 4–5, 9; Lichtenstein and Harris, *Industrial Democracy in America*, 5; Fraser, "The 'Labor Question,'" 57–58.

36. McCartin, "'An American Feeling,'" 67–86, esp. 68–69.

37. Ibid., 69 n. 6, 76; Rodgers, *Work Ethic in Industrial America*, 57–58; Howell John Harris, "Industrial Democracy and Liberal Capitalism," 51–66.

38. McCartin, "'An American Feeling,'" 73–81.

39. Chester M. Culver, General Manager, "A Resume of the Last Year in Industrial Detroit," Annual Report to the Employers' Association of Detroit, excerpts, 1–2, accession #940, box 5, folder: "Labor Detroit Organization, 1914–1925," BFRC.

40. Fraser, "The 'Labor Question,'" 57–58.

41. Peterson, *American Automobile Workers*, 115–117; Meyer, *Five Dollar Day*, 169–188; Bernstein, "Auto Industry, Post-War Developments," 20–45; Peterson, *American Automobile Workers*, 115 n.15; Davidson, "Industrial Detroit after World War I," 44–47; Culver, "Reminiscences," 40, BFRC; Frank Marquart, *An Auto Worker's Journal*, 27; Report of Op. 15, 1 October 1919, on meeting of "English speaking Branch no. 1 of Michigan Socialist Party," Report of Op. 15, 22 October 1919, on meeting of branch no. 1, Report of Op. 15, 17 November 1919, Report of Op. 15, 1919, on meeting at Auto Worker's Hall under auspices of Political Amnesty league and Socialist Party of Detroit, all in Espionage Papers, accession #940, box 5, folder: "Labor: Detroit organizations, 1914–1925," BFRC.

42. Davidson, "Industrial Detroit after World War I," 44–47. Report of Op. 15, November 1919, on meeting at Auto Worker's Hall under auspices of Political Amnesty league and Socialist Party of Detroit, Espionage Papers, accession #940, box 5, folder: "Labor: Detroit organizations, 1914–1925," BFRC.

43. Quoted in Fraser, "The 'Labor Question,'" 58.

44. "What of the Melting Pot?" *Dearborn Independent*, 8 March 1919, 4.

45. Ibid., 4, 14.

46. Ibid., 14.

47. Ibid., 4.

48. Ibid.

49. Nevins and Hill, *Ford: Expansion*, 200, 279.

50. Sorensen, *My Forty Years with Ford*, 165, 170.

51. Van Deventer, "Ford Principles and Practice at River Rouge," 196.

52. Sorensen, *My Forty Years with Ford*, 152.

53. Bailer, "The Negro Automobile Worker," 419, 421.

54. Meyer, *Five Dollar Day*, 170–71.

55. "Ford's Page," *Dearborn Independent*, 21 October 1922, 5 ("a human being"); for races working as partners, see Tom Phillips, "Reminiscences," 13, quoted in David L. Lewis, "History of Negro Employment in Detroit Area Plants," 10.

56. Quotes from "Ford's Page," 21 October 1922, 5. See also editorials, 5 August 1922, 4 July 1925, 20 February 1926, 14 November 1925, and "Ford's Page," 17 June 1922, 5, all in *Dearborn Independent*.

57. *Dearborn Independent*, 10 December 1921, 4, cited in Levine, "'Expecting the Barbarians,'" 145.

58. Meyer, *Five Dollar Day*, 194.

59. Marquis, *Ford*, 148 (soul of the company), 155 (quote).

60. For "hard-boiled" quote, see H. S. Ablewhite, "Reminiscences," accession #65, box 77, file: H. S. Ablewhite, 11, BFRC. For profitability considerations, see Marquis, *Ford*, 155.

61. Nevins and Hill, *Ford: Expansion*, 280–82.

62. Marquis, *Ford*, 10.

63. Bryan, *Clara*, 144; Nevins and Hill, *Ford: Expansion*, 612–13.

64. For Ford's wish for nonmaterial things, see Marquis, *Ford*, 43; for outliving usefulness, see ibid., 153–54.

65. Nevins and Hill, *Ford: Decline*, 497; Nevins and Hill, *Ford: Expansion*, 540; David L. Lewis, "History of Negro Employment in Detroit Area Plants," 9; Meier and Rudwick, *Black Detroit*, 11.

66. Arnesen, "Up from Exclusion," 146–74; Wesley, *Negro Labor in the United States*; Greene and Woodson, *Negro Wage Earner*; Spero and Harris, *Black Worker*; Cayton and Mitchell, *Black Workers and the New Unions*; Bloch, "Craft Unions and the Negro"; Bloch, "Labor and the Negro."

67. Douglas Brinkley, *Wheels for the World*, xiv. For more on Ford's reappraisal of the very world he helped create, see Grandin, *Fordlandia*, 71–72.

68. For quotes from Ford, see his *My Life and Work*, 250–51. Welliver, "Henry Ford, Dreamer and Worker," 492. Ford's dream for his black workers was tied to his belief that African Americans were loyal Americans who would be grateful for opportunities he opened up. He appeared to have little understanding of the intense desire for citizenship that fueled the migration process and inspired the initial gratitude black workers and the black community had for jobs at Ford Motor Company.

69. Richard Hofstadter explains Ford's anti-Semitism in terms of the "foibles of a Michigan farm boy who had been liberally exposed to Populist notions," in *Age of Reform*, 81; Sward, *Legend of Henry Ford*, 143–51; Watts, *People's Tycoon*, 382–83; Baldwin, *Henry Ford and the Jews*, 27–35.

70. Ford, *My Life and Work*, 250–51.

71. *Dearborn Independent*, 6 August 1921, 5, and 27 May 1922, 12; Watts, *People's Tycoon*, 383. The *Dearborn Independent* attributed the "abandoned sensuousness of sliding notes" to Jewish origins and a "degenerated animalism," contrasting jazz with plantation melodies it described as "harmony in its highest form" (27 May 1922, 12). Samuel S. Marquis suggested that Ford's mind did not "move in logical grooves. It does not walk, it leaps. It is not a trained mind. It does not know how to think consecutively, and I doubt if it would do so if it could." See Marquis, *Ford*, 50.

72. Schlesinger, *Crisis of the Old Order*, 73; Douglas Brinkley, *Wheels for the World*, 134–35; McCartin, "'An American Feeling,'" 82; Graebner, *Engineering of Consent*.

73. Marquis, *Ford*, 154–55.

74. Bailer, "Negro Labor in the Automobile Industry," 113, 142–43; Sernett, *Bound for the Promised Land*, 149; Bates, *Pullman Porters and the Rise of Protest Politics*, 45–48; Dickerson, "Black Church in Western Pennsylvania," 329–30, 333; Cayton and Mitchell, *Black Workers and the New Unions*, 389–93.

75. "Remarks by R. L. Bradby," 28 September 1931, reel 3, microfilm, SBCP.

76. David L. Lewis, "History of Negro Employment in Detroit Area Plants," 17.

77. Shelly, "Bradby's Baptists," 5–7, UM-HS.

78. David L. Lewis claims that the lunch date was in 1918, drawing from information several decades later in an interview with the Reverend Robert L. Bradby on 13 May 1954. See David L. Lewis, "History of Negro Employment in Detroit Area Plants," 16–17. A more likely date is 1919, right after World War I, when Ford began hiring African Americans in earnest. See "Remarks" by R. L. Bradby, 28 September 1931, reel 3, SBCP.

79. Rev. Bradby quoted in Lewis, "History of Negro Employment in Detroit Area Plants," 17.

80. Robert L. Bradby to Charles Sorensen, 5 November 1926, 1, accession #572, box 28, folder: 12.7.3, BFRC.

81. Nevin and Hill, *Ford: Expansion*, 168; Douglas Brinkley, *Wheels for the World*, 276–78; Grandin, *Fordlandia*, 69.

82. For another interpretation, see *Five Dollar Day*, 194, where Stephen Meyer argues that "for all practical purposes, Ford paternalism ceased to exist" with the inauguration of Ford's new American Plan, "based upon militant anti-unionism, the open-shop, and a network of spies and informants."

83. For donations to the NAACP, see Bates, "New Crowd Challenges the Old Guard," 358.

84. In 1919, according to Douglas Brinkley (*Wheels for the World*, 276), there were approximately 150 investigators on the staff of the Sociological Department.

85. Shelly, "Bradby's Baptists," 25.

86. For church for the masses, see David L. Lewis, "History of Negro Employment in Detroit Area Plants," 19; for church for the classes, see ibid., 20; for Rev. Peck's congregation, see Dillard, *Faith in the City*, 32.

87. Willis F. Ward, "Reminiscences," 7–8, accession #65, BFRC; Lacey, *Ford*, 368–70; Douglas Brinkley, *Wheels for the World*, 289; Nevins and Hill, *Ford: Expansion*, 296, 298, 540; Grandin, *Fordlandia*, 70–71.

88. David L. Lewis, "History of Negro Employment in Detroit Area Plants," 22; Willis Ward, "Reminiscences," 12–13.

89. Accession #23, box 14, folder: Mr. Ford's Personal Notes, BFRC.

90. Meier and Rudwick, *Black Detroit*, 17; Bailer, "Negro Labor in the Auto Industry," 165–66.

91. Foote, Whatley, and Wright, "Arbitraging a Discriminatory Labor Market," 500; Klug, "Employers' Strategies in the Detroit Labor Market," 63. It should be noted that white workers, during the peak of the Five Dollar Day plan, also displayed their plant badges with all the "ostentation of Masonic lodge members in their regalia," according to Robert Lacey, *Ford*, 139.

92. Report, John Dancy to Charles S. Johnson, on specific figures on the migration of blacks to Detroit since 1920, 18 August 1926, 1, box 1, folder: July–December 1926, DULP.

93. David Moore quoted by Stepan-Norris and Zeitlin in *Talking Union*, 56–57.

94. Quill Pettway, interviewed by author, 20 December 2006.

95. Willis Ward, "Reminiscences," 9. One exception was the George Washington Trade School, created by the WPA in the late 1930s. It is not clear how long this school was in operation in Detroit. See Moon, *Untold Tales*, 151.

96. David L. Lewis, "Training the Tradesmen Who Made the Model T," 30; Bailer, "Negro Labor in the Automobile Industry," 151–53.

97. Maloney and Whatley, "Making the Effort," 470.

98. Mayor's Inter-racial Committee, *Negro in Detroit* (1926), sec. 3, 4. Bailer, "Negro Labor in the Automobile Industry," 44.

99. Foote, Whatley, and Wright, "Arbitraging a Discriminatory Labor Market," 499; Sundstrom, "Color Line," 382–97; Bailer, "Negro Automobile Worker," 421; Hawley, "Mobility of Southern Migrants in Detroit," 1–3, MKP.

100. Ticknor, "Motor City," 168–69; Elmer Akers, "Southern Whites in Detroit," MKP; Adamic, "Hill-Billies Come to Detroit," 177–78, and 305. For management's reluctance to integrate black and white workers, see Bailer, "Negro Labor in the Automobile Industry," 80.

101. For analysis of wage differentials and working conditions, see Foote, Whatley, and Wright, "Arbitraging a Discriminatory Labor Market," 494.

102. The analysis that informs this section relies heavily on the work of Christopher L. Foote, Thomas N. Maloney, Warren C. Whatley, and Gavin Wright. Their findings from their analyses of the FMC's employment records stored in the Ford Motor Company Industrial Archive are in Maloney and Whatley, "Making the Effort," and Foote, Whatley, and Wright, "Arbitraging a Discriminatory Labor Market."

103. Maloney and Whatley, "Making the Effort," 486.

104. For concept of workers as "Ford Mules," see Young, *Hard Stuff*, 21.

105. Maloney and Whatley, "Making the Effort," 479, 486, 490 (first quote), 489 (second quote). Young, *Hard Stuff*, 21.

106. Maloney and Whatley, "Making the Effort," 478–83.

107. Denby, *Indignant Heart*, 35.

108. Cuningham, *J8: Chronicle of Neglected Truth*, 34, BHL.

109. Sward, *Legend of Henry Ford*, 324–25; *Detroit Free Press*, 14 September 1939.

110. Cuningham, *J8: Chronicle of Neglected Truth*, 15–16, 23, 40, BHL.

111. Nevins and Hill, *Ford: Expansion*, 518–19.

112. Klann, "Reminiscences," quoted in Nevin and Hill, *Ford: Expansion*, 519.

113. Dunn, *Labor and Automobiles*, 70.

114. Bonosky, *Brother Bill McKie*, 31.

115. Foote, Whatley, and Wright, "Arbitraging a Discriminatory Labor Market," 500.

116. Bailer, "Negro Labor in the Automobile Industry," 60.

117. Whatley and Wright, "Race, Human Capital, and Labour Markets," 287–89.

118. Bailer, "Negro Labor in the Automobile Industry," 60–61.

119. Ibid., 62–63; report by Louis I. Dublin and Robert J. Vane Jr., *Causes of Death by Occupation*, U.S. Bureau of Labor Statistics, R. 507 (1930), 49–50, cited in Bailer, "Negro Labor in the Automobile Industry," 62–63.

120. Whatley and Wright, "Race, Human Capital, and Labour Markets," 287–89.

121. Nevins and Hill, *Ford: Expansion*, 431–32, 405, 442, 451, 437. There is some question about how many Model T's were actually produced. Some put the actual figure at 15,458,781; others at 15,457,868. See Nevins and Hill, *Ford: Expansion*, 432 n. 29.

122. Denby, *Indignant Heart*, 35–36.

123. Northrup, *Negro Employment in Basic Industry*, 53.

124. Licht, *Getting Work*, 45, 141, cited in Whatley and Wright, "Race, Human Capital, and Labour Markets," 282.

125. Earnings in excess of $3,000 per year for any particular employee were excluded from these figures. The data were based on a 20 percent sample, according to Bailer, "The Negro Automobile Worker," 419–20.

126. Maloney and Whatley, "Making the Effort," 466.

127. Nevins and Hill, *Ford: Expansion*, 381.

128. Bailer, "Negro Labor in the Automobile Industry," 165.

129. Young, *Hard Stuff*, 20–21.

130. Wolcott, *Remaking Respectability*, 93.

131. Engelmann, "Separate Peace," 53.

132. Wolcott, *Remaking Respectability*, 95.

133. Young, *Hard Stuff*, 17.

134. Wolcott argues this point exceptionally well in *Remaking Respectability*; see especially 93–126.

135. Dancy, *Sand against the Wind*, 114.

CHAPTER THREE

1. "The Good Citizenship League," Annual Report, 1, box 1, folder 9; J. L. Porter to Officers and Members of the Detroit Board of Commerce, 11 March 1918, 2–3, box 1, DULP, BHL.

2. Marcus Garvey quoted in Levine, *Internal Combustion*, 102.

3. Mayor's Inter-racial Committee, *Negro in Detroit*, sec. 11, 6.

4. Robert Lincoln Poston and his brother Ulysses, as Richard Thomas shows, published the *Detroit Contender*, which was cited by the UNIA newspaper, *Negro World*, for helping black Detroiters challenge the status quo in a city it claimed posed "the strongest opposition that has been encountered in any northern city." See Richard Thomas, *Life for Us Is What We Make It*, 197, also, 194–202. Dillard, *Faith in the City*, 47; Levine, *Internal Combustion*, 100–101; Wolcott, *Remaking Respectability*, 125–27; Stein, *World of Marcus Garvey*, 230–31; Boyle, *Arc of Justice*, 118–19.

5. Marable, *Malcolm X*, 29.

6. Smith-Irvin, *Footsoldiers of Universal Negro Improvement Association*, 59–60.

7. Stein, *World of Marcus Garvey*, 229. See also Dillard, *Faith in the City*, 48, and Richard Thomas, *Life for Us Is What We Make It*, 197.

8. Richard Thomas, *Life for Us Is What We Make It*, 196–97; for the number of members, see Mayor's Inter-racial Committee, *Negro in Detroit* (1926), sec. 11, 7; Dillard, *Faith in the City*, 47.

9. Stein, *World of Marcus Garvey*, 230–31.

10. Quote from Smith-Irvin, *Footsoldiers of the United Negro Improvement Association*, 41.

11. Craigen's speech from the *Owl* (Detroit), 21 January 1927, quoted in Levine, *Internal Combustion*, 101. See also Stein, *World of Marcus Garvey*, 231.

12. Stein, *World of Marcus Garvey*, 276.

13. Berlin, *Making of African America*, 19.

14. In 1922 Ford's "total Detroit-area employment accounted for over 45 percent of black male employment," according to Maloney and Whatley, "Making the Effort," 470.

15. Dillard, *Faith in the City*, 47–50; Levine, *Internal Combustion*, 103.

16. Quote from interview of Ruth Smith in Smith-Irvin, *Footsoldiers of the United Negro Improvement Association*, 60.

17. Boyle, *Arc of Justice*, 119.

18. Richard Thomas, *Life for Us Is What We Make It*, 195.

19. Ibid., 197–99.

20. Dillard, *Faith in the City*, 48, 70–71; Stein, *World of Marcus Garvey*, 231; Meier and Rudwick, *Black Detroit*, 32–33; Richard Thomas, *Life for Us Is What We Make It*, 265–66; Smith, *To Serve the Living*; Charles C. Diggs Jr., interviewed by Blackside, Inc., 6 November 1986.

21. Mayor's Inter-racial Committee, *Negro in Detroit* (1926), sec. 11, 7.

22. *Detroit News*, 26 June 1918, 1; *Detroit Times*, 26 June 1918, 1.

23. Dancy, *Sand against the Wind*, 103–4. Nevins and Hill, *Ford: Expansion*, 9–11; Lacey, *Ford*, 76–77, 176–78.

24. *Messenger*, August 1919, 20; September 1919, 21; October 1919, 31; Editorial, "*Messenger* Editors Receive Ovation," *Messenger*, March 1920, 13. Cynthia Taylor, *A. Philip Randolph*, 53.

25. "Some Negro Ministers," *Messenger*, March 1920, 3. I am especially grateful to Cynthia Taylor for bringing this article to my attention.

26. Ibid.

27. Shelly, "Bradby's Baptists," 28, UM-HS.

28. Richard Thomas, *Life for Us Is What We Make It*, 273. See also Levine, *Internal Combustion*, 97–98.

29. Shelly, "Bradby's Baptists," *Michigan Historical Review*, 17.

30. *Detroit Tribune*, 15 July 1917, quoted in Sernett, *Bound for the Promised Land*, 148.

31. Shelly, "Bradby's Baptists," 5, UM-HS.

32. Harmon, "Reverend Robert L. Bradby," 20–25.

33. Ibid., 49.

34. Ibid., 20.

35. Ibid.

36. Dillard, *Faith in the City*, 15.

37. Harmon, "Reverend Robert L. Bradby," 40–42.

38. Dillard, *Faith in the City*, 9–10.

39. Best, *Passionately Human, No Less Divine*, 4, 72.

40. For the connection between Bradby and Ransom, see Harmon, "Reverend Robert L. Bradby," 49; Best, *Passionately Human, No Less Divine*, 74.

41. Luker, *Social Gospel in Black and White*, 174; Harmon, "Reverend Robert L. Bradby," 49–51, 84.

42. Harmon, "Reverend Robert L. Bradby," 17.

43. Mayor's Inter-racial Committee, *Negro in Detroit* (1926), sec. 11, 7.

44. Fragnoli, *Transformation of Reform*, 185, 199.

45. Ibid., 197.

46. Wolcott, *Remaking Respectability*, 101–2.

47. Fragnoli, *Transformation of Reform*, 197, 207, 209, 211–13; Fine, *Frank Murphy*, 93.

48. *Civic Searchlight*, July 1920 and August 1920, cited in Fragnoli, *Transformation of Reform*, 227–29.

49. Detroit Citizens League to Harry Bennett (FMC, Office Manager), 25 August 1920, box 6, folder: H.M., 1920, DCLP.

50. I am grateful to scholars who have mapped the political landscape in Detroit during the 1920s. Raymond Fragnoli's excellent study of the Detroit Citizens League, *The Transformation of Reform*, is indispensable for grasping the coordinates and mechanics of municipal reform. Sidney Fine's *Frank Murphy*, Kevin Boyle's *Arc of Justice*,

and David Allan Levine's *Internal Combustion* help us understand how African Americans negotiated their way into the political process.

51. *Civic Searchlight*, November 1920, 2.

52. *Detroit Contender* 31 October 1920, Additional Papers, box 14, DCLP, cited in Fragnoli, *Transformation of Reform*, 224. Thomas Solomon, "Participation of Negroes in Detroit Elections," 66–67.

53. For results on the 1920 election of judges for Recorder's Court, see Fragnoli, *Transformation of Reform*, 232, esp. Fragnoli's ward-level voting data contained in table 5, appendix, 405.

54. Fragnoli, *Transformation of Reform*, 258–64. See *Detroit Times*, 25 January 1922, 3 March 1923.

55. Higham, *Strangers in the Land*, 288.

56. Ibid., 286.

57. Evans, "Klan's Fight for Americanism," 33–63.

58. Jackson, *Ku Klux Klan in the City*, 128–32; Zunz, *Changing Face of Inequality*, 402.

59. Jackson, *Ku Klux Klan in the City*, 128–29.

60. Ticknor, *Motor City*, 171–84.

61. Fifteenth Census (1930), vol. 2, population, 540; Levine, *Internal Combustion*, 12.

62. Ticknor, *Motor City*, 168. Although Ticknor refers to the presence of large numbers of Appalachian whites among the newcomers, it is difficult to know whether his statistics, drawn from older studies, referred to Appalachian southerners or white southerners. I use the term "southern whites" in reference to the limited material I located from contemporary sources (those from the 1920s and 1930s). The problem has been highlighted recently through the research of J. Trent Alexander, James N. Gregory, and others. My concern has been to identify how many southern whites worked at the FMC during the twenties and thirties. What has complicated that effort has been the way that white migrants from the South were identified both within communities in Detroit and within industry. Membership in the group called white southerners was frequently determined by "dialect, by social and economic status of parents and by attitudes toward vaccination and immunization." The Detroit Department of Health, for example, identified southern whites as those who were against vaccines. One of the largest automobile factories in the area had foremen who could give out the number of "Southern Whites" in their respective departments, "although no data are recorded regarding the state of birth of employees." Recognition of southern whites by observation is not a satisfactory tool for scholars. For more on the complexities surrounding the question of southern white migrants—who they were, where they were from, where they worked, how well they fared in the North—see Beynon, "Southern White Laborer Migrates to Michigan," 336 (above quotes); Gregory, "Southern Diaspora and the Urban Dispossessed"; Alexander, "Defining the Diaspora."

63. Mayor's Inter-racial Committee, *The Negro in Detroit* (1926), sec. 2, 2–3; Carlson, "The Negro in the Industries of Detroit," 67, table 6 (1).

64. John Dancy, "Negro Achievement in Detroit," 2, box 70, folder: Detroit Civic Rights, DULP.

65. Jackson, *Ku Klux Klan in the City*, 129–34; *Detroit News*, 7 November 1923, quoted in Levine, *Internal Combustion*, 137.

66. Jackson, *Ku Klux Klan in the City*, 129.

67. Fragnoli, *Transformation of Reform*, 257–72.

68. Fine, *Frank Murphy*, 91–96; Boyle, *Arc of Justice*, 138.

69. Fragnoli, *Transformation of Reform*, 265–73; Fine, *Frank Murphy*, 101–8.

70. Fragnoli, *Transformation of Reform*, 265–72; Fine, *Frank Murphy*, 100–110.

71. *Detroit News*, 16 March 1923, 4.

72. *Detroit News*, 17 March 1923, 2.

73. Quotes from *Detroit News*, 15 March 1923, 1, and 14 March 1923, 1. See also *Detroit Free Press*, 15, 16, 18, 20 March 1923.

74. *Detroit News*, 15 March 1923, 1.

75. *Detroit News*, 16 March 1923, 1.

76. *Detroit News*, 15 March 1923, 1; *Detroit Times*, 15 March 1923, 1.

77. *Detroit Times*, 17 March 1923, 1, 2; Fine, *Frank Murphy*, 112.

78. *Detroit News*, 17, 18 March 1923, 1; quote from 17 March.

79. *Detroit Times*, 25 March 1923, 1.

80. *Detroit News*, 15 March 1923, 1.

81. Fragnoli, *Transformation of Reform*, 271–72.

82. Address of Frank Murphy, Armory, Detroit, Michigan, 29 March 1923, 1–2, reel 141, Frank Murphy Papers, BHL.

83. Ibid., 2.

84. Ibid., 6.

85. Ibid., 7.

86. Ibid., 8.

87. Ibid., 10–11.

88. Ibid., 6.

89. Ibid., 8.

90. W. P. Lovett to "Pastor," 28 March 1923; Detroit Civic League to "Dear Friend," 28 March 1923; Lovett to Dear Friend, 29 March 1923; Lovett "telegram" warning about "vital issues affecting Christian people," Correspondence, box 10, folder: 1923 circulars; Lovett to Rev. William B. Gantz, 28 March 1923, Correspondence, box 10, folder: "g" 1923, DCLP. Fragnoli, *Transformation of Reform*, 272–73; Fine, *Frank Murphy*, 112–13; *Detroit Times*, 31 March 1923.

91. *Detroit News*, 2 April 1923, 1.

92. *Detroit News*, 3 April 1923, 20 (ward and precinct breakdown of election results); Fine, *Frank Murphy*, 114–15.

93. William P. Lovett to Honorable Harry Olson, 23 March 1923, p. 1, Correspondence, box 11, folder: "N, O, P, Q," 1923, DCLP.

94. Lovett to Harry Olson, 3 April 1923, Correspondence, box 11, folder: "1923 N, O, P, Q," DCLP.

95. Lovett to Harry Olson, 17 April 1923, Correspondence, box 11, folder: "1923 N, O, P, Q," DCLP.

96. Arch Mandel to Lovett, 11 April 1923, Correspondence, box 11, folder: "1923 M," DCLP.

97. Lovett to Arch Mandell, 7 April 1923, box 11, folder: "1923 M"; Lovett to H. W. Dodds, 6 April 1923, box 10, folder: "D," DCLP.

98. Frank Murphy had been known as an "organization Democrat" during the years leading up to his run for judgeship on Recorder's Court. He had also run as a Democratic candidate in the early twenties for a seat in Michigan's First Congressional District. He was a Democrat with a capital D, exemplifying the link between Americans of Irish descent and the Democratic Party. He spoke often and passionately about the Irish question—i.e., the social and political rights of Irish Americans. See Fine, *Frank Murphy*, 79–81.

99. Fine, *Frank Murphy*, 114–18; Boyle, *Arc of Justice*, 140.

100. Jackson, *Ku Klux Klan in the City*, 134.

101. Ibid., 132–33.

102. Ibid., 133–36; Levine, *Internal Combustion*, 139.

103. Fragnoli, *Transformation of Reform*, 308; Boyle, *Arc of Justice*, 141–42; Jackson, *Ku Klux Klan in the City*, 135–36; Levine, *Internal Combustion*, 137–39.

104. Fragnoli, *Transformation of Reform*, 310, 313; Boyle, *Arc of Justice*, 141.

105. Levine, *Internal Combustion*, 140–41. *Detroit News*, 5 November 1924, 23, and 8 November 1924, 1.

106. Fragnoli, *Transformation of Reform*, 313.

107. *Detroit News*, 5 November 1924, 23; *Detroit News*, 8 November 1924, 1; Thomas Ralph Solomon, "Participation of Negroes in Detroit Elections," 190; Levine, *Internal Combustion*, 140; Jackson, *Ku Klux Klan in the City*, 136–37; Boyle, *Arc of Justice*, 143.

108. Jackson, *Ku Klux Klan in the City*, 142.

109. *Detroit News*, 20 October 1925; Fragnoli, *Transformation of Reform*, 317–18.

110. Niebuhr, *Leaves from the Notebook of a Tamed Cynic*, 144.

CHAPTER FOUR

1. Violence erupted on several occasions, as early as 1917, but it rarely developed into large-scale rioting. Zunz, *Changing Face of Inequality*, 373; Boyle, *Arc of Justice*, 96–99; David Levering Lewis, *W. E. B. Du Bois: Biography of a Race*, 536–40; Tuttle, *Race Riot*, 130–51.

2. Walter White, "Negro Segregation Comes North," 459; Martin, *Detroit and the Great Migration*, 50; Boyle, *Arc of Justice*, 24. For evidence of execution-style shootings by police, see reports taken from Records of the Homicide Squad in Mayor's Inter-racial Committee, *Negro in Detroit* (1926), sec. 9, 32–37.

3. For the claim that the KKK recruited members of Detroit's Police Department, see Walter White, "Negro Segregation Comes North," 459. Also Boyle, *Arc of Justice*, 24.

4. "Minutes of the Urban League Board," 13 January 1921, and "Report," 18 September to 9 October 1919, both in box 11, DULP; Lett, "Migration Difficulties in Michigan," 235; Washington, *Negro in Detroit* (1920), part, "The Effect on Realty Values of Negro Invasion," section, "Housing the Negro in Detroit," BHC.

5. In *The Negro Ghetto* (22), Robert Weaver argues that the "treatment of the Chinese on the West Coast during the latter decades of the Nineteenth Century was a straw in the wind." Practices against the Chinese "were of strategic importance in sanctioning the spread of segregation. . . . and gave rise to the first American ghettos—Chinatowns, where ethnic islands of Orientals were soon to be established."

6. Boyle, *Arc of Justice*, 24; Levine, *Internal Combustion*, 3, 156–58; Jackson, *Ku Klux Klan in the City*, 139.

7. Harold Rabinowitz, a leading scholar of the urban South during this era, concluded that by 1890 "separate black and white neighborhoods dominated the urban landscape." See Rabinowitz, *Race Relations in the Urban South*, 97–124. Perhaps a more accurate portrayal distinguishes between clustering and concentration. Using "linear blocks" to measure residential separation by race may not capture the full measure of daily interaction between the races. For the clustering effect, see Kellogg, "Negro Urban Clusters in the Post-Bellum South."

8. The outstanding exception to this pattern in the South was Birmingham, Alabama. Soon after the city was founded in 1871, a land company and a railroad company joined forces to develop the region's coal and iron resources. At the same time, real estate companies and industrial corporations combined efforts to develop a "sharply segregated residential pattern" for the city. Large corporations controlled the coal, iron, steel, and machinery production in Birmingham and depended on black workers to carry out hot, dirty, dangerous work. By 1900, 65 percent of Alabama's iron and steel workers were African American. In Birmingham, blacks made up more than 90 percent of the labor force in occupations such as iron-mine operative, unskilled laborer in iron foundries, and general unskilled laborer. Since Birmingham was a new city, it did not carry the weight of racial etiquette that kept Old South cities under the social control of Jim Crow codes. Thus, the "father" of the new city of Birmingham imposed residential segregation from above in order to keep a lid on friction between white and black workers. See Woodward, *Origins of the New South*, 126–27, 136; Carl Harris, "Reforms in Government Control of Negroes in Birmingham, Alabama," 569–71; Norrell, "Caste in Steel," 671; Worthman, "Black Workers and Labor Unions in Birmingham, Alabama," 378.

9. Hirsch, "With or Without Jim Crow," 68–69; Kusmer, "Black Urban Experience in American History," 108–9; Massey and Denton, *American Apartheid*, 20, 24–26.

10. Katzman, *Before the Ghetto*, 94, 159–61; Massey and Denton, *American Apartheid*, 22; Zunz, *Changing Face of Inequality*, 378; Levine, *Internal Combustion*, 51.

11. Zunz, *Changing Face of Inequality*, 139, 352.

12. Ibid., 137.

13. Ibid., 151, 160; Katzman, *Before the Ghetto*, 75.

14. Haynes, *Negro Newcomers in Detroit*, 9.

15. Compare studies made by Haynes, *Negro Newcomers in Detroit*, 9, and Washington, *Negro in Detroit* (1920), "Housing of the Negro in Detroit," BHC. See also Zunz, *Changing Face of Inequality*, 352–53.

16. Jerome Thomas, "City of Detroit," 96–98; Levine, *Internal Combustion*, 125; Mayor's Inter-racial Committee, *Negro in Detroit* (1926), sec. 5, 2; *Detroit Realtor (special edi-*

tion), 20–27 May 1922, 8; *Detroit News Tribune*, 29 April 1917; *Realtor Sales Letter*, January 1923, in "Realtor Sales Letter" envelope, BHC; *Detroit Free Press*, 28, 30 July 1927, plus 21, 22, 24 June 1925 on the boom spirit occasioned by a national convention of 6,000 real estate brokers in Detroit.

17. "Negro Population of Detroit," box 74, folder: Histories of Negro Population of Detroit, 10, DULP; Mayor's Inter-racial Committee, *Negro in Detroit* (1926), sec. 5, 2, 18; Jerome Thomas, "City of Detroit," 98–100; Levine, *Internal Combustion*, 125.

18. Washington, *Negro in Detroit* (1920), part, "Relation of rents to income," section, "Housing of the Negro in Detroit," BHC.

19. John Dancy, "Negro Housing," paper presented at the Ohio State Conference of Social Work, 26 April 1924, Dayton, Ohio, 1, box 1, folder 13, DULP.

20. Miles, "Home at Last," 134–35; Dancy, *Sand against the Wind*, 56; Kocher, "Economic and Physical Growth of Detroit," 77, MHC.

21. Dancy, "Negro Housing," 26 April 1924, 1–2, box 1, folder 13, DULP; Victoria Wolcott highlights the comparison between Detroit and New York City rentals in *Remaking Respectability*, 60. See also Washington, "Report of Secretary to First Meeting of Joint Committee," 17 July 1916, 4, box 34, folder 19, United Community Services Papers, Central Files, ALUA; for descriptions of housing available to African American migrants, see Jerome Thomas, "City of Detroit," 99–107; Richard Thomas, *Life for Us Is What We Make It*, 89–102.

22. "Urban League Report," 3 August 1926, 5, box 1, DULP; Len G. Shaw, "Detroit's New Housing Problem," *Detroit Free Press*, 3 June 1917, 1. For comparison of rents paid by blacks and by the general population, see Washington, *Negro in Detroit* (1920), part, "Comparison of rents paid by Negroes and population in general," section, "Housing of the Negro in Detroit," BHC.

23. Dancy, *Sand against the Wind*, 56–57; Washington, *Negro in Detroit* (1920), part, "Comparison of rents paid by Negroes and population in general," section, "Housing of the Negro in Detroit."

24. Washington, *Negro in Detroit* (1920), "Housing of the Negro in Detroit," BHC; "Report to the Urban League Board," October and November 1922, box 1, DULP; Levine, *Internal Combustion*, 38–39, 125.

25. For the focus of industrialists, including Ford, on shaping a new industrial order, see Zunz, *Changing Face of Inequality*, 309–18; J. H. Porter (Good Citizenship League) to Officers, Detroit Board of Commerce, 11 March 1918, box 1, folder: Executive Secretary's General File, DULP; Levine, *Internal Combustion*, 44–45, 136.

26. *Detroit Free Press*, 3 June 1917.

27. *Detroiter Magazine*, 15 December 1919, 1–2, reprinted in Black, "Restrictive Covenants," 8.

28. Peterson, "Black Automobile Workers in Detroit," 182–83.

29. Niebuhr, *Leaves from the Notebook of a Tamed Cynic*, 143.

30. Niebuhr, "How Philanthropic is Henry Ford?" 1516–17, and "Race Prejudice in the North," 583–84; radio interview of Niebuhr, 1–4, Reinhold Niebuhr Papers, LC, posted on the web: http://being.publicradio.org/programs/niebuhr-rediscovered/b8.

31. Niebuhr, "How Philanthropic Is Henry Ford?" 1517.

32. For the quote from Henry Ford, see his *My Life and Work*, 128. For the attempt to alert Ford to consequences of poor housing, see Nevins and Hill, *Ford: Expansion*, 347–48. For locating the FMC outside the city limits, see Zunz, *Changing Face of Inequality*, 291; Levine, *Internal Combustion*, 16–18; Grandin, *Fordlandia*, 272.

33. Marquis, *Henry Ford*, 146. Ford did attempt at least one housing project in the 1920s. In 1919 the Dearborn Realty and Construction Company, under the control of Clara and Edsel Ford, was formed to buy land and build employee housing. During the next year, about 250 houses were built on a large parcel located in West Dearborn. The houses each had three and four bedrooms. Since those who were unemployed could not make payments during the winter of 1920–21, the enterprise lost a considerable amount of money, discouraging the Fords from pursuing other housing adventures for almost a decade. See Nevins and Hill, *Ford: Expansion*, 347–49.

34. Moon, *Untold Tales*, 27–29; Levine, *Internal Combustion*, 130–31; Richard Thomas, *Life for Us Is What We Make It*, 26, 30; Boyle, *Arc of Justice*, 106.

35. Dancy, *Sand against the Wind*, 55.

36. Massey and Denton, *American Apartheid*, 188; Charles Johnson, *Negro Housing*, 42.

37. "Restrictions for B. E. Taylor's Properties," Ads for "Kenmoor" development, Greenlawn and Birwood Park," E and M, Detroit Real Estate, BHC; Black, "Restrictive Covenants in Detroit," 6, 24–28, 29–30; Boyle, *Arc of Justice*, 144.

38. On the declaration of an "invasion" and the connection in the public's mind of depreciation of property and black residents in neighborhoods, see Mayor's Inter-racial Committee, *Negro in Detroit* (1926), sec. 5, 30–32; 46–47. See also Fulton, "Russel Woods: A Study of Response to Negro Invasion," 18–21; Mayer, "Russel Woods," 200–201.

39. Mayor's Inter-racial Committee, *Negro in Detroit* (1926), sec. 5, 30.

40. Ibid., sec. 5, 25.

41. Ibid.

42. Ibid., 60–62; Detroit Real Estate Board, "Why a Realtor Is a Dependable Real Estate Man," in Detroit Real Estate Board, envelope marked "1924, Miscellaneous material," box 1, BHC; Levine, *Internal Combustion*, 131.

43. "Plan of Boulevard in Kenmoor," advertising brochure, 1919, Detroit Real Estate, Miscellaneous Material, E&M files, BHC.

44. "Restrictions for B. E. Taylor's Properties," Monmoor Subdivision No. 3, p. 30, Detroit Real Estate, Miscellaneous Material, E&M files, BHC.

45. Mayor's Inter-racial Committee, *Negro in Detroit*, sec. 2, 10; Conant Gardeners, *Conant Gardens*, 5, 7; Sugrue, *Origins of the Urban Crisis*, 36–37.

46. Dancy, *Sand against the Wind*, 58; Lindsey, "Fields to Fords," 26.

47. Bostick, *Roots of Inkster*, 31–37.

48. Ibid., 40.

49. Lindsey, "Fields to Fords," 33–34.

50. Ibid., 37; Willis F. Ward, "Reminiscences," 41, accession #65, BFRC.

51. For Ford's offer to build a high school for the Inkster district in 1922, see Lindsey,

"Fields to Fords," 31. For proposed "high-class" development, see *Detroit Times*, 11 April 1923, 1.

52. *Detroit Times*, 11 April 1923, 1.

53. Lindsey, "Fields to Fords," 31.

54. Zunz, *Changing Face of Inequality*, 373.

55. McCartin, "'An American Feeling,'" 77; for Dancy providing strikebreakers, see Spero and Harris, *Black Worker*, 140; for poor relations between black and white labor, see Washington, *Negro in Detroit* (1920), chap. 5 of section, "Negro in the Industries of Detroit," BHC.

56. Nevins, *Ford: Expansion*, 167.

57. Mayor's Inter-racial Committee, *Negro in Detroit* (1926), sec. 3, "Industry," 3–4; Carlson, "Negro in the Industries of Detroit," 115.

58. Rubio, *There's Always Work at the Post Office*, 9.

59. Ibid., 18–27.

60. Post office jobs were highly contested. If black applicants scored high on the civil service examination, according to Rubio, "they still faced rejection by the 'rule of three' that allowed personnel officers to pick one of the three applicants from each batch of applications for a postal position." Ibid., 28. See also Mayor's Inter-racial Committee, *Negro in Detroit* (1926), sec. 3, "Industry," 6, 11–12.

61. Carlson, "Negro in the Industries of Detroit, 134–35.

62. Mayor's Inter-racial Committee, *Negro in Detroit* (1926), sec. 5, "Housing," 61; "Code of Ethics" adopted by National Association of Real Estate Boards, 6 June 1924, part III, article 34, p. 7, copy in "miscellaneous material," Detroit Real Estate Board Papers, BHC.

63. Vose, *Caucasians Only*, 122–23.

64. Boyle, *Arc of Justice*, 150–53. For further discussion, see ibid., 370 n. 47, where Boyle points out that "contrary to common perception, the mob was not made up exclusively of the working class. Among the leaders of the Tireman Avenue Improvement Association were the Turners' next-door neighbor, Christian Schollenberger, a building contractor, and a man who lived down the block, Ruel Caldwell, an executive in an engineering firm." See also "House Stoned, Negro Quits It," *Detroit News*, 25 June 1925; "Mob of 5,000 Forces Negro to Quit Home," *Detroit Free Press*, 24 June 1925; Levine, *Internal Combustion*, 154–55. John Dancy points out that a few black doctors (in addition to Dr. Turner) were allowed to take their patients to white hospitals, but they had to wear sleeveless gowns to differentiate them from the white doctors who did the operating. See Dancy, *Sand against the Wind*, 146.

65. Martin, *Detroit and the Great Migration*, 31; Levine, *Internal Combustion*, 156–58; *Detroit Free Press*, 8–10 July 1925; 11 July 1925, 1, 4.

66. Boyle, *Arc of Justice*, 155–56; Levine, *Internal Combustion*, 157. *Detroit Free Press*, 10 July 1925, 1, 3; "Negroes Shoot White Youth in New Home Row," *Detroit Free Press*, 11 July 1925, 1, 4.

67. Quote from Boyle, *Arc of Justice*, 157; *Detroit Free Press*, 12 July 1925, 1, 4; Levine, *Internal Combustion*, 157–58.

68. Quotes from Boyle, *Arc of Justice*, 157–58.

69. Ibid., 15, 148–49.

70. Ibid., 334–46; Fine, *Frank Murphy*, 156–62; Martin, *Detroit and the Great Migration*, 31.

71. For the first two quotes, see Boyle, *Arc of Justice*, 225, 241; see also 219. For the third quote, see "The Battles of Washington and Detroit," *Crisis*, December 1925, 68–69, 71.

72. Boyle, *Arc of Justice*, 193–95.

73. Levine, *Internal Combustion*, 165–66; *Detroit Times*, 13 September 1925, 1–2.

74. Schneider, *"We Return Fighting,"* 305–6; Boyle, *Arc of Justice*, 181, 196.

75. John C. Dancy to E. K. Jones, 12 May 1926, box 1, folder 17, DULP; Boyle, *Arc of Justice*, 326.

76. *Detroit Times*, 7 October, 1, and 8 October 1925, 1; Boyle, *Arc of Justice*, 227.

77. *Detroit Times*, 31 October 1925, 1; Boyle, *Arc of Justice*, 263–64.

78. *Detroit Times*, 31 October 1925, 1.

79. Levine, *Internal Combustion*, 173.

80. Boyle, *Arc of Justice*, 334–46; Fine, *Frank Murphy*, 156–62; Martin, *Detroit and the Great Migration*, 31–32.

81. Fine, *Frank Murphy*, 151, 167; Boyle, *Arc of Justice*, 341.

82. Boyle points out that the Garland Fund (officially named the American Fund for Public Service) agreed to create an NAACP Legal Defense Fund by contributing $15,000 dollars if the NAACP could raise $15,000. Thus, the outpouring of contributions for the Sweet case provided the moment that made the birth of the Legal Defense Fund possible. Boyle, *Arc of Justice*, 206, 302–3, 337, 342.

83. Ibid., 263.

84. "Facts Concerning Negroes in Detroit Industrially, Politically, Educationally, Socially, etc." 21 November 1925, 6–7, box 1, folder 15, DULP. A month earlier, Walter White referred to a similar belief connecting freedom of housing with democratic rights. See White, "Negro Segregation Comes North," 459.

85. Quoted in Fine, *Frank Murphy*, 163; *Detroit News*, 26 November 1925.

86. Lilienthal, "Has the Negro the Right to Self-Defense?" 724–25.

87. Quote from Boyle, *Arc of Justice*, 149. During the 1920s, the usual real estate loan was limited to 50 percent of the value of the house, with a requirement that the mortgage be repaid within five years. See Jackson, *Crabgrass Frontier*, 128–37, 190–95.

88. John Dancy, "Negro at the Crossroads," 3 March 1927, 1–4, box 1, folder 19, DULP.

89. Berlin, *Making of African America*, 183–84; Drake and Cayton, *Black Metropolis*.

90. Sugrue, *Sweet Land of Liberty*, 16–17; quote, 16.

91. James Weldon Johnson, quoted in Myrdal, *American Dilemma*, 2:808.

92. Thomas Sugrue makes this point in *Sweet Land of Liberty*, 17.

93. Rev. Bradby to Chief of Police, 20 December 1926, reel 3, SBCP.

94. Sward, *The Legend of Henry Ford*, 230, 232–38.

95. "Colored Civic Pride League," 1926, box 1, folder 16, DULP.

96. "Read and Think," *Detroit Independent*, 7 October 1927, 5; 14 October 1927, 4.

97. Mrs. Eva Radden Jackson to Frank Murphy, September 23, 1930, L. L. Scott to FM, 23 September 1930, James C. Traylor to FM, 25 September 1930, reel 37, FMP.

CHAPTER FIVE

1. Kennedy, *Freedom from Fear*, 22–23.

2. Douglas Brinkley, *Wheels for the World*, 333; Jennings and Brewster, *The Century*, 103; David L. Lewis, "Sex and the Automobile," 129.

3. Nevins and Hill, *Ford: Expansion*, 409–21; Ford, *My Life and Work*, 67–72.

4. Douglas Brinkley, *Wheels for the World*, 336–37.

5. Nevins and Hill, *Ford: Expansion*, 416–26; Douglas Brinkley, *Wheels for the World*, 338–43.

6. Douglas Brinkley, *Wheels for the World*, 338–43; Nevins and Hill, *Ford: Expansion*, 416–26.

7. Douglas Brinkley, *Wheels for the World*, 347.

8. Ibid., 348–52.

9. Nevins and Hill, *Ford: Expansion*, 431–36; Douglas Brinkley, *Wheels for the World*, 347–52.

10. Moon, *Untold Tales*, 40.

11. Carlson, "The Negro in the Industries of Detroit," 99; "Mass Production Poverty," *New Republic*, 7 March 1928, 86.

12. Niebuhr, "Ford's Five-Day Week Shrinks," 713; Levin, "Ford Unemployment Policy," 101.

13. Niebuhr, "Ford's Five-Day Week Shrinks," 713; Levin, "Ford Unemployment Policy," 103.

14. Fine, *Frank Murphy*, 202–3; Davidson, "Industrial Detroit after World War I," 134–40.

15. Niebuhr, "Ford's Five-Day Week Shrinks," 713; for caseload figures, see Fine, *Frank Murphy*, 203.

16. Niebuhr, "How Philanthropic Is Henry Ford?" 1516.

17. Niebuhr, *Leaves from the Notebook of a Tamed Cynic*, 112, 116–17.

18. Niebuhr, "How Philanthropic Is Henry Ford?" 1517.

19. Watts, *People's Tycoon*, 401, 422–23.

20. Ibid., 425.

21. Ibid., 401–3.

22. Nevins and Hill, *Ford: Expansion*, 573–74. For the perpetuation of the impression that Henry Ford thought of history as bunk, see Sward, *Legend of Henry Ford*, 100–110. For a more complicated interpretation, see Watts, *People's Tycoon*, 422–23.

23. Quoted in Watts, *People's Tycoon*, 424.

24. Nevins and Hill, *Ford: Expansion*, 573–75. Downward pressure on real wages occurred at the FMC as Ford kept skilled workers who would naturally receive high wages and discharged less skilled workers. Thus the public relations regarding Ford's seven dollar a day plan in late 1929 must be understood in conjunction with the fact that the company subcontracted an increasing proportion of its jobs to suppliers who paid much lower wages than Ford Motor Company. See ibid., 531–34, 578–79. The Edsel Ford quote is from Douglas Brinkley, *Wheels for the World*, 378.

25. Fine, *Frank Murphy*, 201.

26. Ibid.; Haber, "Fluctuations in Employment," 144, 148; Lent D. Upson to Clark Branion, 8 May 1930, MOR; C. C. McGill, Secretary, Public Affairs Bureau, Detroit Board of Commerce, Radio Talk, Station WXYZ, 22 September 1930, 4, FMP.

27. Helen Hall, "When Detroit's Out of Gear," 9.

28. *Detroit Saturday Night*, 3, 10 May 1930.

29. "Ford Output Gains 138%," *New York Times*, 8 January 1930, 20; Nevins, *Ford: Expansion*, 570–71. For Ford's pumping up of sales, see Nevins and Hill, *Ford: Expansion*, 579–83. For employment figures, see Levin, "Ford Unemployment Policy," 101; Douglas Brinkley, *Wheels for the World*, 381.

30. Nevins and Hill, *Ford: Expansion*, 572, 596.

31. Douglas Brinkley, *Wheels for the World*, 387.

32. Ibid., 338, 387–88.

33. Ibid., 382, 388.

34. Nevins and Hill, *Ford: Expansion*, 588; Douglas Brinkley, *Wheels for the World*, 382.

35. Nevins and Hill, *Ford: Expansion*, 587.

36. Fine, *Frank Murphy*, 203.

37. Levin, "Ford Unemployment Policy," 107; Helen Hall, "When Detroit's Out of Gear," 10.

38. For quote, see Fragnoli, *Transformation of Reform*, 336; see also *Detroit Times*, 18 November 1929.

39. William Lovett quoted in Fragnoli, *Transformation of Reform*, 340–41.

40. Ibid., 347, 349.

41. Quotes from Confidential Memo by W. P. L [Lovett], 25 April 1930, Candidate Files, box 3, DCLP. For identification of Harold Emmons, see Fragnoli, *Transformation of Reform*, 341.

42. Engelmann, "Separate Peace," 69. See also Player, "Gangsters and Politicians," 362; *Nation*, 6 August 1930, 138–39.

43. Nevins and Hill, *Ford: Expansion*, 589; Willis Ward, "Reminiscences," accession #65, BFRC.

44. Nevins and Hill, *Ford: Expansion*, 586–92, quote 586.

45. Widick, *Detroit*, 46–47. Dillard, *Faith in the City*, 57.

46. Dillard, *Faith in the City*, 56–57; Roger Keeran, *Communist Party and the Auto Workers Union*, 96–147; *Auto Workers News*, July, September, and October 1927; Mark Solomon, *The Cry Was Unity*, 190–96.

47. Fine, *Frank Murphy*, 250.

48. Joseph Billups and Rose Billups, interview by Herbert Hill, Shelton Tappes, and Roberta McBride, 27 October 1967, 6, BLM.

49. Dillard, *Faith in the City*, 50–51; Wolcott, *Remaking Respectability*, 126–30, 172–83.

50. Fine, *Frank Murphy*, 214.

51. Rothman, "Detroit Elects a Liberal."

52. *Detroit Times*, 2, 7, 9, 10 August 1930.

53. Frank Murphy, "Transcript of Stenographic Notes of Address by Honorable Frank Murphy at the Fort Wayne Hotel, Detroit, Michigan, 19 August 1930," 4–5, reel 141, FMP.

54. Ibid., 7–10, 14, 11, 15, 18; for "lifting eyes to a new dawn," see 11; for "common herd," see 15. While we today may view the term "common herd" as a pejorative, at the time the working men and women Murphy appealed to did not see the term as such.

55. Ibid., 19.

56. Ibid., 14, 18.

57. "Murphy Asks for Votes Bowles Scorns," *Detroit Times*, 21 August 1930, reel 163, FMP.

58. *Detroit News*, 6 September 1930; *Detroit Times*, 5, 7, 8, 9 September 1930.

59. Murphy to Beulah Young, n.d., reel 8, FMP.

60. Murphy to Oscar DePriest, 26 November 1930, DePriest to FM, 13 September 1930; Walter White to Murphy, 2 September 1930; Moses L. Walker to Murphy, 10 September 1930; John Dancy to Murphy, 13 September 1930; Sismae Bagley to Murphy, 4 September 1930; Rev. C. W. Clark to FM, 3 September 1930; all from reel 6, FMP.

61. "Negroes to Hold Murphy Meeting," *Detroit Times*, 31 August 1930, reel 163, FMP; *Second Baptist Herald*, 19 October 1930, 1, reel 10, SBCP.

62. Murphy to Oscar DePriest, 26 November 1930, DePriest to FM, 13 September 1930; Walter White to Murphy, 2 September 1930; Moses L. Walker to Murphy, 10 September 1930; all from reel 6, FMP. Thomas Solomon, "Participation of Negroes in Detroit Elections," 89; Fine interview of Harry Mead, 15 August 1963, 3–4, 8, box 1, Frank Murphy Oral History Project, BHL.

63. "Vote Cast at the Primary Election Held September 9, 1930," reel 6, FMP.

64. Murphy to Walter White, 13 September 1930, reel 6, FMP.

65. Fine, *Frank Murphy*, 220.

66. The existence of political organizations and networks found in the Frank Murphy Papers may raise more questions than it answers. The FMP, especially its large holdings of news clippings, reveal robust political networks in black Detroit. The 1930 campaign was able to tap into a rich political infrastructure within black Detroit to get out the black vote. Stationery and letterheads were not just created at a moment's notice during the late summer of 1930. The frustration lies with the newspaper sources that no longer exist for the twenties. We may never know what secrets may be buried in those sources.

67. Mrs. Eva Radden Jackson to Murphy, 23 September 1930; L. L. Scott to Murphy, 23 September 1930; James C. Traylor to Murphy, 25 September 1930; all from reel 7, FMP.

68. RJK to Murphy, 28 May 1931, reel 8, FMP.

69. Rev. C. W. Clark (signed "colored") to Murphy, 13 September 1930; Mrs. G. C. Jefferson (signed: "a colored moral Citizen, and Civic worker") to Murphy, 14 September 1930; both from reel 6, FMP.

70. Eva Radden Jackson and Bumella Holley to Murphy, 23 September 1930; James C. Traylor to Murphy, 25 September 1930; both from reel 7, FMP.

71. Beulah Young to Murphy, 14 September, 24 November 1930, reel 7, FMP; Fine, *Frank Murphy*, 240.

72. "Political Leadership Assembly," *Detroit People's News*, 28 December 1930.

73. Jim Lee to Murphy, 30 September 1930, reel 7, FMP.

74. W. P. Lovett to Alvan Macauley Jr., 19 January 1931, reel 8; see also Alvan Macauley to Murphy, 22 January 1931, a letter that includes a copy of the correspondence from Lovett to Macauley, reel 8, FMP.

75. Fine, *Frank Murphy*, 225.

76. Text of radio address by Frank Murphy, 1931, 1–2, reel 141, FMP.

77. Ibid., 6, 3, 7.

78. With regard to Hans Kohn's claim, see Fine, *Frank Murphy*, 226. For more on this claim, see Muller, "Frank Murphy: Ornament of the Bar," 182.

79. Fine, *Frank Murphy*, 190.

80. Ibid., 190, 262.

81. Ibid., 263.

82. Text of radio talk by C. C. McGill, secretary, Public Affairs Bureau, Detroit Board of Commerce, 22 September 1930, 4–5, reel 95, FMP.

83. Fine, *Frank Murphy*, 288–89.

84. Ibid., 286–87; *Crisis*, December 1931, 414; Dancy to Walter White, 9 March 1932, DULP; FM to Ballenger, 9 January 1932, and Ballenger to FM, 13 January 1932, MOR.

85. Fine, *Frank Murphy*, 263–64, 307; Lewis to FM, 19 June 1931, and undated typed sheet [1931], MOR.

86. Fine, *Frank Murphy*, 302, 304–5; C. C. McGill radio talk, 10 May 1931, and Lovett to Murphy, 1 May 1931, and enclosed resolution, MOR. The Detroit Department of Public Welfare published annual reports for 1929 and 1930, but not for 1931–39. To fill out the gaps, Sidney Fine recommends Egbert S. Wengert, *Financial Problems of the City of Detroit in the Depression* (Detroit, 1939) and William J. Norton, "The Relief Crisis in Detroit," *Social Science Review* 7 (March 1933): 1–10. Consult "Bibliographic Note" in Fine, *Frank Murphy*, 575, for a deeper discussion. See also Walker, "Down and Out in Detroit," and Dos Passos, "Detroit," 280–82.

87. Fine, *Frank Murphy* 302, 305–6.

88. "Expert Attacks Ford Policy on Unemployment Situation," 12 March 1931, newspaper clipping, reel 155, FMP.

89. Levin, "Ford Unemployment Policy," 107.

90. Ibid., 105.

91. Ibid., 107. *Detroit News*, 12, 13 June 1931.

92. *Detroit News*, 17, 19–27 June, 2 July 1931; Josephine Gomon, "Mayoral Reelection," unpublished manuscript, 28, JGP; Levin, "Ford Unemployment Policy," 107–8.

93. Sward, *Legend of Henry Ford*, 226.

94. Editorial, *New Republic*, 7 October 1931, 191. The discussion of the dire straits that Detroiters were in continued. A Wayne County Coroner's official (Detroit is in Wayne County) objected to the editorial, claiming there had been no deaths from starvation. The October editorial was based on information from a physician in a Detroit hospital who would not give his name for fear of losing his job. The editors of the *New Republic* suggested that one reason for the difference in interpretation may be that "while a diagnosis by medical authorities assigns a specific disease as the cause of death, undernourishment is an important contributing factor." The Michigan Department of Health

specifically directed doctors "never to report mere symptoms, or terminal conditions . . . when a definite disease can be ascertained as the cause." See editorial, *New Republic*, 25 November 1931, 29–30.

95. Fine, *Frank Murphy*, 311.

96. Louis B. Ward to Murphy, 24 June 1931, 1–2, and Murphy to Louis Ward, 25 June 1931, reel 8, FMP.

97. Ward to Murphy, 24 June 1931, 1–2, and Murphy to Ward, 25 June 1931, reel 8, FMP.

98. "Revolt in U.S. Seen by Priest: Fr. Coughlin Blames Ford for Forcing Workers into Communist Party," *Detroit News*, July 26, 1930, in accession #572, box 30, folder: 12.18, "Radicals," BFRC. See discussion and analysis by Alan Brinkley, *Voices of Protest*, 102–3.

99. Josephine Gomon, "Mayoral Reelection," 34, JGP.

100. "Detroit's Duel over Doles," *Literary Digest*, 11 July 1931, 11; Fine, *Frank Murphy*, 302–3 (Gomon quote, 303); *Detroit News*, 30, 31 May, 7, 9, 12, 15–18, 25–27, 29, 30 June, and 1 July 1931.

101. "Detroit's Duel over Doles," 11.

102. William L. Stidger to Murphy, 2 July 1931, and Murphy to Byron Foy, 3 June 1931, reel 8, FMP.

103. Fine, *Frank Murphy*, 432–33.

104. Josephine Gomon, "The Unusual Events of Labor Day in 1931," box 8, folder: Gomon writings, Murphy misc., JGP.

105. For a report on Frank Murphy's campaign appearance on 14 September 1931 at Second Baptist Church and all quotes, see *Second Baptist Church Herald*, 20 September 1931, 1, 8, 10, accession #572, box 28, folder: 12.7.3, "Policies," BFRC.

106. Bradby to Sorenson, 24 September 1931, accession #572, box 28, folder: 12.7.3, "Policies," BFRC.

107. Ibid., 2.

108. Ibid.

109. David L. Lewis, "History of Negro Employment in Detroit Area Plants," 21–26.

110. Bradby to Sorenson, 17 November 1931, 2, accession #572, box 28, folder: 12.7.3, "Policies," BFHC.

111. R. L. Bradby, "Remarks" 28 September 1931, reel 3, SBCP.

112. Rev. Tyra Mopping and Beulah Young to "Dear Sir," 18 July 1931, and Rev. Tyra Mopping to Frank Murphy, July 21, 1931; reel 8, FMP. See also Fine, *Frank Murphy*, 240.

113. "Political Leadership Assembly," *Detroit People's News*, 28 December 1930.

114. James C. Traylor to Murphy, 23 October 1931, reel 10, FMP.

115. *Detroit Times*, 16 September 1931, reel 156, FMP.

116. The Tenth Councilman, "Murphy's Colored Supporters Make Staff Shiver," *Detroit Saturday Night*, 26 September 1931, reel 156, FMP.

117. Murphy to Beulah Young, n.d. [1930]; Young to Murphy, 21 July 1931, reel 8, FMP. See also Young to Murphy, 14 September, 24 November 1930, 7 January 1931, reel 8. FMP. For sanitation workers' band, see "Reported Meetings by Murphy," reel 141, FMP.

118. Fine argues that the "leading newspaper" in black Detroit advised African Ameri-

cans not to vote for Murphy because he was a Democrat. While that may have been the case, the advice was ignored. For this suggestion and more on the reelection campaign, see Fine, *Frank Murphy*, 432–37.

119. Text of Radio Campaign Speech, Frank Murphy, October 1931, 6–7, reel 141, FMP.

120. Citizens' Fact Finding Committee, "How and Why are You Voting, November 3rd?" Campaign of 1931, "Publicity," Frank Murphy MS, BHC. With regard to the suggestion that the KKK authored the pamphlet, see Fine, *Frank Murphy*, 438.

121. Fine, *Frank Murphy*, 439.

122. Ibid., 231.

123. Robert L. Bradby to Murphy, 17 November 1931, reel 3, SBCP.

124. Ibid.; W. Hayes McKinney to Murphy, 23 November 1931, box 4, folder: Ford Motor Co., 1931, MOR.

125. "A Friend" [writer is afraid to give his name fearing for his job] to R. L. Bradby, n.d. [most likely, given content, 16 November 1931]; J. H. Wilson to Dr. R. L. Bradby; both in accession #572, box 28, folder: 12.7.3, "Policies," BFRC.

126. Murphy to Harry Bennett, 31 December 1931, box 4, folder: Ford Motor Company, MOR.

127. Fine, *Frank Murphy*, 262.

CHAPTER SIX

1. Sward, *Legend of Henry Ford*, 229–30.

2. Nevins and Hill, *Ford: Expansion*, 325.

3. Sward writes that Ford "commandeered the entire village of Inkster for a localized experiment in 'self-help' and rehabilitation"; *Legend of Henry Ford*, 229. See also Conot, *American Odyssey*, 356–57; Lacey, *Ford*, 322–23; Meier and Rudwick, *Black Detroit*, 15; Watts, *People's Tycoon*, 435; Georgakas and Surkin, *Detroit*; Widick, *Detroit*, 31. The FMC perpetuated the idea that Inkster was an all-black suburb. See, for example, Edward J. Cutler, "Reminiscences," March 1952, vol. 2, 159–60, Oral History, BFRC.

4. Cobb, "The Negro in the Inkster Village Council," 3, UM-HS.

5. Lindsey, "Fields to Fords," 19.

6. Ibid., 30, 32. As Lindsey notes, it is difficult, at best, to ascertain the size of Inkster's population before 1930 because Inkster encompassed parts of two townships in Wayne County, Nankin and Dearborn. See Lindsey, "Fields to Ford," 59 n. 66.

7. Ibid., 30.

8. Lacey, *Ford*, 322; Conot, *American Odyssey*, 356.

9. Lindsey, "Fields to Fords," 36–37.

10. "Report of Inkster, Michigan," 4 February 1931, pp. 1–2, accession #1, box 178, BFRC.

11. Lindsey, "Fields to Fords," 31.

12. Cobb, "The Negro in the Inkster Village Council," 6–12, UM-HS.

13. Ibid.

14. Ibid., 12–13.

15. Ibid., 15.

16. "Inkster Commissary," accession #285, box 1903, folder: 363-111, BFRC.

17. Sward, *Legend of Henry Ford*, 229–30; Lacey, *Ford*, 322–23.

18. Meier and Rudwick, *Black Detroit*, 15, 155; *Detroit Times*, 17 December 1931. On occasion, Ford's Inkster Project extended a "loan" to a family with no record of work at the FMC. But the route to repayment of the loan was still linked to work on the Inkster account. See Lindsey, "Fields to Fords," 79.

19. "Inkster Commissary," Report, accession #285, box 1903, folder: 363-111, p. 2, BFRC.

20. Ibid.

21. For the revived Sociological Department, see Hayward S. Ablewhite, "Reminiscences," 16 May 1951, 11, BFRC. For a discussion of Henry Ford as the "despot of Dearborn" and his view of dirt as offensive, see a copy of the article by Waldemar Kaempffert, "The Mussolini of Highland Park," *New York Times*, 8 January 1928, sec. 5, accession #572, box 7, BFRC. Kaempffert writes that Ford's most violent aversion was to dirt; it could be called an obsession. "No foundries are as clean as Ford's. No locomotives ever gleamed like those of Ford's railroad. Scores of sweepers ply the broom in the shops. Ships are proverbially spick and span, but Ford's tugboats, ore carriers and ocean steamers are scoured, scrubbed, painted and polished with a meticulousness that would win the admiration of a battleship's commander. The vast laboratory at Dearborn has a polished floor as clean and slippery as ice."

22. For investigators' judgments, see "Inkster Commissary," Report, accession #285, box 1903, folder: 363-111, p. 1, BFRC. Investigators forgot to note that purchase of a Ford automobile was thought to be, according to the lore of Ford employees, a requirement for keeping a job at the FMC. As early as 1927, the FMC had a "check list" of the makes of cars in the Parking Grounds of the Fordson Plant. The detailed survey documented forty different makes and the number represented in the parking lot during three successive shifts. The bottom line revealed that 64.59 percent were Fords. See Check List, Fordson Plant, 17 November 1927, accession #572, box 30, folder: 12.12, "General policies," BFRC. For the lore of the work culture at the FMC, see also Bailer, "Negro Labor in the Automobile Industry," 177–78.

23. Conot, *American Odyssey*, 355–59.

24. "Inkster Commissary," Report, accession #285, box 1903, folder: 363-111, p. 1, BFRC.

25. Meyer, *Five Dollar Day*, 149; see also 151.

26. Moon, *Untold Tales*, 37.

27. Liebold, "Reminiscences," quoted by Conot, *American Odyssey*, 357. Ernest G. Liebold had power of attorney for both Henry and Clara Ford and handled practically all Ford business other than that of the FMC. For example, Liebold handled the Peace Ship project during World War I, was general manager of the *Dearborn Independent*, and managed the Dearborn Realty and Construction Company, developing and constructing Henry Ford Hospital. Ford R. Bryan claims that Ford had "sufficient trust in Liebold's integrity to offer him the power of attorney for both himself and Clara Ford on July 13, 1918. This power was used many times in behalf of the Fords during the next twenty-six years." Bryan, *Henry's Lieutenants*, 169–74.

28. For a detailed, comprehensive report on surveillance of white workers by the Sociological Department, see Meyer, *The Five Dollar Day*.

29. "Sociological Activities," report by E. D. Brown, 26 February 1936, accession #285, box 1903, folder: 363-111, BFRC.

30. For example, accession #55, box 116, "Welfare Correspondence," BFRC.

31. For a good discussion of the social agenda promoted by Henry Ford with his Five Dollar Day project, see Watts, *People's Tycoon*, 199–200.

32. Lindsey, "Fields to Ford," 74, 103–4; E. D. Brown's report noted by Charles Wartman, "Henry Ford and the Negro," *Chicago Defender*, 24 October 1953, 9.

33. Wartman, "Henry Ford and the Negro."

34. See Lindsey, "Fields to Ford," 102–14.

35. See cases in "Welfare" files, accession #55, box 116, BFRC.

36. "Sociological Activities," report by E. D. Brown, 26 February 1936, accession #285, box 1903, folder: 363-111, BFRC.

37. "Departmental Communication," to E. D. Brown, 24 March 1939: the writer reports on four deceased men from the Inkster Welfare Ledger, wondering whether other family members might be able to "pay off this balance"; "Dept. Communication," to Brown, 29 March 1938; H. M. Evans to E. D. Brown, cc: H. S. Ablewhite, Sociological Department, Departmental Communication, 10 June 1942, Welfare Correspondence, accession #55, box 116, BFRC.

38. "Departmental Communication," to E. D. Brown, 29 December 1938, accession #55, box 116, folder: miscel. Welfare, BFRC.

39. Laurie B. Green, *Battling the Plantation Mentality*. See also Honey, *Going Down Jericho Road*, 11. It was not uncommon for black Ford workers from the thirties to refer to the FMC as "the plantation"; more recent employees have done so as well. For references to the FMC as "the plantation," see David Moore, interview by author, 16 December 2007; Quill Pettway, interview by author, 20 December 2006; General G. Baker, interview by author, 8 December 2003.

40. See, for example, "Dr. Carver Had Great Friend in Henry Ford," *Pittsburgh Courier*, 19 April 1947, 22, which honored Henry Ford at the time of his death as a philanthropist who generously aided blacks in Inkster, or the remembrance more than two decades after the beginning of Ford's Inkster Project by Charles Wartman, "Henry Ford and the Negro," *Chicago Defender*, 24 October 1953, 9.

41. Lindsey, "Fields to Ford," 87.

42. H. S. Abelwhite's reflections quoted in Wartman, "Henry Ford and the Negro," 9.

43. Candler, *America's Greatest Depression*, 44.

44. Nevins and Hill, *Ford: Expansion*, 587.

45. Conot, *American Odyssey*, 367.

46. Nevins and Hill, *Ford: Decline*, 5

47. Ibid., 2–4, 478 (Appendix 1); Chandler, *Giant Enterprise*, 3.

48. The Model A had lost its appeal, leading to loss in sales of a little less than 1 million Ford passenger cars between 1930 and 1931. At the same time, the FMC faced competition from improved models of Chevrolet and Plymouth. Both General Motors and

Chrysler forced Ford to upgrade the Model A. Lacey, *Ford*, 321; Nevins and Hill, *Ford: Decline*, 3–4, 7 (figures); Douglas Brinkley, *Wheels for the World*, 385. *Fortune* reported a $140 million loss for the FMC from 1931 to 1933; see Watts, *People's Tycoon*, 427. For tables compiled from U. S. Department of Commerce statistics, see Chandler, *Giant Enterprise*, 3–7.

49. "Mr. Ford Doesn't Care," *Fortune*, December 1933, 62–69, 122, 125, 126, 128, 131, 132–34; quote on 63.

50. Klann, "Reminiscences"; *New York Times*, 17 February 1923, 10 August 1924; cited in Nevins and Hill, *Ford: Expansion*, 526–27, 578–79.

51. "Ford's Wage Rise Comes as a Surprise," *New York Times*, 22 November 1929; "Ford Announces Immediate Wage Increase," *Detroit Free Press*, 22 November 1929; "Henry Ford on Unemployment," *Business Week*, 8 June 1932, 19; Watts, *The People's Tycoon*, 427–32; Ford, *Moving Forward*, 12–13; Lacey, *Ford*, 320.

52. William Cameron quoted by Lacey, *Ford*, 322.

53. Levin, "Ford Unemployment Policy," 105; Douglas Brinkley, *Wheels for the World*, 388; Nevins and Hill, *Ford: Expansion*, 586–96.

54. Figures cited in Nevins and Hill, *Ford: Expansion*, 687.

55. Ibid., 599; Douglas Brinkley, *Wheels for the World*, 388.

56. Cuningham, *J8: Chronicle of Neglected Truth*, 9, BHL.

57. "Relief Fund Needs Money, *Detroit News*, 6 March 1932, 3.

58. *Detroit News*, 3 January 1933, cited in Sward, *Legend of Henry Ford*, 223–24.

59. The figure for March 1929 does not include the Lincoln plant, located in the city of Detroit. Including Lincoln brings the total employed to 128,142. Levin, "The Ford Unemployment Policy," 101–8. Douglass Brinkley, *Wheels for the World*, 388; Nevins and Hill, *Ford: Expansion*, 573–93.

60. McCormick, "Ford Seeks a New Balance for Industry," 4; Ford quoted in Douglass Brinkley, *Wheels for the World*, 389.

61. Baskin, "Ford Hunger March," 335; Lacey, *Ford*, 359.

62. Peterson, "Auto Workers Confront the Depression," 57; for quotes by Albert Goetz, see Sugar, *Ford Hunger March*, 32–34; Bonosky, *Brother Bill McKie*, 76; David Moore, Interview, January 1984, 4, TU-OH.

63. Sugar, *Ford Hunger March*, 34–37; Baskin, "Ford Hunger March," 336–38.

64. Sugar, *Ford Hunger March*, 34–37; Baskin, "Ford Hunger March," 336–39. Several sources refer to the young Bussell as Joseph, yet both the *New York Times* and Christopher Alston, who was at the march with Bussell when he was killed, call him George Bussell. *New York Times*, 9 March 1932, 3; Mary Schroeder, "'32 Marcher Remembers Friend Who Fell to Guns," *Detroit Free Press*, 3 March 1982, box 1, CMAP.

65. David Moore interview, "Ford Hunger March," 28 May 1996, VT: 209, tape 2, Audiovisual Collections, ALUA; David Moore, interview by author, 10 December 2007, Detroit, Mich.

66. Bonosky, *Brother Bill McKie*, 71–73; Peterson, "Auto Workers Confront the Depression," 57; Ruth Seymour, "Union Honors Martyrs," *Detroit News*, 21 June 1979, box 1, folder 4, CMAP. For more on the Ford Hunger March, in addition to above citations,

see *New York Times*, 8 March, 1932; *Detroit Times*, 8 March 1932; William Lovett Memo, 8 March 1932, DCLP; Sugar, "Bullets—Not Food—for Ford Workers"; Fine, *Frank Murphy*, 403–12.

67. David Moore, interview by Judith Stepan-Norris, January 1984, Detroit, 4–5, TU-OH.

68. Bonosky, *Brother Bill McKie*, 76, 79.

69. Moon, *Untold Tales*, 107.

70. Baskin, "Ford Hunger March," 347.

71. See, for example, issues of *Detroit Free Press* and *Detroit Times*, 9–11 March 1932; *Detroit News*, 9 March 1932, 4.

72. Dos Passos quoted in Douglas Brinkley, *Wheels for the World*, 392; see also, Lacey, *Ford*, 365; Watts, *People's Tycoon*, 195–96.

73. Joseph and Rose Billups, interview by Roberta McBride, 9 September 1967, 1–4, BLM; Baskin, "Ford Hunger March," 357.

74. For "something had to be done," see David Moore interview, "Ford Hunger March," 28 May 1996, VT: 209, tape 2, Audiovisual Collections, AULA; my thanks to Tom Featherstone for leading me to this tape. Another source is David Moore, interview by Judith Stepan-Norris, 5 January 1984, TU-OH. For the impact of the Hunger March on Moore's life, see Moore, interview by author, 10 December 2007.

75. Shelton Tappes interview, n.d., p. 1, box 54, folder 7, MSP; Moon, *Untold Tales*, 107.

76. Mary Schroeder, "'32 Marcher Remembers Friend," *Detroit Free Press*, 3 March 1982, box 1, CMAP.

77. Wilson, "Despot of Dearborn," 26.

78. Nevins and Hill, *Ford: Expansion*, 607.

79. Cruden, *End of the Ford Myth*, 3.

80. Nevins and Hill, *Ford: Expansion*, 524; Douglas Brinkley, *Wheels for the World*, 384–85; Watts, *People's Tycoon*, 447; Sward, *Legend of Henry Ford*, 293–98, 305.

81. O'Brien, "Henry Ford's Commander in Chief," 67–68; Douglas Brinkley, *Wheels for the World*, 385; Watts, *The People's Tycoon*, 445–46; *New York Times*, 26 June 1937, quoted by Sward, *Legend of Henry Ford*, 293.

82. See, for example, "Labor Espionage: B. J. Liccardi" and "Labor, Radicals, Socialist Party in Detroit, 1919–1920," Reports of Op. [operative] 15, Labor Detroit organization 1914–1925, Espionage Papers, accession #940, box 5; Memo: E. G. Liebold to Harry Bennett, 14 May 1931, accession #285, box 1310, BFRC. The Liebold memo documents the names and addresses of registered voters from School District No. 5, employed at the Rouge, FMC. Much of the information kept by the FMC treated private civil matters as company concerns. For invasion of privacy as a policy, see, for example, Henry Shearer to Charles S. Sorensen, 9 March 1933; 6 March 1933, 1–3; 8 March 1933, Reports, p. 1; all in accession #572, box 33, folder: 18.10, "Espionage," BFRC.

83. Lacey, *Ford*, 362–63; quotes from O'Brien, "Henry Ford's Commander in Chief," 69–70.

84. Meyer, *Five Dollar Day*, 6–7; Ford, *My Life and Work*, 11.

85. Whatley and Mahoney, "Making the Extra Effort," 490.

86. Whatley, Wright, and Foote, "Arbitraging a Discriminatory Labor Market" (2001), 16–17.

87. Ibid.

88. Foote, Whatley, and Wright demonstrate "upward pressure on the foundry wage" when employment growth at the firm was high. See Foote, Whatley, and Wright, "Arbitraging a Discriminatory Labor Market" (2003), 513. See also Whatley, Wright, and Foote, "Arbitraging a Discriminatory Labor Market" (2001), 17.

89. Foote, Whatley, and Wright, "Arbitraging a Discriminatory Labor Market" (2003), 524.

90. David Moore from interview by author, 10 December 2007.

91. Whatley, Wright, and Foote, "Arbitraging a Discriminatory Labor Market" (2001), 17.

92. Ibid., 19–21.

93. Maloney and Whatley, "Making the Effort," 465–93, 470.

94. Nevins and Hill, *Ford: Decline*, 133.

95. Foote, Whatley, and Wright, "Arbitraging a Discriminatory Labor Market" (2003), 527.

96. McCormick, "Ford Seeks a New Balance for Industry," 4.

97. Ibid., 5.

98. Ibid.

99. Ibid., 4. See also McCormick, "Future of the Ford Idea," 2; Henry Ford, *Today and Tomorrow*, 8–9.

100. Sward, *Legend of Henry Ford*, 465; Douglas Brinkley, *Wheels for the World*, 402, 404; Downs, *Diego Rivera*, 25, 34, 171. Quotes from Rivera, *My Art, My Life*, 186.

101. Rivera, *My Art, My Life*, 187; Downs, *Diego Rivera*, 186.

102. Sterne, "Museum Director and the Artist," 98, 88; Downs, *Diego Rivera*, 29.

103. Sterne, "Museum Director and the Artist," 88, 98–99; Downs, *Diego Rivera*, 21–25. Quotes from Rivera, *My Art, My Life*, 183.

104. Downs, *Diego Rivera*, 165.

105. Grandin, *Fordlandia*, 246; Lacey, *Ford*, 341–42; Downs, *Diego Rivera*, 167.

106. Downs, *Diego Rivera*, 165.

107. Ibid., 166, 186.

108. Lacey, *Ford*, 335.

109. Rivera, *My Art, My Life*, 188–200.

110. Downs, *Diego Rivera*, 21–22, 175; Rivera, *My Art, My Life*, 197.

111. Rivera, *My Art, My Life*, 198.

CHAPTER SEVEN

1. Dillard, *Faith in the City*, 48–49.

2. Young, *Hard Stuff*, 38.

3. Bailer, "Negro Labor in the Automobile Industry," 177–78.

4. Willis Ward, Chronology, iii, Oral History, accession #65, box 21, BFRC.

5. For service men searching for labor "agitators," see Nevins and Hill, *Ford: Expansion*, 592. For Ford's response to section 7A of the NIRA, see Nevins and Hill, *Ford: Decline*, 16, 38–40.

6. Watts, *People's Tycoon*, 491.

7. Nevins and Hill, *Ford: Decline*, 40; Douglas Brinkley, *Wheels for the World*, 424.

8. Nevins and Hill, *Ford: Decline*, 2, 7, 16–17, 26–27; Nevins and Hill, *Ford: Expansion*, 589.

9. Sitkoff, *New Deal for Blacks*, 145–46; Dillard, *Faith in the City*, 60; Weiss, *Farewell to the Party of Lincoln*, 42; Naison, *Communists in Harlem*, 65–66.

10. Naison, *Communists in Harlem*, 58–59, 61–62; Carter, *Scottsboro*, 52–54, 56, 61–63.

11. Naison, *Communists in Harlem*, 62 (Walter White quote and communists' retort to White). For ILD controlling the Scottsboro case, see ibid., 66. For more on Scottsboro, see Goodman, *Stories of Scottsboro*; Miller, *Remembering Scottsboro*; Pennybacker, *From Scottsboro to Munich*.

12. Gunnar Myrdal called the NAACP branches the "lifeline of the Association," adding that "the National Office is constantly struggling to maintain them in vigor and to found new branches." Myrdal, *An American Dilemma*, 2:822; Bunche, "The Programs, Ideologies, Tactics," 52, Carnegie-Myrdal Study of the Negro in America Papers, Schomburg, New York Public Library; Bates, "New Crowd Challenges Old Guard," 358.

13. *Detroit Tribune*, 22 April 1933, 8.

14. See, for example, the coverage in the *Detroit Tribune*, 14 April 1933, 1, 3, when Samuel Lebrowitz, chief counsel for the defense, got Ruby Bates to recant all her testimony against the Scottsboro Boys.

15. *Detroit Tribune*, 22 April 1933, 8.

16. Joseph Billups and Rose Billups, interview by Herbert Hill, Shelton Tappes, and Roberta McBride, Detroit, 27 October 1967, 6–7, BLM; used by permission of Herbert Hill. Naison, *Communists in Harlem*, 75.

17. Editorial, "Communism and Colored America," *Detroit Tribune Independent*, 10 March 1934, 8. By early 1934, the *Detroit Tribune* became the *Detroit Tribune Independent*.

18. Bates, "New Crowd Challenges the Old Guard," 343–44.

19. Meier and Rudwick, *Black Detroit*, 17. For economic nationalism in the BTWTA, see Dillard, *Faith in the City*, 51–53; Wolcott, *Remaking Respectability*, 176–79.

20. For principles of the BTWTA and the Detroit Housewives' League, see pamphlet, Detroit, Michigan, 1935, box 1, folder: "Declaration of Purpose 1935"; and "History and Purpose of Housewives League," by Mrs. F. B. Peck, Housewives Page, May 1, 1934, p. 2, box 1, folder: "History," in Housewives' League of Detroit Papers, BHC; quote from Wolcott, *Remaking Respectability*, 176–77.

21. For the role of boosters, see Richard Thomas, *Life for Us Is What We Make It*, 215–18, and Wolcott, *Remaking Respectability*, 178.

22. Wolcott, *Remaking Respectability*, 183.

23. See handwritten history by Mrs. F. B. Peck, 1932, p. 2, box 1, folder: "History"; *Constitution and By-Laws of Housewives' League of Detroit*, *Declaration of Principles of the Constitution and By-Laws of the Booker T. Washington Trade Association*, box 1, folder:

"History," Housewives' League of Detroit Papers, BHC; Meier and Rudwick, *Black Detroit*, 18.

24. *Detroit Independent*, 16 July and 23 April 1932, both cited in Thomas Solomon, "Participation of Negroes in Detroit Elections," 55–56.

25. Beulah Young to Murphy, 8 June 1932, box 6, folder: "Interracial," MOR.

26. Fine, *Frank Murphy*, 442–48.

27. Nevins and Hill, *Ford: Decline*, 11–12. David L. Lewis mentions Ford's attempts to "swing the Detroit's Negro vote"; see Lewis, "History of Negro Employment in Detroit Area Plants," 37–38.

28. Fine, *Frank Murphy*, 448–49.

29. Ortquist, "Depression Politics in Michigan," 192–93; Fine, *Frank Murphy*, 448.

30. Figures are drawn from Fine, *Frank Murphy*, 450, and Litchfield, *Voting Behavior in a Metropolitan Area*, 39.

31. Dillard, *Faith in the City*, 70–71; Meier and Rudwick, *Black Detroit*, 32–33; Richard Thomas, *Life for Us Is What We Make It*, 265; Solomon, "Participation of Negroes in Detroit Elections," 22–23.

32. "J. A. Craigen Wins Oratorical Contest," *Detroit Tribune*, 10 June 1933, 1; see obituaries, *Detroit News* and *Detroit Free Press*, 23 June 1982; "Petitions Ask Negro Judge: J. A. Craigen Urged for Federal Bench," *Detroit News*, 3 November 1948, in Joseph A. Craigen, Reading Room File, BHC.

33. Levine, *Internal Combustion*, 101.

34. Harold E. Bledsoe to Walter White, 10 February 1933, I-G-96, folder: "Det. Jan–Mar, 1933," and news release, "Detroit NAACP Frees Cary Baylis Wrongly Accused of Murdering a White Man," 23 December 1932, I-G-96, folder: "July–December 1932," Detroit; both in NAACPP.

35. Thomas Solomon, "Participation of Negroes in Detroit Elections," 56; Dillard, *Faith in the City*, 71.

36. See Diggs's column in *UAW*, 29 October 1938, ALUA.

37. Richard Thomas, *Life for Us Is What We Make It*, 266–67; Dillard, *Faith in the City*, 71–72.

38. Watts, *People's Tycoon*, 436, 440; Nevins and Hill, *Ford: Decline*, 11–18. See the article on the Ford-Roosevelt standoff in *New York Times*, 3 September 1933.

39. *Detroit Tribune*, 22 April 1933, 2.

40. *Detroit Tribune*, 29 April 1933, 1, 8.

41. *Detroit Tribune*, 22 April 1933, 1, and 29 April 1933, 1–2.

42. Snow F. Grigsby, interview by Roberta McBride, 12 March 1967, 6, BLM; Grigsby to "Dear Friend [Walter White]," "confidential," 19 January 1933, and White to Grigsby, 20 January 1933, I-G-96, folder: "Jan–Mar, 1933" Detroit, NAACPP.

43. Grigsby, interview by McBride, 12 March 1967, 2.

44. Ibid., 3.

45. If the activism of Grigsby and Peck represents the beginning of a process of securing opportunities for black municipal employees in the urban North, the next stage of the challenge arose in the early 1960s as African Americans battled against the limita-

tions of public sector civil service policies. For more on the later struggle, see Green, *Battling the Plantation Mentality*; Ryan, *AFSCME's Philadelphia Story*; Honey, *Going Down Jericho Road*.

46. Rubio, *There's Always Work at the Post Office*, 2, 52, 70–71.

47. "Memorandum" aired Monday, 30 March 1981, over WJR Radio by newsman Bill Black, printed in *Michigan Chronicle*, 4 April 1981; Program, Funeral Services, Snow F. Grigsby, 26 March 1981; both in Reading Room File, BHC.

48. Grigsby, interview by McBride, 12 March 1967, 2.

49. *Detroit Free Press*, 11 February 1981, 3C.

50. Grigsby, interview by McBride, 12 March 1967, 4.

51. Ibid., 6.

52. Snow F. Grigsby, "The Negro Hospital Situation in the City of Detroit," *Detroit Tribune*, 2 September 1933, 8.

53. "Detroit Civic Group Hits at City Hospital," *Detroit Independent*, 3 March 1934, 1, 4.

54. "Local Ministers to Make Strong Plea for Justice," *Detroit Tribune Independent*, 1; Editorial, "An Appeal to the Race," *Detroit Tribune Independent*, 10 February 1934, 8.

55. Snow F. Grigsby, "An X-Ray Picture of Detroit," Bulletin No. 1 (December 1933), 4, BHL.

56. Ibid., BHL.

57. "Grigsby's Pamphlet Arouses Interest," *Detroit Tribune*, 23 December 1933, 1.

58. "Grigsby Goes Gunning," *Detroit Tribune*, 16 December 1933, 8.

59. Grigsby, "X-Ray Picture of Detroit," 8–9, BHL.

60. Dillard, *Faith in the City*, 54; Richard Thomas, *Life for Us Is What We Make It*, 236, 243; Wolcott, *Remaking Respectability*, 211–12.

61. *Michigan Chronicle*, 28 March 1981, 1, Reading Room File, BHC.

62. Roosevelt is quoted on NIRA in Wolters, *Negroes and the Great Depression*, 90; see also 169–70.

63. Kirby, *Black Americans in the Roosevelt Era*, 41–42; Wolters, *Negroes and the Great Depression*, 135–68; Jesse Thomas, "Will the New Deal Be a Square Deal for the Negro?" 308.

64. Sitkoff, *New Deal for Blacks*, 34–57; Wolters, *Negroes and the Great Depression*, 151–55.

65. For example, the following items in the *Detroit Tribune*: Editorial, "Firing Negroes and Hiring Whites," 17 June 1933, 8; Editorial, "Negro Patronage Not Wanted," 24 June 1933, 8; "Rev. Peck at Head of NRA," "Levee Contractors to Increase Wages," and "Consider Race on NRA Board," all 12 August 1933, 1; "NRA Violated by Whites to Hamper Group," 19 August 1933, 1.

66. Kirby, *Black Americans in the Roosevelt Era*, 155; for a review of "The Negro Faces the New Deal," see *Detroit Tribune Independent*, 31 March 1934, 8. The *Detroit Tribune* and the *Detroit Tribune Independent* were the same newspapers. The *Detroit Tribune* became the *Tribune Independent* in late December 1933. The *Tribune Independent* went back to its original name, the *Detroit Tribune*, in October 1935. See *Detroit Tribune Independent*, 14 September 1935, 1.

67. Davis quoted in Kirby, *Black Americans in the Roosevelt Era*, 156–57.

68. Editorial, "Economic Self-Defense," *Detroit Tribune*, 19 August 1933, 8. See also Editorial, "Ousting Negro Employees," *Detroit Tribune*, 2 December 1933, 8.

69. Editorial, "Forward, March," *Detroit Tribune*, 26 August 1933, 8.

70. Theodore R. Barnes, "The New Deal,—A Myth or Reality," *Detroit Tribune*, 3 June 1933, 8.

71. Frank Murphy, "The Procession of Forgotten Men," address delivered over radio station WJR, Detroit, 7 November 1932, reel 156, FMP.

72. Theodore R. Barnes, "The New Deal,—Our Beer," *Detroit Tribune*, 10 June 1933, 8. As John Davis and black Americans waited for the wings of the NRA's Blue Eagle to lift them to the level of other citizens, Grigsby's CRC appeared to be more suited than ever for the times. John Davis continued his mission, as Mark Solomon notes, with an "uncompromising assault upon New Deal racial policies," and the local press passed along his findings. For the quote, see Mark Solomon, *Cry Was Unity*, 236, and for analysis of Davis's mission, ibid., 235–37; see also Sullivan, *Days of Hope*, 49–50.

73. Editorial, "Uncovering the Truth," *Detroit Tribune Independent*, 17 March 1934, 8.

74. For the earlier split between Bradby and Grigsby, see Grigsby to Walter White, 17 October; Grigsby to White, 23 October; Grigsby to Bradby, 5 November; Bradby to Grigsby, 6 November; Grigsby to L. C. Blount and officers of the local branch, NAACP, 9 November; all 1931, from I-G-96, folder: "July-December 1931, Detroit, Michigan," NAACPP. For the united front that Peck and Grigsby sought to form, see "Civic Rights Group Plans Mass Meeting," *Detroit Tribune Independent,* 31 March 1934, 1.

75. "Rev. Bradby and Mahoney Speak at Y," *Detroit Tribune Independent*, 14 April 1934, 2.

76. David L. Lewis, "History of Negro Employment in Detroit Area Plants," 18–21.

77. Ibid., 20–21.

78. Quote from J. H. Wilson to Rev. Bradby, 16 November 1931; see also A. Friend to Rev. R. L. Bradby, n.d., probably early November 1931, accession #572, box 28, folder: 12.7.3. "Policies," BFRC.

79. Rev. Bradby to Charles Sorensen, 12 January 1925; Bradby to Sorenson, 5 November 1926; Bradby to Sorenson, 17 November 1931; accession #572, box 28, folder: 12.7.3. "Politics," BFHC. David L. Lewis, "History of Negro Employment," 21–23.

80. Wolters, *Negroes and the Great Depression*, 170.

81. Granger, "The Negro—Friend or Foe of Organized Labor?" 142.

82. Spero and Harris, *Black Worker*, 40–45; Philip Foner, *Organized Labor and the Black Worker*, 47–63.

83. Spero and Harris, *Black Worker*, 133; Grossman, *Land of Hope*, 230–35. For the theory of the vicious circle, see Myrdal, *American Dilemma*, 1:75–78; Fusfeld and Bates, *Political Economy of the Urban Ghetto*, 67.

84. Reid, *Negro Membership in American Labor Unions*, 33.

85. Wolters, *Negroes and the Great Depression*, 94.

86. William Harris, *Harder We Run*, 104–5; Wolters, *Negroes and the Great Depression*, 98–106; Reed, *Not Alms but Opportunity*, 108–9.

87. Schulman, *From Cotton Belt to Sunbelt*, 24–25.

88. Weaver and Moton quoted in Wolters, *Negroes and the Great Depression*, 104.

89. Ibid.

90. Reed, *Not Alms but Opportunity*, 125.

91. For John Dancy speaking in Detroit on unions, see "Speakers Tell Advantages of the Unions," *Detroit Tribune*, 24 February 1934, 1, 8. See also Fine, "Origins of the United Automobile Workers," 258; Meier and Rudwick, *Black Detroit*, 30–31, 233 n. 74; Kirby, *Black Americans in the Roosevelt Era*, 158.

92. "Urban League Starts Bureau for Workers," *Detroit Tribune Independent*, 29 September 1934, 1.

93. Meier and Rudwick claim that Dancy's position toward organized labor "remained unchanged." *Black Detroit*, 20. Moreover, they state that "it was not before 1936 that the first significant voices on behalf of the union appeared among the city's Negro elite." Ibid., 22.

94. Christopher Alston, interview by N. Charles Anderson, n.d., box 1, folder 7, pp. 3, 10, CMAP.

95. *Detroit Tribune Independent*, 29 September 1934, 1.

96. Editorial, "The Power of Race Unity," *Detroit Tribune Independent*, 31 March 1934, 8.

97. Ibid.

98. Sitkoff, *New Deal for Blacks*, 34–57.

99. Editorial, "The Power of Race Unity," *Detroit Tribune Independent*, 31 March 1934, 8.

100. Reed, *Not Alms but Opportunity*, 123.

101. *Detroit Tribune*, 19 October 1935, 1; Bailer, "Negro Labor in the Automobile Industry," 192–93.

102. Dillard, *Faith in the City*, 54.

103. CRC, "Second Education Lesson," 1–4, box 10, MSP; *Detroit Tribune Independent*, 14 April 1934, 2.

104. CRC, Educational Lesson No. 15: "The Way to Economic Betterment," 2, 1938, box 13, folder 4, MSP.

105. *Civil Rights Bulletin*, 1, no. 1 (April 1935): 1, BHC.

106. "Committee on Civil Rights Formed Here," *Detroit Tribune*, 23 December 1933, 1.

107. See Detroit CRC, "Open Letter," 19 July 1935, and Sugar's response, "Maurice Sugar to Detroit CRC," 19 September 1935, box 10, folder 19, MSP.

108. Ibid.

109. "Detroit Civic Rights Committee Writes Open Letter to Councilmen of the City of Detroit," 19 July 1935, 2, box 10, folder 19, MSP.

110. For endorsements, see "Sugar Fights for Rights of All Oppressed People," *It's about Time*, 1 April 1935, 2, box 10, folder 17, MSP.

111. Sitkoff, *New Deal for Blacks*, 55.

CHAPTER EIGHT

1. Weiss, *Farewell to the Party of Lincoln*, 205–7.

2. *Detroit Tribune Independent*, 22 September 1934, 1, and 10 November 1934, 8; *Civic Rights Bulletin* 1, no. 1 (April 1935): 2, 3, 4, 7, 8, BHC.

3. Thomas R. Solomon, "Negro Detroit Becomes of Age," *Civic Rights Bulletin* 1, no. 1 (April 1935), 6, BHC.

4. *Black Worker*, 1 September 1935, 3; John P. Davis, "Why a National Negro Congress?" 28–29, NNC Papers.

5. Keynote Address of A. Philip Randolph, *Official Proceedings of the National Negro Congress*, 14–16 February 1936, 8, 11, A. Philip Randolph Papers, box 34, LC.

6. Ibid.

7. Davis, "Why a National Negro Congress?" 30–31.

8. From the records of the NNC, we know Davis compiled an extensive list of black newspapers located in major cities. The list for Detroit included three other newspapers—the *Detroit People's News*, the *Goodwill Ambassador*, and the *Guardian*—whose records are now extinct. For a listing of black newspapers, see *Negro Newspapers and Periodicals in the United States*, Bulletin no. 1 (Washington, D.C., February 1937), 3, reel 11, NNC Papers. For the name change of the *Detroit Tribune* to the *Detroit Tribune Independent*, see chapter 7, n. 66.

9. Editorial, "A Serious Situation," *Detroit Tribune Independent*, 17 August 1935, 1, 8.

10. Snow F. Grigsby to John P. Davis, 16 August 1935, reel 5, NNC Papers.

11. Robert Crump, "Crowd Packs Church to Hear Grigsby," *Detroit Tribune*, 5 October 1935, 1, 4.

12. Snow Grigsby to J. Davis, 10 October 1935, gives Davis an update on the progress of the 3-day conference, reel 5, NNC Papers. "Economic Conference to Be Held at Great Bethel A.M.E. Church," 12 October 1935, 1; "Workers to Hear Plans for Union," 19 October 1935, 1, 4; "Economic Conference Closes," 26 October 1935, 1, 4; Editorial, "A Challenge to Colored Detroit," 2 November 1935, 4; all in *Detroit Tribune*. For remembrances of arbitrary firings by Donald Marshall, see interview of Shelton Tappes, 26–27, box 54, folder 7, MSP.

13. "Economic Conference," *Detroit Tribune*, 12 October 1935, 1, and 19 October 1935, 1, 4.

14. "Ford Plant Stops Shipment of Trucks to Italian-Africa," *Detroit Tribune,* 26 October 1935, 7.

15. J. Davis to Snow Grigsby, 15 October 1935; Snow Grigsby to Davis, 28 October 1935; John Davis to Snow Grigsby, 12 November 1935; John Davis to Lester Granger, 27 November 1935; all reel 5, NNC Papers.

16. Grigsby, *White Hypocrisy and Black Lethargy*, 58, ALUA; LeBron Simmons, interview by Bill McKie, 1, box 33, folder 15, NGC, series VI, ALUA.

17. Wolters, *Negroes and the Great Depression*, 360. John Davis to Snow Grigsby, 28 January 1936, reel 5, NNC Papers.

18. J. Davis to Snow Grigsby, 15 October 1935; Snow Grigsby to Davis, 28 October 1935; John Davis to Snow Grigsby, 12 November 1935; John Davis to Lester Granger, 27 November 1935; all reel 5, NNC Papers.

19. John Davis to Snow Grigsby, 12 November 1935, reel 5, NNC Papers; C. LeBron Simmons, interview by Norman McRae, ca. 1969, 1, BLM.

20. Young, *Hard Stuff*, 112–13; Simmons, interview by McRae, 6; Dillard, *Faith in the City*, 87.

21. Meier and Rudwick, *Black Detroit*, 40.

22. Dillard, *Faith in the City*, 1, 87–88.

23. Ibid., 88.

24. Simmons, interview by McRae, 3–5.

25. Bishop J. A. Bray, Bishop R. Carter, and Bishop W. J. Walls, "Church Leaders in Opposition to the Program of the National Negro Congress," NNC Folder, 4 November–24 December 1936, I-C-383, NAACPP.

26. Grigsby, *White Hypocrisy and Black Lethargy*, 20.

27. Angela Dillard makes this point well in *Faith in the City*, 86–87.

28. For a view of the NNC as a communist front, see Record, *Negro and the Communist Party*; Record, *Race and Radicalism*; and Sitkoff, *New Deal for Blacks*, 258–59. For the suggestion that the Detroit local was formed at the "express instructions of the Communist Party," see Meier and Rudwick, *Black Detroit*, 32, citing testimony before the House Un-American Activities Committee by ex-communist and former UAW organizer William Odell Nowell. For a comprehensive assessment of the relationship between John P. Davis and the Communist Party, see Erik Gellman, *Death Blow to Jim Crow*, especially, 55–58, 121, 143–44, 149–64.

29. Jeanette Worlds to John Davis, 4 December 1935, 1, box 8, NNC Papers.

30. Meier and Rudwick, *Black Detroit*, 29.

31. Ibid. For Dillard's assessment of Rev. Charles Hill and others in the NNC, see Dillard, *Faith in the City*, 13–14, 88–89. For Needleman's observations, see Needleman, *Black Freedom Fighters in Steel*, 187. For the legacy that shaped African American resistance, see Robinson, *Black Marxism*, xxx–xxxi. For more on the Social Gospel, see Luker, *Social Gospel in Black and White*; Ronald White, *Liberty and Justice for All*; Clarence Taylor, *Black Religious Intellectuals*, 11–38; Cynthia Taylor, *A. Philip Randolph*; D'Emilio, *Lost Prophet*, 39–71; Sugrue, *Sweet Land of Liberty*, 41–44.

32. Robert J. Evans to Co-workers, 31 January 1936; Dred Scott Neusom to John Davis, 20 September 1936; Davis to Neusom, 29 September 1936; all box 7, NNC Papers.

33. Davis to Robert Evans, 9 May 1936, reel 4; List of Executive Council of the NNC, reel 11, NNC Papers.

34. Lichtenstein, *Walter Reuther*, 63.

35. Simmons, interview by McKie, 1–2.

36. Meier and Rudwick, *Black Detroit*, 34–38; Lichtenstein, *Walter Reuther*, 104–8; Barnard, *American Vanguard*, 73–110.

37. From 19 February 1937 NAACP Press Release, folder: press releases, I-C-322, NAACPP.

38. *Pittsburgh Courier*, 27 March 1937, 7; Lloyd Bailer, "Negro Labor in the Automobile Industry," 198.

39. Francis A. Henson to Davis, 8 July 1937, reel 10, NNC Papers; Hanson to Walter White, 8 July 1937, and White to Henson, 14 July 1937, I-C-323, NAACPP.

40. George S. Schuyler, "Detroit Awaiting Ford Crisis," *Pittsburgh Courier*, 4 September 1937, 14; Meier and Rudwick, *Black Detroit*, 40.

41. Griffler, *What Price Alliance*, 176–77; Francis A. Henson to Davis, 8 July 1937, reel

10, NNC Papers; Hanson to Walter White, 8 July 1937, and White to Henson, 14 July 1937, I-C-323, NAACPP; Meier and Rudwick, *Black Detroit*, 40–42.

42. George S. Schuyler, "Detroit Awaiting Ford Crisis," *Pittsburgh Courier*, 4 September 1937, 14.

43. *United Automobile Worker*, 30 October 1937, 3; *Detroit Tribune*, 30 October 1937, 1; Meier and Rudwick, *Black Detroit*, 53.

44. Drake and Cayton, *Black Metropolis*, 330–33.

45. Fusfeld and Bates, *Political Economy of the Urban Ghetto*, 69–70; Whatley, "African-American Strikebreaking from the Civil War to the New Deal," 525–58.

46. Barnard, *American Vanguard*, 71; Cayton and Mitchell, *Black Workers and the New Unions*, 255–79; Zieger, *CIO*, 85. For reports from black newspapers, see George Schuyler's reporting in the *Pittsburgh Courier*, 31 July 1937, 14, and 12 August 1937, 14, and the *Chicago Defender*, 12 September 1936, 4.

47. Galenson, *CIO Challenge to the AFL*, 129–30.

48. Lichtenstein, *Walter Reuther*, 72–73; Nevins and Hill, *Ford: Decline*, 133–36.

49. *New York Times*, 8 April 1937, 1.

50. Sorensen, *My Forty Years with Ford*, 259.

51. Nevins and Hill, *Ford: Decline*, 136.

52. Quote from Sorensen, *My Forty Years*, 260; Nevins and Hill, *Ford: Decline*, 138.

53. Watts, *People's Tycoon*, xiii. E. G. Pipp quoted in Edmund Wilson, "Despot of Dearborn," 30.

54. Henry Ford quoted in Lacey, *Ford*, 391.

55. Watts, *People's Tycoon*, 447.

56. "Mr. Ford Doesn't Care," *Fortune*, December 1933, 131; Watts, *People's Tycoon*, 446–47; Nevins and Hill, *Ford: Decline*, 110–12.

57. Nevins and Hill, *Ford: Decline*, 136–37.

58. Sorensen, *My Forty Years*, 260.

59. Nevins and Hill, *Ford: Decline*, 139.

60. Ibid., 139–41; Lichtenstein, *Walter Reuther*, 83–85.

61. Lichtenstein, *Walter Reuther*, 86; Nevins and Hill, *Ford: Decline*, 150; Wilson, "Despot of Dearborn," 24–35; Watts, *People's Tycoon*, 444–62.

62. Benjamin Stolberg quoted in Nevins and Hill, *Ford: Decline*, 150–51.

63. "Reich Honor Is Bestowed," *Detroit News*, 31 July 1938. Watts, *People's Tycoon*, 397. For more on the relationship, see Ernest J. Liebold Papers, accession #64, box 1, Correspondence 1931–1951, BFRC.

64. The analysis of the FBI connection is discussed in Lacey, *Ford*, 391–92.

65. Civil Rights Federation, "FBI Detroit: The Facts Concerning the FBI raids in Detroit," 1940, 1–16, box 89, folder 35, Workers Defense League Papers, ALUA.

66. Willis F. Ward, "Reminiscences," 5–19, accession #65, BFRC.

67. Father Malcolm Dade, interview by Jim Keeney and Roberta McBride, 17 September 1969, 3–5, 13–14, BLM; Bailer, "Negro Labor in the Automobile Industry," 165–68.

68. Bailer, "Negro Labor in the Automobile Industry," 201–3.

69. For October 1937 black employment at the Rouge plant, see Bailer, "Negro

Automobile Worker," 418. For comparison with 1935, see "Colored Count as of 12-4-35 at Rouge and Local Branches," accession #572, box 28, folder: Policies, BFRC.

70. Shelton Tappes, interview by Bill McKie, 14–17, box 54, folder 7, MSP. Tappes's figures regarding black/white proportions in the Rouge foundry match the change from a largely white to a largely black pattern cited earlier by Maloney, Whatley, and Wright, even if the idea of what constitutes "virtually black" may differ. See Whatley and Wright, "Race, Human Capital, and Labour Markets," 287–89, esp. figs. 13.6 and 13.7, and Maloney and Whatley, "Making the Effort," 489.

71. Nevins and Hill, *Ford: Decline*, 150–53.

72. Quill Pettway, interview by Duncan, Lindberg, and author, 3 February 2001.

73. Nevins and Hill, *Ford: Decline*, 124–28; Douglas Brinkley, *Wheels for the World*, 443; Ford R. Bryan, "A Prized Friendship," 90–95, Vertical File, George Washington Carver, BFRC; Richmond Hill, 1–6, accession #940, box 8, folder: "Henry Ford—Educational: Antiquarian Interests in Georgia Schools," BFRC. Watts, *People's Tycoon*, 484–87; Grandin, *Fordlandia*, 333–42.

74. Nevins and Hill, *Ford: Decline*, 110–17.

75. Douglas Brinkley, *Wheels for the World*, 442.

76. *Crisis*, May 1937, 150; *Pittsburgh Courier*, 27 March 1937; Meier and Rudwick, *Black Detroit*, 38, 50.

77. *Pittsburgh Courier*, 5 June 1937, 1, 8, and 28 August 1937, 1, 4; *Detroit Tribune*, 12 June 1937, 1, 11.

78. Galenson, *CIO Challenge to the AFL*, 131–32.

79. *Detroit Tribune*, 10 July 1937, 1.

80. Richard Thomas, *Life for Us Is What We Make It*, 288. Thomas's analysis relies on quotes from a black UAW worker whose reflections were reported in Ernest Calloway's article "Negro and Unionism" in *United Automobile Worker*, 9 October 1937, 2.

81. "Detroit Conference Largest in History," *Crisis* 44 (August 1937), 242, 244–46.

82. Meier and Rudwick, *Black Detroit*, 45–48. Shelton Tappes, interview by Herbert Hill, Detroit, 27 October 1967, #1, pt. 1, 36, BLM; LeBron Simmons, interview by Nat Ganley, 9, box 33, folder 15, NGC.

83. Carl Haessler, interview by Jack W. Skeels, 27 November 1959–24 October 1960, 261, UAW-OH.

84. Shelton Tappes, interview by Jack Skeels, 12 July 1961, 19, 22, UAW-OH.

85. Editorial, "New Labor Developments," *Pittsburgh Courier*, 23 January 1937, 10.

86. Zieger, *CIO*, 31–32, quote on 37; Barnard, *American Vanguard*, 71; Cayton and Mitchell, *Black Workers and the New Unions*, 255–79; Bates, "New Crowd Challenges the Old Guard,"362–67; Cohen, *Making a New Deal*, 333–34. For reports from black newspapers, see n. 46 above.

87. Galenson, *CIO Challenge to the AFL*, 132–33; Zieger, *CIO*, 36–39, 46–54, 80–85, 97–100, 121–23.

88. Walter Hardin and Paul Kirk wrote columns for the UAW in both the *Detroit Tribune Independent* and the *Michigan Chronicle* during the summer of 1937. See *Detroit Tribune Independent*, 12 June, 26 June, and 17 July 1937. Files of the *Michigan Chronicle*

are missing for this period, but Meier and Rudwick, based on an interview with Louis Martin (21 October 1976), confirm that the *Chronicle* also published columns by these two black organizers for the UAW during this period. See Meier and Rudwick, *Black Detroit*, 237 n. 31.

89. See Walter Hardin, "Remnants of Ford Myth Still Exist," *United Automobile Worker*, January 1938, 3.

90. Dave Moore, interview by author, 16, 18 December 2007.

91. *United Automobile Worker*, 13 September, 13 November 1937, quoted in Meier and Rudwick, *Black Detroit*, 49.

92. Paul Boatin quoted in Stepan-Norris and Zeitlin, *Talking Union*, 53

93. Meier and Rudwick, *Black Detroit*, 48–50.

94. Griffler also addresses this question in his important study of the roots of the black-labor alliance that emerged in the mid-1930s. See Griffler, *What Price Alliance?* 174–75.

95. Ziegler, *CIO*, 97–98; Akers, "Social-Psychological Interpretation of the Black Legion," 5–6, Elmer Akers folder, MKP; Fraser, "The 'Labor Question,'" 72–73; Bernstein, *Turbulent Years*, 508.

96. John P. Davis to Francis A. Henson, 17 September 1937; Walter Hardin to John Davis, 4 October 1937; Davis to Hardin, 6 October 1937; John Davis to John L. Lewis, 19 October 1937; all in box 10, NNC Papers; *Detroit Tribune*, 30 October 1937; Meier and Rudwick, *Black Detroit*, 41, 53.

97. John Davis to Walter Hardin, 6 October 1937, box 10, NNC Papers.

98. John Davis to John L. Lewis, 19 October 1937, 2, box 10, NNC Papers.

99. Bates, *Pullman Porters and the Rise of Protest Politics*, 126. Randolph requested a conference between representatives of the NNC and the NAACP during the NAACP conference in Detroit; see NNC, 11 July 1937, NAACP Board Minutes, I-A-11, NAACP Papers.

100. Bailer, "Negro Labor in the Automobile Industry," 166.

101. "Local Meet Is Addressed by Randolph," *Detroit Tribune*, 14 August 1937, 1.

102. *Detroit Tribune*, 21 August 1937, 1.

103. Editorial, "We Doff Our Hats to Pullman Porters," 18 (City Edition), *Chicago Defender*, 18 September 1937.

CHAPTER NINE

1. "Negro Congress Will Meet in Philadelphia," *Detroit Tribune*, 24 July 1937, 11; news about the NNC broadcast in *Detroit Tribune*, 9 October 1937, 4.

2. A. Philip Randolph, Speech, Second National Negro Congress, October 1937, box 11, NNC Papers.

3. "Civic Rights Group to Open Fall Program," *Detroit Tribune*, 11 September 1937, 3; "Civic Rights Group Seeks Jobs for Negro Firemen," *Detroit Tribune*, 10 October 1937, 1; *Detroit Tribune*, 23 October 1937, 1.

4. "Two Scottsboro Boys Coming to Detroit," *Detroit Tribune*, 13 November 1937, 1. Other groups actively challenging the FMC in the late 1930s included Detroit's Civil

Rights Federation, which began in 1935 as the Conference for the Protection of Civil Rights and merged with the Civil Rights Congress in the late forties. The Civil Rights Federation was an interracial effort; rather than originating in black Detroit, it was nurtured in Detroit's liberal-left community. Its stature within black Detroit grew through joint efforts with the NNC local and members like Eleanor Maki, who belonged to both organizations. For a fuller discussion, see Dillard, *Faith in the City*, 16, 84, 103.

5. C. LeBron Simmons, interview by Bill McKie, 10, box 33, folder 15, NGC, series VI.

6. Shelton Tappes, interview by Jack Skeels, 12 July 1961, 13, folder: Shelton Tappes, UAW-OH.

7. Ibid., 18.

8. Shelton Tappes, interview by Herbert Hill, 27 October 1967, Detroit, Interview #1, pt. 1, 36, BLM; Simmons, interview by McKie, 9.

9. Shelton Tappes, interview by Bill McKie, 27–30, box 54, folder 7, MSP.

10. Stepan-Norris and Zeitlin, *Talking Union*, 231; Tappes, interview by McKie, 22.

11. Bonosky, *Brother Bill McKie*, 158.

12. Tappes, interview by McKie, 19.

13. Bonosky, *Brother Bill McKie*, 166; Joseph and Rose Billups, interview by Herbert Hill, Shelton Tappes, and Roberta McBride, 27 October 1967, pt. 2, 6, BLM.

14. Ibid., 6–7.

15. Ibid.

16. Simmons, interview by McKie, 13.

17. Rev. Charles A. Hill, interview by Roberta McBride, 8 May 1967, 6, BLM. For more on Hill's prominent role organizing UAW Local 600, see Dillard, *Faith in the City*, esp. 7, 13–16, 63–106.

18. Shelton Tappes, interview by Judith Stepan-Norris, transcript: tape #2, 28, TU-OH.

19. Meier and Rudwick, *Black Detroit*, 42–44.

20. Tappes, interview by Skeels, 12 July 1961, 24.

21. Bernstein, *Turbulent Years*, 562; Zieger, *CIO*, 99.

22. John Davis to John L. Lewis, 19 October 1937, box 10, NNC Papers.

23. Horace A. White, "Who Owns the Negro Churches?" 176–77; Malcolm Dade, interview by Roberta McBride and Jim Keeney, 17 September 1969, 20, BLM.

24. Dillard, *Faith in the City*, 70; Editorial, *Detroit Tribune*, 8 January 1938, 8; "Rev. Pittman Issues Statement," *Detroit Tribune*, 15 January 1938, 1.

25. "Rev. H. White Gives Views in Broadcast," *Detroit Tribune*, 8 January 1938, 8.

26. White, "Who Owns the Negro Churches?" 176.

27. Bailer interview with Rev. Peck, Detroit, Michigan, 6 March 1940, in Bailer, "Negro Labor in the Automobile Industry," 166.

28. Ibid.

29. "Grigsby Goes On with Meet," *Detroit Tribune*, 15 January 1938, 1.

30. "Dr. Mordecai Johnson Lauds Labor Unions," *Detroit Tribune*, 29 January 1938, 1.

31. Editorial, *Detroit Tribune*, 8 January 1938, 8.

32. Georgia S. Schuyler, "Negro Editor Condemns Ford's Uncle Toms: Finds Ford Propaganda Machine Eager to Divide Workers," *United Automobile Worker*, 5 March 1938, 6.

33. Barnard, *American Vanguard*, 128.

34. Davis to Walter White, 15 April 1938, 2, box 15, NNC Papers; NNC "mass meeting" Program, 23 April 1938, Detroit, Mich., 1–3; LeBron Simmons to John Davis, 13 April 1938; Davis to LeBron Simmons, 14 March 1938; L. B. Spradley, Trade Union Director, and C. LeBron Simmons to "Dear Friends," 10 May 1938; all on reel 14, box 15, NNC Papers.

35. John P. Davis to LeBron Simmons, 7 June 1938, reel 14, box 15, NNC Papers.

36. C. LeBron Simmons to John Davis, 8 February 1938, 1, reel 14, box 15, NNC Papers.

37. Ibid.

38. Simmons to Davis, 8 February 1938, 2; Simmons to Davis, 19 June 1938; both reel 14, box 15, NNC Papers.

39. Simmons to Davis, 8 February 1938, reel 14, box 15, NNC Papers.

40. LeBron Simmons to John Davis, n.d. [summer 1938], reel 14, box 15, NNC Papers.

41. Mark Solomon, *Cry Was Unity*, 304–7; Singh, *Black Is a Country*, 83–85. Community sentiments during the Popular Front were generally positive toward the CP. The community may have had a more complicated response to the CP at a later time. To the extent that communists helped build organization among black workers, they were welcomed as allies in the struggle for social justice. For a discussion of relationships between the CP and African Americans over a longer time span, see Arnesen, "No 'Graver Danger,' . . . ," 13–52, 75–79.

42. Jeanette Worlds to John Davis, 4 December 1935, box 8, NNC Papers.

43. Drake and Cayton, *Black Metropolis*, 735–36.

44. "Lynch Law Is Worse Than Communism," *Detroit Tribune Independen*t, 23 February 1935, 8.

45. Quoted in Drake and Cayton, *Black Metropolis*, 735.

46. Quoted in Singh, *Black Is a Country*, 110. See also "Negro Editors Look at Communism," *Crisis*, May 1932, 13.

47. Du Bois, *Darkwater*, 49.

48. Sorensen, *My Forty Years*, 260–61.

49. Galenson, *CIO Challenge to the AFL*, 164–65; Nevins and Hill, *Ford: Decline*, 158; Barnard, *American Vanguard*, 136; Sward, *Legend of Henry Ford*, 380–83; *New York Times*, 12 October 1938, 8, and 19 October 1938, 3. For much greater detail, see Kraus, *Heroes of Unwritten Story*, 375–401.

50. Barnard, *American Vanguard*, 136–37; Galenson, *CIO Challenge to the AFL*, 165–67.

51. Galenson, *CIO Challenge to the AFL*, 165–71.

52. Canute Frankson, "Negro's Role in Labor Discussed by Congress," *Michigan Chronicle*, 11 February 1939, 12.

53. Canute Frankson, "Discrimination in Union Is Discussed," *Michigan Chronicle*, 4 March 1939, 12; Galenson, *CIO Challenge to the AFL*, 167–68; Meier and Rudwick, *Black Detroit*, 64.

54. *Detroit Tribune*, 29 April 1939, 12; 6 May 1939, 10; 2 December 1939, 12. Charles W. Lowery, "Negro Congress in Mass Move against Discrimination," *Michigan Chronicle*, 15 July 1939, 4; Meier and Rudwick, *Black Detroit*, 65–66.

55. Meier and Rudwick, *Black Detroit*, 66.

56. "Auto Union Head Speaks to Leaders," *Michigan Chronicle*, 1 July 1939, 5.

57. Lichtenstein, *Walter Reuther*, 129–31, 183–89, 191–92; Galenson, *CIO Challenge to the AFL*, 172; Barnard, *American Vanguard*, 139–43; Meier and Rudwick, *Black Detroit*, 82.

58. Hodges Mason, interview by Herbert Hill, Detroit, 28 November 1967, 21–22, BLM.

59. Galenson, *CIO Challenge to the AFL*, 173–76; Lichtenstein, *Walter Reuther*, 132–33; Barnard, *American Vanguard*, 141–43.

60. Lichtenstein, *Walter Reuther*, 132–33.

61. Ibid., 153, 132–53, 178.

62. Barnard, *American Vanguard*, 144–46; Lichtenstein, *Walter Reuther*, 133–38.

63. Barnard, *American Vanguard*, 146–47; Meier and Rudwick, *Black Detroit*, 67; Winn, "Labor Tackles the Race Question," 348–49.

64. Barnard, *American Vanguard*, 146–47.

65. "Labor and Negro Groups Seek Peace," 2 December 1939, 1; C. LeBron Simmons, "NNC Say Negroes are Victims of Propaganda," 2 December 1939, 11; Editorial, "Our New Negroes," 2 December 1939, sec. 2, 10; all in *Michigan Chronicle*; Meier and Rudwick, *Black Detroit*, 68–71; Barnard, *American Vanguard*, 146.

66. Editorial, "Our New Negroes," *Michigan Chronicle*, 2 December 1939, 10.

67. Meier and Rudwick, *Black Detroit*, 72; Bailer, "Negro Automobile Worker," 421.

68. Winn, "Labor Tackles the Race Question," 343.

69. William Lattimore, interview by Roberta McBride, 11 March 1969, 1, BLM.

70. Joseph and Rose Billups, interview by Herbert Hill, Shelton Tappes, and Roberta McBride, pt. 1, 27 October 1967, 14, BLM.

71. "Attention Negro Workers," flier, box 20, folder: Strikes and Lockouts-Chrysler (#3), Joe Brown Papers, ALUA.

72. Bailer, "Negro Labor in the Automobile Industry," 279–81; Meier and Rudwick, *Black Detroit*, 74.

73. "Ford Loyal Workers Sponsor Big Meeting," *Detroit Tribune*, 30 October 1937, 2.

74. Meier and Rudwick, *Black Detroit*, 76.

75. From a Lloyd H. Bailer interview of a Packard worker, 4 February 1940, quoted in Bailer, "Negro Automobile Worker," 421.

76. Quill Pettway, interview by author, 20 December 2006.

77. Snow Grigsby, interview by Roberta McBride, 12 March 1967, 5–6, BLM.

78. For Detroit NAACP membership figures, see Meier and Rudwick, *Black Detroit*, 79; Grigsby, interview by Roberta McBride, 5–6, BLM.

79. Cohen, *Making a New Deal*, 324, 333–49, 365.

80. "Memo re Situation in Ford Local 600, UAW-CIO," 1–2, ACTUC; Bonosky, *Brother Bill McKie*, 160–62; Stepan-Norris and Zeitlan, *Talking Union*, 14–18.

81. David Moore, interview by author, 10 December 2007; Moore, telephone interview by author, 25 June 2009.

82. Stepan-Norris and Zeitlin, *Talking Union*, 119; Arthur McPhaul, interview by Herbert Hill, n.d., Detroit, tape #1, 5 of transcript, BLM.

83. Joseph and Rose Billups, interview by Herbert Hill, #1, 14–15, #2, 1–2, BLM; Galenson, *CIO Challenge to the AFL*, 167.

84. Joseph and Rose Billups, interview by Roberta McBride, 9 September 1967, 10, BLM.

85. Meier and Rudwick also note the fact that "only rarely do the surviving sources illuminate the role of blacks in the intense day-to-day maneuvering . . . during this period." See *Black Detroit*, 63.

86. "Memorandum re: Situation in Ford Local 600 UAW-CIO," 1, box 24, folder: Local 600, 1939–1945, ACTUC.

87. Veal Clough, news articles from *Michigan Chronicle*, 5 June 1943, and *Ford Facts*, 23 July 1960, Vertical File, Biography, ALUA.

88. Tappes, interview by Stepan-Norris, transcript: tape #2, 28.

89. Ibid., transcript: tape #3, 1. William Chafe noted in another context behaviors that emerged from a politics of civility when "white people dictated the ground rules, and the benefits went only to those who played the game." See Chafe, *Civilities and Civil Rights*, 7–8; Bates, *Pullman Porters and the Rise of Protest Politics*, 1–12.

90. Tappes, interview by Skeels, 12 July 1961, 13–14.

91. Tappes, interview by Stepan-Norris, transcript: tape #2, 31–32.

92. Ibid.

93. See the discussion in chapter 8 regarding the historical origins of the support of unions within black Detroit. Dillard, *Faith in the City*, 13–14.

94. Tappes, interview by McKie, 26.

95. Galenson, *CIO Challenge to the AFL*, 180.

96. David Moore, interview by *Political Affairs*, March 5, 2007, 5, online edition, www .politicalaffairs.net/article/articleview/4956/1/246; for Rev. Hill acting as chairman of the "Negro Organizing Committee," see Tappes, interview by McKie, 28.

97. Widman quoted in Bonosky, *Brother Bill McKie*, 165.

98. Moore, interview by author, 10, 16 December 2007.

99. Tappes, interview by Skeels, 19, 22; Barnard, *American Vanguard*, 3–4.

100. When UAW Local 600 emerged from underground, it was, in a sense, a Pyrrhic victory for many of those who had been committed to organizing the FMC for years. Homer Martin's intention, when he created Local 600 out of Local 98, was to dilute the influence of organizers like Bill McKie. Martin hoped his adversaries would disappear. McKie, Clough, Tappes, Moore, and others did just that, using Local 600 as a cover. They used the union local for their own organizing activities, operating in secrecy within the community, with little interference from the politics of UAW officials. See Bonosky, *Brother Bill McKie*, 158–59.

101. Tappes interviewed by Stepan-Norris, tape #2, 16. Not all would have described the transition in terms of "turning" positions over from the local to the international. The Association of Catholic Trade Unionists (ACTU), a faction within the UAW, called Widman's maneuver a "takeover" of Local 600 by the Left involving many communists. Leaders within the ACTU especially disagreed with the means by which Percy Llewellyn "quickly assumed complete command of the local's political machinery."

See "Memo re Situation in Ford Local 600 UAW-CIO," 1–2, ACTUC. For the role of the Catholic caucus, backed by Archbishop (later Cardinal) Mooney, in attempting to "obstruct" the Unity caucus and "pave its way to power," see Carl Haessler, interview by Jack Skeels, 262, UAW-OH. See also Lichtenstein, *Walter Reuther*, 178–79; Barnard, *American Vanguard*, 160, 162, 163.

102. Nevins and Hill, *Ford: Decline*, 159–61; Lichtenstein, *Walter Reuther*, 178–79; Widick, *Detroit*, 80–81; Sward, *Legend of Henry Ford*, 402.

103. Nevins and Hill, *Ford: Decline*, 159; Bonosky, *Brother Bill McKie*, 167; Stepan-Norris and Zeitlin, *Talking Union*, 64.

104. Al Smith quoted in Nevins and Hill, *Ford: Decline*, 159–60.

105. Tappes, interview by McKie, 29–30.

106. Lichtenstein, *Walter Reuther*, 178.

107. Tappes, interview by McKie, 37.

108. Ibid., 34.

109. Ibid., 34–38.

110. Ibid., 39.

111. Nevins and Hill, *Ford: Decline*, 161.

112. Widick, *Detroit*, 80–82; Bonosky, *Brother Bill McKie*, 171; Lichtenstein, *Walter Reuther*, 133, 153.

113. Nevins and Hill, *Ford: Decline*, 161; Bonosky, *Brother Bill McKie*, 171; Tappes interview by McKie, 29–37; Moore, interview by author, 18 December 2007.

114. Bailer, "Negro Labor in the Automobile Industry," 216; Lichtenstein, *Walter Reuther*, 178; Nevins and Hill, *Ford: Decline*, 161; Meier and Rudwick, *Black Detroit*, 87.

115. Widick, *Detroit*, 82; Bonosky, *Brother Bill McKie*, 171; Lichtenstein, *Walter Reuther*, 178–79.

116. Widick, *Detroit*, 81–82.

117. *Michigan Chronicle*, 5 April 1941, 1; Preis, *Labor's Giant Step*, 104–6.

118. Moore, interview by author, 10 December 2007.

119. Widick, *Detroit*, 82.

120. Bonosky, *Brother Bill McKie*, 178; Meier and Rudwick, *Black Detroit*, 87; Bailer, "Negro Labor in the Automobile Industry," 220.

121. Meier and Rudwick, *Black Detroit*, 88.

122. Bailer, "Negro Labor in the Automobile Industry," 214–16.

123. Walter White to James McClendon, 12 April 1941, II-A-334, NAACPP. For the link between union victory and the reputation of the NAACP, see White to Muste, 15 April 1941, folder: Ford Strike, II-A-333, NAACPP. See also White's autobiography, *Man Called White*, 214–16.

124. Rev. Charles Hill, interview by Roberta McBride, 8 May 1967, 4–5, BLM; Stepan-Norris and Zeitlin, *Talking Union*, 17; Babson, *Working Detroit*, 110; Widick, *Detroit*, 85; Bonosky, *Brother Bill McKie*, 178.

125. Moore, interview by author, 10, 18 December 2007.

126. Maloney and Whatley, "Making the Effort," 468 (table 2), 469–70.

127. Tappes, interviewed by Hill, pt. 2, 44–45, BLM; Richard Thomas, *Life for Us Is*

What We Make It, 305; "Why We Chose the CIO," ca. 1941, UAW Organizing Committee, folder: "Miscellaneous Publications," ALUA.

128. Meier and Rudwick, *Black Detroit*, 105.

129. Maloney and Whatley, "Making the Effort."

130. Lichtenstein, *Walter Reuther*, 179.

131. See, for example, "'Join the CIO,' Robeson Urges Negro Workers," *Ford Facts*, 19 April 1941, 4, and Alston, *Henry Ford and the Negro People*. Special thanks go to General G. Baker and David Goldberg for these archival gems.

132. *Detroit News*, 20 May 1941, 6.

133. Geraldine Bledsoe interview by Norman McRae, 5–6, 1970, BLM.

EPILOGUE

1. Ford, *My Life and Work*, 2.

2. Marquis, *Henry Ford*, 153–54.

3. "Ford-C.I.O. Contract Protects Race Workers," *Michigan Chronicle*, 28 June 1941, 1; Korstad and Lichtenstein, "Opportunities Found and Lost," 796.

BIBLIOGRAPHY

ARCHIVAL MATERIALS

Ablewhite, Hayward S. "Reminiscences." Benson Ford Research Center, The Henry Ford. Dearborn, Michigan.

Addes, George. Collection. Archives of Labor and Urban Affairs, Walter P. Reuther Library, Wayne State University, Detroit.

Akers, Elmer. "A Social-Psychological Interpretation of the Black Legion." Presented before the American Sociological Society, Atlantic City, N.J., 29 Dec. 1937. Elmer Akers folder. Milton Kemnitz Papers, Bentley Historical Library, University of Michigan, Ann Arbor.

———. "Southern Whites in Detroit." 1937. Milton Kemnitz Papers, Bentley Historical Library, University of Michigan, Ann Arbor.

Akers, Elmer, and Milton Kemnitz. "Southern White Migration: Summary of Census Materials," 1937. Milton Kemnitz Papers, Bentley Historical Library, University of Michigan, Ann Arbor.

Alston, Chris and Marti. Papers. Archives of Labor and Urban Affairs, Walter P. Reuther Library, Wayne State University, Detroit.

Alston, Christopher C. *Henry Ford and the Negro People*. Washington, D.C.: National Negro Congress, 1940. Special Collections Library, University of Michigan, Ann Arbor.

Americanization Committee of Detroit. Papers. Bentley Historical Library, University of Michigan, Ann Arbor.

Asher, Cash. Papers. Bentley Historical Library, University of Michigan, Ann Arbor.

Association of Catholic Trade Unionists Collection. Archives of Labor and Urban Affairs, Walter P. Reuther Library, Wayne State University, Detroit.

Avery, Burniece. Papers. Burton Historical Collection, Detroit Public Library, Detroit.

Bell, John. "Reminiscences." Benson Ford Research Center, The Henry Ford, Dearborn, Michigan.

Blacks in the Labor Movement. Oral Histories. Archives of Labor and Urban Affairs, Walter P. Reuther Library, Wayne State University, Detroit.

Brown, Joe. Papers. Archives of Labor and Urban Affairs, Walter P. Reuther Library, Wayne State University, Detroit.

Bumgardner, Eleanor M. Papers. Bentley Historical Library, University of Michigan, Ann Arbor.

Bunche, Ralph J. "The Programs, Ideologies, Tactics, and Achievements of Negro

Betterment and Interracial Organizations." 1940. Carnegie-Myrdal Study of the
Negro in America Papers. Schomburg Center for Research in Black Culture, New
York Public Library, New York.

Cameron, William J. "Reminiscenses." Benson Ford Research Center, The Henry Ford,
Dearborn, Michigan.

Carnegie-Myrdal Study of the Negro in America Papers. Microfilm. Schomburg Center
for Research in Black Culture, New York Public Library, New York, and Library of
Congress, Washington, D.C.

Civic Rights Bulletin. Burton Historical Collection, Detroit Public Library, Detroit.

Civil Rights Congress. Papers. Archives of Labor and Urban Affairs, Walter P. Reuther
Library, Wayne State University, Detroit.

Cobb, Anita Smith. "The Negro in the Inkster Village Council." 18 January 1959. Paper
for Professor Sidney Fine, Seminar #335. University of Michigan, History Seminars,
Department of History. Bentley Historical Library, University of Michigan,
Ann Arbor.

Culver, Chester M. "Reminiscences." Benson Ford Research Center, The Henry Ford,
Dearborn, Michigan.

Cuningham, Walter M. *J8: Chronicle of Neglected Truth.* Detroit: W. M. Cuningham,
ca. 1931. Bentley Historical Library, University of Michigan, Ann Arbor.

Cutler, Edward J. "Reminiscences." Benson Ford Research Center, The Henry Ford,
Dearborn, Michigan.

Dade, Malcolm. Papers. Burton Historical Collection, Detroit Public Library, Detroit.

Detroit Bureau of Governmental Research. Papers. Burton Historical Collection,
Detroit Public Library, Detroit.

Detroit Citizens League. Papers. Burton Historical Collection, Detroit Public Library,
Detroit.

Detroit Real Estate Board. Papers. Burton Historical Collection, Detroit Public
Library, Detroit.

Detroit Urban League. Papers. Bentley Historical Library, University of Michigan,
Ann Arbor.

"Ford Hunger March," VT #209. Audiovisual Collections, Archives of Labor and
Urban Affairs, Wayne State University.

Frank Murphy Oral History Project. Bentley Historical Library, University of
Michigan, Ann Arbor.

Ganley, Nat. Collection. Archives of Labor and Urban Affairs, Walter P. Reuther
Library, Wayne State University, Detroit.

Gellein, Hilmer. Papers. Bentley Historical Library, University of Michigan,
Ann Arbor.

Gomon, Josephine. Papers. Bentley Historical Library, University of Michigan,
Ann Arbor.

Grigsby, Snow F. *White Hypocrisy and Black Lethargy.* Box 1, vertical file: African
Americans in Detroit, 1930s. Archives of Labor and Urban Affairs, Walter P.
Reuther Library, Wayne State University, Detroit.

Haldeman-Julius, Marcet. Papers. Bentley Historical Library, University of Michigan, Ann Arbor.

Hawley, A. H. "Mobility of Southern Migrants in Detroit." Report submitted for partial fulfillment of requirements for Sociology 262, "The Metropolitan Community," June 1937, University of Michigan. Milton Kemnitz Papers, Bentley Historical Library, University of Michigan, Ann Arbor.

Housewives' League of Detroit. Papers. Burton Historical Collection, Detroit Public Library, Detroit.

Human Resource Association. Papers. Bentley Historical Library, University of Michigan, Ann Arbor.

Kemnitz, Milton. Papers. Bentley Historical Library, University of Michigan, Ann Arbor.

Klann, William C. "Reminiscences." Benson Ford Research Center, The Henry Ford, Dearborn, Michigan.

Kraus, Henry. Collection. Archives of Labor and Urban Affairs, Walter P. Reuther Library, Wayne State University, Detroit.

Labadie, Joseph A. Collection. Harlan Hatcher Graduate Library, University of Michigan, Ann Arbor.

Liebold, Ernest G. Papers. Benson Ford Research Center, The Henry Ford, Dearborn, Michigan.

———. "Reminiscences." Benson Ford Research Center, The Henry Ford, Dearborn, Michigan.

Likert, Rensis. Papers. Bentley Historical Library, University of Michigan, Ann Arbor.

Mayor's Office Records. 1928–1935. Burton Historical Collection, Detroit Public Library, Detroit.

Metropolitan Detroit Council of Churches. Collection. Archives of Labor and Urban Affairs, Walter P. Reuther Library, Wayne State University, Detroit.

Michigan Historical Collections. Bentley Historical Library, University of Michigan, Ann Arbor.

Michigan Politics and Labor. Oral Histories. Archives of Labor and Urban Affairs, Walter P. Reuther Library, Wayne State University, Detroit.

Murphy, Frank. Papers. Bentley Historical Library, University of Michigan, Ann Arbor.

National Association for the Advancement of Colored People. Papers. Library of Congress, Washington, D.C.

National Negro Congress. Papers. Microfilm. Schomburg Center for Research on Black Culture, New York Public Library, New York, and Library of Congress, Washington, D.C.

Phillips, Tom. "Reminiscences." Benson Ford Research Center, The Henry Ford, Dearborn, Michigan.

Randolph, A. Philip. Papers. Library of Congress, Washington, D.C.

Raushenbush, Carl. Papers. Bentley Historical Library, University of Michigan, Ann Arbor.

Searle, Frederick E. "Reminiscences." Benson Ford Research Center, The Henry Ford, Dearborn, Michigan.

Second Baptist Church. Papers. Bentley Historical Library, University of Michigan, Ann Arbor.

Shelly, Cara. "Bradby's Baptists." Seminar Paper for Sidney Fine. University of Michigan, History Seminars, Department of History. Bentley Historical Library, University of Michigan, Ann Arbor.

Simpson, Howard. "Reminiscences." Benson Ford Research Center, The Henry Ford, Dearborn, Michigan.

Sugar, Maurice. Papers. Archives of Labor and Urban Affairs, Walter P. Reuther Library, Wayne State University, Detroit.

Talking Union. Oral Histories. Archives of Labor and Urban Affairs, Walter P. Reuther Library, Wayne State University, Detroit.

Tappes, Shelton. Collection. Archives of Labor and Urban Affairs, Walter P. Reuther Library, Wayne State University, Detroit.

UAW Oral Histories. Archives of Labor and Urban Affairs, Walter P. Reuther Library, Wayne State University, Detroit.

United Automobile Worker. Holdings. Archives of Labor and Urban Affairs, Walter P. Reuther Library, Wayne State University, Detroit.

United Auto Workers, International. Collection. Archives of Labor and Urban Affairs, Walter P. Reuther Library, Wayne State University, Detroit.

United Auto Workers, Local 600. Collection. Archives of Labor and Urban Affairs, Walter P. Reuther Library, Wayne State University, Detroit.

United Auto Workers, Walter P. Reuther. Collection. Archives of Labor and Urban Affairs, Walter P. Reuther Library, Wayne State University, Detroit.

United Auto Workers Political Action Committee, Roy Reuther. Collection. Archives of Labor and Urban Affairs, Walter P. Reuther Library, Wayne State University, Detroit.

United Community Service Papers, Central Files. Archives of Labor and Urban Affairs, Walter P. Reuther Library, Wayne State University, Detroit.

University of Michigan, History Seminars, Department of History. Bentley Historical Library, University of Michigan, Ann Arbor.

Vertical Files. Burton Historical Collection, Detroit Public Library, and Archives of Labor and Urban Affairs, Walter P. Reuther Library, Wayne State University, Detroit.

Walker, Moses. Papers. Bentley Historical Library, University of Michigan, Ann Arbor.

Ward, Willis F. "Reminiscences." Henry Ford Archives, Benson Ford Research Center, The Henry Ford, Dearborn, Michigan.

Washington, Forrester B. *The Negro in Detroit: A Survey of the Conditions of a Negro Group in a Northern Industrial Center during the War Prosperity Period.* 1920. Burton Historical Collection, Detroit Public Library, Detroit, and Bentley Historical Library, University of Michigan, Ann Arbor.

INTERVIEWS

Alston, Marti. Interview by author. Detroit. 11 December 1999.

Baker, General G. Interview by author. Detroit. 8 December 2003; 17 February 2004.

Baker, General G. Interview by Todd Duncan, Kathryne V. Lindberg, and author. Detroit. 26 September 2002.

Boggs, Grace Lee. Interview by author. Detroit. 13 December 2000; 6 December 2006.

Boggs, Grace Lee. Interview by Todd Duncan, Kathryne V. Lindberg, and author. Detroit. 26 September 2002.

Fraser, Douglas. Interview by author. Detroit. 6 June 2003.

Fraser, Douglas. Interview by Todd Duncan, Kathryne V. Lindberg, and author. Detroit. 26 September 2002.

Jeffrey, Mildred. Interview by Todd Duncan, Kathryne V. Lindberg, and author. Detroit. 26 September 2002.

Maddox, James. Interview by author. Detroit. 16 April 2003.

Mahaffey, Maryann. Interview by Todd Duncan, Kathryne V. Lindberg, and author. Detroit. 26 September 2002.

Moore, David. Interview by author. Detroit. 10, 16, and 18 December 2007. Telephone by author, 25 June 2009.

Pettway, Quill. Interview by author. Detroit. 20 December 2006.

Pettway, Quill. Interview by Todd Duncan, Kathryne Lindberg, and author. Detroit. 3 February 2001; 22 January 2002; 26 September 2002.

Smith, Lasker. Interview by author. Encorse, Mich. 16 January 2000; 14 February 2002.

Smith, Lasker. Interview by Todd Duncan, Kathryne V. Lindberg, and author. Detroit. 26 September 2002.

NEWSPAPERS AND PERIODICALS

Afro-American (Baltimore)

Amsterdam News

Auto Workers News

Black Worker

Chicago Defender

Christian Century

Civic Rights Bulletin

Civic Searchlight

Crisis

Daily Worker

Dearborn Independent

Detroit Contender

Detroiter

Detroit Free Press

Detroit Independent

Detroit Journal

Detroit News

Detroit People's News

Detroit Saturday Night

Detroit Times

Detroit Tribune

Detroit Tribune Independent

Ford Facts

Fortune

Forum and Century

It's About Time

Literary Digest

Messenger

Michigan Chronicle

Nation

New Republic

New York Times

New York Times Sunday Magazine
North American Review
Opportunity, Journal of Negro Life
Pipp's Weekly
Pittsburgh Courier

Southern Workman
Survey
Survey Graphic
United Automobile Worker

GOVERNMENT DOCUMENTS

Bernstein, Irving. "The Automobile Industry: Post-War Developments, 1918–1921." *Historical Studies* 52 (September 1942): 20–45. Washington, D.C.: U.S. Department of Labor, Bureau of Labor Statistics.

Kocher, Eric. *Economic and Physical Growth of Detroit, 1701–1935*. Division of Economics and Statistics, Federal Housing Administration. Washington, D.C.: Federal Housing Administration, 1935. Copy at Bentley Historical Library, University of Michigan, Ann Arbor.

Mayor's Inter-racial Committee (Rev. Reinhold Niebuhr, Chairman, Bishop William T. Vernon, Dr. E. A. Carter, Fred M. Butzel, Fred G. Dewey, Frederick C. Gilbert, Donald J. Marshall, W. Hayes McKinney, Mrs. Charles Novak, Mrs. C. S. Smith, Walter H. Stowers, and Jefferson B. Webb) with a Special Survey Staff under the direction of Forrester B. Washington. *The Negro in Detroit*. Detroit: Detroit Bureau of Governmental Research, Inc., 1926.

U.S. Bureau of Labor Statistics. "Standard of Living of Employees of Ford Motor Company in Detroit." *Monthly Review* 30, 6 (June 1930): 1209–51.

U. S. Department of Commerce, Bureau of the Census. *Abstract of the Fifteenth Census of the United States, 1930*. Washington, D.C. Government Printing Office, 1933.

———. *Abstract of the Fourteenth Census of the United States, 1920*. Washington, D.C. Government Printing Office, 1923.

———. *Abstract of the Thirteenth Census of the United States, 1910*. Washington, D.C. Government Printing Office, 1913.

BOOKS, ARTICLES, AND THESES

Adamic, Louis. "The Hill-Billies Come to Detroit." *Nation*, 13 February 1935, 177–78; 13 March 1935, 305.

Addington, Wendell Phillips. "Reds at the Rouge: Communist Party Activism at the Ford Rouge Plant, 1922–1952." M.A. thesis, Wayne State University, 1997.

Alexander, J. Trent. "Defining the Diaspora: Appalachians in the Great Migration." *Journal of Interdisciplinary History* 37, 2 (Autumn 2006): 219–47.

———. "Demographic Patterns of the Great Black Migration (1915–1940)." In *Encyclopedia of the Great Black Migration*, edited by Steven A. Reich, 1:236–39. Westport, Conn.: Greenwood Press, 2006.

Amidon, Beulah. "Battle of Detroit." *Survey Graphic*, April 1942, 198.

Anderson, Jervis. *A. Philip Randolph: A Biographical Portrait*. Berkeley: University of California Press, 1972.

Andrew, William D. "Factionalism and Anti-Communism: Ford Local 600." *Labor History* 20 (1979): 227–55.

Aptheker, Herbert, ed. *A Documentary History of the Negro People in the United States.* Vol. 4: *1933–1945.* 1974; reprint, New York: Carol Publishing Group, 1992.

——, ed. *Writings in Periodicals Edited by W. E. B. Du Bois: Selections from the Crisis.* Vol. 1: *1911–1925.* Millwood, New York: Kraus-Thomson Organization Limited, 1983.

Arnesen, Eric. *Brotherhoods of Color: Black Railroad Workers and the Struggle for Equality.* Cambridge, Mass.: Harvard University Press, 2001.

——. "Following the Color Line of Labor: Black Workers and the Labor Movement before 1930." *Radical History* 55 (Winter 1993): 53–87.

——. "No 'Graver Danger': Black Anticommunism, the Communist Party, and the Race Question" and "The Red and the Black: Reflections on the Responses to 'No Graver Danger'" [roundtable essay with responses by John Earl Haynes, Martha Biondi, Kenneth Janken, and Carol Anderson). *Labor: Studies in Working-Class History of the Americas* 3, no. 4 (Winter 2006): 13–52, 75–79.

——. "Up from Exclusion: Black and White Workers, Race, and the State of Labor History." *Reviews in American History* 26 (March 1998): 146–74.

——. *Waterfront Workers of New Orleans: Race, Class, and Politics, 1863–1923.* 1991; reprint, Urbana: University of Illinois Press, 1994.

——, ed. *Black Protest and the Great Migration: A Brief History with Documents.* Boston, Mass.: Bedford, 2003.

——, ed. *The Black Worker: A Reader.* Urbana: University of Illinois Press, 2007.

Asher, Cash. *Sacred Cows: A Story of the Recall of Mayor Bowles.* Detroit: Cash Asher, 1931.

Asher, Robert, and Ronald Edsforth (with assistance of Stephen Merlino), eds. *Autowork.* Albany: State University of New York, 1995.

Babson, Steve. *Building the Union: Skilled Workers and Anglo-Gaelic Immigrants in the Rise of the UAW.* New Brunswick, N.J.: Rutgers University Press, 1991.

Babson, Steve, with Ron Alpern, Dave Elsila, and John Revitte. *Working Detroit: The Making of a Union Town.* 1984; reprint, Detroit: Wayne State University Press, 1986.

Badger, Anthony J. *The New Deal: The Depression Years, 1933–1940.* New York: Hill and Wang, 1989.

Bailer, Lloyd H. "The Automobile Unions and Negro Labor." *Political Science Quarterly* 59 (December 1944): 548–77.

——. "The Negro Automobile Worker." *Journal of Political Economy* 51 (October 1943): 415–28.

——. "Negro Labor in the Automobile Industry." Ph.D. diss., University of Michigan, 1943.

Bailey, Beth L. *From Front Porch to Back Seat: Courtship in Twentieth-Century America.* Baltimore, Md.: The Johns Hopkins University Press, 1989.

Baldwin, Neil. *Henry Ford and the Jews: The Mass Production of Hate.* New York: Public Affairs, 2001.

Barnard, John. *American Vanguard: The United Auto Workers during the Reuther Years, 1935–1970*. Detroit: Wayne State University Press, 2004.

Baskin, Alex. "The Ford Hunger March—1932." *Labor History* 13:3 (Summer 1972): 331–60.

Bates, Beth Tompkins. "A New Crowd Challenges the Agenda of the Old Guard in the NAACP." *American Historical Review* 102, 2 (April 1997): 340–77.

———. *Pullman Porters and the Rise of Protest Politics in Black America, 1925–1945.* Chapel Hill: University of North Carolina Press, 2001.

Bennett, Harry. *We Never Called Him Henry.* New York: Fawcett, 1951.

Berlin, Ira. *The Making of African America: The Four Great Migrations.* New York: Viking, 2010.

Bernstein, Irving. *Turbulent Years: A History of the American Worker, 1933–1941.* Boston: Houghton Mifflin, 1971.

Best, Wallace D. *Passionately Human, No Less Divine: Religion and Culture in Black Chicago, 1915–1952.* Princeton, N.J.: Princeton University Press, 2005.

Beynon, Erdmann Doane. "The Southern White Laborer Migrates to Michigan." *American Sociological Review* 3, no. 3 (1938): 333–43.

Biondi, Martha. *To Stand and Fight: The Struggle for Civil Rights in Postwar New York.* Cambridge, Mass.: Harvard University Press, 2003.

Black, Harold. "Restrictive Covenants in Relation to Segregated Negro Housing in Detroit." M.A. thesis, Wayne State University, 1947.

Bloch, Herman D. "Craft Unions and the Negro in Historical Perspective." *Journal of Negro History* 43 (1958): 10–33.

———. "Labor and the Negro, 1966–1910." *Journal of Negro History* 50 (1965): 163–84.

Bonosky, Phillip. *Brother Bill McKie: Building the Union at Ford.* New York: International Publishers, 1953.

Bostick, Alice J. *The Roots of Inkster.* Inkster, Mich.: Inkster Public Library and Historical Commission, 1986.

Boyd, Melba J. *Discarded Legacy: Politics and Poetics in the Life of Frances E. W. Harper, 1825–1911.* Detroit: Wayne State University Press, 1994.

———. *Wrestling with the Muse: Dudley Randall and the Broadside Press.* New York: Columbia University Press, 2003.

Boykin, Ulysses W. *A Handbook on the Detroit Negro.* Detroit: Minority Study Associates, 1943.

Boyle, Kevin. *Arc of Justice: A Saga of Race, Civil Rights, and Murder in the Jazz Age.* New York: Henry Holt and Company, 2004.

———. "Building the Vanguard: Walter Reuther and Radical Politics in 1936." *Labor History* 30 (Summer 1989): 433–48.

———. "'There Are No Union Sorrows That the Union Can't Heal': The Struggle for Racial Equality in the United Automobile Workers, 1940–1960." *Labor History* 36, no. 1 (Winter 1995): 5–23.

Brinkley, Alan. *Liberalism and Its Discontents.* Cambridge, Mass.: Harvard University Press, 1998.

———. *Voices of Protest: Huey Long, Father Coughlin, and the Great Depression.* New York: Vintage Books, 1982.

Brinkley, Douglas. *Wheels for the World: Henry Ford, His Company, and a Century of Progress, 1903–2003.* New York: Penguin Books, 2004.

Brophy, Anne. "'The Committee . . . has stood out against coercion': The Reinvention of Detroit Americanization, 1915–1931." *Michigan Historical Review* 29, no. 2 (Fall 2003): 1–39.

Brown, Elsa Barkley, and Gregg D. Kimball. "Mapping the Terrain of Black Richmond." In *The New African American Urban History*, edited by Kenneth W. Goings and Raymond A. Mohl, 66–114. Thousand Oaks, Calif.: Sage, 1996.

Brown, Nikki. *Private Politics and Public Voices: Black Women's Activism from World War I to the New Deal.* Bloomington: Indiana University Press, 2007.

Bryan, Ford R. *Clara: Mrs. Henry Ford.* Dearborn, Mich.: Ford Books, 2001.

———. *Henry's Lieutenants.* Detroit: Wayne State University Press, 1993.

Bunche, Ralph J. "A Critique of New Deal Social Planning as It Affects Negroes." *Journal of Negro Education* 5, no. 1 (January 1936): 59–65.

Candler, Lester V. *America's Greatest Depression, 1929–1941.* New York: Harper and Row, 1970.

Carlson, Glen E. "The Negro in the Industries of Detroit," Ph.D. diss., University of Michigan, 1929.

Carter, Dan T. *Scottsboro: A Tragedy of the American South.* New York: Oxford University Press, 1971.

Cayton, Horace R., and George S. Mitchell. *Black Workers and the New Unions.* Chapel Hill: University of North Carolina Press, 1939.

Chafe, William H. *Civilities and Civil Rights: Greensboro, North Carolina, and the Black Struggle for Freedom.* New York: Oxford University Press, 1980.

Chandler, Alfred D., Jr. *Giant Enterprise: Ford, General Motors and the Automobile Industry.* New York: Harcourt, Brace and World, 1964.

Chavis, John M. T. "James Couzens: Mayor of Detroit, 1919–1922." Ph.D. diss., Michigan State University, 1970.

Chicago Commission on Race Relations. *The Negro in Chicago: A Study of Race Relations and a Race Riot.* Chicago: University of Chicago Press, 1922.

Chinoy, Ely. *Automobile Workers and the American Dream.* Garden City, N.Y.: Doubleday, 1955.

Cohen, Lizabeth. *Making a New Deal: Industrial Workers in Chicago, 1919–1939.* New York: Cambridge University Press, 1990.

Conant Gardeners. *Conant Gardens: A Black Urban Community, 1925–1950.* Detroit, Mich.: Self-published, 2001.

Conot, Robert. *American Odyssey.* New York: Bantam Books, 1974.

Countryman, Matthew J. *Up South: Civil Rights and Black Power in Philadelphia.* Philadelphia: University of Pennsylvania Press, 2006.

Craig, Scott Ian. "Automobiles and Labor: The Transformation of Detroit's Black Working Class, 1917–1941." M.A. thesis, Wayne State University, 1986.

Cruden, Robert L. *The End of the Ford Myth*. New York: International Pamphlets, 1932.

Cruse, Harold. *Plural but Equal: A Critical Study of Blacks and Minorities and America's Plural Society*. New York: William Morrow, 1967.

Dancy, John C. *Sand against the Wind: The Memoirs of John C. Dancy*. Detroit: Wayne State University Press, 1966.

Davidson, Gordon W. "Industrial Detroit after World War I, 1919 to 1921." M.A. thesis, Wayne State University, 1953.

Davis, John P. "A Survey of Problems of the Negro under the New Deal." *Journal of Negro Education* 5, no. 1 (Jan. 1936): 9–11.

D'Emilio, John. *Lost Prophet: The Life and Times of Bayard Rustin*. New York: Free Press, 2003.

De Jong, Greta. *A Different Day: African American Struggles for Justice in Rural Louisiana*. Chapel Hill: University of North Carolina Press, 2002.

Denby, Charles. *Indignant Heart: A Black Worker's Journal*. 1978; reprint, Detroit: Wayne State University Press, 1989.

Dickerson, Dennis C. "The Black Church in Industrializing Western Pennsylvania, 1870–1950." *Western Pennsylvania Historical Magazine* 64 (October 1981): 329–44.

Dillard, Angela D. *Faith in the City: Preaching Radical Social Change in Detroit*. Ann Arbor: University of Michigan Press, 2007.

Dittmer, John. *Local People: The Struggle for Civil Rights in Mississippi*. Urbana: University of Illinois Press, 1994.

Dos Passos, John. "Detroit: City of Leisure." *New Republic,* 27 July 1932, 280–82.

Downs, Linda Banks. *Diego Rivera: The Detroit Industry Murals*. New York: Detroit Institute of Arts in association with W. W. Norton, 1999.

Drake, St. Clair, and Horace R. Cayton. *Black Metropolis: A Study of Negro Life in a Northern City*. 1970; reprint, Chicago: University of Chicago Press, 1993.

Du Bois, W. E. B. *Darkwater: Voices from Within the Veil*. 1920; reprint, New York: Schocken Books, 1969.

Dunn, Robert W. *Labor and Automobiles*. New York: International Publishers, 1929.

Engelmann, Larry. "A Separate Peace: The Politics of Prohibition Enforcement in Detroit, 1920–1930." *Detroit in Perspective* 1, no. 1 (Autumn 1972): 51–73.

Evans, Hiram Wesley. "The Klan's Fight for Americanism." *North American Review* 123 (March–April–May 1926): 33–63.

Farmer, Silas. *History of Detroit and Wayne County and Early Michigan*. 1890; reprint, Detroit: Gale Research, 1967.

Feuer, Rosemary. "William Sentner, the UE, and Civic Unionism in St. Louis." In *The CIO's Left-Led Unions*, edited by Steve Rosswurm, 95–117. New Brunswick, N.J.: Rutgers University Press, 1992.

Fine, Sidney. *Frank Murphy: The Detroit Years*. Ann Arbor: University of Michigan Press, 1975.

———. "The General Motors Sit-down Strike: A Re-examination." *American Historical Review* 70 (April 1975): 691–713.

———. "Origins of the United Automobile Workers, 1933–1935." *Journal of Economic History* 18 (September 1958): 249–82.

Fitch, John A. "Making the Job Worthwhile." *Survey* 27 April 1914, 87–89.

Foner, Eric. *Free Soil, Free Labor, Free Men: The Ideology of the Republican Party before the Civil War.* 1970; reprint, with a new introduction by the author, New York: Oxford University Press, 1995.

———. *Nothing But Freedom: Emancipation and Its Legacy.* Baton Rouge: Louisiana State University Press, 1983.

———. *The Story of American Freedom.* New York: W. W. Norton, 1998.

Foner, Philip S. *Organized Labor and the Black Worker, 1619–1973.* New York: Praeger Publishers, 1974.

Foote, Christopher L., Warren C. Whatley, and Gavin Wright. "Arbitraging a Discriminatory Labor Market: Black Workers at the Ford Motor Company, 1918–1947." *Journal of Labor Economics* 21, no. 3 (2003): 493–531.

Ford, Henry, with Samuel Crowther. *Moving Forward.* New York: Kessinger Publishing, 1930.

———. *My Life and Work.* Garden City, N.Y.: Doubleday, 1923.

———. *Today and Tomorrow.* 1926; reprint, Cambridge, Mass.: Productivity Press, 1988.

Fragnoli, Raymond R. "Progressive Coalitions and Municipal Reform: Charter Revision in Detroit, 1912–1918." *Detroit in Perspective: A Journal of Regional History* 4 (Spring 1980): 119–42.

———. *The Transformation of Reform: Progressivism in Detroit—and After, 1912–1933.* New York: Garland, 1982.

Fraser, Steve. "The 'Labor Question.'" In *The Rise and Fall of the New Deal Order, 1930–1980,* edited by Fraser and Gerstle, 55–84.

Fraser, Steve, and Gary Gerstle, ed. *The Rise and Fall of the New Deal Order, 1930–1980.* Princeton, N.J.: Princeton University Press, 1989.

Fujita, Kuniko. "Black Workers' Struggles in Detroit's Auto Industry, 1935–1975." M.A. thesis, Michigan State University, 1977.

Fulton, Lester Robert. "Russel Woods: A Study of a Neighborhood's Initial Response to Negro Invasion." Ph.D. diss., Wayne State University, 1959.

Fusfeld, Daniel R., and Timothy Bates. *The Political Economy of the Urban Ghetto.* Carbondale: Southern Illinois University Press, 1984.

Galenson, Walter. *The CIO Challenge to the AFL: A History of the American Labor Movement, 1935–1941.* Cambridge, Mass.: Harvard University Press, 1960.

Gartman, David. *Auto Slavery: The Labor Process in the American Automobile Industry, 1897–1950.* New Brunswick, N.J.: Rutgers University Press, 1986.

Garvey, Amy Jacques. *Garvey and Garveyism.* New York: Macmillan, 1970.

Gavrilovich, Peter, and Bill McGraw, eds. *The Detroit Almanac: 300 Years of Life in the Motor City.* Detroit: Detroit Free Press, 2001.

Gellman, Erik S. *Death Blow to Jim Crow: The National Negro Congress and the Rise of Militant Civil Rights.* Chapel Hill: University of North Carolina Press, 2012.

Georgakas, Dan, and Marvin Surkin. *Detroit: I Do Mind Dying: A Study in Urban Revolution.* New York: St. Martin's Press, 1975.

Giddings, Paula. *When and Where I Enter: The Impact of Black Women on Race and Sex in America.* 2d ed. New York: Harper Paperbacks, 1996.

Goodman, James E. *Stories of Scottsboro.* New York: Random House, 1995.

Gottlieb, Peter. *Making Their Own Way: Southern Blacks' Migration to Pittsburgh, 1916–1930.* Urbana: University of Illinois Press, 1987.

Graebner, William. *The Engineering of Consent: Democracy and Authority in Twentieth-Century America.* Madison: University of Wisconsin Press, 1987.

Grandin, Greg. *Fordlandia: The Rise and Fall of Henry Ford's Forgotten Jungle.* New York: Picador, 2009.

Granger, Lester B. "The Negro—Friend or Foe of Organized Labor?" *Opportunity, Journal of Negro Life* 13, no. 5 (May 1935): 142.

Green, Laurie Beth. *Battling the Plantation Mentality: Memphis and the Black Freedom Struggle.* Chapel Hill: University of North Carolina Press, 2007.

Greene, Lorenzo J., and Carter G. Woodson. *The Negro Wage Earner.* New York: Russell and Russell, 1930.

Gregory, James N. *The Southern Diaspora: How the Great Migrations of Black and White Southerners Transformed America.* Chapel Hill: University of North Carolina Press, 2005.

———. "The Southern Diaspora and the Urban Dispossessed: Demonstrating the Census Public Use Microdata Samples." *Journal of American History* 82, no. 1 (June 1995): 111–34.

Griffler, Keith P. *What Price Alliance? Black Radicals Confront White Labor, 1918–1938.* New York: Garland, 1995.

Grossman, James R. "Blowing the Trumpet: The *Chicago Defender* and Black Migration during World War I." *Illinois Historical Journal* 78, no. 2 (Summer 1985): 82–96.

———. *Land of Hope: Chicago, Black Southerners, and the Great Migration.* Chicago: University of Chicago Press, 1989.

Haber, William. "Fluctuations in Employment in Detroit Factories, 1921–1931." *Journal of the American Statistical Association* 27 (June 1932): 141–52.

Hahn, Steven. *A Nation under Our Feet: Black Political Struggles in the Rural South from Slavery to the Great Migration.* Cambridge, Mass.: Harvard University Press, 2003.

Hall, Helen. "When Detroit's Out of Gear." *Survey,* 1 April 1930, 9–14, 51–54.

Hall, Jacquelyn Dowd. "The Long Civil Rights Movement and the Political Uses of the Past." *Journal of American History* 91, no. 4 (March 2005): 1233–63.

Halpern, Rick. *Down on the Killing Floor: Black and White Workers in Chicago's Packinghouses, 1904–1954.* Urbana: University of Illinois Press, 1997.

Harmon, Julia Robinson. "Reverend Robert L. Bradby: Establishing the Kingdom of God among Migrants, Women and Workers, 1910–1946." Ph.D. diss., Michigan State University, 2002.

Harris, Carl V. "Reforms in Government Control of Negroes in Birmingham, Alabama, 1890–1920." *Journal of Southern History* 38, no. 4 (November 1972): 567–600.

Harris, Howell John. "Industrial Democracy and Liberal Capitalism, 1890–1925." In *Industrial Democracy in America: The Ambiguous Promise*, edited by Nelson Lichtenstein and Howell John Harris, 51–66. New York: Cambridge University Press, 1993.

Harris, William H. *The Harder We Run: Black Workers since the Civil War.* New York: Oxford University Press, 1982.

Haynes, George Edmund. *Negro Newcomers in Detroit, Michigan: A Challenge to Christian Statesmanship, a Preliminary Survey.* 1918; reprint, New York: Arno Press and the New York Times, 1969.

Helper, Rose. *Racial Policies and Practices of Real Estate Brokers.* Minneapolis: University of Minnesota Press, 1969.

Herron, Jerry. *AfterCulture: Detroit and the Humiliation of History.* Detroit: Wayne State University Press, 1993.

Higginbotham, Evelyn Brooks. *Righteous Discontent: The Women's Movement in the Black Baptist Church, 1880–1920.* Cambridge, Mass.: Harvard University Press, 1993.

Higham, John. *Stranger in the Land: Patterns of American Nativism, 1860–1925.* New Brunswick, N.J.: Rutgers University Press, 1988.

Hill, T. Arnold. "The Plight of the Negro Industrial Worker." *Journal of Negro Education* 5, no. 1 (January 1936): 40–47.

Hirsch, Arnold R. "With or Without Jim Crow: Black Residential Segregation in the United States." In *Urban Policy in Twentieth-Century America*, edited by Arnold R. Hirsch and Raymond A. Mohl, 65–92. New Brunswick, N.J.: Rutgers University Press, 1993.

Hofstadter, Richard. *Age of Reform: From Bryan to F.D.R.* New York: Vintage, 1955.

Holloway, Jonathan Scott. *Confronting the Veil: Abram Harris Jr., E. Franklin Frazier, and Ralph Bunche, 1919–1941.* Chapel Hill: University of North Carolina Press, 2002.

Holt, Thomas C. "The Political Uses of Alienation: W. E. B. Du Bois on Politics, Race, and Culture, 1903–1940." *American Quarterly* 42 (June 1990): 301–23.

Honey, Michael Keith. *Black Workers Remember: An Oral History of Segregation, Unionism, and the Freedom Struggle.* Berkeley: University of California Press, 1999.

———. *Going Down Jericho Road: The Memphis Strike, Martin Luther King's Last Campaign.* New York: W. W. Norton, 2007.

Horowitz, Roger. *"Negro and White, Unite and Fight!": A Social History of Industrial Unionism in Meatpacking, 1930–1990.* Urbana: University of Illinois Press, 1997.

Hunter, Tera W. "'The Brotherly Love for Which This City Is Proverbial Should Extend to All': The Everyday Lives of Working-Class Women in Philadelphia and Atlanta in the 1890s." In *W. E. B. DuBois, Race, and the City: The Philadelphia Negro and Its Legacy*, edited by Michael B. Katz and Thomas J. Sugrue, 126–51. Philadelphia: University of Pennsylvania Press, 1998.

———. *To 'Joy My Freedom: Southern Black Women's Lives and Labors after the Civil War.* Cambridge, Mass.: Harvard University Press, 1997.

Jackson, Kenneth T. *Crabgrass Frontier: The Suburbanization of the United States.* New York: Oxford University Press, 1985.

———. *The Ku Klux Klan in the City, 1915–1930*. New York: Oxford University Press, 1967.

Jennings, Peter, and Todd Brewster. *The Century*. New York: Doubleday, 1998.

Johnson, Charles S. *Negro Housing: Report of the Committee on Negro Housing*. Chaired by Nannie H. Burroughs. 1932; reprint, New York: Negro Universities Press, 1969.

Johnson, Christopher H. *Maurice Sugar: Law, Labor, and the Left in Detroit, 1912–1950*. Detroit: Wayne State University Press, 1988.

Johnson, James Weldon. "Harlem: The Culture Capital." In *The New Negro*, edited by Alaine Locke, 301–11. 1925; reprint, New York: Macmillan Publishing Co., 1992.

Jones, LeRoi. *Blues People: Negro Music in White America*. New York: William Morrow, 1983.

Jordan, William. *Black Newspapers and America's War for Democracy, 1914–1921*. Chapel Hill: University of North Carolina Press, 2001.

Katzman, David M. *Before the Ghetto: Black Detroit in the Nineteenth Century*. Urbana: University of Illinois Press, 1973.

Katznelson, Ira. *When Affirmative Action Was White: An Untold History of Racial Inequality in Twentieth-Century America*. New York: W. W. Norton, 2005.

Kazin, Michael, and Joseph A. McCartin, eds. *Americanism: New Perspectives on the History of an Ideal*. Chapel Hill: University of North Carolina Press, 2006.

Keeran, Roger. *The Communist Party and the Auto Workers Union*. Bloomington: Indiana University Press, 1980.

Kelley, Robin D. G. *Hammer and Hoe: Alabama Communists during the Great Depression*. Chapel Hill: University of North Carolina Press, 1990.

———. "'We Are Not What We Seem': Rethinking Black Working-Class Opposition in the Jim Crow South." *Journal of American History* 80, no. 1 (June 1993): 75–112.

Kellogg, John. "Negro Urban Clusters in the Post-Bellum South." *Geographical Analysis* 67 (1977): 310–21.

Kennedy, David. *Freedom from Fear: The American People in Depression and War, 1929–1945*. New York: Oxford University Press, 1999.

Kenyon, Amy Maria. *Dreaming Suburbia: Detroit and the Production of Postwar Space and Culture*. Detroit: Wayne State University Press, 2004.

Kinzie, Stuart. "Mr. Ford Lends a Hand." *Scribner's Commentator*, April 1941, 21–26.

Kirby, John B. *Black Americans in the Roosevelt Era: Liberalism and Race*. Knoxville: University of Tennessee Press, 1980.

Klug, Thomas. "Employers' Strategies in the Detroit Labor Market, 1900–1929." In *On the Line: Essays in the History of Auto Work*, edited by Lichtenstein and Meyer, 42–72.

Korstad, Robert Rogers. *Civil Rights Unionism: Tobacco Workers and the Struggle for Democracy in the Mid-Twentieth-Century South*. Chapel Hill: University of North Carolina Press, 2003.

Korstad, Robert, and Nelson Lichtenstein. "Opportunities Found and Lost: Labor, Radicals, and the Early Civil Rights Movement." *Journal of American History* 75, nos. 3–4 (December 1988): 786–811.

Krass, Judith. "Detroit as a Center of Commerce, 1880–1900." M.A. thesis, Wayne State University, 1962.

Kraus, Henry. *Heroes of Unwritten Story: The UAW, 1933–1939*. Urbana: University of Illinois Press, 1993.

Kurashige, Scott. *The Shifting Grounds of Race: Black and Japanese Americans in the Making of Multiethnic Los Angeles*. Princeton, N.J.: Princeton University Press, 2008.

Kusmer, Kenneth L. "The Black Urban Experience in American History." In *State of Afro-American History*, edited by Darlene Clarke Hine, 91–122. Baton Rouge: Louisiana State University Press, 1986.

Lacey, Robert. *Ford: The Men and the Machine.* New York: Ballantine Books, 1986.

Lasker, Bruno. "The Negro in Detroit." *Survey*, 15 April 1927, 72–73, 123.

Lawrence, Charles Radford. "Negro Organizations in Crisis: Depression, New Deal, World War II." Ph.D. diss., Columbia University, 1953.

Lee, John R. "The So-Called Profit Sharing System in the Ford Plant." *Annals of the American Academy of Political and Social Science* 65 (May 1916): 297–310.

Lemke-Santangelo, Gretchen. *Abiding Courage: African American Migrant Women and the East Bay Community*. Chapel Hill: University of North Carolina Press, 1996.

Lett, Harold A. "Migration Difficulties in Michigan." *The Southern Workman* 56, no. 5 (May 1927): 231–36.

Leuchtenburg, William E. *Franklin D. Roosevelt and the New Deal, 1932–1940*. New York: Harper & Row, 1963.

Levin, Samuel M. "The End of Ford Profit Sharing." *Personnel Journal* 6 (October 1927): 161–70.

———. "Ford Profit Sharing, 1914–1920, I. The Growth of the Plan." *Personnel Journal* 6 (August 1927): 75–86.

———. "The Ford Unemployment Policy." *American Labor Legislation Review* (June 1932): 101–8.

Levine, David Allan. "'Expecting the Barbarians': Race Relations and Social Control, Detroit, 1915–1925." Ph.D. diss., University of Chicago, 1970.

———. *Internal Combustion: The Races in Detroit, 1915–1926*. Westport, Conn.: Greenwood Press, 1976.

Lewis, David L. "History of Negro Employment in Detroit Area Plants of Ford Motor Company, 1914–1941." Seminar Paper, History 344, University of Michigan, 1954.

———. "Sex and the Automobile: From Rumble Seats to Rockin' Vans." In *The Automobile and American Culture*, edited by David L. Lewis and Laurence Goldstein, 123–33. Ann Arbor: University of Michigan Press, 1980.

———. "Training the Tradesmen Who Made the Model T." *Model "T" Times*, May–June 1974, 30.

———. "Working Side by Side." *Michigan History Magazine*, January–February 1993, 24–30.

Lewis, David Levering. *W. E. B. Du Bois: Biography of a Race, 1868–1919*. New York: Henry Holt, 1993.

———. *W. E. B. Du Bois: The Fight for Equality and the American Century, 1919–1963.* New York: Henry Holt, 2000.

———. *When Harlem Was in Vogue.* New York: Oxford University Press, 1979.

Lewis, Earl. *In Their Own Interests: Race, Class, and Power in Twentieth-Century Norfolk, Virginia.* Berkeley: University of California Press, 1991.

Licht, Walter. *Getting Work: Philadelphia, 1840–1950.* Cambridge, Mass.: Harvard University Press, 1992.

Lichtenstein, Nelson. "Another Time, Another Place: Blacks, Radicals and Rank and File Militancy in Auto in the 30s and 40s." *Radical America* 16 (January–April 1982): 131–37.

———. *Labor's War at Home: The CIO in World War II.* 1982; reprint, Philadelphia: Temple University Press, 2003.

———. "Life at the Rouge: A Cycle of Workers' Control." In *Life and Labor: Dimensions of American Working-Class History,* edited by Charles Stephenson and Robert Asher, 237–59. Albany: State University of New York Press, 1986.

———. *Walter Reuther: The Most Dangerous Man in Detroit.* New York: Basic Books, 1995.

Lichtenstein, Nelson, and Howell John Harris, eds. *Industrial Democracy in America: The Ambiguous Promise.* New York: Cambridge University Press, 1993.

Lichtenstein, Nelson, and Stephen Meyer, eds. *On the Line: Essays in the History of Auto Work.* Urbana: University of Illinois Press, 1989.

Lieberman, Robert C. *Shifting the Color Line: Race and the American Welfare State.* Cambridge, Mass.: Harvard University Press, 1998.

Lilienthal, David. "Has the Negro the Right to Self-Defense?" *Nation,* 23 December 1925, 724–25.

Lindsey, Howard O'Dell. "Fields to Fords, Feds to Franchise: African American Empowerment in Inkster, Michigan." Ph.D. diss., University of Michigan, 1993.

Litchfield, Edward H. "A Case Study of Negro Political Behavior in Detroit." *Public Opinion Quarterly* 5 (June 1941): 267–74.

———. *Voting Behavior in a Metropolitan Area.* Ann Arbor: University of Michigan Press, 1941.

Litwack, Leon F. *Trouble in Mind: Black Southerners in the Age of Jim Crow.* New York: Vintage Books, 1999.

Logan, Rayford W. *The Betrayal of the Negro: From Rutherford B. Hayes to Woodrow Wilson.* New York: Da Capo Press, 1997.

Luker, Ralph E. *The Social Gospel in Black and White: American Radical Reform, 1885–1912.* Chapel Hill: University of North Carolina Press, 1991.

Maloney, Thomas N., and Warren C. Whatley. "Making the Effort: The Contours of Racial Discrimination in Detroit's Labor Markets, 1920–1940." *Journal of Economic History* 55:3 (Sept. 1995): 465–93.

Marable, Manning. *Malcolm X: A Life of Reinvention.* New York: Viking, 2011.

Marks, Carole. *Farewell—We're Good and Gone: The Great Black Migration.* Bloomington: Indiana University Press, 1989.

Marquart, Frank. *An Auto Worker's Journal: The UAW from Crusade to One-Party Union.* University Park: Pennsylvania State University Press, 1975.

Marquis, Samuel S. *Henry Ford: An Interpretation.* Toronto, Canada: Thomas Allen, 1923.

Martin, Elizabeth Anne. *Detroit and the Great Migration, 1916–1929*, Bulletin, no. 40. Ann Arbor: Bentley Historical Library, University of Michigan, 1993.

Massey, Douglas S., and Nancy A. Denton. *American Apartheid: Segregation and the Making of the Underclass.* Cambridge, Mass.: Harvard University Press, 1993.

Mayer, Albert J. "Russel Woods: Change without Conflict: A Case Study of Neighborhood Racial Transition in Detroit." In *Studies in Housing and Minority Groups*, edited by Nathan Glazer and Davis McEntire, 190–202. Berkeley: University of California Press, 1960.

McCartin, Joseph A. "'An American Feeling': Workers, Managers, and the Struggle over Industrial Democracy in the World War I Era." In *Industrial Democracy in America*, edited by Lichtenstein and Harris, 67–86.

McCormick, Anne O'Hare. "Ford Seeks a New Balance for Industry." *New York Times Magazine*, 29 May 1932, section 5, 3–6.

———. "The Future of the Ford Idea." *New York Times Magazine*, 22 May 1932, section 5, 2–5.

McKenzie, Roderick D. *The Metropolitan Community.* New York: McGraw-Hill Book, 1933.

McMillen, Neil R. *Dark Journey: Black Mississippians in the Age of Jim Crow.* Urbana: University of Illinois Press, 1989.

McPherson, William H. *Labor Relations in the Automobile Industry.* Washington, D.C.: Brookings Institution, 1940.

Meier, August, and Elliott Rudwick. *Black Detroit and the Rise of the UAW.* New York: Oxford University Press, 1979.

Meyer, Stephen. "Adapting the Immigrant to the Line: Americanization in the Ford Factory, 1914–1921." *Journal of Social History* 14 (Fall 1980): 67–82.

———. *The Five Dollar Day: Labor Management and Social Control in the Ford Motor Company, 1908–1921.* Albany: State University of New York Press, 1981.

———. "Red Scare in the Factory: Shop Militants and Factory Spies at Ford, 1917–1920." *Detroit in Perspective* 6 (Fall 1982): 21–45.

Miles, Norman Kenneth. "Home at Last: Urbanization of Black Migrants in Detroit, 1916–1929." Ph.D. diss., University of Michigan, 1978.

Miller, James A. *Remembering Scottsboro: The Legacy of an Infamous Trial.* Princeton, N.J.: Princeton University Press, 2009.

Minchin, Timothy J. *The Color of Work: The Struggle for Civil Rights in the Southern Paper Industry, 1945–1980.* Chapel Hill: University of North Carolina Press, 2001.

———. *Hiring the Black Worker: The Racial Integration of the Southern Textile Industry, 1960–1980.* Chapel Hill: University of North Carolina Press, 1999.

Moon, Elaine Latzman. *Untold Tales, Unsung Heroes: An Oral History of Detroit's African American Community, 1918–1967.* Detroit: Wayne State University Press, 1991.

Morris, Aldon. *The Origins of the Civil Rights Movement: Black Communities Organizing for Change*. New York: Free Press, 1984.

Morrison, Toni. *Song of Solomon*. New York: Alfred A. Knopf, 1987.

Muller, Carl. "Frank Murphy: Ornament of the Bar." *Detroit Lawyer* 17 (September 1949): 181–83.

Murage, Njeru. "Making Migrants an Asset: The Detroit Urban League–Employers Alliance in Wartime Detroit, 1916–1919." *Michigan Historical Review* 26 (22 March 2000): 67–104.

Murch, Donna Jean. *Living for the City: Migration, Education, and the Rise of the Black Panther Party in Oakland, California*. Chapel Hill: University of North Carolina Press, 2010.

Murphy, Frank. "The Detroit Plan." In *Plain Talk* (October 1932): 36–37.

Myrdal, Gunnar. *An American Dilemma*. Vol. 1: *The Negro in a White Nation*. 1944, 1962; reprinted, New York: McGraw-Hill, 1964.

———. *An American Dilemma*. Vol. 2: *The Negro Social Structure*. 1944, 1962; reprint, New York: McGraw-Hill, 1964.

Naison, Mark. *Communists in Harlem during the Depression*. New York: Grove Press, 1983.

Needleman, Ruth. *Black Freedom Fighters in Steel: The Struggle for Democratic Unionism*. Ithaca, N.Y.: Cornell University Press, 2003.

Neumann, Amber Cooley. "Twenty-Five Years of Negro Activity in Detroit, 1910–1935." M.A. thesis, University of Detroit, 1935.

Nevins, Allan, and Frank Ernest Hill. *Ford: Decline and Rebirth, 1933–1962*. New York: Charles Scribners' Sons, 1963.

———. *Ford: Expansion and Challenge, 1915–1933*. New York: Charles Scribners' Sons, 1957.

———. *Ford: The Times, the Man, the Company*. New York: Charles Scribners' Sons, 1954.

Niebuhr, Reinhold. "Ford's Five-Day Week Shrinks." *Christian Century*, 9 June 1927, 713–14.

———. "How Philanthropic Is Henry Ford?" *Christian Century*, 9 December 1926, 1516–17.

———. *Leaves from the Notebook of a Tamed Cynic*. Hamden, Conn.: Shoe String Press, 1956.

———. "Race Prejudice in the North." *Christian Century*, 12 May 1927, 583–84.

Norrell, Robert J. "Caste in Steel: Jim Crow Careers in Birmingham, Alabama." *Journal of American History* 73, no. 3 (December 1986): 669–94.

———. *Reaping the Whirlwind: The Civil Rights Movement in Tuskegee*. Chapel Hill: University of North Carolina Press, 1998.

Northrup, Herbert R. *Negro Employment in Basic Industry: A Study of Racial Policies in Six Industries*. Philadelphia: University of Pennsylvania Press, 1970.

Norton, William J. "The Relief Crisis in Detroit." *Social Science Review* 7 (March 1933): 1–10.

Nye, David E. *Henry Ford: "Ignorant Idealist."* Port Washington, N.Y.: Kennikat Press, 1979.

O'Brien, John H. "Henry Ford's Commander in Chief: Harry Bennett and His Private Army." *Forum and Century*, February 1938, 67–72.

Ortquist, Richard Theodore, Jr. "Depression Politics in Michigan, 1929–1933." Ph.D. diss., University of Michigan, 1968.

Osofsky, Gilbert. *Harlem: The Making of a Ghetto.* 2nd edition. Chicago: Elephant Paperback, 1996.

Painter, Nell Irvin. *Exodusters: Black Migration to Kansas after Reconstruction.* 1976; reprint, New York: W. W. Norton, 1992.

Parkins, Almon Ernest. *Historical Geography of Detroit.* Lansing: Michigan Historical Commission, 1918.

Payne, Charles. *I've Got the Light of Freedom: The Organizing Tradition and the Mississippi Freedom Struggle.* Berkeley: University of California Press, 1995.

Pennybacker, Susan D. *From Scottsboro to Munich: Race and Political Culture in the 1930s.* Princeton, N.J.: Princeton University Press, 2009.

Peterson, Joyce Shaw. *American Automobile Workers, 1900–1933.* Albany: State University of New York Press, 1987.

———. "Auto Workers and Their Work, 1900–1933." *Labor History* 22 (Spring 1981): 213–36.

———. "Auto Workers Confront the Depression, 1929–1933." *Detroit in Perspective* 6 (Fall 1982): 47–71.

———. "Black Automobile Workers in Detroit, 1910–1930." *Journal of Negro History* 64, no. 3 (Summer 1979): 177–90.

Phillips, Kimberley L. *AlabamaNorth: African American Migrants, Community, and Working-Class Activism in Cleveland.* Urbana: University of Illinois Press, 1999.

Pipp, Edwin, G. *The Real Henry Ford.* Detroit: Pipp's Weekly, 1922.

Player, Cyril Arthur. "Gangsters and Politicians in Detroit." *New Republic*, 13 August 1930): 361–63.

Poole, Mary. *The Segregated Origins of Social Security: African Americans and the Welfare State.* Chapel Hill: University of North Carolina Press, 2006.

Preis, Art. *Labor's Giant Step: Twenty Years of the CIO.* New York: Pioneer Publishers, 1964.

Rabinowitz, Harold N. *Race Relations in the Urban South, 1865–1890.* 1978; reprint, Urbana: University of Illinois Press, 1980.

Ralph, James R., Jr. *Northern Protest: Martin Luther King, Jr., Chicago, and the Civil Rights Movement.* Cambridge, Mass.: Harvard University Press, 1993.

Ramsey, Maurice M. "Some Aspects of Non-Partisan Government in Detroit." Ph.D. diss., University of Michigan, 1944.

Randolph, A. Philip. "The Trade Union Movement and the Negro." *Journal of Negro Education* 5, no. 1 (Jan. 1936): 54–58.

Raper, Arthur. *Preface to Peasantry.* Chapel Hill: University of North Carolina Press, 1936.

Record, Wilson. *The Negro and the Communist Party*. Chapel Hill: University of North Carolina Press, 1951.

———. *Race and Radicalism: The NAACP and the Communist Party in Conflict*. Ithaca, N.Y.: Cornell University Press, 1964.

Reed, Touré F. *Not Alms but Opportunity: The Urban League and the Politics of Racial Uplift, 1910–1950*. Chapel Hill: University of North Carolina Press, 2008.

Reich, Steven A. "The Great Migration and the Literary Imagination." *Journal of the Historical Society* 9, no. 1 (March 2009): 87–128.

———. "The Great War, Black Workers, and the Rise and Fall of the NAACP in the South." In *The Black Worker: A Reader*, edited by Eric Arnesen, 147–77. Urbana: University of Illinois Press, 2007.

———. "Soldiers of Democracy: Black Texans and the Fight for Citizenship, 1917–1921." *Journal of American History* 82, no. 4 (March 1996): 1478–1504.

———, ed. *Encyclopedia of the Great Black Migration*. Vol. 1: *A–L*. Westport, Conn.: Greenwood Press, 2006.

Reid, Ira De A. *Negro Membership in American Labor Unions*. New York: Negro Universities Press, 1930.

Rice, Roger L. "Residential Segregation by Law, 1910–1917." *Journal of Southern History* 34 (May 1968): 179–99.

Rivera, Diego, with Gladys March. *My Art, My Life*. New York: Citadel Press, 1960.

Robinson, Cedric. *Black Marxism: The Making of the Black Radical Tradition*. Chapel Hill: University of North Carolina Press, 2000.

Rodgers, Daniel T. *The Work Ethic in Industrial American, 1850–1920*. Chicago: University of Chicago Press, 1979.

Rosengarten, Theodore, comp. *All God's Dangers: The Life of Nate Shaw*. New York: Alfred A. Knopf, 1974.

Ross, Joyce B. *J. E. Spingarn and the Rise of the NAACP, 1911–1939*. New York: Atheneum, 1972.

Rothman, R. "Detroit Elects a Liberal." *Nation*, 15 October 1930, 400–401.

Rubio, Philip F. *There's Always Work at the Post Office: African American Postal Workers and the Fight for Jobs, Justice, and Equality*. Chapel Hill: University of North Carolina Press, 2010.

Ryan, Francis. *AFSCME's Philadelphia Story: Municipal Workers and Urban Power in the Twentieth Century*. Philadelphia, Pa.: Temple University Press, 2011.

Salem, Dorothy. *To Better Our World: Black Women in Organized Reform, 1890–1920*. Brooklyn, N.Y.: Carlson Publishing, 1990.

Schlesinger, Arthur M., Jr. *The Crisis of the Old Order, 1919–1939*. Boston: Houghton Mifflin, 1957.

Schneider, Mark Robert. *"We Return Fighting": The Civil Rights Movement in the Jazz Age*. Boston: Northeastern University Press, 2002.

Schulman, Bruce J. *From Cotton Belt to Sunbelt: Federal Policy, Economic Development, and the Transformation of the South, 1938–1980*. Durham, N.C.: Duke University Press, 1994.

Schwartz, Jonathan. "Henry Ford's Melting Pot." In *Ethnic Groups in the City: Culture, Institutions, and Power*, edited by Otto Feinstein, 191–98. Lexington, Mass.: D.C. Heath, 1971.

Scott, Emmett J. "Additional Letters of Negro Migrants of 1916–1918." *Journal of Negro History* 4 (October 1919): 412–65.

———. *Negro Migration during the War*. 1920; reprint, New York: Arno Press, 1969.

Self, Robert O. *American Babylon: Race and the Struggle for Postwar Oakland*. Princeton, N.J.: Princeton University Press, 2003.

Self, Robert O., and Thomas J. Sugrue. "The Power of Place: Race, Political Economy, and Identity in the Postwar Metropolis." In *A Companion to Post–1945 America*, edited by Jean-Christophe Agnew and Roy Rosenzweig, 20–43. Malden, Mass.: Wiley-Blackwell, 2002.

Sernett, Milton C. *Bound for the Promised Land: African American Religion and the Great Migration*. Durham, N.C.: Duke University Press, 1997.

Shelly, Cara L. "Bradby's Baptists: Second Baptist Church of Detroit, 1910–1946." *Michigan Historical Review* 17, no. 1 (Spring 1991): 1–33.

Singh, Nikhil Pal. *Black Is a Country: Race and the Unfinished Struggle for Democracy*. Cambridge, Mass.: Harvard University Press, 2004.

Sitkoff, Harvard. *A New Deal for Blacks: The Emergence of Civil Rights as a National Issue: Volume I: The Depression Decade*. New York: Oxford University Press, 1978.

Smith, Suzanne E. *To Serve the Living: Funeral Directors and the African American Way of Life*. Cambridge, Mass.: Harvard University Press, 2010.

Smith-Irvin, Jeannette. *Footsoldiers of the Universal Negro Improvement Association*. Trenton, N.J.: Africa World Press, 1989.

Solomon, Mark. *The Cry Was Unity: Communists and African Americans, 1917–1936*. Jackson: University Press of Mississippi, 1998.

Solomon, Thomas Ralph. "Participation of Negroes in Detroit Elections." Ph.D. diss., University of Michigan, 1939.

Sorensen, Charles E., with Samuel T. Williamson. *My Forty Years with Ford*. 1956; reprint, Detroit: Wayne State University Press, 2006.

Spear, Allan H. *Black Chicago: The Making of a Negro Ghetto, 1890–1920*. Chicago: University of Chicago Press, 1967.

Spero, Sterling D., and Abram L. Harris. *The Black Worker: The Negro and the Labor Movement*. New York: Columbia University Press, 1931.

Staff. "Mr. Ford Doesn't Care." *Fortune*, December 1933, 62–69, 121–22, 125–28, 131–34.

Stein, Judith. *The World of Marcus Garvey: Race and Class in Modern Society*. Baton Rouge: Louisiana State University Press, 1986.

Stepan-Norris, Judith, and Maurice Zeitlin. *Talking Union*. Urbana: University of Illinois Press, 1996.

Sterne, Margaret. "The Museum Director and the Artist: Dr. William R. Valentiner and Diego Rivera in Detroit." *Detroit in Perspective* 1, no. 2 (Winter 1973): 88–110.

Strauss, Anselm L. *Images of the American City*. Glencoe, Ill.: Free Press of Glencoe, 1961.

Sugar, Maurice. "Bullets—Not Food—for Ford Workers." *Nation* 23 (March 1932): 333–35.

———.*The Ford Hunger March*. Berkeley, Calif.: Meiklejohn Civil Liberties Institute, 1980.

Sugrue, Thomas J. *The Origins of the Urban Crisis: Race and Inequality in Postwar Detroit*. Princeton, N.J.: Princeton University Press, 1996.

———. *Sweet Land of Liberty: The Forgotten Struggle for Civil Rights in the North*. New York: Random House, 2008.

Sullivan, Patricia. *Days of Hope: Race and Democracy in the New Deal Era*. Chapel Hill: University of North Carolina Press, 1996.

Sundstrom, William A. "The Color Line: Racial Norms and Discrimination in Urban Labor Markets, 1910–1950." *Journal of Economic History* 54 (June 1994): 382–97.

Sward, Keith. *The Legend of Henry Ford.* New York: Holt, Rinehart and Winston, 1948.

Taylor, Clarence. *Black Religious Intellectuals: The Fight for Equality from Jim Crow to the Twenty-first Century*. Oxford, U.K.: Routledge, 2002.

Taylor, Cynthia. *A. Philip Randolph: The Religious Journey of an African American Labor Leader.* New York: New York University Press, 2006.

Taylor, Quintard. "The Civil Rights Movement in the American West: Black Protest in Seattle, 1960–1970." *Journal of Negro History* 80, no. 1 (Winter 1995): 1–14.

Theoharis, Jeanne F., and Komozi Woodard, eds. *Freedom North: Black Freedom Struggles outside the South, 1940–1980*. New York: Palgrave, 2003.

Thomas, Jerome Gale. "The City of Detroit: A Study in Urban Geography." Ph.D. diss., University of Michigan, 1928.

Thomas, Jesse O. "Will the New Deal Be a Square Deal for the Negro?" *Opportunity, Journal of Negro Life* 11:10 (October 1933): 308.

Thomas, Richard W. *Life for Us Is What We Make It: Building Black Community in Detroit, 1915–1945*. Bloomington: Indiana University Press, 1992.

Thompson, Heather A. *Whose Detroit? Politics, Labor, and Race in a Modern American City*. Ithaca, N.Y.: Cornell University Press, 2001.

Ticknor, Thomas James. "Motor City: The Impact of the Automobile Industry upon Detroit, 1900–1975." Ph.D. diss., University of Michigan, 1978.

Trotter, Joe William. *Black Milwaukee: The Making of an Industrial Proletariat, 1915–45.* Urbana: University of Illinois Press, 1985.

———. *Coal, Class, and Color: Blacks in Southern West Virginia, 1915–1932*. Urbana: University of Illinois Press, 1990.

———. "From a Raw Deal to a New Deal?" In *To Make Our World Anew: A History of African Americans*, edited by Robin D. G. Kelley and Earl Lewis, 409–44. New York: Oxford University Press, 2000.

———, ed. *The Great Migration in Historical Perspective: New Dimensions of Race, Class, and Gender*. Bloomington: Indiana University Press, 1991.

Tuck, Stephen. *We Ain't What We Ought to Be: The Black Freedom Struggle from Emancipation to Obama*. Cambridge, Mass.: Belknap Press of Harvard University Press, 2010.

Tuttle, William M., Jr. *Race Riot: Chicago in the Red Summer of 1919*. New York: Atheneum, 1970.

Van Deventer, John H. "Ford Principles and Practice at River Rouge: II—Mechanical Handling of Coal and Coke." *Industrial Management: The Engineering Magazine*, October 1922, 195–201.

Vose, Clement E. *Caucasians Only: The Supreme Court, the NAACP, and the Restrictive Covenant Case*. Berkeley: University of California Press, 1967.

Walker, Charles R. "Down and Out in Detroit." *Forum and Century*, September 1931, 129–36.

Ward, Stephen M., ed. *Pages from a Black Radical's Notebook: A James Boggs Reader*. Detroit: Wayne State University Press, 2011.

Watkins, Myron W. "The Labor Situation in Detroit." *Journal of Political Economy* 28 (December 1920): 840–52.

Watts, Steven. *The People's Tycoon: Henry Ford and the American Century*. New York: Alfred A. Knopf, 2005.

Weaver, Robert. *The Negro Ghetto*. New York: Harcourt Brace, 1948.

Weiss, Nancy J. *Farewell to the Party of Lincoln: Black Politics in the Age of FDR*. Princeton, N.J.: Princeton University Press, 1983.

Welliver, Judson C. "Henry Ford, Dreamer and Worker." *American Review of Reviews* 64 (November 1921): 481–95.

Wells, Ida B. *Crusade for Justice: The Autobiography of Ida B. Wells*. Chicago: University of Chicago Press, 1970.

Wells-Barnett, Ida B. "A Red Record: Tabulated Statistics and Alleged Causes of Lynchings in the United States, 1892–1893–1894." In *Selected Works of Ida B. Wells-Barnett*, edited by Trudier Harris, 138–252. New York: Oxford University Press, 1991.

Wesley, Charles H. *Negro Labor in the United States, 1850–1925: A Study in American Economic History*. New York: Vanguard Press, 1927.

Whatley, Warren. "African-American Strikebreaking from the Civil War to the New Deal." *Social Science History* 17, no. 4 (Winter 1993): 525–58.

Whatley, Warren, and Gavin Wright. "Race, Human Capital, and Labour Markets in American History." In *Evolution of Labour Markets,* edited by George Grantham and Mary Mackinnon, 270–91. Toronto: Routledge, 1994.

Whatley, Warren C., Gavin Wright, and Christopher L. Foote. "Arbitraging a Discriminatory Labor Market: Black Workers and the Ford Motor Company, 1918–1947." Working Papers 01009, Department of Economics, Stanford University (2001): 1–47.

White, Horace A. "Who Owns the Negro Churches?" *Christian Century*, 9 February 1938): 176–77.

White, Ronald C., Jr. *Liberty and Justice for All: Racial Reform and the Social Gospel, 1877–1925*. Philadelphia: University of Pennsylvania Press, 2002.

White, Walter F. *A Man Called White: The Autobiography of Walter F. White*. Bloomington: Indiana University Press, 1970.

———. "Negro Segregation Comes North." *Nation*, 21 October 1925, 458–60.

Widick, B. J. *Detroit: City of Race and Class Violence*. 1972; reprint, Detroit: Wayne State University Press, 1989.

Wik, Reynold M. *Henry Ford and Grass-roots America*. Ann Arbor: University of Michigan Press, 1972.

Wilkerson, Isabel. *The Warmth of Other Suns: The Epic Story of America's Great Migration*. New York: Random House, 2010.

Williams, Chad L. *Torchbearers of Democracy: African American Soldiers in the World War I Era*. Chapel Hill: University of North Carolina Press, 2011.

Williams, Rhonda Y. *The Politics of Public Housing: Black Women's Struggles against Urban Inequality*. New York: Oxford University Press, 2004.

Wilson, Edmund. "The Despot of Dearborn." *Scribner's Magazine*, July 1931, 24–36.

Winn, Frank. "Labor Tackles the Race Question." *Antioch Review* 3, no. 3 (1943): 341–60.

Wittner, Lawrence S. "The National Negro Congress: A Reassessment." *American Quarterly* 22 (Winter 1970): 883–901.

Wolcott, Victoria W. *Remaking Respectability: African American Women in Interwar Detroit*. Chapel Hill: University of North Carolina Press, 2001.

Wolters, Raymond. *Negroes and the Great Depression: The Problem of Economic Recovery*. Westport, Conn.: Greenwood Press, 1970.

Woodard, Komozi. *A Nation within a Nation: Amiri Baraka and Black Power Politics in Newark*. Chapel Hill: University of North Carolina Press, 1999.

Woodruff, Nan Elizabeth. "African-American Struggles for Citizenship in the Arkansas and Mississippi Deltas in the Age of Jim Crow." *Radical History Review* 55 (Winter 1993): 33–51.

Woodward, C. Vann. *Origins of the New South, 1877–1913*. Baton Rouge: Louisiana State University Press, 1951.

Work, Monroe N., ed. *Negro Year Book, An Annual Encyclopedia of the Negro, 1918–1919*. Tuskegee, Ala.: Negro Year Book Publishing, 1919.

Worthman, Paul B. "Black Workers and Labor Unions in Birmingham, Alabama, 1897–1904." *Labor History* 10 (Summer 1969): 375–407.

Wright, Richard. *12 Million Black Voices*. 1941; reprint, New York: Basic Books, 2008.

———. *Black Boy: (American Hunger)*. New York: Harper Perennial, 1993.

Young, Coleman, with Lonnie Wheeler. *Hard Stuff: The Autobiography of Coleman Young*. New York: Viking, 1994.

Zieger, Robert H. *The CIO: 1935–1955*. Chapel Hill: University of North Carolina Press, 1995.

———. *For Jobs and Freedom: Race and Labor in America Since 1865*. Louisville: University Press of Kentucky, 2007.

Zunz, Olivier. *The Changing Face of Inequality: Urbanization, Industrial Development, and Immigrants in Detroit, 1880–1920*. Chicago: University of Chicago Press, 1982.

ELECTRONIC SOURCES

Diggs, Charles Jr. Interview conducted by Blackside, Inc., 6 November 1986, for *Eyes on the Prize: America's Civil Rights Years* (1954–1965). library.wustl.edu/units/spec/filmandmedia/collections/henry-hampton-collection/eyes1/eyes1interviews.html.

Moore, David. Interview by *Political Affairs*, 5 March 2007. Online Edition: www.politicalaffairs.net/article/articleview/4956/1/246.

Murage, Njeru. "Making Migrants an Asset: The Detroit Urban League–Employers Alliance in Wartime Detroit, 1916–1919." *Michigan Historical Review* 26 (Spring, 2000). www.http://findarticles.com/p/articles/mi_7021/is_1_26/ai_n28819471/.

Niebuhr, Reinhold. Radio interview of Niebuhr, n.d. (probably 1950s), pp. 1–4, Reinhold Niebuhr Papers, Library of Congress, taken from the web: http://being.publicradio.org/programs/niebuhr-rediscovered/b8.

INDEX

of, 57, 151, 154–56, 226; political networks of, 69, 115, 124, 129–30, 172–86
passim, 231, 255; and Marcus Garvey,
69–70, 124; old guard, 70, 223, 228,
229–30; and KKK, 83; and Democratic
Party, 87, 179–82; and housing, 92–114;
and Great Depression, 123–24, 145,
160–63, 172–74; and New Deal, 187–89,
200; new crowd, 194–98, 199, 224, 254;
and unions, 208, 235
—black vote: 1920, 79–80; 1923, 80–87;
1930, 128–29; 1931, 141–43
Black Ford workers: and unions, 5, 6, 8, 9,
60, 200, 238–40, 242; and loyalty, 5, 6,
37–38, 54, 60, 68, 72, 219, 224, 229, 251,
254; and economic opportunity, 6, 10,
37–38, 39, 42, 54, 57, 60, 69, 72, 172, 248,
251; surveillance of, 56–57, 165, 200,
213–14, 225, 253; and white Ford workers, 63–64; and foundry, 64–65, 165–67,
214–15, 248, 253–54; and Marcus Garvey, 69, 70, 72; and Great Depression,
172–73; and UAW, 200, 207–8, 216–18,
222, 234, 246–49, 254; and Ford strike,
245–46. *See also* American Federation
of Labor; Ford, Henry—industrial relations; Ford Hunger March
Black freedom struggle, 5, 10, 12, 18–20,
54, 68, 69, 72, 90–91, 115, 172–73, 256;
and World War I, 18, 29–30, 36–38, 41;
and Sweet case, 111, 113–15; and unions,
241, 246–49, 255–56
Black ministers, 54–57
Black urbanization, 11, 74, 112–13; and
housing, 32–34; and new crowd, 180
Bledsoe, Geraldine, 181, 201, 203, 243, 249
Bledsoe, Harold, 180, 193, 243
Blount, Louis C., 196, 201, 230
Boatin, Paul, 219
Booker T. Washington Trade Association
(BTWTA), 178, 183, 194
Bowles, Charles S., mayoral campaigns

of, 88–90, 105–6, 109, 122–23, 126–27,
129
Bradby, Rev. Robert L., 5, 7, 8, 9, 75–78;
and Henry Ford, 8, 182, 189, 247–48; as
a progressive, 9, 182, 189, 196–98; and
FMC, 55–57, 75, 138–40, 189, 216, 221;
and rights of citizenship, 75, 113–14,
139–40; theology of, 76–78; and Sweet
case, 108; and Frank Murphy, 128,
138–40, 142–43; as old guard, 181–82;
and Donald Marshall, 189–90
Brewster Community Center, 203, 229,
232–33
Brotherhood of Sleeping Car Porters
(BSCP), 221–22, 227, 240–41
Brown, John, 20
Buchanan v. *Warley* (1917), 99
Bussell, George, 163

Cadillac Motor Car Company, 34, 61
Cadillac Square, 83, 249
Cameron, William, 158
Charles A. Young Post of the American
Legion, 129
Chatham, Canada, 20, 76
Chevrolet, 61, 116–17, 121, 157
Chrysler, 225, 241; compared to FMC, 2,
57, 156–57; black workers at (1926), 61;
and UAW, 207, 220; and Dodge Main
strike (1939), 235
Civic Rights Committee (CRC), 173–74,
182–83, 241, 254; protest tactics of,
184–86, 188–89, 195–97, 199; as bridge
to unionism, 186, 194–95, 220–22; and
NNC local, 200–223 passim; and Detroit Edison, 223, 237–38
Civil rights unionism. *See* Labor-oriented
civil rights
Clough, Veal: and NNC local, 204, 227,
238; organizing strategy of, 234, 240–
41, 243, 247; and black Ford workers,
238–39, 242

Garvey, Marcus, 69, 70, 73, 124, 173, 197;
and black industrial workers, 71–72;
and black Democrats, 73, 180–81
General Motors, 2, 207, 220, 241, 227;
compared to FMC, 57, 116, 121, 156–57;
and Walter Reuther, 234–35
Goetz, Albert, 160
Gomez, Rev. Joseph, 74–75
Gomon, Josephine, 135–38
Good Citizenship League, 69, 70
Granger, Lester B., 190, 202; and Work-
ers' Councils, 193–94
Great Depression, 65, 68, 115, 156–59. *See
also* Black Detroiters; Ford, Henry;
Ford Hunger March
Greenfield Village, 119–20
Griffin, David T., 146–47
Grigsby, Snow F., 178–79, 189, 194, 197;
and CRC, 182, 184–85, 194–96, 199,
201, 223–24; biography of, 183–86; and
Maurice Sugar, 197; collaboration with
John Davis, 202–3, 223–24; and black
ministers, 203–5; and communists,
205; and Detroit Edison, 237–38

Haber, Professor William, 131
Hardin, Walter, 124, 235; and FMC's poli-
cies, 219; as UAW organizer, 233
Harper, Frances E. W., 20
Hartford Avenue Baptist Church, 194,
203, 226
Haynes, George, 33, 95
Haywood, William D., 48
Henry Ford Trade School, 57–60
Herndon, Angelo, 177, 231
Highland Park plant, 43, 99, 117–18
Hill, Charles: and FMC, 12, 226, 243,
246–47; and CRC, 186, 194–96, 201;
and unions, 193; and NNC local, 203,
205, 230, 241; theology of, 205
Housing and neighborhoods: racial cov-
enants in, 6, 32, 99–101, 105; and racial
restrictions, 13, 31–32, 69, 92–93, 95–97,

105–6, 108, 111, 114; and black ghetto,
33, 34, 36–38, 92–93, 96–97, 112–13;
Henry Ford on, 51, 99; southern patterns of, 93–94, 276 (n. 8); and black
and white workers, 103–5, 110–11; and
promise of America, 110
Hughes, Langston, 195–96

Immigration, 48–49, 61, 82
Industrial Workers of the World (IWW),
47, 48, 218
Inkster, Mich.: settlement of, 101–2,
146–47; and Ford's project in, 144–56,
172, 287 (n. 21); "plantation mentality"
of, 154–55
International Labor Defense (ILD), 9,
175–78, 196, 224

Jayne, Judge Ira W., 142
Johnson, James Weldon, 107, 112–13
Johnson, Dr. Mordecai, 229, 254
Johnson, William, 238
Jones, Eugene Kinckle, 30
Jones, Theodore T., 230

Keyes, Percy, 235, 238
Kirk, Silas Paul, 124, 203, 207, 216, 238
Klann, William C., 63
Ku Klux Klan, 7, 13, 41, 87, 90, 92, 142;
principles of, 81–82; and Detroit
membership, 82, 88; and DCL, 83–84,
122–23. *See also* Bowles, Charles

Labor-oriented civil rights: civil rights
unionism, 1, 13, 249, 255; formation
of, 3, 10, 12, 126–49, 254–55; and CRC,
194–98; and NNC/CRC, 200, 223
Lampkin, Daisy, 237
Lawrence, Charles, 102, 156
Lee, John R., 28
Leland, Henry Martyn, 34
Lenin, Vladimir, 40
Lewis, John L., 218, 220, 242

Wagner Act, 210

Walker, Moses L., 128

Ward, Louis, 134–35

Ward, Willis, 60, 174; and surveillance of black Detroiters, 212–13

Washington, Forrester B., 16, 17, 74; and racial status quo, 31–32, 95–96

Waterworks Association, 107

Weaver, Robert, 191

Wells-Barnett, Ida B., 19

Westside Improvement Association, 228

White, Horace (pastor): and NNC local, 203, 235, 246; and critique of black churches, 228; support for strike at Dodge Main, 235

White, Walter, 128–29; support for Ford strike, 245–46

Widman, Mike, 226; and Ford Organizing Drive, 241–45; and Paul Robeson, 249

Wilkins, Roy, 207

Williams, A. D., 70

Williams, Curtis, 161–62

Winn, Frank, 236

Woodson, Carter, 41, 201

Woodson, Wilbur C., 213, 230, 235

Work, Monroe N., 18

Workers' Councils of NUL, 190; labor-oriented agenda, 193–94; and cross-fertilization, 196, 202

World War I, 3, 4, 17, 18, 21, 28, 33, 36, 39, 40, 41, 44, 46; and opportunities, 3, 5, 17, 18; and immigration, 16, 17, 48–49; and migration, 20; and Americanization, 28–29; and housing, 32; and industrial relations, 40, 46–47; and lynchings, 41; and radicals, 46–51

World War II, 3, 39, 60, 195

Wright, Richard, 15, 20–21, 29

Young, Beulah, 128, 130; and Political Leadership Assembly, 130, 141–42; and Murphy for Mayor Clubs, 141; and black Democrats, 179; as voice of new crowd, 202

Young, Coleman A.: migration, 16–18; and Ford wages, 66–67; and depression, 172–73; and NNC local, 203, 238

YWCA, Lucy Thurman Branch of, 192

Zampty, Charles, 71–72